THE SHAPING OF THE ARABS

THE SHAPING OF THE ARABS

A Study in Ethnic Identity

BY

JOEL CARMICHAEL

The Macmillan Company, New York
Collier-Macmillan Ltd., London

Library of Congress Catalog Card Number: 67-14416

FIRST PRINTING

The Macmillan Company, New York
Collier-Macmillan Canada Ltd., Toronto, Ontario

Printed in the United States of America

A few paragraphs from the Prologue and the Epilogue have appeared in *Foreign Affairs* and *Problems of Communism.*

CONTENTS

THE SHAPING OF THE ARABS

PROLOGUE

WHAT IS AN ARAB?

THE word "Arab" is ambiguous. That is because Islam, which has only recently become Westernized, does not recognize distinctions of nations or races as important. It is Islam that constitutes an all-embracing community for its adherents. Since the overwhelming majority of Arabs are Muslim, the Western concept of nationality has had to compete with the religious concept of Islam as a locus of crystallization for group feeling. The consequence is that Islam contains a welter of ethnic types that also permeate the Arab world, types ethnically distinct only to the mind of a Westerner preoccupied with differences of race and nationality.

It has not been possible for a thousand years and more to speak of an Arab community based on any biological similarities. Even at the time the Arabs burst out of their peninsula, they do not appear to have been a physically homogeneous stock. But whatever their unity may have been founded on at that time, the combined effects of Islam and the persistently nomadic movements of Arabs throughout north, central, and east Africa have converted the Arabic-speaking world into a genuine melting pot in which all origins are forgotten, or, rather, all origins are granted a more or less fictitious "Arab" character. At present if one were told that a given individual was an "Arab," one would not know in advance whether he was coal-black, blond, tall, or short.

From the point of view of nationalism, the most concrete achievement of the Muslim conquests, initially borne abroad by Bedouin (the original meaning of "Arab"), was the spread of Arabic. The Arabs' language and literature created a vast cultural unity. The Arabs' language, at the height of Islam merely the learned language of the universal Islamic society, eventually contracted with the political decay of Islam to the confines of populations speaking it as a vernacular—populations in which there existed scarcely more than a few drops of "Arab" blood in the old sense.

More than 4.5 million square miles in Africa and Asia are Arabic-speaking; the extent of this area is the background for the equivocal character of the word "Arab."

The definition so often strained for is in reality a metaphysical distinction, a definition shaped to fit into some sort of logical scheme. There is no need for such a definition. What is required is precision in referring to certain living individuals and communities who are called or call themselves "Arabs." For most purposes it will be found that the best criterion is language, with the exception of certain communities in whose case some other criterion acquires decisive importance, such as the Jews and some other minorities. This "definition" will comprise the Arabian Peninsula, Iraq, Syria, Jordan, Egypt, the Sudan (with the exception of the pagan Negro region in the south), Libya, Tunisia, Algeria, and Morocco (perhaps debatable, because of the strong Berber population). There are of course borderline cases, as in the Somalilands.

Every physical type is represented in "Arab" communities. Some are entirely white; some are almost entirely black. The Hijaz is one of the most racially mixed communities on earth; Mecca has been a city of mulattoes and quadroons, of all racial blends, since the fourteenth century.

This book is essentially an attempt to outline the profile, so to speak, of an ethnic community as it has changed from the beginning, some thirteen hundred years ago, through the Middle Ages down to the present day.

As the Arabs gave birth to Islam, so they were, in a way, formed by it. Yet, as we know, they are not at all coextensive with it. Accordingly, I have tried to extricate them from the far larger community of Islam, and so have concentrated on the fortunes of people who may be or have been called Arabs, and have described the shifting point of view from which the word itself would be meaningful, both to ourselves and to the people it has referred to.

An "Arab" today, in short, is not what an "Arab" has been over the centuries. I hope this book will convey the dynamics of both the continuity of the word and its changing significance.

I

ORIGINS: MUHAMMAD AND THE QURAN

THE history of people called "Arabs" begins, appropriately enough, in Arabia, but the scattered references to them that are familiar to us from as long ago as the eighth century B.C. became consolidated, so to speak, only with the launching of Islam, the last of the great world religions, some thirteen hundred years ago.

For it was with Islam that the Arabs became a factor of world history, and even though Islam was to expand far beyond the Arabic-speaking community and has come to embrace a sixth of mankind, the fate of the Arabs was fused with that of Islam itself, at least in its beginnings, and cannot be considered apart from it.

Arabia—or the "island of the Arabs," as it is called in Arabic—is a vast rectangle of granitic land, steppe and desert, some million square miles in area, bordered by mountains, and with a tropical climate, by and large, accentuated by the desiccation that seems to have been characteristic of it since time immemorial. An older generation of scholars considered it a womb of nations and thought that for ages it had been pouring out to the northeast and northwest its children, who founded various civilizations of antiquity—the Assyrians, the Babylonians, the Phoenicians, the Hebrews, the Arameans. According to this fashionable theory, the Arabian heartland had ejected these various peoples successively over a period of millennia, and the Arab eruption of the seventh century was merely the final phase of an ancient process that was due to natural phenomena, such as cycles of desiccation or a contraction of the economy.

A certain element of surmise is, to be sure, inevitable in discussing Arab origins. The history of people living in the Arabian Peninsula goes back so far and the written records are so scanty—for all practical purposes nonexistent—that the Arabs are bound to be considered in connection with kindred peoples that may be better known. The Bible may well turn out to be a valuable source for the Arabs as well as for other ancient peoples, but before we can assess its testimony we must avoid the pitfall of one of the most persistent myths of our age—the notion of a Semitic "race" as distinct from a family of languages.

The romanticism of the nineteenth century made it attractive to deal with the word "Semitic"—originally an eighteenth-century German professorial coinage referring solely to languages—as though it had some biological significance. A characteristic scholarly conceit envisioned the "Semites" as having a monotheism without mythology because of their all having come from the desert. This notion, though utterly refuted the moment the archeologists discovered a very complex mythology written in various Semitic languages, still lingers on, perhaps because of its endearingly harmonious simplicity.

Indeed, the ancient peoples that spoke different Semitic languages are quite well known by appearance from their pictures as well as from their remains. They did not look remotely like each other, and their socioeconomic circumstances seem to have been even more various. Whatever might have been common to them in the way of literary or religious ideas is quite simply explained by cultural diffusion, which, however obscure, does not in any case require any biological modality.

If Biblical testimony is accepted on this point, or at least the tradition held by both Jews and Arabs that Abraham's son Ishmael was the father of the Arabs, it may give us a hint of an ancient migration that did in fact produce Arabs, Arameans, and Hebrews as branches of an ultimately identical stock. If the content of the word "Arab" is reduced to the notion of dwellers in the deep desert who bred camels, carried out raids, and specialized in long-range businesses and overland transport, then we may consider the Biblical "Ishmaelites" as well as "Midianites" as having been Arabs or proto-Arabs. This notion, as we shall see, was to play a role in the origins of Islam.

There is scarcely any doubt but that the idea of ancient "Semitic" peoples bursting out of the Arabian Peninsula over whole millennia and establishing civilizations on the borderlands north of the peninsula is mere theory. It is based on no records at all and is, in fact, modeled on the historic eruption of the Arabs themselves in the seventh century and then retrojected to fit an unknown situation.

There are, after all, actual records of the emergence of some of the great Arabian tribes from the desert and of the settlement of some Bedouin in the cultivated area north of Arabia. If there are records of even such minor colonizing movements, it seems unlikely that such immensely important, comprehensive, and far-reaching events as the successive conquests of such huge areas as Babylonia, Assyria, or Phoenicia by Arabian tribes would not have been commemorated in one way or another.

One of the by-products of this general theory of the successive ejection of whole peoples from the Arabian steppelands is also applied directly to the ancient Hebrews. For generations it has been a popular theory that the Hebrews were merely Bedouin transformed in the conventional manner through settlement in agricultural regions. The theory is a very old one, perhaps because of an agreeable symmetry that made it appeal to the Jews themselves, who adopted it when they became familiar with Arabic after the Muslim conquests.

Yet strangely enough, however appealing, the theory does not seem to have the smallest factual foundation. The one "objective" fact underlying it is generally taken to be the record of the ancient Hebrews' having been divided into tribes—the "Twelve Tribes." This is often taken to imply an originally Bedouin background behind the agricultural atmosphere of the People of Israel in the Bible, which is evident from the earliest possible times, that is, at the very least from the time of the Book of Judges onward. Tribal organization, however, by no means implies a nomadic background; many sedentary societies show signs of it with no Bedouin origins at all.

This misconception doubtless underlies the further misconception of Abraham himself as a "Bedouin Shaykh." There is a quite fundamental difference between seminomads engaged in the husbandry of sheep and cattle, wandering about like the Biblical Patriarchs and occasionally settling down to a farming life in an area already more or less under cultivation, and real nomads living "outside" all sedentary areas—in Arabic *"Bedu"* (whence "Bedouin") means "outside"—far off in the great steppelands, the best breeding grounds for dromedaries.

The Bible gives no indication whatever that the Hebrews were ever camel-breeding nomads, or that they even came out of Arabia at all. If anything were needed to demonstrate this, it is precisely the way in which the Bible refers to Israel's sojourn in the desert, taken to be the birthplace of Judaism.

Israel's sojourn in the desert, while vital in the mythology of the Jewish people and of Judaism, is explicitly declared to be a short *episode* in between the basic phases of sedentary life in Egypt and then in Canaan, where the Hebrews took root. The reason the stay in the desert was such an ordeal for the Hebrews was just because they were not used to it; life in the desert is very painful for farmers. If the internal evidence of the Bible is then examined, in addition to explicit statements, it shows even more clearly that within human memory the Hebrews were never anything but farmers. If the Bible is compared with classical Arabic literature, which was actually written down generations later by a society that merely remembered its own mythological past and by people who while speaking Arabic were not Arabs in any sense, the language even in recall shows unmistakable evidence of the desert past of the people who spoke it originally. Everything in the language—metaphors, similes, themes, indeed the actual vocabulary—demonstrates that the Bedouin had originally lived in the great Arabian steppelands. The Bible shows quite the contrary: it is wholly redolent of a life of farming, including the husbandry of small animals like sheep and cattle.

But if we treat the Biblical account with caution, it may allow us to take the name Abraham as a reference to an ancient migration from Mesopotamia toward Palestine, perhaps after some great calamity. If Palestine at the time was too crowded to take in the entire migration, some of the "Abrahamites" might have moved into the farmlands east and south of Palestine, whereas some others—the "Midianites" and "Ishmaelites" of the Bible—took to the great caravan routes from Beersheba eastward and southward into the great Arabian Peninsula.

What then created the Arabs as a people, the special circumstance they owed their future national identity to, was the titanic fact of the domestication of the one-humped camel, which probably took place in the latter part of the second millennium B.C. This singled out various desert tribes and enabled them to become long-range businessmen, merchants, and raiders. Though there is no actual evidence for this schematic reconstruction, it seems to account for undeniable similarities between Arabs and Jews historically, as well as to give full weight to the Biblical accounts that in so many other respects have been borne out by recent archeological testimony.

Though the origin of the word "Arab" itself remains somewhat obscure, some authoritative opinion tends to regard it as probably derived from an ancient Semitic root implying nomadism—*i.e.*, "*'abar,*" or "pass," from which the word "Hebrew," too, is ultimately to be derived. This is all the likelier since Arabic-speaking people themselves have always used this word, from the very earliest times on, to refer to nomadic Bedouin as distinct from Arabic-speaking town- and village-dwellers. Indeed, down to our own day this continues to be the case. I shall go into this later; it seems to me a vital point in tracing the outline of the Arab ethnic profile.

There was thus an early cleavage between the concept of "Arabs," meaning Bedouin, and the speakers of Arabic. In the Quran, for instance, there are some clearly slighting references to the (Arab) Bedouin, while at the same time the unique excellence of the Arabic tongue is made much of. When Islam was borne abroad by the great tribes of Arabia, a basic ambiguity in the general attitude toward the Bedouin was extended very far afield, intensified by the concomitant feeling that in spite of everything it was somehow the Bedouin who also spoke the best Arabic. This prejudice grew unshakable roots in the generation after Muhammad, partly because of his own tribal connections and partly because of the Bedouin paramountcy in the first few generations after the institution of Islam.

Ultimately, as we shall see, this primordial cleavage between the "Arabs," or Bedouin, and the speakers of Arabic was to assume decisive importance, some thirteen centuries later, to be sure. In our own day, when individuals are socially adrift and society is given over to the broadest of abstractions, language has become a major classifier of people. Thus classical Arabic, which was, perhaps, somewhat artificial to begin with and in the beginning provided a common cultural medium for otherwise disparate communities, has now become a cementing factor in the contemporary movement for the unification of the Arabic-speaking peoples and the emblem of potential nationhood.

It must be said that there is something mysterious about the role played by the Arabic language in the very beginnings of Arab self-consciousness. There seems to be an almost miraculous element in the very existence of the poetic idiom current over such a wide area among tribesmen who in most respects were quite primitive. Not merely was the idiom itself very strange as a product of nomadic camel-breeders, but it was in actual use among perfectly illiterate people throughout the Arabian Peninsula, which covers, after all, more than a million square miles. Long before Islam this idiom seems to have evolved—though we are quite unaware of any stages in its evolution—into a remarkably complex means of expression, with a matchless wealth of vocabulary, a remarkable strictness of form, and a ramified precision of detail. Since the Arab tribes of the peninsula were bound together by nothing else, the stellar role in their formation as a nation must be ascribed to their language.

• • •

The first actual use of the word "Arab" in history is to be found in an Assyrian inscription of 853 B.C., commemorating the defeat of a mutinous chieftain called "Gindibu the Arab" (the name means locust), among others. Fittingly, Gindibu's contribution to the rebellion was a thousand camel riders, and he was associated, piquantly enough from our point of view, with King Ahab of Israel, who contributed ten thousand foot soldiers and two thousand war chariots.

Arabs are then mentioned quite often, until the sixth century B.C., in various inscriptions that indicate a state of vassalage to the Assyrians; the campaigns against the "Aribi" are obviously punitive sallies, intended to keep the nomads cowed and the Assyrian borderlands and lines of communication secure. These inscriptions do not mention the Arabic-speaking peoples of southwestern Arabia at all.

The place-name "Arabia" occurs for the first time in Greek

writings, modeled on "Italia," etc. Herodotus, followed by most other Greek and Latin writers, extended the terms "Arabia" and "Arab" to the whole peninsula and everything in it, even including the eastern desert of Egypt between the Red Sea and the Nile. Around this time the word was apparently used to cover all desert areas inhabited by people speaking Semitic languages. The word "Saracen," first used in Greek literature too, is a transcription of an Arabic word meaning "easterner." In Greek and Latin, and in the Talmudic literature of the Jews, it was applied to nomads generally; later on, in Byzantium and in the Medieval West, it referred to all Muslim peoples.

I shall use this word "Saracen" myself later to refer to the inhabitants of the Islamic world in contradistinction historically to the Arabs (Bedouin) who launched Islam on the one hand and to the contemporary Arab nationalist movement of our own day.

As for the Arabs' use of the word, it occurs for the first time in the ancient epigraphical material originating in southern Arabia, where it is clearly used for Bedouin, with the corollary of "raider." In any case, it referred to the nomadic, not the sedentary, population. In the north the word is used for the first time in the fourth century A.D., in one of the oldest records of the language that became classical Arabic.

By the early seventh century A.D., with the rise of Islam, we can see how the word was used in the central and northern parts of the peninsula. For Muhammad and his contemporaries, the "Arabs" were exclusively the desert-dwelling Bedouin, never the town-dwellers of Mecca, Medina, and other cities. Still, the language of them all, as of the Quran itself, is referred to as Arabic; hence the ambiguity mentioned above, which has survived to this day. On the other hand, though the word was thus synonymous in the narrower sense with the great nomadic tribes, similarities of language and perhaps genealogy extended it also to the sedentary settlements of southern Arabia. Yemen—the Arabia Felix of the classical geographers—was by far the best known of these.

This division into north Arabs and south Arabs has been, indeed, a motif running throughout the Arabs' historical awareness of themselves. Its importance is hard to assess with any precision, but it played a legendary role during the initial expansion of Islam and to some extent down to the present day. It may represent a fixed attitude of the Arabs of Muhammad's time; with the success of his enterprise, it was generalized very broadly in the vastly expanded horizons of the Arabs after Islam.

The division may be rooted in the factual situation of the nomadism of the peoples of the north and the sedentary and agricultural condition of the south. This division was felt to be so strong, indeed, that it served the fourteenth-century Arab historian Ibn Khaldun as the framework of his whole view of world history, which he conceived of as the result of the reciprocal interaction between the Bedouin and the city-dwellers.

There is, of course, no need to make this distinction hard-and-fast. Even if one accepts the accuracy of genealogy, so long an obsession of the Arabs, it seems clear that some originally "southern" tribes actually lived in the north and led a nomadic life, while some "northern" tribes were rooted in the south. There were, in short, settled communities in the north and tribal elements in the south.

Yet by and large the distinction may be valid. It is of importance in tracing the history of the Arabs because it is only against the background of northern tribalism that the career of Muhammad, with its incalculable consequences for world history, can be understood.

The history of the southern Arabs, that is, of the general complex encompassed by the classical phrase "Arabia Felix," may be far more interesting, at least potentially, than the history of the northern tribes—which, in the absence of any monuments, complex institutions, or records, is not history in our sense but is best understood as a sustained continuity of tradition against the background of an immutable nature. Yet the chapter of south Arabian history is forever closed; it has left no descendants, and while the actual life led in the southern settlements of the Arabian Peninsula has doubtless remained in some respects unchanged from time immemorial until very recently, it has been totally encapsulated within the civilization rooted in the conquests of the north Arabian tribesman and generalized by the spread of Islam.

There are monumental remains still awaiting adequate excavation and an impressive amount of epigraphical material, both of which indicate the complexity of life in Yemen, spanning many centuries before and after the appearance of Christianity. There was a proliferation of monarchical government institutions, a highly complex society, and intense commercial activity—in short, a stable and cultivated way of life. Several states seem to have succeeded each other and to have coexisted. The archeological and epigraphical data flesh out the accounts of classical authors, and it was, indeed, this Arabia that early established itself in the minds of all those who read the classical authors as an arresting contrast with the squalor of life in the northern and central deserts, where the Bedouin, who remained exotic curiosities until they burst out of these deserts, led humdrum lives submerged in the monotonous flux of the seasons.

This millennium of a wholly vanished society comes down to us only faintly, an aromatic whiff of the spices that constituted its principal commerce and the source of its prosperity. These spices, which sound exotic to us today—frankincense, labdanum, myrrh—were given intensive cultivation through highly sophisticated techniques. They found their way to the Mediterranean basin in convoys that also transported the products of India and of Somalia, on the coast of East Africa. The whole life of society, ruled by a monarch and an executive of elders, depended on this spice trade. Spiritually it was sponsored by the local gods, a pantheon of astral deities served by a priesthood.

All this comes to us through the south Arabian epigraphs, the only written monument to this rich and cultivated society. They tell us of the organization of public life, of the religious cults, of the family structure, which seems to have been monogamous, and of its economy and laws. The epigraphs were written in monumental characters, quite different from the north Arabian script and language we are familiar with.

It is a voice from a dead past, a past, moreover, that is separated from us by the almost total obliteration imposed on it through the later successes of Islam and has been pieced together only by the antlike labors of the last few generations of Oriental scholars. The recollections and genealogies of the north Arabs who launched Islam are laughably misleading and inadequate; for Muslim tradition, everything that preceded the explosion of Islam had a merely quaint interest and became the subject of fantasies like those embodied in fabulist literature like *The Arabian Nights*. Without the painstaking labors of European scholarship, this whole period of history would have passed without leaving an echo.

The spices and precious woods produced or forwarded by the

south Arabian kingdoms reached the Mediterranean over a dual route: one entirely on land, going from southwestern Arabia through Transjordan to Palestine and Syria; the other by river, going up the Euphrates from the Persian Gulf. After the merchandise on this route was unloaded in the entrepôt station of Dura-Europos, it then went on to Syria across the desert by caravan.

These two caravan routes were responsible for the fortunes of two other Arab states that have since vanished without more than an epigraphical trace. One was Petra in Transjordan (the ancient Edom of the Bible), the capital of the Nabatean kingdom that blossomed from the fifth century B.C. on. There seems to have been no doubt of the Arab origins of the Nabateans, but they were culturally subordinate to the far more cultivated Arameans and in fact used Aramaic for the inscriptions that have come down to us. The alphabet, too, was Aramaic and was to serve as the basis for what we now know as the Arabic alphabet.

At one time the Nabatean kingdom extended from the Gulf of Aqaba to the Dead Sea and also took in part of the northern Hijaz. It was subjugated by Rome in the first century B.C. and ultimately absorbed by it completely in 105 A.D., when the Emperor Trajan established the Provincia Arabia. Its imposing ruins, as well as its inscriptions and coins, are all that have survived of this once-flourishing society.

The other Arab state, Palmyra in Syria, was also intimately involved with Rome. This society was also strongly Aramaicized, which at this time meant Hellenized. Its strategic location athwart the caravan routes from the Euphrates to Syria gave it effective control of all transport. Aside from this, the kingdom was largely given over to banking and commercial operations; it became famous, too, for hiring out its legendary archers as mercenaries. Palmyra was given special privileges by Rome as a reward for its consistent loyalty, which continued until the third century A.D., when one of its leaders attempted to make Palmyra independent. His ambitions were continued after his death by his widow, Zenobia, the only personage of proto-Arab history whose memory is preserved in Muslim tradition. In 273 A.D. the Emperor Aurelian destroyed Zenobia's dreams, after which Palmyra declined rapidly.

These northern Arab states, more or less masked culturally by their use of Aramaic, were of considerable importance insofar as they furnished the north, or Bedouin, Arabs the contacts with Hellenistic civilization that ultimately percolated through to Muhammad's milieu. Together with the kingdoms in the south of the peninsula, they were the only states of consequence to precede the singular outburst of the Arabian tribes in the wake of Muhammad's revelation.

Between the third and the sixth century A.D., the Roman power in the north, like that of the states in the south of Arabia, waned steadily. One of the consequences this entailed, or conceivably was caused by—historical causality is slippery terrain—was a radical shift in the relations between the nomads in the interior and the civilized or semicivilized states on the periphery. Nomadism seems to have engulfed some of the buffer states in the north and spread up to the borders of Persia and of Byzantium, the successor state of the Roman Empire. What may be considered a barbaric tide was contained by these empires anew through the formation of other buffer states based on Arab peoples, such as the Ghassanids along the Byzantine border, who were maintained by the Byzantine rulers as "phylarchs," *i.e.,* tribal princelings, and the Lakhmids, who were tributaries of the Persian Great King.

These two tiny states lasted down to the beginning of the seventh century A.D. and were a sort of transmitting chamber between the cultivated life of Syria and Mesopotamia and the nomadic life of the great deserts of central and northern Arabia. From the point of view of the Bedouin in contact with them southeast or southwestward, they represented the life of a higher sedentary civilization. For their Byzantine and Persian masters, on the other hand, they themselves were not much better than their outrightly nomadic kinsmen.

It was in this way that elements of foreign culture seeped into the nomadic world. Technically, the Ghassanids and the Lakhmids were Christians; the Bedouin could observe their rites, their convents, and their hermitages with the deference they might have felt for something beyond them. In the numerous taverns the Bedouin could also enjoy the effects of wine drinking. The Ghassanids and the Lakhmids were mutually hostile, like their sponsors, and were in a constant state of skirmishing, which was blown up by Bedouin rhetoric and legendarized far into the deserts, quite out of proportion to the modest political realities.

From the point of view of the later evolution of Islam, both the Ghassanids and the Lakhmids performed a function of mediation; their buffer states filtered the relatively advanced civilization of Hellenistic western Asia into the primitive nomadism of pre-Islamic Arabia.

The matrix of Islam was these Bedouin, timelessly roaming throughout the vast deserts of the peninsula. Indeed, Bedouin tribalism is the hallmark of the crucial period preceding the emergence of Islam. The pressure of nature, whose harsh realities are the mold of nomadic society, made the tribe a highly cohesive entity in which the individual's rights were understood only in terms of his group membership. The mechanisms of this cohesiveness revolved around one material factor—the need for self-defense in the teeth of desert rigors and dangers—and one spiritual, or mythological, factor—the theory of blood kinship, based on the blood tie between all members of the tribe, or clan, through descent in the male line. This conception of blood kinship was the underlying social bond of the group.

The tribes depended for their livelihood on two things: the flocks and herds, which would have to be taken from one grazing area to another in accordance with the shifting of the seasons; and the raids that would be launched against the sedentary neighbors and such caravans as ventured across the wilder deserts. Through these raids the tribes acted as conductors for all the various commodities and ideas that penetrated the area at any point and gradually seeped through the whole of the peninsula. Private property in land was unusual; the tribe simply exercised a collective control over grazing areas, wells, and so on. Apparently, too, the flocks and herds were often the property of the tribe collectively; only movable objects could be privately owned.

The tribes were headed by individuals called *Shaykhs* (Elders) or *Sayyids* (Lords). These were elected and seem to have generally enjoyed no more than the authority of a premier among peers. The rulers lacked the authority to assign duties or to punish anyone; rights and duties were part of the area of authority not of the tribe but of the individual family within the tribe. Indeed, the government by the tribal chieftain consisted generally of acting as umpire, rather than commander. In nomad society the very notions of such things as authority, monarchy, public penalties, etc., were quite unknown. The Shaykh was simply elected by the tribal elders, though generally, to be sure, he came from a single family that might be recognized as inherently superior, in some undefined sense. His advisers consisted of the *Majlis,* the council of family heads and clan spokesmen within the tribe, all together representing "public opinion." A feeling seems to have been prevalent that some clans were more aristocratic than others; indeed, the Bedouin at all times seem to have regarded themselves, quite unaccountably from a sedentary point of view, as inherently superior to absolutely everyone.

This nomadic feeling of superiority independent of personal attributes or merits may be accounted for by the seclusion in the emotional universe constituted by the magical bond uniting the tribespeople. It made it natural for the Bedouin to establish themselves, later on, as a topmost aristocratic layer above all foreigners, including the highly civilized foreigners they were to conquer. Because of this, during the initial phase of Arab hegemony in Islam, the new community carried abroad by the Arabian tribesmen was characterized by the aristocratic virtues of ignorance and lineage, that is, by the mere *fact* of being a certain kind of person. This seems to have given the Bedouin the morale they required to squat, as they were to do, on the cultivated societies they overran.

Just as in their external lives the tribes were held in the iron grip of the seasonal flux, so their inner lives were confined within the *Sunna* (immemorial ancestral custom), which was propped up on nothing more than the recognition by public opinion of the authority of ancient precedent and whose sole instrument of articulation was the tribal Majlis. Public law was nonexistent; the sole regulation of what would otherwise have been anarchy was the *lex talionis* found in the oldest stratum of the Old Testament—the "eye for an eye and tooth for a tooth." In practice this meant that the kin of someone murdered or injured had the duty of exacting vengeance from any one of the culprit's kinfolk.

The nomads had, of course, religious beliefs, which revolved around the notion of petty deities, or demons, inhabiting or patronizing particular places, trees, fountains, and specific stones held to be sacred. There were also a few gods, that is, deities that transcended tribal boundaries. The most important cults were those of Manāt, 'Uzza, and Allāt (the last is mentioned by Herodotus). But these three goddesses were subordinate to a still higher deity, generally referred to as Allah. There was no priesthood among the tribes; the gods were simply transported by the nomads under a sort of red tent, which was taken into battle with them. The tribal god was the center of the faith and was generally symbolized in some object, perhaps a stone. Part of the prestige of the house of a Shaykh consisted of the duty of protecting the cultic object. The cult was the tribal emblem of identity, the only way in which the cohesiveness of the tribe could find some form of organized spiritual or "ideological" expression. Loyalty to the tribe, as well as its converse, treason, was thus expressed as a function of allegiance to the tribal cult.

The incessant peregrinations of the tribes found an occasional interruption in the few oases scattered about the endless deserts. Settlement in an oasis enabled the formation of a skeleton political organization, headed by an eminent family, that might even extend its authority beyond the oasis to neighboring tribes and, ephemerally, even to another oasis. The only noteworthy, though equally ephemeral, regime was that of the Arab Kinda kingdom, which in the late fifth and early sixth century flourished in northern Arabia, but soon came to an end because of its inability to withstand the pressures exerted by the Persian and Byzantine empires. Kinda was important not so much because of its political foreshadowing of the infinitely more successful Islamic expansion, but because of its helping to form a poetic language and convention that became standard for the various Bedouin tribes of the peninsula, thus giving them, above their bickerings, a single tradition and culture that on the eve of Islam had reached its zenith.

It was poetry that enabled the Arabian tribes to transcend their varying tribal identities in the awareness of a heritage common to them all. Poetry, doubtless a primordial impulse of mankind, in the Arabian desert flowered as perhaps never before or since. It was, of course, deeply religious in impulse, in the sense in which all solemn rhythmic activities can stimulate and enhance the feeling of awe and control. Magic is an integral part of all primitive religion, and poetry is an integral part of magic. Words, it is said with great significance, have *power,* which means magical power. In the poetry of the Arabian desert the power that had always been inherent in blessings and cursings gradually was transformed into the wounding capacities of satire, in which both tribes and personalities could be made fun of and so substantially dwarfed in the minds of an appreciative audience. The poets sang of sexual love, too, though often as a prelude to the basic theme of a given poem—self-glorification, or the glorification of a tribe. Professional poets could also produce eulogies for payment.

A classic form of tendentious poem was the *qasidah,* long-established in tribal custom. This might begin with the throbbing regret for vanished bliss in love; then, before coming to his essential theme, the poet would pause to delight his hearers with lush and detailed descriptions of nature, especially, of course, the boundless desert and its animals, primarily the camel. Arabic poetry is celebrated for the extraordinary opulence and wealth of imagery and vocabulary attendant on its obsession with these themes. There was a substantial impersonal element in all this; the poet was generally constrained to make use of ancient traditional forms. Hence, poetry was not an occasion for the display of any individuality, but enabled the poet simply to make a show of his virtuosity in the handling of ancient themes.

Viewed sociologically, Arabic poetry was not merely an ornament of life; the role it played in unifying the tribes was more than incidental. The poetic dialect, common to all the tribes, understood throughout the peninsula and as far as the interior of Mesopotamia, and in fact the primary source of unity in Arabia, gave rise to classical Arabic, which was transformed into a world language by the expansion of Islam. Arabic was to become the vernacular speech of the whole of the Middle East, the whole of the southern Mediterranean coast, and down along the East African coast and far into the African interior, with incalculable consequences for the world of today. Arabic was also to provide a massive proportion of the technical vocabulary for the huge family of nations that were to become Islamicized—Turkey, India, Indonesia, Persia, and the speakers of Swahili.

Some important towns even evolved out of the Bedouin fluctuation of Arabia. The most important one was, and is, Mecca, in the Hijaz. In Mecca each clan retained its own identity, that is, its own Majlis and its own sacred object, but the clans were united in a sort of federation, expressed in a central shrine with a symbol common to all. This common shrine was known as the Ka'ba, a large meteorite whose worship was eventually assimilated into Islam. In Mecca, and the few other towns in Arabia, the authority of each

Shaykh was conditioned by the evolution of a sort of family oligarchy that overshadowed its constituent clans.

One of the ways in which Persian and Byzantine influence infiltrated into the peninsula was through the establishment of foreign colonies. Jewish and Christian settlements were scattered throughout Arabia, busy radiating both Aramaic and Hellenistic culture. There were, indeed, Jews and Judaized Arabs everywhere, principally craftsmen and farmers, who seem to have been a predominant element in a number of important oases: Tayma, Khaybar, Yathrib, and Fadak. Their origins are obscure. They may have come to Arabia in the eighth or the sixth century B.C., *i.e.,* from the first dispersion of the Jews following the fall of Samaria in 721 B.C., or from the much more widespread dispersion following the establishment of the great Jewish settlements in Mesopotamia, which have survived to the present day. Another date that has often been suggested, the first and second centuries A.D., is perhaps the most probable, since the Romans systematically uprooted all Jewish life in Palestine, and Arabia was a natural refuge. The existence of Jews along the trade routes from south to north Arabia is quite well known from the Hellenistic period. It is also likely that there was a more or less steady influx of Jews from the eighth century B.C. down to the emergence of Islam.

The important Jewish colony in the Yemen surely dates from the fourth century A.D. at least. It had led a well-organized communal existence there for centuries, and it came to an end, indeed, only with the establishment of the State of Israel in 1948 and the removal thither of the whole of the Yemenite Jewish community.

On the eve of Islam, in any case, the Jews seem to have dominated the economic life of the Hijaz. At Yathrib, to which Muhammad fled from Mecca and where he established himself, the Jews must have formed at least half the population. In the Hijaz generally, they seem to have made many converts among the Bedouin.

Christianity, too, was very widespread in the Arabian Peninsula. If Syria is included as part of the great north Arabian desert, Christianity's first roots were put forth in Arabia, and by the time of Muhammad a large number of Arabs were Christians, however superficial their Christianity may be thought. It is true that though the great Bedouin tribes in the north were very close to the settled

Aramean population, long since Christianized, most Bedouin were thoroughgoing pagans, but they were surrounded by others, often on the borders of their territories, who had accepted one version of Christianity or another. In addition to some scattered Christian communities, there were three big centers: Yemen in the south, and Syria and Hira in the north and east respectively. In addition, the relatively neighboring country of Abyssinia was Christian, allied with the Egyptian church. The Hijaz was invaded by a Christian general, for instance, in about 570 A.D.; the Quran mentions the battle in a celebrated passage ("The Elephant"). In Mecca itself only individuals, curiously enough from Muhammad's own clan, are referred to as Christians. There are some indications that upon Muhammad's triumphal entry into Mecca (in 630) he found some paintings of Jesus and the Virgin Mary on the walls of the inner shrine.

Arabian Christianity was split up in a conventional manner, complicated by the internecine warfare between the greater states to the north, which made use of many Arab auxiliaries. Its major divisions were Greek Orthodox, Monophysite, and Nestorian. These divisions are still alive, though of course their relative situation is quite different today. Christology, the basic source of the entanglements of Christian theology, is so complex that it cannot be gone into here. The only point worth making is that the split between the Monophysites and the Nestorians revolved around the nature of the Christ: Did he have one nature, as a God-Man, or two, as a Man and as a God? The Monophysites held that there was only one: Christ was the eternal Logos incarnate. The Nestorians took the view that though the Christ was completely human, still he was, at the same time, born of the Virgin Mary as God and hence combined two natures within himself.

Both Monophysites and Nestorians had been showing extraordinary zeal in their proselytizing among the Arabs, including the Bedouin of the desert. Churches, schools, and monasteries were founded; Nestorian monks were a common sight, praying toward the east.

The eastern and western Arabs were generally at war, reflecting, through the Lakhmid and Ghassanid houses, the contending allegiances to Persia and the Byzantine Empire in Syria. The Lakhmids, though vassals of Persia, had gone over to the Christianity of the town-dwellers. In Syria there was a constant campaign of persecution directed by the Greek Orthodox Byzantine Empire against the Arabs of the west who were Monophysites, steadfast in their refusal to accept the Orthodox notion of the two natures of the Christ. They were treated with remarkable cruelty. Communities were terrorized and bishops and monks expelled; even ordinary laymen were compelled to take refuge in Persia.

In some ways Monophysite Arab Christianity seems to have held an element of a return to unity as a prerequisite for the True God. There is an episode of an Arab chief, an ally of the Byzantine Empire, who after defending the fortunes of his patrons with conspicuous success was finally alienated by his inability to swallow the intricacies of Byzantine theology. The Greek Byzantine Empire, by consistently misusing the Arab Monophysite Christians who were their faithful allies for some time, ultimately paved the way for the success of Islam. The Greeks in fact alienated the Arab Christians to such a degree that when the Muslims arrived they were to be regarded as liberators.

In short, the Arabs of the peninsula were by no means isolated from the civilized world outside, most proximately in the form of Byzantium and Persia. Materially, the Arabs acquired arms and learned their use, as well as strategic and organizational principles. Arab auxiliaries were trained by Byzantine and Persian teachers in the border provinces of the north; this training spread gradually throughout the peninsula. The Arabs were also gradually influenced by the spread of textiles, food, wine, and, doubtless, writing. It was in a spiritual way, especially, that the thinking of the Arabs was influenced by the religions of the Middle East, more particularly by monotheism, which was, indeed, the indispensable background for the success of Muhammad's activity later on. It was precisely in the sedentary population of the Hijaz, where Muhammad was born, that the response to these various foreign stimuli, material and intellectual, was most marked.

For though it was the Bedouin who bore abroad primitive Islam, it was among the sedentary populations of the peninsula, especially south Arabia and the Hijaz, that the real preparation for it had taken place.

It was ultimately, doubtless, the evolution of the trade routes that conditioned the zigzags and fluctuations in Arabian history. In the second half of the sixth century A.D., for instance, the Euphrates-Persian trade route, which had hitherto benefited by the commerce between the Mediterranean and the further east lands, was encumbered and made dangerous by the constant friction between the Byzantine and Persian empires, with concomitant tariffs, political rivalries, and general chaos. Since Egypt too was somewhat disorganized, it could no longer provide an alternative route. Businessmen were obliged to fall back again on the more difficult, though more peaceful, route leading from Syria down through western Arabia to the Yemenite ports that served the Indian trade. Yemen itself was governed by foreigners, and by this time Palmyra and Nabatea in the north had quite disappeared.

This provided a socioeconomic vacuum that Mecca had a chance to leap into. Mecca had doubtless arisen in the first place because of its location along the spice route leading from southern to northern Arabia; it was probably a way station, favored as the hub of lines leading to the Mediterranean, the Persian Gulf, the Red Sea through Jidda, and overseas to Africa.

Some time before the emergence of Islam, Mecca came under the control of the north Arabian tribe of the Quraysh, which was soon transformed at least partially into a community of merchants that turned the old way station into an important commercial center. The Quraysh traders had substantial agreements with the Byzantine, Persian, and even Abyssinian border authorities. In the society of the time, they were men of considerable substance. Great caravans would be organized by them twice a year, going north and south. These enterprises were cooperative, owned and controlled by syndicates of merchants and investors. In addition, there was a constant succession of smaller caravans in various directions and some overseas trade with Africa. The neighborhood of Mecca also served as background for a number of fairs, which spread the influence of the city very considerably among the surrounding Bedouin.

Mecca was something of a hotchpotch in the way of nationality. The governing element in the city itself became known as the "Quraysh of the Inside"—a sort of business aristocracy consisting of traders and bankers in control of the transit commerce. This aristocracy was supplemented by the "Quraysh of the Outside," consisting of petty traders of humbler standing and more recent origin. In addition, there was a sort of rabble of outlanders and

Bedouin, while outside the city proper there were the Bedouin tribes directly dependent on it—the "Arabs of the Quraysh."

Mecca has been described as a merchant republic governed by a syndicate of rich businessmen, but of course there was no question of any rigidly organized institutions. The city still recalled its nomadic origins: There was a maximum of individual liberty, with as little centralized authority as possible. There was a sort of urban equivalent of the tribal Majlis, but essentially its authority consisted of an awareness of mutual interests on the part of the merchant aristocracy. Probably the experience and skill embodied in this functioning merchant aristocracy provided the capacities later on that, after first being turned against Muhammad, were later used in the administration of the vast empire that was to come under its control after the rise of Islam.

More immediately, Mecca was to serve as the background for the career of Muhammad, Prophet of Islam, the Envoy of God.

• • •

Though it is doubtless true, indeed banal, that great movements in history are not created by individuals alone, still the name of Muhammad, regarded by a sixth of mankind as the initiator of all real history, must be thought of as opening a new age. For it is with the emergence of Muhammad as the spiritual and later the secular organizer of a new Arab community that Arabs as such make their appearance in the mainstream of world history and are no longer merely given peripheral or individual mention in the histories of other peoples. Paradoxically, Muhammad, by founding a world religion, forged the Arabs into a people.

The career of this remarkable man is unique among religious innovators in that it unfolded in broad daylight, before the eyes of his contemporaries, and was partly recorded in a self-written book, highly personal, that became the holy book of a new religion. On the other hand, not much is known of Muhammad's ancestry or early life. For that matter, the little that was once thought to be known has been steadily whittled away by Western scholarship. One fact after another, long regarded by Muslim tradition as steadfast, has been brought into question, and a living, breathing portrait of a real man eludes our grasp. Though his humanity is incontestable, despite the legends it has accumulated, though there is an occasional throb of life from some of the accounts, and though the Quran itself pulsates with a life of its own, Muhammad's personality remains irrecoverable.

He was born in Mecca, apparently, sometime around 570 A.D., or in the following decade, a member of a reputable though not a leading family of the Quraysh aristocracy. An impoverished orphan, he seems to have been brought up by his grandfather. He ultimately improved his social position by marrying a rich widow a few years older than himself. He may have had some connection with business, though this impression emerges more from the occasional knowledgeability shown in the Quran with respect to commercial terminology and from the character of Mecca itself than from any positive information.

Though he was obviously familiar with many Jewish and Christian ideas, it is far from certain that he ever traveled outside Arabia. It is, on the other hand, quite unmistakable that Muhammad himself, whether or not he could read—Muslim tradition makes him illiterate, but many scholars consider that to be making some symbolical point—had not actually read the Bible, though much of, indeed almost all, the Quran itself is clearly drawn from Biblical sources. The form in which Muhammad clothes his knowledge of the Bible implies that he had acquired that knowledge indirectly, perhaps from unorthodox Jewish and Christian travelers who might have been subject to exegetical or apocryphal influences. Tradition suggests the existence of some people (*Hanifs*) who while dissatisfied with current Arabian idolatry were not quite prepared to accept either of the two locally available alternatives, Christianity and Judaism.

What Muhammad interpreted quite literally as a "call" came to him around his fortieth year. At this distance it is impossible to say whether it resulted from a long-drawn-out psychological process or from a sudden upsurge of emotion, as suggested by the Quran itself. At first his early preaching, which was extremely simple and devoid of anything that could be called a doctrine, aroused no particular opposition from the townspeople, and while still in Mecca he himself does not seem to have considered his own revelation in the least original. Indeed, his claims did not go beyond the assertion that he was doing no more than repeat in Arabic the original message of the One God that had been revealed to others before him. The chapters written in Mecca emphasize only the One God, the perniciousness of idol worship, and the imminence of the Day of Judgment.

In the beginning he did not win much support for his somewhat bare religious claims. The first people he converted were his wife and a cousin, who later became the fourth of his successors. As his views took on a clearer outline and were preached by him with growing vehemence, he gradually aroused the opposition of the rulers of the city, ultimately making their hostility unyielding.

In line with the materialist explanations of history that have been commonplace since the nineteenth century, attempts have sometimes been made to explain the beginnings of Muhammad's movement as a reflection of a conflict between haves and have-nots. Muhammad is sometimes presented as a spokesman for the poor—or "underprivileged"—who expressed their deeply felt resentment of the pretensions and exploitation of the oligarchy in control of the city's economy. This may be exaggerated, but it reflects one particular aspect of Muhammad's early support, which was drawn to some extent from the lower classes, while the resistance on the part of the Meccan oligarchy may be explained as economic in motivation, revolving around the fear of risking Mecca's privileged economic position if its cult were to be destroyed. There may also have been an element of outrage in the pretensions of someone who did not stem from the higher strata of the community.

In any case, the conflict grew irreversible. Muhammad was gradually driven to action, doubtless as a result of the increasing persecution of the Muslims, which led a group of them to flee to Abyssinia. On the other hand, the new faith, called Islam—*i.e.*, "surrender" (to the will of God)—kept winning new adherents, though at the same time Muhammad's failure to make a really sizable dent in his own community discouraged him to the point of making him cast about for a new arena of activity. This ultimately took the form of his accepting an invitation to the city of Yathrib, some 280 miles northeast of Mecca, which had originally been settled by Jewish tribes coming from the north. Yathrib, a relatively opulent city, served as a magnet for many pagan Arabs who kept drifting into the town and who had finally come to dominate the Jews. The city lacked any stable authority. It was kept in a state of explosive division by the clan rivalries of two great Arab tribes, with the Jews acting only as counterweights in the fluctuating balance of power. While the Jews were materially and culturally superior to their neighbors, they were not particularly liked, it seems, and the moment the Arabs became unified, as they were through the success of Islam, the Jews were set upon and finally eliminated altogether, as they were to be from the entire peninsula.

This flight of Muhammad from Mecca to Yathrib gives us the first certain date in Muslim history. The flight—or the Hijra (Hegira), as it is called in Arabic—took place in 622 A.D.; it is the start of the Muslim calendar. This is surely in accordance with the importance of the event, for with the Hijra Muhammad's mission led directly to the formation of a new community based on new principles.

The significance of this move was not assessed at the time with the perspective given us by hindsight. The Quraysh made no fuss about Muhammad's departure, which took place only after he had suggested to his followers that they precede him to Yathrib (later to be called Medina—*i.e.,* "The City" [of the Prophet])—doubtless so that Muhammad might arrive there not as a mere individual, however eminent, but as the head of a specific, organized community.

The Medinese did not have the vested economic interests of the Meccans, so this element of opposition to Muhammad's new teaching was missing. On the other hand, they were not converts to Muhammad's views either. They apparently wanted him there because of his powerful character and temperament, as one who could help referee their constant internal disputes. Islam, too, was looked upon by them not as a religion but as a means of imposing law and order. Since they lacked the Meccan economic interest in the maintenance of paganism, they could look on the new religion quite without bias, though they did not actually adopt it in serious numbers until much later. In Muslim tradition the Medinese who were agitating for Muhammad to be brought in from "outside" as an umpire are called the Helpers (*Ansar*), while those who opposed this are called the Hypocrites (*Munafiqun*). It was only in the perspective of later piety, however, that the division between the Medinese acquired this religious tinge.

The transformation of Muhammad's activities was fundamental. He moved from the plane of prophecy to that of statesmanship. He was actually a governor, even though for the time being only a small community was under his authority. In spite of all the difficulties he was to encounter, however, this psychopolitical transformation of Muhammad marked the first genuine revolution within the nascent religion of Islam; it was the springboard for its unprecedented expansion.

Yet in the beginning these difficulties were formidable. During the early part of his stay in Medina, Muhammad was preoccupied primarily with the problem of his relations with the Jews. In his own mind, after all, he was not originating a new message or a new revelation, but was simply translating the message of monotheism into Arabic for the benefit of his heathen countrymen. Hence it was quite natural for him to appeal directly to the Jews as the source of his own contribution and to try to enlist their aid in disseminating the monotheistic doctrines embodied in their ancient books.

From their point of view, on the other hand, he was, of course, thoroughly superfluous. If it was their message he was broadcasting, what was he himself needed for? For that matter, they spoke Arabic too and were doubtless perfectly capable of conveying the message of the One God in Arabic to the neighboring pagans—and had, indeed, already done so.

Muhammad seems to have attempted to arrange a suitable compromise by adopting some of the Jewish ritual. He took over the fast of Yom Kippur, for instance, the holiest day in the Jewish calendar, and whereas in Mecca his followers had to pray only twice a day, after they got to Medina he initiated the custom of praying three times daily, in imitation of the Jews. He also started calling his followers to public prayers, somewhat like both Jews and Christians, though here he made a point by contrast of using only the human voice, appointing a professional caller to prayer (the muezzin). He also laid down a day of public prayer, Friday, modeled on the Jewish Sabbath, though again by contrast the day as a whole, after prayers, was a normal worldly day. He also had his followers turn toward Jerusalem when praying.

In spite of everything, however, Muhammad soon fell out with the Jews. It is true that he had modeled his message on the monotheism of the Hebrew Scriptures, yet since he had never actually read them and was wholly untrained in such matters, his ignorance could not but arouse the scorn of the Jews even in a remote place like Medina, and since he clung to his own version of the Jewish message in spite of his failure to persuade the Jews, he soon came to the conclusion that what was wrong was with the Jewish tradition and not with his own ideas. He developed the view that the Jews, and for that matter the Christians, had simply corrupted the original tradition. The mere charge of ignorance was not enough to make him doubt the authenticity of his own convictions. Since he was gripped by the assurance of having received a revelation originating directly with God, any deviation from that revelation could be ascribed only to corruption or malevolence.

Once Muhammad gave up his hopes of a compromise with the Jews, he turned away from them altogether. He decided to bypass them, so to speak, by returning to Abraham as the source of all revelation—Abraham, who now became for him not merely one of the many ancient prophets whose authority was acceptable but more specifically the inspirer of Islam itself. As the father of Ishmael, Abraham could be regarded as the ancestor of the Arabs as well as of the Jews—though this idea is itself a Jewish theory, or tradition, not vouched for by the Hebrew Scriptures—and so, once Muhammad had secured Abraham as a direct source of Islam, there was no longer any need for him to be dependent on the Jews at all. Abraham was claimed as the founder of the Meccan sanctuary, which he had needed for Ishmael, and hence as the author of the pilgrimage there. Accordingly, all that had to be done to restore the divinely sanctioned tradition initiated by Abraham in its integrity was to purify Mecca of some of its pagan perversions. Thus, through Muhammad—the "Seal of the Prophets"—an independently validated tradition was to be revived and launched once again.

At this time Muhammad's primary goal was the imposition of Islam on his pagan countrymen. His community in Medina consisted of followers who had come with him from Mecca—the Emigrants (*Muhajirun*)—and the Medinese Helpers. The former were still bound by ancient, pre-Islamic conceptions of honor, while the Helpers were reluctant to start any trouble with the powerful Meccan oligarchy on behalf of a mere religious view. This purely spiritual incentive, however, which may be thought of as specifically Muhammad's, was soon supplemented by a material motive—the cupidity aroused by the thought of the opulent caravans going to and fro outside Medina. Muhammad's believers, who as newcomers in a settled community had no particular source of income, soon felt the pinch of need, and in any case were constantly being reminded by Muhammad of all the injustices they were suffering. In the very first year of his stay in Medina, and in the beginning of the second, Muhammad seems to have undertaken a number of abortive raids. He was not successful until later in the second year, during the sacred month of Rajab, when "God's truce" was supposed to prevail. A party he sent out with sealed orders succeeded in intercepting a particularly rich caravan lulled into carelessness by the assurance of the holy truce, and in bringing back exceptionally heavy booty. Muhammad's suppleness was demonstrated here by his denial, in the face of the general indignation aroused in Medina itself by the breach of the holy truce, of having had any responsibility for it. He said it had all been a regrettable misunderstanding of his intentions and instructions. Later, however, when the size of the booty overshadowed the heinousness of the breach of tribal custom, Muhammad had a revelation that justified the spoliation of unbelievers even in the holy month of Rajab.

This episode concisely illustrates Muhammad's practicality as expressed against the background of contemporary custom, which of course saw nothing remotely reprehensible in the piracy that had its roots deep in the desert.

But Muhammad proved adept as a diplomat and statesman, too. Though as the governor of his own small community of believers he had a certain amount of political authority, he was careful from the beginning not to allow his merely political power to obtrude itself on the Medinese community. He transformed the political power he exercised over his own followers into a sort of religious authority. In one of the earliest documents that have come down to us—a primitive constitution for the early Islamic community in Medina—he informed his own followers, that is, the Helpers and the Emigrants, of an agreement he was making with the Jews, a sort of treaty confirming their right to exercise their religion freely and outlining conditions for coexistence. The document was exceedingly circumspect, constituting in effect a description of the relations to be observed between the Emigrants from Mecca and the tribes in Medina, and between both these groups and the Jews. It laid down, in fact, a ground plan for the Islamic community (*Umma*), based on the pre-Islamic town, but with a few basic changes that pointed to the later development of Islamic society.

Though all the underlying ideas of this document retained the structure of a tribal order of society, as well as many pre-Islamic practices relating to property, marriage, and intratribal relations, a fundamental change was introduced through the substitution of the new faith for blood as the element binding the community together. This development, though it must have seemed to replace the old tribe with the new Umma while retaining the same general structure, in fact pointed the way both to the universalism of the nascent religion and to the despotism that was later to become characteristic of Islamic society.

In the pre-Islamic tribe the identity of the tribe had been defined by the tribal cult, the tribe being held together by the mystical bond of the blood tie. When this was replaced by faith, the blood feud was suppressed within the Umma, and its unity was regulated by the arbitration of Muhammad himself, conceived of as dependent on the will of God exercising itself through his chosen Envoy. Muhammad, that is, became the new Shaykh of the Umma, which meant that his authority, deriving as it did from the will of God, was not contingent. It did not depend on consent, but had absolute authority for all converts to the new faith. The public opinion that in the pre-Islamic tribe had been the ultimate source of sanction was replaced by the absolute authority of God.

The implications of this were to become clear with the expansion of the Umma later into an Islamic society that theoretically could take in the whole of mankind. The Umma was on the one hand a sort of new tribe with Muhammad as Shaykh; at the same time it functioned as a sort of theocracy. The tribe, that is, was constituted by an act of faith; this entailed a form of society that from the Western point of view was and remains an essential unity in which religious and political authority are formally identical. The separation of church and state is quite irrelevant to this concept. In the Arabia of Muhammad's time no other form of social expression was possible, since religion could be organized only on political lines. At the same time, it was indispensable to obliterate the tribal antagonisms that would otherwise have been insurmountable, since only religion could create among Arabs an authority that hitherto had been exercised by the tribal structure.

The successful raids against the caravans coming from Mecca helped keep Mecca under curb until it could be subjugated by the new Umma; on the other hand, it also vastly increased the wealth and hence the power of the Umma. One of the most important victories of this kind took place in March 624, when a small party of no more than three hundred Muslims under Muhammad's personal leadership surprised a very rich caravan at Badr, a battle that is mentioned reverently in the Quran as a sign of divine favor. This particular raid gave the Umma considerable stability. In the Quran it marked the beginning of Muhammad's transition from the lonely prophet, prophesying timelessly, to the man of affairs, regulating pressing current problems. It was then that agitation against the Jews began; the Christians, too, were now accused of having falsified *their* scriptures in order to keep people in the dark about Muhammad's mission.

From now on Muhammad's preaching overtly conveyed a new religion. His own status, "Seal of the Prophets," was confirmed. Having turned away completely from the Jews and Christians, Muhammad's religion became entirely Arab. Jerusalem was no longer the place to turn to, but Mecca, with the Ka'ba being adopted as the center of a new cult and a place of pilgrimage.

All this implied, of course, that Mecca became a primary target of the Umma. After a temporary setback in March 625, when Muhammad was attacked by the Quraysh, irritated at the incessant brigandage of the Umma, and defeated (at Uhud), Muhammad attacked the Quraysh in turn, without, however, any decisive results. In the spring of 627, a large Meccan army (of ten thousand men—enormous in the circumstances) besieged Medina, but a simple technical innovation—a ditch!—baffled the Meccans completely and the Quraysh withdrew after a siege that had lasted some forty days. (These various battles generally had as a sequel the destruction of one Jewish tribe or another.)

In the spring of the following year, Muhammad risked a direct attack on Mecca, but while en route it seemed apparent that he lacked the power to take it. In a celebrated compromise (at Hudaybiyya) the Muslim leaders negotiated a truce to last ten years, with the Muslims having the right to make the pilgrimage to Mecca the following year.

Though some of the more ardent among Muhammad's followers were disappointed, their resentment was assuaged by an attack on a Jewish oasis. This constituted the first formal interaction between the Muslim community, considered as a state entity, and a non-

Muslim group; it served as a pattern for subsequent dealings with unbelievers. The Jews were allowed to keep their land, but had to pay a tribute of 50 per cent.

The next year Muhammad, with two hundred companions, made the pilgrimage to Mecca, where the new faith, lustrous now with power and prestige, made many new converts, including Khalid ibn al-Walid and Amr ibn al-As, two great generals who were to play a paramount role in the conquests the Umma was soon to embark on.

In January 630, finally, Muhammad took advantage of what was apparently a purely private murder of a Muslim and conquered Mecca once and for all. The capture of Mecca, at once the biggest city in Arabia and the shrine of the new faith, was really the peak of Muhammad's political career. The Quraysh were forced to submit; Muhammad's subjugation of the peninsula was assured. It is true that the spiritual conquest of the Bedouin tribes was not completed —to this day the Bedouin are not, perhaps, as devout as they theoretically should be. Muhammad's entire ethos was, after all, radically opposed to everything in Bedouin life; it was only his diplomacy that enabled him to persuade them to compromise with his claims as a prophet.

But though he never really converted the Bedouin of the peninsula to the new faith in terms that were acceptable to himself, his specific immediate objective, the overcoming of the influence of the Quraysh in his own favor, was ultimately achieved. This gave him the needed framework for the consolidation of the Umma and ultimately for its extension after his death beyond the borders of Arabia. To achieve this he had become accustomed to placating the tribes by not demanding too much from them. He insisted merely that they acknowledge the paramount position of Medina, leave the Muslims in peace, and accept the religious tax. Muhammad was perfectly content to allow remote tribes to remain neutral, though after the conquest of Mecca and of the Quraysh even these began volunteering delegations to acknowledge the political hegemony of the new and growing power. As far as the tribes themselves were concerned these delegations were purely political in nature, but Muhammad of course took advantage of them to expose them to his own religious propaganda. On the political plane they would form a personal contract with Muhammad as the ruler of Medina.

Very remote tribes, under the influence of Byzantium and Persia, were not, for the time being, affected at all, though here too there were many delegations, now of religious-minded people, who were hearkening to the new message being preached by Muhammad.

• • •

Muhammad died in June 632. His personal achievement was remarkable: He had introduced the monotheism of Judaism, with some accretions from Christianity, and with it replaced the idolatry of his countrymen. He had accomplished this through the personal composition of a revealed book, the Quran, which was to become the bedrock of belief for untold millions of followers in the generations to come. In addition, he had created a new state, or rather a new community founded on a new state principle, a community that was to prove itself capable of expanding without limit, of encompassing territories and peoples undreamed of by its founder, and of eventually serving as framework for an empire far greater than the Roman.

It is of course difficult to disentangle the figure of Muhammad the man from the dense web of emotion that surrounds him, woven of different materials by believers and enemies. For the Muslims he is, of course, a quite unquestionable figure. Though he never claimed to be anything more than human, his election as the mouthpiece of the Divine Will made it possible for the pious of later generations to envelop this purely human figure in a network of legend and fantasy felt to be fitting for the final and greatest Envoy of God, following in the footsteps of Abraham, Moses, and Jesus as the Seal of the Prophets and bringing to the human race the final revelation of God's Word.

This is of course the opposite of the curiously monstrous image the West has always formed of Muhammad. The endless prejudice of Christian dogmatists and the altogether silly slanders of medieval polemics have shaped a figure of repulsive fantasy, an archheretic or vulgar charlatan too contemptible to be worthy of any consideration at all. There has been so much theological prejudice even in Western scholarship, not always acknowledged by those whose thought it has impaired, that it requires an active effort of the mind to free oneself from the tendentious opinion expressed behind the façade of scholarly prose.

Yet to our own history-minded generation it is obvious that Muhammad, whatever his personal qualities, was clearly expressing with greater success a general movement that found parallel expression elsewhere. The need for unity and the desire for expansion had already been reflected in the brief career of the Arab Kinda empire. For that matter, Judaism and Christianity had both been spreading along the borders of Arabia. Even while Muhammad was still alive, other Arabian tribes produced their own "false" prophets, whose role seemed to be only partly modeled on that of Muhammad; in part it was an obvious parallel. Muhammad's own doctrine was, indeed, so simple that there was nothing in the nature of things to prevent almost any temperamental and outstanding person from magnifying his own person as the spokesman of the One God against the background of disintegrating idol worship and the steady spread of monotheistic ideas. Muhammad, in short, triggered what seems now to have been a latent movement of revival and expansion on the part of the hitherto atomized Arab tribes.

But clearly, things were not so cut-and-dried. If we consider the spiritual background Muhammad found himself opposed to, the deep contradiction between the religiosity he was imbued with and the immemorial code of honor of Bedouin chivalry, we may see what a revolution he effected.

The Bedouin who were ultimately to be converted, however superficially, to the austere simplicity of Muhammad's version of monotheism were essentially interested in nothing so much as the delights of this life—fighting, drinking, gambling, and lovemaking. This was in sharp contrast to an occasional outburst of religiosity among individual Arab poets, and especially to the culture of the south Arabian centers, where a definite interest and attachment to religious things was unmistakable. This contrast highlights the extreme earthiness of the Bedouin themselves.

Bedouin realism had nothing to do with the projection of bliss into the other world, or with transcendental mysticism of any kind. When Muhammad spoke of salvation or of the Final Judgment the words were quite meaningless for the Bedouin, wrapped as they were in the most immediate contact with the stark realities of the desert. The Quran's references to "good tidings" and to "redemption," insofar as they meant anything at all to the nomads, had to do with material advantages of one kind or another. Even the Bedouin who accepted Islam simply regarded it as a system for procuring the good things of life, by which they meant handsome foals from their mares, well-shaped infants, and the multiplication of their possessions. If they had all these, they congratulated themselves on Islam; if, after adhering to Islam, they discovered that they were still subject to shifts of fortune, they would curse Islam and turn their backs on it.

It is this crass materialism, or realism, on the part of the Bedouin that must account for the mistrust shown them in the Quran itself. Muhammad regarded them as inherently vacillating with respect to the new doctrines. If one considers the Bedouin virtues, this is only natural. For in the sense of the new ideals conveyed by Muhammad to the society of his time, the highest ethical perfection as understood in the desert was moral vileness for the new dispensation. The personality of Muhammad was itself almost the antithesis of what the nomads had been accustomed to accepting as the ideal of manliness. All Muhammad's basic ideas were the negation of the ideals of the Bedouin, if only because they went directly counter to the traditions of their ancestors. This was the most powerful argument Muhammad had to meet from them, and throughout the Quran it keeps exasperating him. "If they are told, 'Obey the law God sends you!' they reply, 'We obey the customs of our fathers!' "

Just as the Bedouin plumed himself on living in accordance with the customs of his noble forebears, so he would refuse to accept anything new in the way of morality.

From this point of view the absence of any originality in Muhammad's thought is of small significance sociologically. The fact is that it was his personality that somehow enabled the ethical ideas and the general world view drawn from Judaism, and to some extent from Christianity, to penetrate the consciousness of at least a few of the desert-dwellers after making a much stronger impact on the sedentary and semisedentary Arabians. If we recall that Christianity had a great many footholds in Arabia, it is all the more astonishing that its effects were so superficial. The core of the Arabs confronted Christianity as a whole with detachment and indifference. But it was Muhammad, by fusing these alien ideas into a new form that was channeled into Arab society in a way they could understand, who first enabled the Arabs to express their distaste for these novel ideas. That is, what had been detachment with respect to Christianity, which had simply not been assimilated into Arab thinking at all, became active revulsion when Muhammad presented to the Arabs, in a tangible, concentrated form, his own new ethic, grounded in that of Christianity and Judaism.

This profound contradiction between the monotheistic ethic preached by Muhammad and the pagan world view of the Bedouin is best summed up in two simple words—*"Din"* and *"Muruwwa."*

Din is the religion of Muhammad; *Muruwwa,* the exact equivalent of the Latin *virtus,* is what the Bedouin understood as all the glory inherited from their noble forebears and the obligations it imposed on them, the fulfillment of all those duties revolving around family ties, hospitality, and the great law of blood vengeance. Underlying the whole structure were two notions: fidelity and self-sacrificing devotion on behalf of all those linked to the clan.

Forgiveness, a virtue according to the ethic based on Judaism and Christianity and the Islam preached by Muhammad, was a vice to the Bedouin. Irreconcilability with respect to injury and insult—such was the pagan ideal. Failure to pay back an insult was regarded by the pre-Islamic Arab world—during the *Jahiliyya,* the "Ignorance"—as a symptom of vulgar cowardice that covered the whole tribe with shame. In the Quran, of course, a principal condition of God's forgiveness is that a man forgive those who have wronged him and forget injuries he has suffered (24:22). This ethical claim of Muhammad was thus in flagrant contradiction with a major motivation in Bedouin life.

With respect to pleasure, too, Muhammad's limitations ran counter to all the ideals of Bedouin life, particularly the "Two Good Things"—wine and women. The Bedouin had always taken the view that the endless fasting in the tomb dispensed them of any obligation to asceticism in this life. Thus the idea instituted by Muhammad of fasting for the month of Ramadan lacked appeal, as did Muhammad's restrictions on sexual license, which, though they may seem laughably overgenerous to the West, imbued, sometimes unconsciously, with the Christian notion of hatred of the flesh and the general desirability of chastity, could not but seem to the Bedouin an outrageous invasion of their right to enjoy themselves. Since the Muruwwa of Muhammad's pagan contemporaries was based on the traditions of their ancestors, and these traditions allowed unbounded sexual license, Muhammad's restrictions were extremely vexatious.

Muhammad's restrictions with respect to food and drink, too, were found deeply repulsive by the pagan Bedouin. Tippling—though not, to be sure, solitary tippling—was regarded by them all as a delicious pastime. Wine was thought to lead to virtue, honor, and generosity. Muhammad was summoning all those who believed in this to regard it as a filthy sin and the work of the devil! The "real Arabs" remembered with delight all their drinking bouts; they boasted of their prowess as tipplers and made a point of getting up very early in the morning so as to be able to drink their fill before their women would be up and about with their nagging.

Beyond the denial of their traditional pleasures, the Bedouin were also required by Islam to indulge in all sorts of pietistic exercises, especially prayer, which of all Muhammad's requirements seemed to them the most tiresome and abhorrent. The pagan Arabs must of course have had occasion to make invocations to their local deities for specific purposes, but the alienness of Muhammad's institution of regular and systematic prayer at set times during the day is illustrated by his finding it necessary to borrow a foreign word for prayer, despite the celebrated wealth of the Arabic vocabulary. A legend concerning the institution of prayer gives an amusing sidelight on the inherent Arab distaste for the whole thing.

The legend is that once, when Muhammad ascended to Heaven, he visited the six lower Heavens, to greet the other prophets, Adam, Abraham, Moses, and Jesus, and then went to the seventh Heaven, where God ordered fifty prayers daily for the Arabs. When Moses heard of this he advised Muhammad to go back to God and tell him it was out of the question for the Arabs to pray that much. Muhammad did this, and God waived half the prayers. But Moses was shocked at this, too, and persuaded Muhammad to go back to God once again, since the Arabs were quite incapable of accomplishing this either. Muhammad managed to get God to come down to five prayers a day, but Moses thought this too was unendurable for Arabs and tried to get Muhammad to go back once more, but here Muhammad balked, saying that this time he himself would really feel too ashamed before God.

This perhaps unintentionally comic legend surely reflects the negative attitude of the pagan Arabs to an institution they must have thought quite senseless. It was a peculiarly irritating detail of the new way of life, a sort of straitjacket, from the point of view of the unbridled life of the desert, that seemed designed to stifle the essential man beneath a fossilized edifice of piety and ritual.

With respect to the basic concept of society, too, Islam ran head-on into the structure of the tribe, which for the individual pagan Bedouin meant the whole universe. If all relations revolved around the concept of a mystical participation in the mystical essence of a unit descended from ancestors whose exploits gave the tribe its claim on esteem, so to speak, what were the Bedouin to make of an attitude toward society that made hash of all their feelings? How could they give up allegiance to their tribes, which is what established their identity both positively, as members of one tribe, and negatively, as nonmembers of all other tribes? How could they surrender that allegiance? Individuals who could not point to any notable ancestors were universally looked down on in Arab society. Even though they dwelled among Arabs and their native tongue was Arabic, such people would find themselves performing menial tasks that debased them still further. The more glorious ancestors one had to enumerate, the greater one's personal nobility. This was not a question of mere vanity; the magical inheritance of attributes was what actually defined the personality of an individual. Just as it was believed that physical qualities were transmitted from one ancestor—male, of course!—to his descendants, so moral qualities were too. In this sense personal glory and personal merit were mere reflections of inherited glory and inherited merit: nobility imposed duties and led to the performance of noble deeds. The glory of the ancestors was a constant incentive to good behavior. Indeed, the concept of *noblesse oblige* was the cornerstone of Bedouin tribal life.

Curiously enough, this general attitude was reflected with particular intensity in the poetry that formed the chief common element of Bedouin culture. The tribes would fight against each other primarily through poetry, in which the glorification of one's own tribe would be counterposed to the vilification of one's opponents. The praises of one's own ancestors would find a counterpoint in diatribes against the ancestors of one's adversaries, since this was the sensitive point in their armor. If effectively worded, an insult directed at the ancestors of an adversary could be shattering—it was his ancestors' honor, after all, that a man's own claim to fame and honor was intimately bound up with. Thus the principal weapons in the armory of two tribes in conflict would be their poets; the battle would be waged largely through reciprocal satire, a sort of seesaw. The recitation of the disgraceful deeds or the stained lineage of one's opponent would be set against the panegyrics directed at oneself, all in the most inflated language. Combat via poetry was thought of as the serious beginning of real warfare, which came to an end only when the reciprocal lampooning stopped. The poets were effective not merely because of their artistic skill—indeed, such a concept would have been quite unthinkable—the poets were wielders of magic, knowers and seers (as their Arabic name indicates). They might be mentioned in the same breath as augurs and well finders. In this way the magical quality of the poet was a reflection of the magical quality of language that made poetry literally effective. Hence, a well-worded lampoon would be thought of as striking its target in a real sense; the mockery would arise out of the destruction of the opponent via the destruction of his family tree.

A similar situation may be seen in the Biblical story of the cursing of the Children of Israel by Balaam at the request of King Balaq: The cursing was not merely rhetorical, but was magically effective in the mouth of the magical poet. A tribal poet among the Bedouin was thus no mere versifier, but a kindler of battle who by the mocking verses he could shoot out at the mockers of his own tribe would undo them. His words would be "possessed of wings" and be "current," *i.e.,* they would make the rounds of the encampments and become universally known. Hence their targets, to wipe away the obloquy that came on them from such humiliating defeats in poetry, would have to do so by flinging shafts of their own back at their enemies that would do the same to them.

It is thus entirely understandable that this intricate association of tribal structure with the mystical sense of personal identity collided very directly with the basic tendency of Islam, that is, the universalizing of relations under the authority of God. The equality and fraternity of all mankind, irrespective of tribal personal origins and arising out of the descent from Adam, were designed to destroy the whole concept of tribalism. The fact of Islam was supposed to level all social and genealogical differences and put a stop to the incessant bickering among the tribes, their unflagging self-glorification, mutual lampooning, and so on. For that matter, no distinction was to be left in Islam even between the noble Arabs and the lowly barbarians once the barbarians accepted Islam, nor were there to be basic differences between freemen and slaves. Islam was to consist of brothers only. In Muhammad's Umma it was to be forbidden even to ask whether anyone was of such and such a tribe, or even a Persian, or an Arab. This was specifically contemned as a relic of the "Ignorance." From the moment Muhammad proclaimed himself the "Prophet of the White and of the Black," a mission that encompassed the human race, the only criterion of distinction among his followers was to be the degree of their piety within Islam.

It is curious to reflect that this universalizing tendency of Islam, which was to become its sociopolitical *raison d'être,* is doubtless to be sought not in the mere abstraction of Muhammad's thought, but in the circumstances that led to his flight from Mecca and to his falling-out with his own tribe, the Quraysh. The necessity he underwent of taking up arms against his fellow tribesmen—felt by all Arabs to be a shameful disgrace—at some point, by an inherent logic, led Muhammad to denounce as worthless the very principle underlying tribal organization and to replace it as a social bond by allegiance to the new faith. The perception of the political necessity for justifying his taking up arms against the Quraysh then led to the further perception of the social advance it implied: "Oh mankind! We have created you man and woman, and have made you into nations and tribes that you may know each other. Verily, the noblest of you, in the sight of God, is he who is most God-fearing" (Quran 49:13).

This statement in the Quran is the source of Islamic egalitarianism and has found universal acceptance among Muslims, with no deviant interpretations. In all its implications it was a total disruption of the traditional Arab view of life and society and was to have revolutionary effects on the Arabs and on the world. Ultimately, indeed, it was to lead to the retreat of the Arabs from the Islamic society whose groundwork they had laid. They left that society flourishing, as it were, without them, and although the nomadic Arabs remained nominal Muslims and still are to this day, they never changed their own way of life, nor did tribal society in Arabia itself change substantially even after the impact of Islam.

The contrast between the tribal system and the nascent religious community remained so strong that in the first phase of Islam the tribes that were busily engaged in carrying Islam abroad did so as discrete units. There was never any mingling of the tribes, who would migrate en masse as independent entities and would have to be quartered in separate encampments. Even in cities where many tribes settled they had to have special quarters assigned them. The municipal authorities would, in fact, be composed of the chiefs of the various tribal city districts. It was only when individual tribes were present in very small numbers that different tribes could be quartered together, and even then only against violent resistance. This separation of the tribes was even maintained at the moment of collective prayer, when presumably the religion would come into the most obvious collision with the hostile tribal traditions. In the conquered provinces each tribe might have a mosque of its own.

Perhaps the culminative phenomenon in this question of tribal feuds and rivalries was to be found in the rivalry I have mentioned above between northern and southern Arabs. This ancient rivalry was reflected in social life, politics, and literature; it was to last far into the Islamic era and has even persisted down to our own day. It was to play an important role in the establishment of the first Arab empire and in its dissolution.

Now, it is true that this antagonism between northern and southern Arabs goes back very far into the prehistory of the Arabs, if we are to judge by tradition. Some scholars believe it to go back to the dawn of Arab consciousness. Yet it now seems far more likely that the development of this systematized opposition between northern and southern Arabs was a reflection of newborn Islam, in the attempt of Muhammad's Medinese Helpers to find points of support in their conflict with the haughty Quraysh. The early and thoroughly political-cum-religious conflict between the Meccan Quraysh and the Medinese Helpers was ideologized, so to speak, against the background of the traditional Arab tribal outlook. Thus, at the very moment that Islam was taking shape as a universal religion, its universalism itself was the reflection of a tactic adopted by Muhammad to offset the haughty genealogical claims of the Meccans while at the same time the opposition was generalized on the most old-fashioned Arab Bedouin tradition of all. Even though Muhammad himself was a northern Arab by birth, a difficult fact to undermine, the Helpers, who were generally regarded as the southern Arab party, found counterarguments that enabled the rivalry to smolder on with great force for centuries. As Islam became more or less assimilated, whether superficially or not, the tribes could vie with each other with respect to their Islamic devoutness and past achievements. Thus, Islam itself, despite all its leveling and universalizing tendencies, became an object of vainglorious boasting in tribal terms. Traditions could even be and were invented in accordance with the general tendency to retroject to Muhammad's day the sociopolitical and religious disputes of later times. Even bogus Quranic verses were contrived, for instance, to put the Helpers in a favorable light with respect to the Quraysh—even to those Quraysh who had become Emigrants together with Muhammad.

It is curious to observe the manner in which Islam, in its initial, Arabian phase, itself became one factor—though ultimately a dominant one—among others in the flux of local society. The genealogical obsession of the Arabs, for instance, a reflection of traditional Arabian particularism, was strong enough to preoccupy the attention of the professional class of Muslim exegetes and jurists—roughly the equivalent of the theologians of the West—and force them to expend their energies in combating it, in the name of Islamic egalitarianism. The Muslim theoreticians—as distinct from the Arabs—were rightly to see in all this emphasis on tribal allegiance and on race in general a fundamental contradiction of the other, dominant, universalizing tendency that was at the core of the religion proper, that was, so to speak, the "real" religion. It is, perhaps, no more than an additional oddity that the Muslim theoreticians themselves sometimes used the system of genealogizing to their own advantage, when, for instance, they found a common ancestor for both northern and southern Arabs in the nebulous figure of Ishmael himself!

In any case, Islam was soon to propel itself beyond Arabia, and very soon beyond the Arabs generally. It is timely to give a short, summary account of Muhammad's handiwork.

• • •

Though in the centuries after Muhammad Islam was to become heavily encrusted with an intellectual development, it was of an altogether pristine simplicity as it emerged from the mind of Muhammad. The whole religion, indeed, could be summed up in the formula by which one can still today become a Muslim: "There is no god but God, and Muhammad is his envoy."

Islam has, properly speaking, no theology, if by theology is meant the extraordinarily complicated systems evolved by Christian thought in its struggle to establish and clarify the relationship between Jesus and God. For all Muslims, of Muhammad's time and now, Muhammad was simply a man. He had been, to be sure, selected by God as a mouthpiece, and in that sense was perhaps closer to the divine than other men. In the minds of simple Muslims he has been enveloped in a dense web of legend and fantasy, but in spite of all fabulist tendencies, and in spite of a perhaps common desire among the simpleminded of all strata of society to feel that special people are nearer God, Muhammad's function never gave rise to any special claims of theological *substance*. His role was clear: He was a man who came to reveal the will of God, who had selected him but had not thereby made him different.

The Quran, which contains the basic teachings of Islam, is unique among the great religious works of mankind in that it was actually composed by Muhammad personally, that is, by an historic individual well known to many thousands of his contemporaries. It is of interest to us here since it also constitutes the beginning of the Arabs as a self-conscious people, though simultaneously—and paradoxically, as we shall see—their subsequent transformation out of all recognition.

Perhaps the chief oddity of the Quran, and indeed of Muhammad's career generally, is that despite its function as the fountainhead of one of the great socioreligious movements in history the Quran is in no sense of the word a religious innovation. Nor was it, as I have said, ever given out as such by its author.

What Muhammad thought he was doing—and in fact did do—was to convey to his own people in their own language the revelation originally given by God to the Jews and Christians. He seems to have been unaware of what his followers later considered to be the incontrovertible idolatrousness of Christianity: the divinity of Jesus, the Trinity, and the actual worship of the figure on the cross, to say nothing of tendencies like Mariolatry. Muhammad seems to have understood Christianity in its Judaistic aspect, as one more stage in the revelation of the One God to mankind. For this reason Jesus finds a place in the list of the authentic envoys of God, that is, the prophets, beginning with Adam and going through Abraham and Moses. Muhammad consummates, so to speak, the list as the "Seal of the Prophets," after whom no other prophet is necessary or for that matter conceivable.

Thus the Quran is one man's version of the books of the Old and the New Testaments. Now, though Muhammad was never thought of as divine—though some later Muslim sectarians believe in his sinlessness—it has always been an article of faith that the Quran itself is divine, in two senses: one, that it consists of God's actual words spoken to one man through the mouth of the Angel Gabriel; and two, in the sense of being no more than a copy or transcription of actual written tablets preserved in Heaven.

Muhammad was in a state of exaltation when actually reciting the verses of the Quran (which itself simply means "recitation"), a state that must have been recognized and acknowledged by those around him, who thus clearly distinguished the Quranic passages from Muhammad's mere remarks. Thus, though Muslim tradition makes Muhammad an illiterate, this may be exaggerated or even downright false. It seems unlikely, since Muhammad must have had to keep business accounts as a young man. The point may be that the words he got from on high bear all the earmarks of divine origin.

Essentially then, if we suspend judgment as to the Quran's having come literally from the mouth of God, it is the literary composition of one individual. It is thus doubtless unique not only as a religious text but as a literary work.

The language itself is often claimed as the absolute and irrefutable proof of its divine origins. It is supposed to be untranslatable. If an outsider points out various obscurities, confusions, or even absurdities in the text, a believing Muslim will simply declare, as an act of faith, that the Quran is absolutely perfect. Its sonorous, rhythmic, poetic prose is supposed to exercise an actually hypnotic effect on those who listen to it. Because of this it has played a unique role in the spread of the Arabic language and in its influence over those who speak it. It is doubtless the most effective monument of the Arabian poetry I have mentioned above.

Though large parts of the Quran sound like a collection of battle cries, simple exhortations, etc., it contains a religious system, rounded out though simple. This rests on the following pillars:

God is the sole Creator of the Universe; He is absolutely One. Hell awaits the idolaters, the unjust, the rich and selfish. As life-giver God will raise up the body after death. Believers will find themselves in Paradise, full of earthly delights, especially luscious fruits and dark-eyed beauties, male and female, and will drink wine from golden bowls. Paradise is constantly contrasted with the horrors of Hell. Though God can be depended on to forgive minor infractions, major sins will be punished ferociously.

The most important statement made by the Quran, after it lays down the utter Oneness of God, is that God had revealed His message to mankind through envoys who actually wrote the message down. Just as Muhammad was the Seal of the Prophets, so the Quran was the last of such messages, completing and occasionally abrogating everything gone before. As it says (4:135): "Believe in God and his envoy, and the book he has sent down to his envoy and the book he sent down formerly. He who disbelieves in God and his angels, his books, and his envoys, and in the Last Day, has strayed far."

The corollary of the belief that the Quran was merely repeating in a perfected form the message formerly revealed to Jews and Christians was that any discrepancies between both these communities or between both of them with respect to Muslims were due to falsification. Hence the primordial situation of purity must be restored—Abraham, the first Muslim, must be gone back to via the revelation Muhammad was now making.

In the Quran God's mercy and knowledge are limitless. While transcendent, he is omnipresent. The Muslim must not be afraid to die: Paradise awaits him. Through all the trials of life the Muslim must trust in God.

The Last Day (Day of Judgment), a dominant theme in the Quran, especially in its early sections, is manifestly Jewish and/or Christian. Only God knows when it will come. There will be a sound of trumpeting, and the graves will give up their dead, whose deeds will be weighed in the divine scales and who will be handed a ledger (this seems original with the Quran). If this ledger is put into their right hand, they will go to Heaven; if the left, Hell.

The Muslim has, of course, duties. The most important obligations in Islam are prayer, almsgiving, fasting, and making the pilgrimage to Mecca.

The Quran itself suggests that only three prayers a day are necessary, but later tradition made it five—sunset, night, dawn, noon, and afternoon. The Muslims are called to prayers by a muezzin, who is supposed to have a powerful voice and who calls from the top of a gallery encircling the minaret of a mosque: "God is most great. I bear witness that there is no god but God. I bear witness that Muhammad is God's Envoy. Come to prayer! Come to security! God is most great!" Worshipers are supposed to face Mecca, and all mosques have a sort of semicircular alcove (*mihrab*) to indicate the direction of Mecca.

Almsgiving is both obligatory and voluntary. Muslim law laid this down as one-fortieth of income, whether in money or possessions. In modern times this duty is now left entirely to the conscience of the individual. Both words for "alms" were taken from Jewish law.

Fasting is derived explicitly from Jewish and Christian practice with the change in the duration of the fast, extending over an entire month (Ramadan, when the Quran was first revealed). It is a rather strict fast, since for the whole of a day, between sunrise and sunset, it is forbidden to eat, drink, or smoke. At high temperatures this entails some suffering, so that travelers and invalids are exempt. On the other hand, the nighttime is quite free.

As for the pilgrimage to Mecca, Muhammad simply took over this custom from time immemorial and made it one of the obligations of the believers. He seems to have launched the theory that Abraham himself made the pilgrimage there, though this seems a quite arbitrary notion. Every Muslim is required to make the pilgrimage at least once in his life. The ritual is traditional, though Muhammad seems to have made some changes—just which ones we do not know.

These four cardinal duties, plus the profession of faith in God and his Envoy, make up the "Five Pillars of the Faith."

There are a number of other prohibitions, directly borrowed from Judaism: Pork is altogether taboo, while idolatry is unpardonable. Though the actual interdiction on wine in the Quran is somewhat ambiguous, usage has hardened it into an absolute. All the Ten Commandments but the second, third, and fourth are found in somewhat different wording. Pretentious waste and pride are condemned, as is unkindness to slaves, though slavery as such is accepted.

Despite many misconceptions, the Quran has a rather puritanical attitude toward sexuality, representing a very considerable modification of the former Arab license. Marriage was regarded as existing for the purpose of procreation; indeed, the word used is the same as "copulation." It is for this reason that it permits a man to have four wives and apparently an unlimited number of concubines, though some Muslims (notably the Wahhabis of Arabia, in modern times) reject concubinage. This permission is somewhat softened, from the woman's point of view, by the obligation of the man to treat all his women in a precisely similar manner and with the same kindness and attentiveness. If he cannot manage this, he is supposed to restrict himself to one. Modern Muslims are fond of denying that the status of women in Islam is in any way inferior to what it is in the West, but though it is true that in recent times women have been treated in a far more humane way, there is no gainsaying that the Quran, though it may have marked an advance over paganism, nevertheless lays down the inherent inferiority of women quite unmistakably (Sura 4).

• • •

Apart from Muhammad's originality as a personality and the uniqueness of his personal contribution, it is clear that the doctrinal and ritual structure of Islam as he conceived it is solidly grounded in Judaism and Christianity. There has been some scholarly dispute as to the precise proportions between the two influences, and it is difficult to specify in detail just which elements influenced Muhammad through just which channels. It is obvious that some Jewish material from the Hebrew Scriptures, for instance, might have come to Muhammad via Christians, while Christian material might have been mediated by Jews who had been influenced in their turn by Christian customs such as vigils, cenobitism, and so on. The Quran, in short, contains a vast mass of material that can be traced to Jewish and Christian sources equally.

In any case the similarities between Islam, Judaism, and Christianity are—if we except Christology!—very striking. If we confine ourselves for the moment to a comparison between Islam and Christianity, between the basic tenets of Islam and, say, the Apostles' Creed, only a few important things would be denied by Muslims: They do not believe that God is the Father, that Jesus is the only

Son of God and Our Lord, or that Jesus is sitting on the right hand of God the Father Almighty. Nor do they, of course, believe in the Holy Catholic Church, or in the Communion of Saints.

Essentially Muslims have the same objections to the Apostles' Creed as Jews: The idea of God being Jesus' father is abhorrent to both because of its implication of a biologically progenitive role being played by the Creator of the Universe, and since it is specifically Jesus' divine role, as later developed into the Trinity and so on, that is indigestible for Muslims and Jews, Islam would seem to be a regression to the situation preceding the advent of Christianity.

Indeed, Muhammad's seeming belief in Jesus is an anachronism altogether, for if he had not heard of or in any case did not believe in Jesus' divine role, or in the redemptive character of the Crucifixion, why was Jesus important to him at all? On the level of reason it is, of course, impossible to say. Historically, however, Muhammad must have been impressed by the presence of so many Christians in Arabia and must have thought them mere monotheists, without ever becoming aware of the weightiness of the Christology. Hence his belief in Jesus as a prophet and even more strikingly his acceptance of the virginity of Mary—which even Saint Paul never heard of!—are no more than foibles, representing a misunderstanding of the nature of Christianity that was quite understandable for someone in Muhammad's position.

The fact, however, that Muhammad believed in the Virgin Mary, and in Jesus' conception by the Holy Ghost, and in His ascension into Heaven, is quite meaningless in the Muslim system, for since the monotheism of Islam is quite rigid, its simplicity being disturbed only by Muhammad's special role, there is simply nothing for the concept of Jesus to accomplish within the thinking of Islam. Muhammad as the Seal of the Prophets consummates the function of all preceding prophets. The resemblances to Christianity do no more than revolve around ideas that are in fact derived from Judaism, that is, the oneness of God as Creator of the Universe, his speaking to people through prophets, and the embodying of both these ideas in a book.

Thus Islam, on closer inspection, can be seen to be structurally a replica of Judaism, with Christian accretions, rather than of Christianity. It is Judaism, of course, without the special role of the Jews: The "Covenant," so to speak, between Muhammad and God supersedes the successive covenants recorded in the Pentateuch between God and the Chosen People. It is curious to reflect that this singular historical event—the impinging of Judaism and of a small segment of the Jewish people on Muhammad's consciousness—was to play a seminal role in the formation of Islam, and in the creation of the Arabs as a people.

A closer look will bear this out.

Muhammad's early biographers thought it a special sign of God's favor that Medina had a large Jewish population that could help guide the Arabs onto the path of monotheism, and it is surely significant that at the crucial moment in the formation of the Arabs as a people there were so many Jewish colonies scattered throughout Arabia. Indeed, the name "Medina" itself was the word for "town" in Aramaic, which was spoken by the Jews who had settled there long before. The majority of the Jews in Arabia, despite some scholarly speculation to the contrary, were doubtless Jews by birth, which seems likely partly on the analogy of the Yemenite Jews, who have so many "Priests"—*Kohanim*—and Levites among them, and partly because the early Muslim historiographers described the Jews of Medina as "priests."

The Quran itself repeatedly refers to Jewish rabbis and scholars who expounded the Torah and were looked up to by the whole community for their scholarship. It often mentions the Sabbath as a day of rest and refers to Jewish dietary and other laws. It contains numerous legends and theological notions from Talmudic literature, and though it is more than likely that the Jews whom Muhammad knew might have had some sectarian groups, there can be no doubt that it was a flourishing community of quite conventional Jews, though of course there is no reason to think all its members particularly pious or learned as individuals. Indeed, there are indications that while the bulk of the Jews absolutely refused to acknowledge Muhammad as a prophet, some did, and it has been suggested that these might have represented a Jewish sect, one that insisted on the exclusive validity of the Torah alone against any "human" emendations such as the Talmud.

Muhammad claimed his message from God merely confirmed earlier revelations made to Jews and Christians. Later on in the Quran he developed Jewish themes, notably in the Joseph Sura, in which he indicated some acquaintance with Genesis as well as with the post-Biblical Jewish treatment of the theme. This may indicate an acquaintance with some more or less scholarly Jews. By going back to Abraham, however, Muhammad was able to find his own warrant for his own version. It must be assumed that it was necessary for him to bypass Jewish opposition by discovering an ancestry for the Arabs parallel to that of the Jews. The slight artificiality of this—that is, the likelihood that the whole idea was a mere device of Muhammad's—seems indicated by the fact that the word "Ishmael" itself does not occur in an Arabic form in the Quran, but in an obvious derivation from Greek or Syriac, which implies that if Ishmael had ever been thought of as a real ancestor of the Arabs the recollection had long since faded from the minds of the Arabians.

As far as Christianity is concerned, Muhammad's knowledge of Christ and Christianity in general does not seem derived from any actual Christian denomination or sect. He never mentions the figure of Christ, or even the name Christ itself in the earliest parts of the Quran, the very parts that have numerous accounts of the holy men of the Old Testament and of Arab antiquity. The impression is unavoidable that Muhammad interested himself in Christianity only at a very late stage in his religious career, which probably accounts for the absence of the edifying stories about Christ which appear in the New Testament. Hence, though Muhammad, as an inhabitant of a big caravan center, doubtless met Christians, the teachers referred to in the Quran from whom he actually received the material for his new religion could not have been professing Christians. The very name of Christ—*i.e.,* al-Masih, the Messiah—was used by him only after his migration to Medina.

It is, on the other hand, Moses who is far and away the predominant figure in the Quran. Though Jesus is mentioned only four times during the formative period of Muhammad's career in Mecca, Moses' name comes up more than a hundred times. What is still more important, stories about Moses pervade the whole of the Quran. Indeed, it was the idea of Moses—*the Prophet with a Book*—that inspired Muhammad, who during his earlier period regarded himself as Moses' direct successor. "Before this book there was Moses' book . . . and this book confirms it in the Arabic tongue" (Quran 46:12).

Perhaps the slightly contradictory evidence of Muhammad's inspiration as having been derived from both Christian and Jewish sources can be explained by the assumption that though the Jews who influenced Muhammad were fundamentally merely orthodox Jews, they had themselves come under the influence of Christian monastic piety and taken over some of its practices, perhaps some of its literature.

The most convincing demonstration of Muhammad's dependence on Jews is the uncompromisingly expressed theme of unswerving monotheism characteristic of Muhammad from the outset of his career. Only pious Jews could have inspired that.

As Muhammad never stopped stressing, it was from Israel that he derived the values that for him were paramount: the belief in the One God, Creator of the world and Architect of human destiny, a God of justice and mercy to whom all men, of all stations, bear a personal responsibility.

Close as the connection is between Muhammad's Quran and Judaism, there is an even more striking parallelism between the two systems of religion as fully developed, in particular between the Muslim religious law (the *Shari'a*) and the older Jewish religious law (the *Halakha*).

Both are religions with a God-given code that regulates in detail all aspects of life—law, worship, ethics, and social behavior. The religious law in both religions is based on an oral tradition in addition to the written. The oral tradition is both legal and moral, and both Muslim and Jewish literature contain this oral law in the form of loosely linked aphorisms and anecdotes.

Muslim religious law, like Jewish, was evolved by a completely free and unorganized republic of scholars. Ancient Muslim rulers never actually created laws, nor did Islam ever have an ecclesiastical hierarchy. In both religions the religious law was shaped finally as different schools or rites, all of them equally orthodox. The logical reasoning underlying the development of the religious law is identical in both religions. Since the religious law is paramount, its study is considered a form of worship; holy men in both Islam and Judaism are not priests or monks, but merely students of the divinely revealed law. It is true that later on in Islam a certain antagonism developed between the legal students and the mystically inclined saints, but in early Islam they were identical.

A consequence of the total inclusivity of the Islamic law was that the mere knowledge of it gave the knower a decisive superiority over the unknower, since in many areas of basic importance the

Shari'a did not remain mere theory but was translated into authoritative law. This lent an otherwise inexplicable authority to the scholars who on the model of the Jewish rabbis took the place in Islam of a Western clergy. It was only the doctors of the law who could implement, for instance, the termination of a marriage. The prestige of this caste was also heightened by the very fact that so many believers were incapable of living even partially up to the law and so looked up to the learned with particular fervor.

Summing up, if one recalls that Judaism was fully developed during the first Arab conquests and that Muslim religious law developed mainly in Iraq, the chief center of Jewish studies, that Islam was in its nature bound to learn from other religions and that Muhammad's strict monotheism doubtless inspired his followers to be instructed by equally strict monotheists, the influence of Judaism not only on Muhammad but on early Islam as a whole must have been well-nigh decisive.

Judaism did not only play a genetic role in the formation of Muhammad's Islam. The parallel between the two religions, on the historical plane, is very striking.

In both cases a religion that was wholly ethnocentric, while retaining its national flavor and content, was assimilated by a great many other peoples. In the case of the Jews the Old Testament, a thoroughly parochial history book recording the history of one people and their meditation on it, became a sacred book for Christianity—a third of mankind—and conserved a special status for Islam, too, another sixth of mankind. The same thing took place with the Quran and Islam. A specifically Arab national spiritual paternity was grafted onto the histories of the many peoples that adopted Islam, with even greater impact, in some ways, because of the failure of Western-style nationalism to mold the peoples outside Christendom. To this day the Arabic element in Islam has retained far more meaningful prestige among Muslim peoples than, say, Latin or Greek has for Christendom.

It is not unlikely that what promoted the worldwide diffusion of both Judaism (through Christianity) and Islam was the primitive democracy characteristic of both the ancient Hebrews and the Arabs of Arabia. The equality of all men and the consequent sanctity of individual rights constitute a natural vehicle for universalism however ethnocentric its focus.

Of course the difference in the actual history of Jews and

Arabs is still more striking. In a way, it illustrates the curiously long-range effect of Jewish monotheism, which worked like a delayed-action bomb.

The evolution of Jewish monotheism itself was a long and painful process. It took some twelve centuries for it to be shaped into a force that served as a springboard for Christianity and Islam. Muhammad's religion was established on the solid groundwork of something already worked out; it simply had to be translated into another idiom, which is just how Muhammad, in his early phase, expressed it: his own message was that of Moses in "clear Arabic." This took no more than one generation, even less—the last half of the life of one man was enough for Islam to be founded, at least as a religion, in such a way as to support the great structure that succeeding generations erected on top of it.

Israel, moreover, developed its own monotheism in a tiny country surrounded by great and ancient civilizations it was in constant conflict with; by the time the Arabian tribes were ready to accept Islam they had already occupied the whole of the Arabian Peninsula, had a lengthy though unwritten history and sense of unity behind them, and had already penetrated into all the countries on their borders—Persia, Iraq, Syria, and Egypt. Contacts between Arabs and other peoples had been in progress for a millennium and a half, since the ninth century B.C., and though some Arab splinter groups were absorbed by the more cultivated societies they penetrated, such as the Nabateans, these losses were made up for by the development of Arabia as a neutral country benefiting greatly from the lucrative role of a commercial middleman between the Roman and the Persian empires, which for centuries were at each other's throats.

Perhaps an equally potent factor in the promotion of the Arab conquests and of Islam was the gradual arabization of the ancient kingdoms of southern Arabia, which had been steadily disintegrating during the centuries preceding the emergence of Islam. Indeed, without the arabization of these ancient centers of civilization, both the Arab conquests and the inner evolution of Islam itself would have been unthinkable. While the pre-Islamic Arabian tribes had a common literary language, as well as the intertribal language of business, their actual spoken dialects were quite distinct.

Thus it was to prove a relatively simple matter for Muhammad to put down local resistance and to unite all the Arabian tribes into a single state and religion, and thus a people. Once this was done on the domestic scene, the Arabs became the single strongest power in the Middle East. Their effectiveness was all the more remarkable because it came into play against the background of the great rickety empires of Persia and Byzantium, debilitated still further by the presence of immense numbers of disaffected subjects.

The history of ancient Israel was quite different. Though all southern Syria and Palestine spoke much the same language, its small tribes and peoples had managed to become settled nations, rooted in their home grounds, with fully developed local states and religions propped up on well-articulated ecclesiastical organizations. Israel's monotheism came into existence when the religions of its neighbors had already been elaborated into fixed forms far too powerful for Israel to affect them seriously.

But perhaps another decisive difference was in the social backgrounds of the Jews and Arabs. As farmers and workmen, the Jews had naturally been more insular and parochial than the Arabs, long-range businessmen who had become used to the handling of customers and thus adept in the arts of propaganda and the manipulation of opinion. This proved to be very useful in the propagation of a new religion and point of view. Muhammad and all his companions, who were to become the caliphs and generals of the Muslim state after his death, had in fact been merchants, busy in the import and export trade between the Byzantine and the Persian empires and southern Arabia. Before the Arabs turned up as conquerors in the various cities of their neighbors in Syria, Egypt, or Mesopotamia, they had already familiarized themselves with them as merchants or caravan escorts. It was a situation in sharp contrast with that of the ancient Israelites, whose ideal had been no more than the cultivation of their own garden.

An odd sidelight on history is given by the puzzling problem of why the Jews failed to accept Muhammad.

Before the pagan rites of the Meccan pilgrimage were incorporated into Islam, there was nothing in the least repugnant to the Jews in Muhammad's religion. In fact, Muhammad's message was described as an act of God's mercy—*i.e.,* a true religion, in a Jewish document widely disseminated a couple of generations after his death.

It is ironical that in this question too, as in the purely local incentives of Muhammad's universalism mentioned above, a wholly parochial situation was to have such far-reaching consequences. For it is more than likely that the Jewish refusal to accept Muhammad was due to his having been in contact not with the orthodox, Talmudic Jews living around Medina, but with a somewhat dissident Jewish group. Thus Muhammad's rejection by the Jews was a mere reflection of an internal Jewish struggle between orthodoxy and sectarianism.

For his own part, on the other hand, Muhammad could scarcely tolerate the proximity of a big monotheistic community with a well-worked-out religion that simply denied his claims as a prophet and doubtless also made fun of his odd blunders about the Hebrew Scriptures.

In addition, Muhammad's Meccan followers were landless refugees and had to be indemnified in some way for the loss of their property in Mecca on their departure. The Jewish castles and plantations of northern Arabia were brilliantly designed for this.

Thus, because of the specific historic constellation, the struggle against the Jews left its mark on the Quran, and though Muhammad rejected Christianity with far greater vigor than Judaism, his actual conflicts with the Jews made him say some disagreeable things about them—for instance, that they were even more hostile to Islam than the Christians. For this very reason it is all the more striking that Muslim law made no distinction between Jews and Christians as far as their legal status in Islam was concerned, even though the Jews were being severely discriminated against in the countries conquered by the Arabs and if the latter had wished they could have found some justification in the Quran for continuing this discrimination. This is probably to be accounted for by the Jewish alliance with the Arabs during the wars of conquest and the formation of Muslim law in Iraq, the center of Jewish studies.

It is very strange that while Christianity was gradually to disappear in most parts of the Muslim Empire, Jewish communities survived and flourished—in Bukhara, formerly a great Christian center; in Yemen, once a Christian bishopric; and in North Africa, the home of Saint Augustine.

• • •

Muhammad's role in Islam was incomparably far below that of Jesus, since the crux of a believer's personal salvation did not depend on him. Nevertheless, he loomed so large in Islam, despite the theoretical acceptance of his mortality, that the circumstances of his life—real or imagined—were regarded as ultimately authoritative. His personality thus became a model for the Islamic community, perhaps in imitation of the elevation of Jesus. The legal foundation, in fact, of the vast community that Islam was to evolve into was by convention grounded in the traditional recollection of what the prophet had done or said. All Islam could not be contained within a short book like the Quran, hence the Holy Book had to be supplemented by the life of the prophet, which provided models for all social behavior. Thus Muhammad's habits and utterances laid down the framework of law in all its forms.

This was doubtless due to the fact that Muslim theory, as well as practice, was based on so little indigenous Arab material. There was so little intellectual preparation for it among the Arabs who brought Islam into the world that the Quran was bound to be abandoned as the sole guide to behavior. The Sunna—the life and conduct of Muhammad and his oldest companions—thus became the second criterion. It proved to be sufficiently flexible to provide an endless series of responses to the complex problems the early Muslim Arabs found themselves encountering once their eruption from the desert made them rulers of a vast empire whose administration was bound to create situations quite unforeseen, and unforeseeable, during the lifetime of Muhammad.

What happened was that a record of Muhammad's habits and remarks was established quite early. This record was in the form of what was called *Hadith* (Tradition); each particular Hadith had a characteristic form: "I was told by so-and-so, who heard from so-and-so, who heard from so-and-so, who heard the prophet say *this.*"

Thus, within a few generations after Muhammad's death a huge body of traditions sprang into being that necessarily extended to every conceivable social and administrative problem, in the form of statements about Muhammad.

It is obvious that in spite of the circumstantiality of the Hadith form, with its apparent scrupulousness in the enumeration of witnesses, it has the flexibility of any written record. In many ways, indeed, it is even more flexible for purposes of interpretation than an apparently fixed text might be, though of course the history of the Bible shows what miracles the interpretation of fixed texts can achieve.

After all, the assembly and setting down of the Hadith did not begin for a couple of generations after Muhammad's death, by which time both the reasons and the occasions for concoction were practically boundless. Inaccuracy could be adequately accounted for by mere human fallibility within the space of a century, and if that fallibility is augmented by special ax-grinding and by the vested interests of all kinds that were bound to grow up with the transformation of the Arab conquerors into an administrative apparatus governing an immense area, it is clear that the mere form of the Hadith could not insulate it against the new sociopolitical and religious interests of the evolving community. The conquered peoples, immensely more cultivated and civilized than the somewhat primitive Bedouin tribes that were governing them, contributed endless new concepts, as well as sociopolitical, legal, and religious difficulties to their new rulers. It was only natural for all the new developments to be retrojected into the life of the prophet via the canonizing form of the Hadith.

The same applied, of course, to the proliferating conflicts between individuals, clans, factions, and sects within the Islamic community. It became the natural form of conflict to invent Hadiths that would support one case against another.

The whole situation became so overgrown with dubiousness that Muslims themselves were perfectly well aware of the snares and defects in this traditional criterion of the Hadith, which hence was supplemented in turn by still another discipline of criticism to discriminate between various Hadiths. This traditional criticism based itself exclusively on the examination of the actual "chain" of witnesses; but of course this led nowhere, from the point of view of content, since, if a tradition depends on the mere enumeration of names, what is to prevent its "chains" from being invented, link by link? Moreover, the application of a criterion of probability to such a chain of witnesses in itself simply implies the acceptance of one criterion of probability, the mere reflection of a particular opinion at a given time, and thus is just as susceptible to analytical criticism as any other form of textual manipulation. Modern scholarship, indeed, has gone so far as to maintain that the entire body of Hadith, including the actual biography of Muhammad, must be handled with cautious reserve and considered as a reflection of a society in flux rather than an objective account of past events or opinions.

What I have said above about Muhammad and his work is, I hope, a fair account. But I think it essential to restore the balance, as it were, by giving a sketch of what pious Muslims have historically considered the most important things about him—just those things, to be sure, that an "objective" historical enquiry would doubtless have a corrosive effect on.

The following is, roughly, a portrait of Muhammad as seen through Muslim eyes; it has been fixed for more than a millennium.

God, in his infinite wisdom and in his determination to save mankind, created the light of Muhammad the prophet long before anything else, as the first of all created things. The light of prophecy, after roving about for generations, was finally embodied in the best of all created beings, in the most aristocratic scion of the most aristocratic clan of the premier people of the world, at the navel of the world, in Mecca. For centuries this marvelous event had been foretold in sacred writings. Miracles accompanied the birth of Muhammad, announcing it to the whole world. Angels opened up his heart to take every evil impulse out of it.

Of course, like all prophets Muhammad too has to contend with hardship. He too herds sheep. Then, when he becomes a businessman, God blesses every one of his undertakings. He grows familiar with the world on long voyages and is revered by noble and God-fearing men, both Jews and Christians, as a future prophet.

In the prime of life he is approached by God through the Angel Gabriel and starts off on his mission. Even though hampered by the sinfulness of mankind, he has religious and then political success, with the help of the divine hosts. He is protected against danger by miracles. He has supernatural powers: he can heal the ill and produce miracles of providing food; he can even awake the dead—for instance, his parents, who had died heathen, were brought to life by him again and the brief moment of their resurrection was long enough for them to become Muslims and thus deserve Paradise.

He makes a miraculous nocturnal trip on a miraculous beast first to Jerusalem, then into Heaven, where he negotiates with God concerning the religious duties of the believers. Finally his life comes to an end in Mecca, after he has ordered the new religion and the state that is identical with it, as well as the life of the believer, by word and example that is still the ideal of the learned to this day. The whole of Islam is Muhammad's handiwork. With prophetic vision he can even foretell the future destinies of Islam, and on the Day of Judgment he will gather his faithful around him in Paradise, after testifying for or against them in the final court.

His grave and relics are to be sought for by the pious, to acquire their blessing. His name is never to be pronounced without a formula of benediction—Muhammad, the noble, good, perfect messenger of God, the divine intercessor, the matchless wonder-worker!

Such is the tone of all Muslim biographies of Muhammad. It cannot be denied that some of the elements in it are clearly modeled on Jesus, though it is equally clear that because of the structure of Islam, Muhammad could never play more than the role of a mortal human being, however aggrandized by legend.

In any case, the importance of Muhammad's role can scarcely be overestimated. Though Islam began outwardly and inwardly as an Arab appendage, it soon overflowed the bounds of the people it had been born into and burst out of the Arabian Peninsula altogether. The paradox of Muhammad's life was that though he formed the Arabs into a people, he did so through a modality that was essentially self-contradictory, by laying the foundations of a universal religion. This ultimately disintegrated the Arabs as a community—in one way—by dissolving them within the cosmopolitan religious community of Islam and thus simultaneously diluting the original Arab Muslim conquerors and transmuting them, over the centuries, into a different people, the people whose identity is being reshaped in our own day simply through their speaking of the Arabic language.

The simple creed composed by Muhammad was systematized, streamlined, and amplified to become the underpinnings of a new kind of community—or rather, it universalized and gave religious sanction to a unitary civilization that had developed in the Middle East from the time of Alexander the Great. It also dressed that civilization in the new garb of the Arabic language and, through that language, created a new and expanded version of an ancient universal civilization.

Muhammad's combination within his own person of the secular quality of political leader and the religious quality of envoy of God led the religion in its first phase to enter into an indissoluble union with the Muslim-Arab state because of the historically quite unprecedented rapidity of evolution of the young political community—the Umma. It was this that was to set the Arab stamp on early Islam and ensure the hegemony of the Arabs for at least a few generations. It also was to make Arabic a world language, with consequences we are undergoing in our own generation.

It must be admitted that Muhammad's intellectual arsenal represents a singular combination of simplicity and efficiency: His message to the Arabs revolved around a couple of ideas, yet these cemented the fractious tribes into a force sufficiently cohesive to puncture the Persian and the Byzantine empires and to enable the Muslim Arabs to encompass a stretch of territory larger than the Roman Empire at its height.

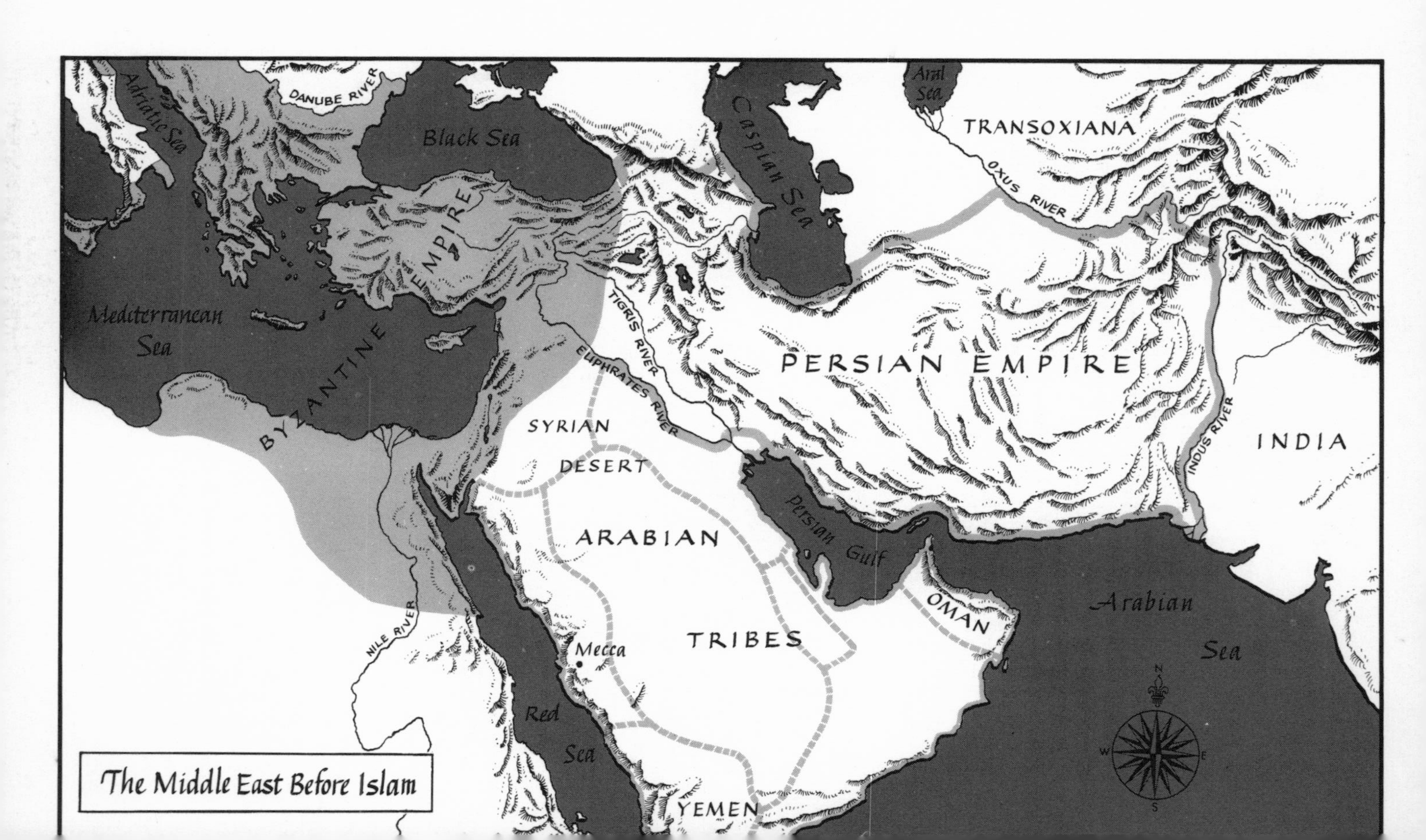

The Middle East Before Islam

II

THE OUTPOURING FROM THE DESERT: THE BEDOUIN CONQUESTS

MUHAMMAD'S death was followed by one of the most remarkable events in history: the conquest, within eighty years, of an area far larger than that amassed by the Romans in eight hundred. And this conquest was accomplished by a number of warriors that was equally remarkable for its small size.

But it would be absurd to think of it as a systematic campaign. It seems to have been begun rather thoughtlessly, as a sort of molecular reaction to local, domestic, and altogether ephemeral events, then to have broadened out, still more or less instinctively, and ultimately to have congealed into a new state form almost before it was realized just what was happening. Later, to be sure, once the conquests were an accomplished fact, they were seen by historians and philosophers as the result of design, though it is incontestable that Muhammad's own thought had never ranged beyond his native Arabia.

Our own view of this event, moreover, has been falsified, perhaps inevitably, by its having been refracted to us through the prism of a religious tradition that has cast it into a purely theological perspective. This religious prism is the creation of both Christian and Muslim writers, so it is only within fairly recent times that we can see the Arab conquests as having been produced by the expansion not of a religious idea or system, but of an ethnic group.

A churchly misconception of the advance of Islam was paralleled by a churchly misconception of the role of the Arabs. Just as the medieval ecclesiastics regarded the incursion of Islam as an alien triumph, so they regarded the eruption of the Arabs as a religious advance.

Yet the extraordinary thing about the remarkably rapid thrusting out of the Arabs from Arabia was precisely that it had nothing to do with religion at all. It was Islam, to be sure, that unified the great Bedouin tribes for the military expeditions against the neighboring states, but in the initial period of the Muslim expansion the important factor was simply that Arabs were united against their military opponents. In spite of the universalist tendencies inherent in the new faith, it was merely an appendage, so to speak, of the Arabs. It may have entailed universal application, but for the time being it was a mere emblem of Arab hegemony. What the Arabs did with their sword was not to spread Islam, in short, but merely their own political rule. Theoretically non-Arabs could adopt Islam and ultimately they did, in vast numbers. But in the beginning of the conquests this not only was not sought after by the Arabs, it was actively distasteful to them.

The Arabs were not, in fact, particularly pious about their religion as such. It was not even part of their faith to make converts; with respect to the Christians and Jews in any case, not conversion but simply tribute was the objective. Christians and Jews were supposed to accept Islam—*or* pay tribute, retaining unmolested their own cults and customs. The Muslim Arabs merely constituted themselves a ruling caste, sitting on top of the older and more cultivated conquered peoples and enjoying the latter's material contributions to the Arab way of life.

Since in their eruption from the desert the Arabs identified Islam with themselves, as a purely Arab institution, indifferent at first to its universal implications, the idea of a non-Arab's becoming a Muslim was utterly strange. Hence there was no modality for conversion; there was no method for anyone's becoming a member of the new faith as such. This is perhaps the most striking demonstration of what may be called the national *structure* of the new religion. A newcomer to Islam could join it, in fact, only by becoming an Arab first—that is, by affiliating himself to some particular Arab tribe. This was the only way of overcoming the rigidity of the Arabian tribal organization as the tribes became an aristocracy squatting on top of the sedentary societies that were to be overrun with bewildering ease.

In nascent Islamic society this category of what were called "Clients"—*Mawāli*—of the Arabian tribes was ultimately to constitute the source of a basic transformation in Islamic society. (See Chapter III.)

Once a man had become a Muslim by becoming a "Client" of an Arab tribe, he would, to be sure, be the equal—*theoretically*—of an Arab as a fellow member of the Muslim community. But that would not blunt the haughtiness of the Arab aristocrats; for generations Arab Muslims were contemptuously superior to other Muslims.

The underlying assumption of this system during the first period of the caliphate—roughly a century after Muhammad—was that while Arab and Muslim were coextensive, the source of the caliph's *authority* was religious. Initially, to be sure, there was no cleavage between religious and secular authority; it remained for a later period to point up the complications. But in any case, the fiscal system, based on the taxation of the vast mass of non-Muslim subjects of the Arab ruling group, was bound to break down once the two assumptions of Arab-Muslim identity and of the universal religious authority of the Muslim caliph were outdistanced by the development of the swiftly evolving Muslim community.

The main problem constituted by this attitude in the primitive phase of Muslim expansion was that if anyone did become converted to Islam he ceased being subject to the taxes levied by the Muslim Arabs on non-Muslims. Hence, the governors of the evolving society were bound to accept such conversions with reluctance. The fact that at a later period it became a custom, perhaps an obligation, among individual pietists to seek converts and that the material advantages of adherence to Islam eventually won over the bulk of the inhabitants of the conquered countries has naturally obscured the initial period, in which the whole outthrust of the Arabs from the peninsula arose for quite different reasons.

The Muslim eruption of the Arabs was basically a folk migration, the emptying out of the peninsula into the bordering areas. For centuries before Muhammad, the Arabs had been milling about; the population seems to have been in a state of constant flux. The Arab-

Muslim migration was a response to socioeconomic factors that can be perceived perhaps dimly but unmistakably.

South Arabian tribes were in control of Medina; others were settled in Syria and Mesopotamia. Legends testifying to the steady worsening of life in south Arabia seem to be confirmed by inscriptions; one of the results was that the great public waterworks underlying the prosperity of the country had fallen into disrepair. This neglect—itself, of course, the result of a more general situation—may have been the immediate cause of the migratory commotion characteristic of pre-Islamic Arabia.

Arabian tribes had been infiltrating Persian terrain as well as Roman. Relations were especially intimate with the Arameans, a people speaking a Semitic language akin to Arabic. It was doubtless as a method of controlling this amorphous flux that both the Persian and the Roman empires had attempted to yoke to their service the Arabian tribes in their border provinces, so as at least to make use of them in the constant strife between the two empires. This may be the functional significance of the two vassal pre-Islamic Arab states of the Ghassanids and the Lakhmids, who worked for the Byzantines and the Persians respectively. The shortsightedness of the Byzantine and Persian overlords, which led to the neglect and eventual alienation of these Arab dynasties, finally left the borders quite unprotected against the Muslim incursion. Had these two dynasties been cultivated as assiduously as originally intended, they could, perhaps, have withstood the newcomers from the desert later on.

The consolidated dynasty of the Ghassanids had been broken up and the Lakhmid princes replaced by various satraps from the center. The great empires had made an attempt to decentralize these tiny Arab states, but the border Arabs retained the ancient tradition of being allowed, in the constant wars between Persia and Byzantium, to ravage the neighboring civilized countries unmolested. As other Arab tribes slowly came to depend on the growing Muslim power, they resumed this old tradition of living off the cultivated sedentary societies, an ancient practice later promoted with growing zeal by the youthful caliphate.

Thus it was not Islam that brought about the folk migration of the Arab tribes, but the folk migration, originating for quite independent reasons, that united them under Islam. The expansion of the Muslim Arabs was the culmination of a long-drawn-out development. What Islam changed was simply the slogan under which the general fighting was conducted, or rather, it gave this general movement a simple slogan capable of drawing all Arabs together in opposition to the great empires, which thus, after mistrusting the small buffer states of the Ghassanids and the Lakhmids, finally found themselves face to face with a far more numerous confederation of Arabian tribes temporarily unified by the simple tenets of primitive Islam.

The predominant incentives that drove the Bedouin out of the peninsula were bodily hunger and greed, natural consequences of the straitened circumstances there and of the endless opportunities for enrichment offered by the cultivated societies they overran. Thus, though there were doubtless also men who "killed for the sake of the hereafter," the masses of tribesmen surely "killed for earthly lust."

The otherworldly aspects of Muhammad's preaching were completely eclipsed during the conquests by the incredible booty that could be won. Thus a Qurayshite notable, who was considered so pious that he was one of the ten men to whom Muhammad could give his personal word during their lifetimes that they would get into Paradise because of their zeal for Islam, left behind an estate whose net worth seems to have been between 35 and 52 million dirhams; he had eleven houses in Medina alone, as well as others in Basra, Kufa, Fustat, and Alexandria. Another of these ten pious men personally promised Paradise by Muhammad owned real property in the amount of 30 million dirhams; on his death his steward had over 2 million dirhams in cash.

The warriors who went on the great campaigns, or glorified Bedouin raids, that carried the banners of Islam far and wide were also richly rewarded. After a campaign in North Africa every rider got three thousand mithqals of gold as booty. There may have been odd exceptions who refused payment for their part in these campaigns, but apparently the prevailing mood was that everyone was entitled to his share by divine guarantee, which was the basis of general complaints when the authorities attempted to limit the booty when it took the form of shares in gold and silver.

Once this process is seen in perspective, it becomes clear how remarkably obtuse is the old, traditional conception of the Arab expansion as being a pietist movement aroused by Muhammad's personal religious zeal. Scholars have even raised the question, perhaps in an excess of materialist zeal of their own, whether the whole movement of Arab expansion might not be wholly explicable without even bringing in the existence of Islam. Even if this goes too far there seems to be no doubt that the last thing the Muslim Arabs were thinking of was converting anyone. More particularly, the pietism that was to become the hallmark of later Islam, at least in certain of its manifestations, was utterly alien to the initial Arab conquerors. It is more easily understood as a concomitant development of the society that was to come into being *through* the success of the Muslim Arabs. The aspect of Islam that prevailed together with the first Arab conquerors was its political aspect, which for that matter is still dominant in some sense in modern Islamic states.

In the very beginning, however, what Islam meant was the hegemony of Medina, first of all, then of the Arab tribes in general. Islam was merely the institution through which Arab dominion was imposed on subject populations because of their political atomization and inner weakness and despite their cultural superiority. The driving force, that is, of the Arabs as a collectivity was a material craving, but it was the spiritual impulse of the nascent religion that unified them and thus enabled them to achieve their goal. This broad, extremely simple notion—of Islam as the emblem of Arab unity and dominion—gave the ethnic eruption of the peninsula some spiritual content; it also turned Medina into a political focus with the same religious base.

Thus the religious impulse of Islam was both chronologically and factually a secondary consequence of the ethnic drive of the Arabian tribes, really more of a political, indeed utopian, ideal at first than a political reality. As the Arabian tribes, long since in movement, began to overflow once again under the umbrella of Islam, they fused with the neighboring population of Aramaic-speaking peoples, oppressed by both Persia and Byzantium, and together they made up what looked like a torrential folk migration throughout the cultivated Middle East and North Africa, bursting asunder in the process the world empires that only a short while before seemed to have most of the known world under firm control.

By the time Islam made its appearance, the Persian and Byzantine empires had been in a state of practically incessant warfare for some three centuries. The administration of the Byzantine Empire was still largely Roman, while its population was Greek-speaking and Christian. It was solidly established on the plateau of Anatolia, now the heart of modern Turkey. Its two chief provinces were Syria and Egypt, where the authority of the central state, centered in Constantinople, encountered widespread resistance in the alien populations, Aramaic-speaking in Syria and Coptic in Egypt. The irritation of these subject populations was exacerbated still further by the religious differences mentioned above: The Monophysites were systematically persecuted by the orthodox regime in Constantinople, on top of having to pay ruinous taxes. In Palestine, also, there were still some Jews, an important element in the population, who were even more terrorized by the Byzantine state than the heretical Monophysites.

The situation of the Persian (Sassanid) Empire was roughly parallel. The empire was solidly established in Persia too on a big plateau, from which an Aryan-speaking people ruled the Semitic-speaking and religiously alien province of Iraq. Persia professed a state religion of a monotheistic, or at least semimonotheistic, kind—Zoroastrianism. In addition, the internal edifice of state power in the Persian Empire lacked the stability of the Byzantine. The country had just emerged from an upheaval by the end of the sixth century. Its ancient feudal order was largely shattered and replaced by a military dictatorship based on a mercenary army. Political affairs were still highly unstable, and the political as well as religious unity of the empire was under attack from many quarters.

The long series of wars between these two great empires had been fought out during the first third of the seventh century. Though the Byzantines seemed to have won, both states were left quite drained, in no condition to withstand the incursion about to reach them from the Arabian desert.

Thus a potent stimulus of the Arab military expansion was the fanatical orthodoxy of the Byzantine Empire, expressed by the persecution of the Aramaic-speaking population in Syria. It helps explain one of the most striking things about the advance of the Muslim armies, which were all relatively miniature: their success against the superior forces of the vastly more civilized Byzantines. The decisive part of this explanation may lie in the deeply rooted hatred of local Christians for the savagely intolerant and obtuse policy of the Byzantine state. They were utterly disaffected and uniformly welcomed the advance of the Muslim tribesmen—all the easier to do since at first the new religion of Islam did not seem to be so very new, after all, especially not to Monophysite Christians. All the Muslim Arabs had to do was to crush a relatively small number of garrison troops who were more or less alienated anyhow. This was exceptionally easy, since in Syria the population as a whole welcomed them as liberators, while they were able to make a separate peace in Egypt, where their insistence on the total eradication of the Byzantine power was cheerfully accepted.

Thus the Arab incursion arose quite naturally, in a quite unplanned way, because of the inner development of the infant Muslim community and because of the various social blights their enemies were suffering from. Viewed from inside, the Muslims were impelled to drift over the borders not in any excess of proselytizing zeal, but because of the logical interaction between the evolution of their own domestic affairs and the increasingly felt debilitation of their adversaries abroad.

• • •

Though Muhammad himself had never pretended to anything more than mortality, nor indeed was anything more ever believed of him, his death came as a quite unexpected blow to the infant Muslim community. In any event Muhammad had never given any thought to the consequences of his death; he had never laid down a code of laws or made any provision for his succession.

His death produced indescribable confusion in Medina. There was, of course, no question of Muhammad's finding a successor in his capacity as prophet. What had to be taken care of was the political guidance of the community, that is, the government. The immediate situation was complicated by the basic division of the youthful Muslim community into Helpers and Emigrants, a split that only Muhammad's personality had been able to bridge over and that now threatened to manifest itself once again.

It would have been impossible for Muhammad to provide for his own succession, simply because of his unique role. On the other hand, the old Arab tradition of choosing a successor from an acknowledged Shaykhly family would have been difficult in the case of Muhammad's own clan, since he had left no sons and in a polygamous society the influence of fathers-in-law and sons-in-law is bound to be diluted.

Hence, the only precedent the Muslim community had to guide it was the principle of election, and the Medinese Helpers did make an attempt to select a candidate from a powerful tribe. The crisis this brought about was nullified practically immediately by the energetic action of some of Muhammad's intimates, including Abu Bakr, his father-in-law, and Umar, who were to be his immediate successors. Abu Bakr was simply put forth as the candidate of this small inner council, and both the Meccan Emigrants and the Medinese Helpers found themselves saddled with him as a *khalifah, i.e.,* successor (of Muhammad), now in all European languages in a form like "caliph."

Abu Bakr's function was already different in important ways from that of a traditional Shaykh. The structure of the Muslim community—the Umma devised by Muhammad to supersede the tribalism of the peninsula—gave Abu Bakr control not only over a community, but over the actual region it inhabited; it also gave him executive authority plus an army. Since Islam from the very beginning implied a state order as well as a religious discipline, it was only natural for Abu Bakr to begin performing the functions of a head of state as well as of a religious leader. Indeed, throughout Islam the two have generally been, at least in theory, indissoluble. As the first caliph, then, Abu Bakr naturally took in hand a situation that in any case was crying out for action.

The initial problem he confronted has come down in Muslim tradition as a religious one. As conceived by the pietistic tendency of later historians, the tribes that had been converted to Islam during Muhammad's lifetime fell away from it the moment he died; hence the movement is known as the Apostasy (*Ridda*). There was, of course, no particular reason for the recently converted tribes to acknowledge the succession of Abu Bakr, since the whole idea of succession was in any case alien to them and more particularly since what they thought they had been doing in embracing Islam was making a contract with Muhammad as an individual. Such a contract obviously came to an end with his death; theoretically a new contract would have to be negotiated with his successor. The tribes that had been very close to Medina had already fused with the Umma, for all practical purposes, so that there is no record of their behavior. More distant tribes saw no reason to go on submitting to Medina once Muhammad was dead; their "apostasy" amounted to no more than the resumption of their immemorial freedom. New treaties had to be freely entered upon, and the tribes far from Medina simply refused. This entailed their military subjugation if Abu Bakr and the Medina center wanted to "reconvert" them.

The Apostasy could thus be looked upon both as a measure of enforcing religious solidarity and as a campaign of military conquest. In any case the wars of the Apostasy involved, almost at once, and in the nature of things, the launching of a campaign of conquest that automatically led beyond the borders of the peninsula. There was indeed no distinction in the execution of this campaign between the reconquest of the disaffected tribes and the new conquest of the bordering provinces: Iraq of the Persian Empire and Syria and Egypt of the Byzantine. It is very likely that the conquest of the Arabian tribes, as a matter of fact, might not have seemed even worth going in for if the accessible opulence of the great settled provinces outside the Arabian desert had not beckoned to the impoverished Bedouin. The first expeditions undertaken to the north, for instance, were certainly not aimed at conquest—the whole idea would have seemed absurd. The expeditions were simply extensions of the time-honored Bedouin raids. It was, indeed, this quality of improvisation inherent in Bedouin raids that was to prove extremely effective against the centralized military control of the two great empires, which found themselves baffled by the Bedouin hit-and-run routines. The further advance into these countries took place only when the Bedouin, following the line of least resistance, finally found themselves drawn into the interior by the unforeseen weaknesses of the enemy as they revealed themselves.

Perhaps the key figure of the Bedouin conquests was Khalid ibn al-Walid, Abu Bakr's chief marshal, a former pagan military leader who had come over to Islam and was to distinguish himself in the new expansion. The petty, individual campaigns against the Arabian Bedouin proved to be relatively quite simple. After restoring the situation at home to what it had been before Muhammad's death, Khalid simply decided, on his own initiative, to move to carry out what in fact swiftly and unexpectedly turned into a military program. The immense expansion of the Arabian tribes may be said to have been launched in central-eastern Arabia by the celebrated battle of Aqraba in 633, where Khalid's clear-cut victory demonstrated to all Arabs, including any waverers, that the regime in Medina, which could by now be regarded as a bona fide government, was stable enough to enforce submission.

This laid the foundations for a whole series of thrusts in a variety of directions. It would be difficult to see in these military advances any initiative of the central government in Medina. In many ways the nascent caliphate simply acquiesced in the decisions taken on the spot by the various commanders, who would make up their minds on the spur of the moment to extend a given raid in accordance with specific circumstances.

In Iraq, for instance, the Banu Wail, a north Arab border tribe that had never submitted to Medina at all and had never even thought of turning Muslim, found itself squeezed between the suddenly expanding Medinese power, after the Muslim success at Aqraba, and the Persian state. It was thus a matter of course for this tribe to invite the newly formed Muslims, who were, after all, related to them in the unusual crisscross of tribal patterns, to join with them in a further advance into the Persian interior. Thus the ancient movement forward of the Bedouin tribes was simply given added impetus by the emergence in the Arabian interior of a local conflict trivial enough to be absorbed into a new enterprise that would both act as safety valve for local pressures and at the same time dangle something attractive before the avid tribesmen.

Khalid instantly took advantage of this suggestion, though there was no question in all this of a conversion of the Banu Wail. Religion in this connection was quite irrelevant; the main point was that by this impromptu alliance the border tribe from then on automatically subsided into the sphere of authority of the now rapidly expanding regime in Medina, which, since it bore by now a tutelary relationship to the sundry Bedouin tribes that were beginning to stir, more or less automatically benefited by any success, however local. The political fusion with the Muslims simply led one border tribe after another to dissolve as political entities to the degree that the Medina regime grew more and more important.

In the beginning Abu Bakr had had no intention of any systematic occupation of Iraq, though he might have been thinking of embarking on some action against the Byzantine Empire in its Syrian province, which was much closer to the interests of Medina.

The proof of the thoroughly improvised campaign against Persia can be seen in the fact that most of Khalid's troops had been called back home for a rest when he, with or without Abu Bakr's knowledge, joined the border Arabs in the first Persian campaign. Khalid had no more than five hundred selected fighters, whom he took eastward in a fast march into Persia.

Khalid and his volunteers crossed over the swamps of the Euphrates from the west. Numbering no more than two or three thousand men, together with the Banu Wail, they were lucky enough to make their way to the provincial capital of Hira, which was fortified well enough to make a siege imperative. Since mere resistance from within the city walls would not have saved the lush lands north of the city, it seemed sensible to the city leaders to ransom themselves, which they did by accepting the laughably small Bedouin demand for cash (sixty thousand dirhams).

The Arabs seem to have been delighted by their success in laying their hands on a sum that for them meant a fortune. They immediately withdrew, and Khalid started flashing back and forth through the countryside in the general direction of Syria, where he arrived very suddenly and unexpectedly, to stand outside the very gates of Damascus (April 24, 634) in one of the most legendary and perhaps decisive military marches in history.

In Syria it was not a thought-through plan of the youthful Muslim regime or the pious wisdom of a proselytizing caliph that drew the Muslim forces over the borders; it was the Christian Arabs in the border provinces who had applied to the new centralized regime in Medina for help. Relations between the Muslims and the great north Arabian tribes are rather obscure for us—an obscurity heightened by the tendentious historiography of later ages—but it seems that for a couple of years before Muhammad's death a friendly footing had been established with at least a few tribes along the southern border of Palestine. The big tribes associated with the Ghassanid dynasty along the Syrian frontiers seem to have preserved their ties with the Byzantine authorities, but some of the tribes south of the Red Sea, which controlled the Medina-Gaza highway, thought it important to be on good terms with the Medina regime.

These tribes had been receiving a subsidy from the Byzantines, but at one point, when Emperor Heraclius was short of money because of a debt he had contracted to the church during his struggle against the Persians, he had cut off the subsidy, doubtless on the theory that in the new circumstances he could get away with it. Probably no Byzantine statesman would have dreamed at this time that the emergence of any centralized power in the heart of Arabia need be feared.

In any event, even though these tribes were Christian and had never previously thought of joining with the Muslims, when their annual subsidy was stopped their attitude shifted abruptly. It now lay in their interest, just as had been the case with the Banu Wail in the east, to join the Muslims from Medina in a generalized raid through the Syrian interior. After Khalid's victories in central Arabia, the north Arabian border tribes in the south of Syria and Palestine also became very restive, like the Banu Wail in the east. They thought a joint raid with their Muslim fellow Arabs would compensate them for the loss of the Byzantine subsidy.

The caliph acquiesced in the new situation, no doubt sensing that a tribal upheaval like this must lead somewhere or other, though it seems clear that even now no systematic campaign was under consideration. In any case, even though the Medinese proper do not seem to have been very enthusiastic for the risks of another campaign against Byzantium, a number of small detachments were despatched against Syria in the autumn of 633. They were uniformly successful, and after a striking victory in February 634, they were in a position to plunder the whole of southern Palestine as far north as Gaza.

When Heraclius heard this surprising news, he gathered together a great army south of Damascus, but since it was practically impossible to divine any systematic plan on the part of the Arabs—chaos was their chief agent—he went forward very tentatively in an attempt to safeguard Jerusalem—now cut off from the sea—as well as Caesarea and Gaza. Khalid, however, turned up outside Damascus after his celebrated march, directly after Heraclius' army had begun its move southward. When Khalid arrived in April 634, Damascus was practically unprotected since the Byzantine troops were already well on their way southward.

Khalid was free to form a general view of the precarious situation of the Arabs in the south of Palestine; he immediately left to join the Bedouin who had made their initial advance into

Syria simply as raiding detachments. When Khalid joined them in the Wadi Arabia, he consolidated his own forces with theirs and then, once again with a united Muslim force, confronted the Byzantine troops, who had taken up a firm position at Ajnadayn, between Jerusalem and Gaza. A savage battle took place on July 30, 634, which ended in an overwhelming Arab victory.

It is likely that Khalid was the real architect of victory, though there seems to be some doubt about just who was in command of the Arab troops at this point, or indeed whether there was any united command at all. But in any case, the Arabs now had in front of them the whole of the flatland; it was some time before they could take the fortified towns. The Arabs still felt themselves to be on a raiding party; the country as a whole seems to have been plunged into total chaos. The Bedouin, in fact, simply disbanded as an organized military force and scattered throughout the country, turning up as far north as Homs (the ancient Emesa) by January 636.

Soon after the victory of Ajnadayn, Abu Bakr died (634) and was succeeded by the energetic, universally authoritative Caliph Umar. During the first six months that followed the Arab victory of Ajnadayn, it must have become apparent that the raiding parties were not leading anywhere in particular. As soon as the central regime in Medina became aware of its growing authority, it must have seemed to the leaders that the raids had to be replaced by more or less systematic occupation. This feeling was doubtless heightened by another aspect of the general Arabian flux that had been evident for some time, as pointed out above: Bedouin from the south of the peninsula, tempted and stimulated by the remarkable successes of the Medina regime, now began crowding northward into Syria, coming not as mere fighting detachments but in the manner of a folk migration, bringing along their wives, children, and possessions, on the quest for advantageous dwelling places.

The initial planlessness of the Muslim overflow is well illustrated by Khalid's rapid and effective campaign from Hira to the gates of Damascus in April 634. Though the campaign itself is generally regarded as a masterpiece, it looks more like a brilliant improvisation made possible by Bedouin mobility and nothing else. In any case, it indicates that the conquest of Persia had not even been thought of; it was in Syria, with its Aramaic population so close to the Arabs themselves, that the infant caliphate was contemplating a general sally. Khalid's expedition against Hira had taken place during a period of great confusion in Persia. As soon as a regime had emerged that was once more in control, with a restoration of central authority under a famous Persian general (Rustam), the Bedouin buccaneers were set upon in their turn. The Banu Wail turned to Medina for assistance just after Abu Bakr's death, when Umar became the second caliph.

Umar could not spare enough forces from his Syrian interests; and in November 634, in a second collision between the Persians and the united Muslim–Banu Wail forces, the Persians won a great victory, which the Muslims recouped, though only partially, the following year. Meanwhile their main forces were being deployed in the west, and only six months after the Ajnadayn battle a general advance began under the leadership of Khalid. Heraclius' last troops had fallen back on Damascus. Despite their concentration, the Muslims, after two brilliant victories (in January and February 635), were outside the walls of the Syrian capital by March 635.

The Arabs, still quite untrained except in old-fashioned desert warfare, could not seriously think of capturing the well-fortified capital by a siege, but even without that, successful attempts were made to isolate the city and to force the garrison troops to surrender. It finally capitulated in early autumn of the same year, through the treachery of the civil authorities.

Once the Bedouin took Damascus, they went on to the occupation of the entire country, giving no further heed, apparently, to the Byzantine authorities. Various local generals resumed their private operations in Palestine and east of the Jordan; even now there was no question of centralization. Khalid himself resumed his sally against Homs, which he occupied at the end of the year. A number of smaller towns were taken, though the big fortified cities like Jerusalem, Caesarea, and the various harbor cities still counted on rescue by Heraclius.

Heraclius set about the reconstruction of an army with immense energy, centering his activities in Antioch and Edessa. Since he had been unable to relieve Damascus, he gathered his forces, mainly consisting, in addition to his Byzantine troops, of Armenians and Arabs, for a major onslaught on the Bedouin in the spring of 636. His newly formed army moved on to Homs, where Khalid was waiting for him. For the first time, the Arabs, under Khalid, had come up against a substantial force, numbering perhaps some fifty thousand men, after having been able to deal hitherto with rather negligible Byzantine units.

Khalid instantly released Homs, and Damascus too, and concentrated all his forces at a strategically favorable point on the eastern side of the Jordan, southeast of the deep Yarmuk valley (north of the present-day Derat), at a midpoint between the northerly and southerly Arab positions. This position was in the lushest section of Syria, at the crossroads of the most important highways leading to the southern part of Transjordan and to the heart of Palestine, covered on the flank by the deep valley clefts of the Yarmuk's tributaries. Even if the Arabs were beaten here, Khalid must have thought, their rear was free; they could always fall back into the desert behind them and eventually to Medina. The swift retreat of the Arabs on this occasion is an indication of the danger they were in; they had scarcely half the numbers of the army approaching.

The Byzantines did not come by way of Damascus, but through Coele-Syria and over the Jordan, to make a stand at Jillin. The armies confronted each other for some time; there was some desultory skirmishing. The Arabs were waiting for reinforcements, while the Byzantines seem to have squandered their energies in squabbling and jockeying for power. In addition, the Byzantines' Arab auxiliaries deserted, encouraging Khalid's army to outflank the Byzantines on the east, cutting off their access to Damascus as well as to the west. The Arabs finally forced the Byzantine troops into the corner of the Yarmuk and the Wadi ar-Ruqqad, slaughtering them with relative ease. In August 636, finally, the Byzantines were thoroughly destroyed. Heraclius' last troops were totally wiped out, and Khalid's Arabs pressed forward so swiftly into Damascus that there was no chance to find any others to withstand them. Thus in the autumn of 636 Damascus was taken by the Arabs for the second time, this time for good. The Byzantines had suffered a most disastrous defeat, which sealed the fate of Syria and set it on the road to the blanket linguistic arabization that has marked it ever since.

The decision taken by the Medina regime the preceding year to replace the chaotic raiding parties of its Bedouin troops by a systematic occupation required the establishment of some sort of stable civil regime. Khalid, despite his remarkable qualities as field marshal, does not seem to have been fitted for this. In any case, Caliph Umar sent out Abu Ubayda, a trusted associate, who had played a decisive role immediately after Muhammad's death. Abu Ubayda arrived before the battle of the Yarmuk, bided his time until Khalid won the victory, then assumed charge of the operation as a whole. He sent the various local commanders throughout the country and moved north together with Khalid. In a short time Baalbek, Homs, Aleppo, Antioch, and the great Arab tribes dwelling in the north of Syria were subjugated, with no particular difficulty. The Amanus became the northern frontier of the caliphate.

In 636 and 637, meanwhile, the interior and most of the seaports had been occupied. The only difficulty the Bedouin met with was at Jerusalem and Caesarea, both of them heavily Hellenized.

It is this small fact that gives us an inkling of the reasons for the Arabs' remarkably swift advance. Throughout Syria, and wherever the Byzantine state had earned the loathing of the local Semitic population, the Arabian tribes were greeted practically as liberators. It is true that the Byzantine emperor's armed forces were in trouble —there was shortage of both people and money—but the main political problem was that Heraclius had made himself so detestable to the Arameans under his rule that the moment they saw there was no longer any reason to fear him they uniformly turned against the state.

Heraclius had had to squeeze the population to the utmost in order to cover his debts. In addition, his church policy had made him terrorize the Monophysites and the Jews still more. This religious oppression contributed heavily to the anti-Greek tendency already prevalent among the Semitic part of the population. When the Bedouin arrived, they were hailed not only by the numerous Christian Arabs but by the Arameans themselves as kinfolk. The Bedouin's demands in the way of tribute were also rather modest, and, in addition, since they were fundamentally indifferent toward religion, they allowed their new subjects complete religious freedom. It was, indeed, mere common sense for them to give active support to the heterodox tendencies of their new subjects.

Because of this, the country simply fell into their laps the moment its despotic regime was defeated in battle. The resistance offered by Jerusalem and Caesarea indicates this process in reverse.

Both cities, thoroughly Hellenized and orthodox to boot, held out with considerable vigor, though they were too isolated to withstand Arab pressure for long; Jerusalem surrendered in 638 and Caesarea somewhat later, through treachery, in 640.

Even before Jerusalem fell, Umar made an appearance in Syria, as a direct result of the new occupation policy decided on by Medina. The victories of the Bedouin had been so remarkable in their scope that a new and systematic method of regulating relations with the occupied countries, as well as of disciplining the raw and illiterate Arab occupation forces, had to be made. Umar came to give his authority to his representative Abu Ubayda and to sponsor the institution of the new regime.

At this time the Muslim army headquarters was still in Jabiya, a little to the north of the Yarmuk battlefield. Umar gathered together all the army heads and seems to have laid down some general principles for the treatment of the newly conquered peoples. He was, of course, establishing a colonial regime. In addition, the money pouring into the central treasury had to be handled in some systematic way, and a whole administrative apparatus established.

Leaving Abu Ubayda behind in charge of Syria, Umar stopped off to visit Jerusalem on his way back to Medina. Abu Ubayda was felled by the plague in 639 and was succeeded by Yazid, a son of Abu Sufyan, the celebrated head of the Umayyad clan. Soon afterward, Yazid succumbed to the disease too, and Umar appointed in his place Mu'awiya, another son of Abu Sufyan's. Abu Sufyan himself had been an obdurate opponent of Muhammad's, but now Mu'awiya was the governor of Syria, a vital position, since Syria later became the center of the youthful caliphate, and through Mu'awiya the house of Umayyad was to be at the helm of Islam for a few generations.

Meanwhile, however, during the various moves against Syria, which at first seemed to Medina the far more important and immediate task, the enterprise against Iraq took second place. Umar could spare hardly any serious forces against Iraq; even a minor victory won at Buwayb in 635 did not prompt him to make any serious follow-up, especially since it had taken place at a time when the Medina regime needed all its available troops to face Heraclius' forces for what turned out to be the battle of the Yarmuk. It was only after this that Umar could pay more attention to Iraq and select a governor of some weight, Sa'd ibn Abi Waqqas. But it was still very difficult to get together the forces needed, and it took Sa'd a whole winter (636–37) to assemble a few thousand men. There was not the smallest evidence of the alleged religious zeal taken for granted by Western scholars and of course by the Muslim historians themselves.

Meanwhile the Persians, very upset by their own defeat at Buwayb and still more disconcerted by the total collapse of the Byzantines in Syria, had decided on an energetic counterattack. The imperial regent Rustam himself led an army to the border of the empire at Qadisiyya. There is no clear report of the size of the armies; the Arabs seem to have been no more than five or six thousand—including Christians and pagans—and it seems unlikely that the Persians numbered many more. In any case, the Persian troops were shattered in a single day, with their leaders killed (637).

Here too, accordingly, the Arabs found themselves looking across at the lush farmland that lay before them completely unprotected, while just as in Syria the Aramean farmers regarded the Bedouin as liberators from the Persian despotism. With no particular opposition, the Arabs pressed north up along the Tigris as far as Ctesiphon—in Arabic *al-Madain,* the "urban complex"; the right bank of the Tigris was cleared and all the bridges smashed. The government fled to the protection of the Iranian plateau, while the city itself, brimming over with treasure, opened its gates to the invaders. The fabulous booty intoxicated them for several weeks, which they spent amusing themselves, from all accounts, in a rather earthy way. Then, after only one more battle, the whole of Iraq dropped into their laps.

Here too it was no accident that the forward thrust of the Bedouin came to a halt at the mountains that constituted the line of demarcation between the Semitic-speaking peoples and the Indo-European Persians. The seat of the newly installed government was made not Ctesiphon, but Kufa, a point near Hira, on the direct orders of the caliph. Kufa was laid out as a vast army encampment that was purely Arab, as a bastion of the new Islamic community against the alien Persians. Kufa and Basra, which had been founded a little before, were to be rival centers of Muslim culture for centuries.

The overwhelming victories at Yarmuk and Qadisiyya opened up the lush farmlands of Syria and Iraq; it was now that the folk migration of the Arabian tribes began in earnest. Even those tribes who had had no particular sympathy for Islam now could at least enjoy the advantages of the civilized countries that had always given them their conception of paradise on earth. It was with the opening up of these great new centers for colonization that Islam entered into its secondary stage. It no longer meant mere political subjugation to a new center in Medina, run by the parvenu Umma of Muhammad and Abu Bakr; it now encompassed such a broad area that it took on the aspect of a pan-Arab community capable of aiming at dominion over the world of the time. From now on, authentic campaigns could be launched in which whole tribes had roles to play.

As a beginning the provinces of Syria and Iraq were fused together, rounded off by the conquest of Mosul in 641. But it was obvious that a systematic conquest had to be directed first of all against Persia proper, that is, the Iranian plateau, where the Persian government had fled. Without the reduction of this plateau there was no security for Iraq, and in fact the whole of Persia was soon summoned to resist any further advances from the desert by the victorious Muslims. In 641, a decisive battle was fought at Nihawand, near ancient Ecbatana, in which the Arabs won a victory that Muslim tradition was to make the source of endless legends. But even this victory still left the Arabs to win control over ancient centers like Ecbatana and Ispahan. In these areas they were not greeted, as they had been in Syria and Iraq, by an indigenous Aramaic-speaking population as liberators, but ran into tenacious resistance.

The Arabs did not get to Khorasan until Persia proper, the province of Fars, was conquered. Soon after the battle of Qadisiyya the Arabs undertook a campaign against Fars via the easiest route, through the Persian Gulf from Bahrayn, the third entryway into the country after Ctesiphon and Basra. Fars put up substantial resistance, and it was not conquered until 649–50. The following year a campaign was undertaken against Khorasan; ultimately Persia as a whole was conquered. In striking contrast to the rapidity of the Arab advances in Syria and Iraq, it took almost an entire decade to eliminate Persian resistance. Even though Persia was eventually thoroughly Islamicized, it never gave up its native speech entirely. Indeed, it was finally restored as a quite independent idiom, though with a huge admixture of Arabic, and Arabs as such never settled there as an independent population. Not only did Arabic never become the vernacular, but even in the sphere of Islam the Persians retained a distinctive attitude—they were to become en bloc the homeland of the greatest single Muslim sect (the Shi'ites) to this day.

These striking military triumphs had as their immediate consequence the shunting away of Medina from the center of the new community to its periphery. Egypt, a major province of Byzantium, was perilously close to both Syria and Medina, and a reconquest based on Egypt was altogether likely, especially since Alexandria's resources as a seaport were supplemented by a substantial military harbor in Clysma (Qulzum, Suez). Egypt as a whole was of vital importance for the Byzantine sea forces; it was probably one of the most important dockworks in the empire. It is very likely that even the Bedouin, utterly strange to sea warfare though they were, must have perceived the vital importance of Egypt from the point of view of naval warfare if they were to be able to defend the coastline of Syria. This perception was doubtless reinforced by the difficulty they had had in seizing Caesarea.

Moreover, Egypt, the granary of the ancient world, must have seemed even more tempting from the supply point of view than Iraq, which was a long way off. The moment Egypt was conquered the import of grain to Medina, with its growing needs, became systemized. Thus the conquest of Egypt formed part of the inherent logic of the Arab expansion as soon as the initial chaotic raids were transformed into a system.

It is highly unlikely, to be sure, that there could have been any awareness among the Muslim leadership of just how easy the conquest of Egypt was going to be. The Persians, who had at one time been in control of the country for about a decade, had been expelled some time before. Their departure had been followed by a vigorous Byzantine reaction based as in Syria on Heraclius' determination to impose a unitary church on the country by suppressing the embittered contest between the Monophysites and the Dyophysites. But his celebrated "peace formula" was frustrated by the bitterness that had grown up between the two parties. In any case, the peace formula was not brought to the Egyptian Monophysites by a peacemaker, but by Cyrus, a sort of fanatical inquisitor who had been bishop of Phasis in the Caucasus and been sent to Alexandria in 631 by Heraclius both as patriarch and as the head of the whole provincial administration. For some ten years Cyrus had been striving, by means of the most stringent measures, to force the Copts of Egypt into accepting Heraclius' peace formula. The Coptic ritual was forbidden and the Coptic priests and organizations were savagely persecuted, and Cyrus moreover had heightened the tax squeeze still further to do his share in alleviating Heraclius' financial plight. Later Coptic tradition regarded Cyrus as an actual anti-Christ.

In December 639 Amr ibn al-As, a field marshal who had distinguished himself in the Syrian campaigns, appeared on the eastern frontier of Egypt with a rather small force, some three or four thousand men; a month later he conquered Pelusium. Then he had to wait for reinforcements before undertaking a really serious battle. Zubayr, the famous companion of the prophet, turned up with five thousand auxiliary troops and Amr embarked on the battle of Heliopolis in July 640, immediately followed by the capture of a suburb of Babylon not far from present-day Cairo. Though not the capital, Babylon was the most important city in the country after Alexandria because of its strategic location at the head of the mouth of the Nile.

Babylon held out for a while, but Cyrus, whose name is enveloped in Coptic tradition by the most scurrilous rumors, entered into negotiations with Amr against the wishes of his own camp and took the proposed treaty with Amr off to Heraclius for approval. The latter was furious, and Cyrus was deported for treachery, but Heraclius himself died soon afterward (641), unloosing once again all the bitter disputes and squabbles of the Byzantine court against a background of widespread personal corruption.

By April 641 Babylon had surrendered. There again the extraordinary corruption in the country, fortified by religious and social dissension, had made any serious campaign against the Muslims quite impossible. The eastern delta and upper Egypt fell into the Muslims' hands. Amr now crossed the Nile and followed its western arm toward Alexandria, but though his progress was substantially eased by the widespread treachery and fear, he could not for the time being expect to conquer the powerful metropolis.

After Heraclius' death, Cyrus was sent back to Egypt by Empress Martina, who was apparently weary of the long-drawn-out warfare with the Muslims. Cyrus was supposed to get from Amr the best possible conditions for surrender. He arrived in Alexandria in September 641 and seemed to embark on a campaign to placate the Copts he had formerly persecuted. He may have been aiming at getting control of the Egyptian primacy under the Muslims, who were by now well known for their tolerance in such matters. In any event, without letting the Alexandrians know, he concluded a separate treaty of surrender with Amr. The city was supposed to be evacuated by the Greeks before the middle of September 642, though the city-dwellers themselves were to be left unmolested, with religious freedom in return for a certain tribute, in accordance with the basic Muslim formula.

When the news got out of Cyrus' action, he seems to have been in mortal danger, but the people eventually saw its wisdom under the circumstances; the city was taken over by the Muslims. After the fall of Alexandria, it seemed advisable to Amr to secure his rear; the following winter (642–43) he set out against Pentapolis and occupied Barqa without a struggle.

In Egypt, too, executive policy was aimed at the isolation of the Arabs from the indigenous population, and Alexandria was not made the capital of the newly conquered province. The Muslims, as they had done in Kufa and Basra, built their own city on the eastern shore of the Nile near Babylon. Their encampment city was called by a Greek word arabicized into Fustat (Tent). The list of quarters, arranged by tribe, shows us that most of the tribes that carried out the conquest of Egypt were south Arabian. Fustat was probably founded even before Alexandria was evacuated (642).

There is a famous anecdote about the Muslim destruction of the Alexandria library (the Serapeum). The story goes that the whole library was wiped out, on the theory that the books it contained were superfluous if they repeated the Quran and pernicious if they contradicted it. The story seems to be a pure fabrication, unmentioned even in Christian documents until the thirteenth century. As a matter of fact, most of the Serapeum had been destroyed by Christians in countless embittered controversies long before the Muslims came on the scene.

Umar repeated in Egypt his behavior in Syria with Khalid. He replaced the conqueror of Egypt by a civil governor, Abdallah ibn

Sa'd ibn Abi Sarh, the moment the conquest was assured, doubtless for fear of allowing a local army commander too much power, but the governor proved helpless because of lack of training and of any prestige with the actual troops. When the Byzantine government, once order had been restored in Constantinople, dispatched a fleet that appeared outside Alexandria in 645, the city opened its gates to its former Byzantine overlords. Umar's successor, Uthman, the third caliph, called back Amr, who by 646 expelled the Byzantines once and for all and this time reduced Alexandria to bondage by military force instead of waiting for it to collapse of itself.

Amr then withdrew once again. It annoyed him to head the army without having the civil administration in his hands as well—largely because the specific objective of the great Arab marshals had always been personal enrichment, an instance of the classical Bedouin attitude toward the taking of booty. Since the only way to get rich in the newly conquered lands was to have the key to the tax office, the only reason for remaining as head of the province was to control the civil administration, with its powers of taxation. In this case the civil governor sent out by the caliph was his own foster brother, hence Amr had only a small chance of enriching himself substantially.

Abdallah ibn Sa'd ibn Abi Sarh distinguished himself not only in the creation of the taxation system that was to prove an immense source of wealth, but also by extending the frontiers of the Egyptian province, settling the troubled border with the Nubians in upper Egypt (April 652), and pushing westward as far as Tripoli.

Abdallah's principal service, however, was the development of a fleet, which the Arabs, doubtless to their own surprise, now found themselves in need of, since they now had a very substantial portion of the eastern Mediterranean coastline, from north Syria to Tripoli. Mu'awiya, who was now established in Syria, was engaged in building ships himself, and Abdallah, who controlled the major shipping works in Alexandria, was able to cooperate with Mu'awiya in a substantial way, providing the ships that enabled the Arabs, novices though they were in naval warfare, to display surprising naval skill.

This adaptability was quite remarkable. It is true that before Islam some Arabs had been thoroughly proficient in navigation and Arab ships had been commonplace long before Islam throughout

the Red Sea and the Indian Ocean, but these Arabs were southern Arabs, based on the sedentary civilizations of south Arabia, while the Bedouin tribes of the north, which carried out the conquests, had no familiarity at all with the sea. The Bedouin of the Hijaz and of the Syrian and Iraqi marches were essentially a continental people and in all probability had never even seen the sea.

Yet within no more than a few years the northern Arabs had familiarized themselves with this specialized art to such a degree that they could cope with the expert navies of the Byzantines and thus give the infant caliphate control of the most vital part of its domain, the Mediterranean Sea. The conquest of Syria and Egypt brought a substantial segment of the Mediterranean coastline under the control of the Arabs; there were many seaports and a large class of people used to seafaring. The significance of sea power for any country on the Mediterranean would have been obvious if only on the basis of common sense; common sense was stimulated by the brief Byzantine reoccupation of Alexandria, which was carried out from the sea in 645.

Unaccountably, Muslim tradition somewhat belittles the naval achievements of the early Arab conquerors, but Western observers were always greatly impressed by them as part of the general Arab success at arms. By the end of the seventh century the building of a navy and the recruitment for it were a principal activity of the civil administration in Egypt.

Mu'awiya needed the ships primarily, of course, against Byzantium. It was clear that as long as the Greeks controlled the sea there could be no expectation of any tranquillity either in Syria or in Egypt. Hence his primary task was now to seize Cyprus, the principal point of support for the Byzantine fleet.

The first naval enterprise of the Arabs took place in the summer of 649 against Cyprus; it was a great success. The Ardus was taken the next year, and five years later, in 655, Mu'awiya undertook the first Arab campaign against Constantinople, which depended to a great extent on ships from Egypt. There was a great battle off Phoenix, on the Lycean coast; its importance is shown by the presence of Emperor Constans II himself as commander.

Though the details of the battle are somewhat obscure, its results were definitive: The whole of the Byzantine fleet, reported as some five hundred ships, was utterly destroyed. For some reason, however, the Arabs lost heart for the campaign against Constantinople, and the Byzantines were spared another strenuous struggle through the assassination shortly afterward of Uthman and the immediately ensuing tussle for the caliphate. Hence Mu'awiya's internal problems now forced him to make an unfavorable peace treaty with the Byzantines.

Mu'awiya and others were to carry on a practically uninterrupted series of campaigns with the intention of occupying both Byzantium and Armenia, but though success wavered back and forth the Arabs never managed to penetrate abidingly beyond north Syria. Their northern border coincided with the areas that had always been Semitic-speaking and came to an end at the foothills of the Taurus Mountains. There were annual expeditions, depending on special tax systems in kind. These systematic caravans went in two directions, one northward toward Asia Minor and Armenia, the other westward toward North Africa and, from 711 on, toward Spain.

Despite all their efforts to take Constantinople, a natural and highly tempting target, the Arabs never succeeded. They carried on a great many campaigns on both land and sea, some of which were relatively successful but none wholly. The Arab frontier proper was to remain the Amanus and the Caucasus, with occasional thrusts beyond that never endured. The agonies of the Byzantine Empire constitute, of course, a complex subject; but as for the Arabs, they reached their "natural" border very quickly and never went beyond.

There is a remarkable resemblance between the strategy of the Bedouin and that of modern sea power. Viewed from the vantage point of nomads, the desert, which only they could make use of, was like a vast ocean on which they controlled the only vessels. The Bedouin could use it for supplies and communications—and as a haven when defeated. They could appear from its depths whenever they wished and slip back again at will. This gave them enormous mobility and resilience as long as they were moving against sedentary communities. This mobility was to remain of incalculable value in the early period down to the very point, indeed, when the Bedouin themselves were to transform the societies surrounding them, whereupon their tactics and strategy inevitably changed. Desert warfare was bound to be superseded as soon as the desert

Arabs came into systematic contact with the Byzantine and Persian armies. The Arabs soon learned to copy the order and discipline of the Byzantine armies, as the Persians for that matter had also tried to do in their time. In the case of the Arabs the transition was natural; the Arabs along the Syrian border had received their military training as Byzantine auxiliaries and were to be of great importance under the Umayyad regime.

A new form of warfare was entailed by the need to cope with big cities. Engineering had to be applied in order to besiege fortified cities and to construct defense fortifications. The rectangular fortified camp that had been used to such advantage by the Romans and the Byzantines was taken as a model for imitation, and in each conquered area the Arabs set up such camp cities, sometimes rather ill-chosen with respect to site. In the beginning the Bedouin were so dependent on the deserts they had come out of that wherever they settled in the conquered provinces they made a point of setting up their encampments at the borders of the desert and the sown. They would use already existing towns only if they suited them; otherwise they could create altogether new ones, like the two great towns in Iraq that were to play a seminal role in the evolution of Islam—Basra (founded around 635 or 637) and Kufa (founded a little later). Fustat in Egypt and Qayrawan in Tunisia were founded for similar reasons.

These garrison towns were the Arab strongpoints, much like the bases maintained by imperial powers today. Throughout the purely Arab phase of the caliphate—the dominion of the Umayyads—these encampments, which originally were simply great army camps quartered out by tribe, were the chief centers of Arab administration.

These camp cities were to acquire special importance under the purely Arab regime of the Umayyads, whose indifference to religion spread from their Syrian headquarters to the co-capitals of Mecca and Medina. Many of the more devout Muslims were to feel put off by the laxity of the Umayyad court and move to one or another of the Iraqi camp cities, which thus became the havens of orthodoxy and ultimately heightened resentment of the Umayyad caliphate because of its secularism.

These purely Arab towns were the instrument by which the Arabic language was so quickly imposed on the conquered populations. Although the Arabs were a tiny minority in the conquered countries at large, in their own encampments they were the great majority; Arabic was naturally the dominant language. Since these encampments, as the ruling centers of the country, were the chief markets for the farm products of the neighboring areas, it was only natural for Arabic to fan out rapidly into the surrounding countryside. The upshot was that each encampment soon created an outer circle of settlements consisting of craftsmen, shopkeepers, and laborers to satisfy the needs of the new Arab ruling class. The urban movement into the towns was promoted by the heavy Muslim taxation on the non-Muslim population in the early period of the caliphate, as well as by the fall in farm prices produced through the systematic distribution of agricultural produce *gratis* among the conquerors.

As has been pointed out, the driving force behind the Muslim Arab conquests was not religious in the least, but a migratory impulse rooted in the millennial condition of the Arabian Peninsula. Men like Khalid and Amr, for instance, were obviously no pietists or mystics; their interests were thoroughly practical.

The decade of Umar's rule was marked by the practical measures he had to take in order to cope with the problems of administering vast subject populations infinitely superior in education and civic ability to the Bedouin themselves, the overwhelming majority of whom could not, of course, read or write. The policy of the caliphate had nothing whatever to do with the actual interests of its subjects, but solely with those of the Muslim Arab aristocracy that was superimposed on the conquered areas.

Though Muslim tradition has piously ascribed to Umar the credit for laying the foundations of the Arab kingdom, it seems clear that his rule lacked the time, as well as the perspective, to establish a novel state principle. What Umar can be claimed as achieving in the first phase of Islam was the subordination to the Arab tribes of the vast mass of newly conquered, taxpaying subjects, while at the same time he forestalled particularism through the introduction of his central fiscal system.

It was because there was not, in fact, a conception, apart from the treasury, of a central administration for the vast realms that were added to the caliphate so quickly during Umar's decade of rule that the caliph largely depended on the decisions of the commanders and authorities on the spot. This was why the Arabs in the beginning merely retained the preceding administrative machinery, even the old currency. In the first phase of Islam the Arabs were still in the grip of the nomad attitude toward sedentary society and did not try to transform anything at all—as long as tribute was paid they were content. It was not until after 640 that Umar saw the need for a new coinage, and it was not until much later that it was actually introduced.

In its first phase, in fact, Islam can be characterized as a trust: The whole of the new empire, almost wholly non-Muslim in its composition, was treated like a chattel of the Muslim community, which at this time meant a small number of Arabs. The exclusive trustee, of course, was the caliph himself.

A note on numbers may be illuminating. At the height of his power Muhammad, on one of his triumphal processions, could assemble, according to tradition, no more than fifty thousand men. Most authorities agree that this implies, in terms of the given circumstances, that what was meant by "Arab" during the opening phase of Islam referred to not more than a few hundred thousand people. After the conquests, accordingly, with the accretion of the densely settled areas of Persia, Syria, Iraq, and Egypt, the Arabs were scattered very thinly indeed over an enormous terrain.

Basically the Arab realm was established through the immense triumphs won under the second caliph, Umar. Curiously enough, it is the very success of the initial Arab advances that shows how torn from within the nascent Arab-Muslim community really was, for if it had been genuinely united the victories won by the handful of Bedouin warriors would surely have been still more astonishing. It is the extraordinary feebleness of the Byzantine regime that shows us to what extent it was not military power that withstood the Bedouin campaigns, but inner conflicts, quickly unfolding after Muhammad's death, that acted as a brake from within on the expansion of the Arabs.

• • •

Umar was assassinated in November 644, quite unexpectedly, by a Persian slave. Though he had been named Abu Bakr's successor with no opposition, as the only really obvious candidate, he himself felt unable to make a sensible choice of successor from among the rather mediocre group of his immediate entourage. He compromised by designating a special council to make the choice. Uthman was chosen, doubtless because he was considered the weakest and most pliable of all, and perhaps, also, because Umar had been so autocratic, severe, and capable that a change was felt to be a relief. In addition, Uthman was doubtless used by his family, the Umayyads, as a springboard for their own advancement, since the Umayyad segment of the old Meccan aristocracy, which had always been hostile to Muhammad but had switched over in time, had even moved to Medina to participate in the triumphs of Islam and to make their own way as men of action at the expense of the unworldly pietists there. The switching over of the Meccan aristocracy to the side of the Muslims is a telling illustration of the swift and irresistible injection of purely secular elements into the earliest enterprises of the Umma, which though formulated on the basis of religion was articulated on the basis of politics.

The Umayyad clan, with the practical sense and outstanding intelligence of many individual members, had successfully integrated themselves into Muhammad's entourage, and Uthman now appointed many Umayyads and their intimates to every post of the slightest consequence—an unabashedly nepotistic procedure that immediately aroused irritation throughout the nascent Muslim realm.

This vexation was closely associated with a consequence of the financial system introduced by Umar and carried on by Uthman, namely, the disposition of the booty accruing from the conquests.

It was the desire for booty, after all, that had magnetized the great Arabian tribes. The limitless loot from the countries that had fallen with such bewildering ease into their laps now belonged to the tribes as such, after deduction of the so-called "prophet's fifth." The question had, of course, instantly arisen: What was to happen to the vast areas that were now in the control of so few people? There was an enormous annual tribute to be paid by the subject populations; who was to get it?

Though the individual conquerors might—logically—have claimed it, it was clear that from the point of view of the central regime this would have led to an impossible situation, what with the fluctuation of the number of Arabs and the dangers inherent in the self-enrichment of local commanders.

It was because of this that Umar had set up a central fiscal system. The actual inhabitants of the vast new army encampments were to be put on a salary or pension, and the excess went to Medina, there to be allocated as pensions to members of the evolving religious hierarchy, at the discretion of the caliph.

Umar himself had been above party, and the booty was so great that there was no occasion for discontent. But by Uthman's time the booty had begun to shrink, and so the centralized fiscal system began to appear to the great Arabian tribes in the provinces as an outrage against them. The opposition arising on these economic grounds was now fortified by the vexation due to Uthman's nepotism; this finally brought things to a head and triggered a revolt directed at his person.

Though it seemed to be the mutinous elements in the provinces that were fermenting, his opponents in Medina itself were also clandestinely pouring fuel on the flames. Finally some five hundred men were sent to Medina by the Arabs in Egypt. After some futile negotiations that dragged on for some weeks, they besieged the old caliph in his house and with no resistance from his own entourage simply killed him at prayer, in June 656.

This assassination was to bear fruit. By giving rise to the Shi'ite schism it brought about a rupture in Islam that has persisted to the present day.

Uthman's natural successor was generally considered to be Ali, Muhammad's son-in-law, but choosing him meant offending the powerful Umayyads, since after all Ali would be benefiting by the assassination of a scion of the Umayyad clan, and in the eyes of all Umayyads, most especially in those of Mu'awiya, an Umayyad and the governor of Syria to boot, would thus bear the taint of murder.

Mu'awiya's position in Syria was so strong that he could easily take the risk of opposing Ali as caliph, especially since Ali had other enemies, including the prophet's widow herself, Ayesha. In December 656, near Basra, at the decisive Battle of the Camel—celebrated for Ayesha's attending it on camel back in the ancient Bedouin manner, as though she were a shrine—Ali was victorious. Now master of Iraq, he moved the seat of the government to Kufa.

This was to prove of long-range historic significance, for it meant that from now on Arabia itself dropped out of the center of events and became a backwater. The nascent Muslim empire now formed two centers that were to carry on as in pre-Islamic times the ancient polarity between Syria and Iraq.

Syrian discipline had ensured a temporary victory over Iraq, but the memory of the short-lived glory of Iraq as the residence of the caliphate was to provide the later Abbasid dynasty with a spiritual claim to the leadership of Islam that it was to retain for many centuries.

After the Battle of the Camel, Ali was in a very strong position vis-à-vis Mu'awiya, since Egypt was still behind Ali and Mu'awiya could do nothing without it. Yet a celebrated trick contrived by Amr, the first conqueror of Egypt, who had now gone over to Mu'awiya, was to lead to Mu'awiya's triumph.

Ali's forces moved against Mu'awiya's. Both armies collided near Siffin, not far from Raqqa on the Syrian border, and in July 657, after a battle that lasted several days, when Ali seemed to be winning the upper hand, Amr conceived the notion of sending his men into battle with copies of the Quran fixed to the points of their lances, as though the divine word were now being called upon for a decision.

Ali was completely undone by this ruse. He had to give in to the pressure of the pietists in his own ranks, and a court of arbitration was agreed to, with Amr acting as Mu'awiya's spokesman while another notable, who was not, in fact, wholly in harmony with Ali's interests, was to speak for Ali's side.

In the event, however, the same pietists who had forced Ali to succumb to Amr's trick now turned away from him, reproaching him for choosing to negotiate through people instead of leaving the decision to God. Several thousands of Ali's troops deserted him, setting up an encampment of their own, which made them known as Secessionists (*Kharijites*). Their revolt is doubtless to be understood as a cropping forth of the ancient freedom-loving anarchy of the Bedouin. They remained obdurate opponents of Ali as well as of the Umayyads, who were soon to govern the empire.

The details of the court of arbitration are somewhat obscure. It seems clear that Amr was wily enough to persuade his colleague to act as though Mu'awiya and Ali were on the same level juridically, though Ali had a caliphate at stake, whereas in theory Mu'awiya was no more than his satrap.

In any case the court of negotiation, which met in 658, came out against Ali, without, of course, being able to enforce any practical decision. The vexation of this result was further heightened by the loss of Egypt, which was reconquered by Amr, who went back there permanently to rule it as practically a viceroy and no mere governor. Since Ali's and Mu'awiya's forces were roughly equal, neither reached for a decision. It was not until July 660 that Mu'awiya had himself proclaimed caliph in Jerusalem, and since Ali was assassinated a half year later Mu'awiya's pretension went unchallenged. Ali's son and successor was simply bought off.

Mu'awiya's victory marks the germination of Umayyad rule. Damascus became the center of the empire; a full-fledged Arab kingdom was launched.

• • •

The progress of the Arab invasion in North Africa was markedly different from what it had been in the Middle East and in Egypt. The Arabs had encountered no resistance to speak of from the Aramaic-speaking population of the Middle East and hardly more from the Egyptian Copts. Both these groups assimilated the Arabic language as well as the Arabs individually, in sharp contrast to Persia, whose population by and large resisted the Arab invasion ethnically and culturally and although ultimately absorbed into the world community of Islam retained its own identity and language, to reemerge as a national entity generations later.

North Africa was an intermediate case. There the Arabs came across the Berbers, warlike nomads like themselves and just as mobile. The Berbers are a people of mysterious origin, many of them tall, blond, and blue-eyed, speaking a Hamitic language related to Ancient Egyptian. The Arabs managed to impose Islam on the Berbers, too, but it received a special stamp in North Africa, and the Berbers never lost their national identity. Ultimately they were to mingle with the Arabs, but they retained their own speech; to this day most Moroccans outside the big cities speak Berber dialects.

The Berbers, moreover, were absolutely vital for the Arab invasion of Europe. Without the Berber masses, for instance, any major Arab enterprise against Spain would have been unthinkable, nor would the long-lived, though episodic rooting of Islam in southern Europe have been realizable without them. In this sense the history of Islam in Europe is intimately linked to its history in North Africa, far more organically than it was with the fate of the eastern caliphate, with which it shared only some cultural features.

The intermingling of Arabs and Berbers that characterized all western Islam took place only slowly, over some centuries, but Arabic-speaking Islam succeeded in doing something that for the Phoenicians and Romans had remained no more than a dream. These two peoples had never done more than establish themselves as thinly settled coastal colonies along the North African littoral, while the flatlands and the hinterland remained steadfastly Berber, Berbers remaining the basic populace long after the Phoenicians and Romans belonged to the past. Ultimately, however, the Arabs were to consolidate the Berber hinterland as well as the coast.

It was not the Byzantines that held up the Arab advance through North Africa, but the resistance of the Berbers, who upon being crowded by the oncoming Arabs would occasionally join forces with their generally detested Byzantine overlords to resist the new danger. The Arabs found it very difficult to demonstrate to the Berbers by force of arms that Islam was on their side and that the Byzantines must be ousted. When the Berbers finally accepted Islam, they then gave it a further stimulus of their own and overran southern Europe under the leadership of the Arabs. In Africa itself Islam kept penetrating Berber life more and more, and as it took shape there assumed a Berber tinge.

When Alexandria was occupied by Amr, it was manifestly necessary to secure the Arab flank by occupying Barqa, a suburb of ancient Pentapolis. In consequence, the whole of the Pentapolis was soon to belong to the Arab sphere of power. Barqa in its turn bordered on the ancient Africa Proconsularis, divided by the Arabs into an eastern half, Tripolis, and a northern half, Carthage, or, as the Arabs called it, Ifriqiyya—Africa *tout court*. After Barqa was occupied, there was a constant stream of raids throughout Tripolitania going as far south as the great desert.

But for the time being, the Arabs were obliged to retain their principal combat units for Alexandria, which was to fall once more into the hands of the Byzantines; hence, there was no question of sending any serious forces farther west than Barqa.

Toward the end of 647, after Alexandria had been reconquered firmly and Abdallah ibn Sa'd ibn Abi Sarh had become governor of Egypt, a great campaign westward was organized. With the disorder in the Byzantine administration, it was not difficult for the Egyptian governor to extend his power very considerably, though not permanently. After a campaign that lasted more than a year (647–48) the expedition was called off, and when confusion broke out upon the assassination of Caliph Uthman, the general expansion westward came to a halt.

With the restoration of some degree of stability, however, under Mu'awiya, when Amr was once again ruler of Egypt, the westward-ranging campaigns of the Arabs started up once again, under Amr's nephew Uqba ibn Nafi, with Barqa as base of operations and with a number of subchiefs conducting their own raiding parties. By 670, after a series of brilliantly successful raids on the strip of oases along the northern border of the Sahara, Uqba undertook a campaign into Africa proper, where he ultimately founded the future Qayrawan, celebrated for Islamic learning, as an Arab army encampment and a strategic strongpoint like Basra and Kufa.

What the Arabs called Africa had at first been a province independent of Egypt; now it was to be reunited with Egypt. Uqba was succeeded by an emancipated slave, Dinar Abu-l-Muhajir, who was a marked contrast to Uqba. The latter had been an old-fashioned Bedouin raider, in the habit of settling all questions by force and of treating Berber backsliders from Islam with undiplomatic severity. Dinar, on the other hand, was to show himself very skillful in reconciling the Berbers to Islam and in conducting operations against the Byzantines. He secured the support of the Berbers, under their leader Kusayla, in a campaign he undertook against the Byzantines in Carthage. Though he failed to take the city, he occupied a number of surrounding areas and then moved westward as far as Tlemsen, which he could do without much risk because of his intimacy with the Berbers.

Uqba meanwhile, after having been thrown into chains before being replaced by Dinar, had managed to get himself reinstated by the caliph as general commander of North Africa (681–82). He revenged himself on Dinar by carrying him in fetters along with him on his campaigns. He removed the chief Muslim headquarters encampment to Qayrawan again and once again began dealing with the Berbers in his characteristically old-fashioned, high-handed Bedouin style. The upshot was foreseeable: He antagonized them systematically. Kusayla began inciting them against Uqba and abandoned him at the first possible chance. Thus, when Uqba began campaigning westward, it was under far more unfavorable conditions than Dinar. To be sure, he got as far as Tangiers by way of Tlemsen and even made his way to the Atlantic Ocean over the Atlas Mountains, but on his way back he, together with his captive Dinar, was killed by some rebel Berbers. Uqba seems to have overestimated the strength of the Arab position throughout the west. He had run the risk of defeat by dividing his army up into small detachments, or he may have overloaded his troops with booty and so was unable to maintain discipline. In any case, he was killed in 683 at Tahudha, near Biskra; he became a martyr in local mythology and is one to this day.

Uqba's death triggered a general insurrection on the part of the Berbers, who leaped back into the arms of the Byzantines, with the result that Africa soon had to be given up by the Arabs. Kusayla could range throughout northwest Africa with impunity.

Thus all Africa, except for Barqa, was lost to Islam again, at least for the time being. It was not until 688–89 that an attempt could be made to restore the power of Islam in North Africa. Here again, however, it was the Berbers, not the Byzantines, who were the target of the Arab forces, since the Byzantines, sitting in their cities, were extremely skillful in using the Berbers as a shield. The first action of the renewed Muslim offensive was to free Muslims who had come under Berber rule in Qayrawan and then to move against Mons Aurasius, Kusayla's base of operations. Kusayla fell in a bloody struggle, and the Arab troops made their way as far as the present-day Kef and perhaps farther, there to come to a stop through the exhaustion of their forces. On the way back the Arab troops were fallen upon by the Byzantines, who had taken advantage of the Arab expedition to attack Barqa once again.

Qayrawan, however, remained in Arab hands. A new leader, Hasan ibn an-Nu'man, the first Syrian prince on African soil, seems to have been a skillful diplomat as well as a disciplinarian. He resumed Dinar's policy of regarding not the Berbers but the Byzantines as the chief enemy of the Arabs. As soon as he got an allowance of auxiliary troops from the caliph he moved against Carthage, which had never yet been conquered. He took it in the summer of 697 and then defeated the united Berbers and Byzantines northeast of Tunis at Satfura, though without being able to prevent their reconcentrating their forces near Bizerta. In any case the Arabs lost Carthage again, but ultimately ensured its possession when they drove off a big Byzantine fleet with a still bigger Arab one in the summer of 698 and sealed the fate of the city.

At first Hasan ibn an-Nu'man was rather unsuccessful against the Berber tribes, which had been rallied into a cohesive force once again by a woman, a seeress called Kahina (Priestess), Kusayla's successor. But although Kahina defeated a major Arab force in the foothills of Mons Aurasius, she was unable to maintain her position over a longer period of time, and Hasan's diplomacy gradually eroded her following. Because of this diplomacy he was able to use the final victory he won over Kahina in Gafes a few years later as a springboard for a durable fusion with the Berbers, which seems to have taken place about 703. The oddity in these campaigns was that the definitive victory of the Arabs was by no means due to the success of their land troops, but to the efficacy of their navy, which made possible the occupation and maintenance of the Byzantine coastal points.

It was thus the peace with the Berbers, rather than any military successes against the Byzantines on land, that brought the Berbers into the Muslim camp and thus sealed the fate of the Byzantine cities that had been holding out. Now it was under the slogans of Islam that the converted Berber tribal chiefs moved in their turn against the still independent Berber chiefs of the west. The prospect of vast booty, plus the acquisition of land, had united the two former enemies, so similar in their way of life. It is true that the countryside was soon to prove too small to contain these two peoples, brought into turbulence by the upheaval of Islam. In any case the Latin and Greek population of the cities seems to have vanished immediately, doubtless to Spain and Sicily; Latin civilization evaporated from North Africa with remarkable rapidity.

The Arab conquest of North Africa was possible only after the Arabs stopped regarding the countryside as a mere arena for plunder and began to settle it in a systematic way, signalized by Uqba's establishment of Qayrawan. At first, however, this meant no more than that the starting point of the countless Arab raids was shifted, and it was not until Dinar laid down a policy of moving against the fortified cities, backed up by a reconciled Berber hinterland, that the Arab settlement of the countryside as a whole was possible. This in its turn depended on the restoration of order at the Syrian center, which provided more troops for use in Africa and also made the fleet available—two circumstances that could be taken advantage of effectively only when a diplomat of Hasan ibn an-Nu'man's skill was in a position to realize Dinar's plans.

Hasan's policy was carried on and amplified by Musa ibn Nusayr, the real pacifier of North Africa and a conqueror of Spain. He seems to have begun his activities in 708, devoting the first years of his governorship to the subjugation of the Berbers in the west, who were destined to carry out the conquest of Spain under Tariq, Musa's emancipated slave and general. The seizure of Spain cannot be explained by the Arab drive toward expansion so much as by the necessity of giving the newly subjugated Berbers in the west something to do, since it was their avidity for booty that had lured them into Islam. At the center of the caliphate itself these far-flung campaigns and enterprises gave rise to some misgivings, but the success of the Arab-Berber campaign against the Visigothic kingdom of Spain, already in a state of some decomposition, took place so quickly that there was no time for the seat of the caliphate to exercise any restraining influence.

The immediate occasion of the Spanish invasion is completely obscure. The last king of the Visigoths, Roderich, is thought to have been a usurper and to have been undone by a mysterious Count Julian, perhaps of Berber origin himself, who invited the Arabs and Berbers into Spain to revenge himself on Roderich for having dishonored Julian's daughter.

In any case, in connection with the frictions around the Gothic throne, and doubtless more with the aim of plunder than of conquest, Tariq moved into Spain with some seven thousand Berbers—later to be supplemented by another five thousand—and landed near the mountain that still bears his name, Gibraltar (Jabal Tariq). His expedition seems to have been embarked on as the result of a successful reconnaissance carried out the year before. Tariq met the forces of King Roderich in the present-day valley of the Salado (Wadi Bakka), and it was here that Roderich, though at the head of a much bigger army, was undone by his internal enemies and defeated by Tariq's soldiers.

This single great success was to initiate an unprecedented triumphal march of the Berbers, which can be explained, doubtless, only on the assumption that the Gothic regime was detested by everyone. Economic and religious measures had inflamed the various elements of the population against each other and thus, in a way similar to what had happened on Byzantine terrain, had prepared for the Berber invasion. The Jews especially, who had been subjected to an unscrupulous campaign of terrorism by the orthodox regime, hailed the Arabs and Berbers as liberators. Only the cities where the Gothic knighthood was concentrated put up any serious resistance.

Tariq seems to have been well informed of the local situation, perhaps by Julian. In any case, success justified his remarkably bold plan of marching directly forward on to Toledo, the capital, and of leaving smaller cities to isolated detachments. Tariq met with serious opposition only at Ecija, where the bitterest battle of the whole campaign was fought. Córdoba and Toledo fell through treachery; the aristocracy and the upper clergy had not even waited for the Muslims to arrive, but had sought refuge beforehand or even joined the conquerors.

By the end of the summer of 711 Tariq already held half of Spain. His successes were unexpected—all his chief, Musa, had expected from his customary summer raid was just another caravan of booty—and Musa was thoroughly disconcerted by the utter destruction of the Gothic kingdom.

Eager to share the glory and the benefits of the conquest of such a rich country, Musa came to Spain himself the following spring with some eighteen thousand men. Deliberately avoiding Tariq's itinerary, he conquered the cities that were still holding out, especially Medina, Sidonia, Carmona, and Seville, the last of which had been the spiritual center of Spain and the seat of the Roman regime for hundreds of years. Even under the Goths it had retained its ancient splendors; its siege was to last several months before it surrendered. It was clear that Tariq's successes, however brilliant, had not destroyed the resistance of the country as a whole and that his conquest of the capital had to be followed up by a long-drawn-out, painful campaign. It is doubtlessly true to say that except for the chaos of the Gothic regime and the consequent absence of cohesion the Muslims would never have managed to conquer Spain at all. The situation was, in short, quite similar to what had given the

Arabs the victory over Byzantium and Persia. Even after Seville fell, Musa still encountered resistance from Mérida, which finally prudently capitulated (June 713).

Musa finally met Tariq again in Toledo, where he vented his wrath on him because of the very excess of his achievement, but Musa himself was soon to be recalled to Damascus. Loaded down by treasure, the old man made his way to Syria with a huge train whose expenses have come down to us in considerable detail. He fell into disfavor in Damascus. His sons, whom he had left in Spain and Africa, did not live long to enjoy the fruits of their father's remarkable exploits; soon afterward they were deposed or assassinated.

A few years later (717 or 718) an expedition conducted by Musa's fourth successor, Hurr, was launched beyond the Pyrenees into the lush countryside of France, where the prevalent internecine strife, plus the fabulous tales of the treasures accumulated in the nunneries and monasteries beckoned to the Arabs and Berbers. There may also have been some notion that Constantinople, the ultimate target of Islam, might be reached overland from France.

In 721, however, when an attempt made by Hurr's successor to capture Toulouse collapsed—the first time the Muslims had ever lost a battle to a Teutonic prince—the tide began to turn against the Arab-Berber invasion.

The bold general expedition that had begun with the breakthrough over the Pyrenees culminated in 732 at the celebrated Battle of Tours (or Poitiers), where Charles Martel ("The Hammer") defeated the Arab-Berber forces in fighting that lasted several days. The light cavalry of the Arabs and Berbers proved to be no match for the unyielding discipline of the Franks, who also showed themselves, according to the chronicles, much superior to their opponents in hand-to-hand combat. It was a catastrophe for the Muslims; a day after their commander had fallen they unexpectedly made off during the night, leaving their entire camp behind as booty for the Frankish victors.

The Battle of Tours has generally been considered an event of primordial consequence in world history. It is assumed that if the Moors had won they might then have gone on to the conquest of all Western Europe.

Yet the stop put to the Muslim push into Europe seems to have been inevitable. The Arab expansion had reached a natural end; the supply lines from the center of the empire in Damascus were strained to their uttermost. The Arabs alone, in any case, would surely have lacked the human resources to undertake even the conquest of Spain without the massive assistance of the Berbers, who by joining the Islamic flood swelled it sufficiently to overflow into a new country, but at the same time, by contributing still another element to the Muslim mixture created further sources of friction, this time between the Arabs and the Berbers. This friction probably broke out just when the high point of the joint advance was reached, so that the Battle of Tours merely coincidentally marks the culminating point of that advance. It was itself the symptom of the inner collapse of the Arab-Berber alliance.

Even inside Spain, after all, the Arab-Berber invasion had not succeeded in mastering the whole peninsula. In its northeast corner a small independent state maintained itself successfully against the Muslim thrust, steadily growing from year to year, and ultimately thrusting an invincible wedge between the Arab and Berber princes and the Pyrenees.

Thus the advances of the Arabs came to a stop for internal reasons. Tours, though a dramatic symbol enshrined in Western literature, is simply the registering of a fact—the cessation of the Arab torrent at its farthest extremity. Even if the Arabs had managed to go on plundering the cities in southern France, that alone could scarcely have led to a permanent establishment of Islam there. The defeat of the Arabs outside Constantinople, on the other hand, was an event of cosmic consequence. If the Arabs had managed to occupy Constantinople, it seems likely that the whole history of the Middle East would have been totally transformed, as indeed it was to be seven hundred years later when another Muslim people—the Ottoman Turks—seized Constantinople and made it the center of a new empire.

The Battle of Tours, accordingly, though it marked the farthest limit of the Arab movement into Western Europe, did not in and for itself bring that movement to a halt, still less to a retreat.

That retreat was caused by growing friction between the Arabs and their unstable allies, the Berbers. The conflict between the two nomadic peoples was all the more serious for the Arabs because of a comprehensive vendetta that had meanwhile broken out in the east, throughout the eastern caliphate, between two great tribal confederations (the Qays and the Kalb), and that had now carried over to the west as well and there too divided the Arab rulers into two hostile parties.

This conflict between the Arab tribes was itself a part of the turmoil that was to plunge the eastern caliphate into a series of upheavals. Though Spain was to emerge from those upheavals a powerful independent state with a brilliant civilization, and countless small successor states were to be formed in North Africa, the real locus for the autonomous evolution of Islam was to remain in the east. The Arab folk migration simply died out at the western end of the Mediterranean.

Islam was also to find a foothold in Sicily, where a curiously intriguing experiment in Muslim-Christian symbiosis was to take place. Both in Sicily and in Spain the implantation of Islam proved to be episodic, though the Spanish episode lasted for centuries. I shall deal with the cultural content of both societies in later chapters.

Summing up, the Arab migration streamlined by Islam utterly transformed the Mediterranean, especially its eastern end and North Africa. It laid the groundwork for the later development of Islam without which a comprehension of the European Middle Ages would elude us.

If we take a bird's-eye view of what emerged from the initial Arab conquests, we shall see how quickly the universe of Islam was established.

After the conquests, the Middle East took only a couple of centuries to become Muslim almost completely. Asia Minor beyond the Oxus and eastward as far as India was islamized very quickly; the Islamic state soon more or less attained its boundaries. Later, the Turks (Seljuqs and Osmanlis) pressed forward into Asia Minor and the Balkans, while in the eleventh century India was heavily islamized, as it still is. In China Islam had found a foothold even before this; it had been carried forward into Turkestan and as far as eastern China, largely by itinerant traders. India and then later Arabia itself were to promote a rapid islamization of the Malay islands.

Africa was to become an arena of massive islamization. After the Mediterranean coast so quickly became part of the Islamic realm, the same process of commercial penetration as in Asia spearheaded a later advance of religious conversion, at least of the ruling classes. By means of trade Islam was to press forward across state borders into the heart of central Africa, starting out from upper Egypt and Morocco and proceeding via the ancient oasis highways of the Sahara.

By 1100 there was a Muslim empire on Lake Chad; by 1400 the whole of North Africa as far as Lake Chad and from Senegal to the Nile was overlaid by a network of Muslim regimes. A Muslim (in this case Arab) settlement and conversion of the whole of the Zanzibar coast down to Madagascar was begun as early as the ninth century. The Muslims at present in South Africa are from Malaysia.

In eastern Europe it was the Ottoman Turks that penetrated far into the heart of the Balkans, through Greece and into Hungary. Nowadays Muslims are left in significant numbers only in Yugoslavia and the Soviet Union, which has perhaps 40 to 50 million Muslim subjects, mostly speaking various Turkish dialects.

At present Islam is about a sixth of mankind, *i.e.*, roughly 500 million; those who speak Arabic may account for 50 to 60 million.

This should provide the framework in time and space within which Islam, evolving and flowering during the Middle Ages, has remained confined.

III

A NEW STATE: THE ARAB KINGDOM AND THE MUSLIM EMPIRE

THE Umayyad regime may be said to have arisen organically out of the original intentions of Muhammad and the first four caliphs. These had all meant Islam to become a theocracy, but what had happened, since in fact all the early Muslims were Arabs, was that the regime rooted in these pious intentions was simply an Arab dynasty organized along national lines. The folk migration had prevailed, for the time being, against the religious impulse; this was given formal expression by the eclipse of Muhammad's pious comrades, by the decline of the Helpers and Emigrants as wielders of authority, and by the rise of the old Arab aristocracy and of the great tribes of Syria and Iraq.

Thus the Arab kingdom, though brought into being through the unifying influence of Islam, actually represented a recrudescence of the primitive Arabism that Muhammad and his pietist entourage had combated. The statesmanlike element that had come into Muhammad's life some time after his flight to Medina, molding his career from then on, was now embodied in an actual state structure, a realization of the dreams of the generation of desert Arabs that had carried out the conquests, not in the interests of their new religion but for the sake of the good things of this world.

The underlying theme of the Arab kingdom was quite in harmony with the worldliness of the early Arab Muslims. Like all nomads who seize hold of sedentary societies, the Arab parvenus were preoccupied only by the *control* of the wealthy lands they had conquered so easily. They had not interest either in the religious conversion of their new subjects or in mingling with them. The colonization practice was in fact similar in many respects to the British occupation regime in Egypt. There was a rigidly exclusive aristocratic caste superimposed on a native population that was not interfered with at all except for administrative purposes. The population was merely milked: There was one simple requirement—tribute. In the beginning Islam made it incumbent on the Arabs only to convert the Christians and the Jews *or* make them pay the taxes due from non-Muslims. For the first few generations after Muhammad, before the great masses of the newly conquered countries had become Muslim, the fiscal theory of the Arab kingdom rested on this simple concept of mulcting the unbelievers on behalf of a treasury on which all Muslim Arabs had a collective claim.

In the beginning the most important of these material privileges was the right to pay and pensions from the office Umar set up to handle the distribution of booty among the Arabs.

The Arabs had begun by appropriating no more than the lands belonging to the enemy state and to actual enemies. If the landowners agreed to accept the new Arab regime, they simply had to pay some taxes; their freehold rights were fully acknowledged. The lands that were confiscated were registered and administered by the state. It was allowable for Muslims to buy lands outside Arabia. Many were given land grants in the form of a certain kind of lease; if the land grants involved unproductive land, they would be given together with capital for development, plus tax remissions and so on. After Umar many caliphs did this as a matter of course; it was a method of paying off their supporters. Outside Arabia Muslim landowners did not pay the full land tax but, after complex debate back and forth, a much smaller tax known as a tithe. The Muslims were also subject to a trivial religious tax, but apart from this all other taxes were levied only on the non-Muslim subjects, who consequently bore the main burden of the state and of the far-flung wars of expansion. The Arabs simply levied a lump sum from each territory, though this was divided, at first purely nominally, into the head tax and the land tax. Local officials were left in charge of the calculation and collection of this lump sum.

No attempt was made to interfere with the local customs, civil or religious, of their new subjects. The Quran had laid it down that the so-called "Peoples of the Book"—*i.e.,* the Christians and Jews, later added to by the acceptance of Persian Zoroastrians as monotheists—were to be regarded as acceptable subjects to the Muslims, if they only paid taxes. Hence the newly conquered populations of the former Byzantine and Persian territories were given this special status. As I have indicated, the Arabs were generally welcomed by those who had been suffering under Byzantine rule, since the new Arab administration was lighter in religious as well as in economic affairs. The Christian populations of Syria and Egypt, in particular, naturally preferred the tolerance of their new Muslim rulers to the fanatical oppressiveness of their former Greek Orthodox rulers. The Arab invaders were often helped, in fact, by the active assistance of both Christians and Jews.

This state of affairs, with its agreeably clear-cut distinction between Muslim Arabs and infidel non-Arabs and its equally clear-cut cleavage in the system of taxation, was not to last long, but during the initial phase of the Arab kingdom the inevitable difficulties were not foreseen.

Under the Umayyad dynasty, accordingly, the internal tasks of the new state consisted primarily of disciplining the ruling class, *i.e.,* the Arab aristocrats themselves—in order to make social life possible—and of systematizing the relationship of that class to its non-Arab subjects.

• • •

Mu'awiya proved to be a remarkably able ruler. While preserving the patriarchal atmosphere of a traditional Arab prince, he was strong-willed, clear-headed, and skillful enough to keep the parvenu state propped up on the playing-off of the contending Arab factions, princelings and tribal chieftains against each other, so that their mutual antagonism kept the edifice of authority in balance. He was so free of pomposity and arrogance that many students have perceived glimmerings of a parliamentary system in his regime, but this seems an overgeneralization of the merits of the primitive democracy that was characteristic of tribal life in Arabia. It is more likely that Mu'awiya's common sense and acumen, and his habit of paying close attention to his counselors, gave the impression of a diffusion of authority. He made a point, also, of leaning away from the nepotism that Uthman had been reproached for; while attending to the needs of his kinsmen, he successfully preserved the state administration from family encroachments.

Perhaps his basic contribution was his success in bridling the traditionally headstrong Arab tribes as they began settling down from their conquests and in establishing a hitherto unknown dynastic principle as the basis of the Arab kingdom, departing both from the old tribal custom of electing the Shaykh as well as from the selective method of the theocracy. In this way the Arab kingdom replaced religious authority with state power.

Installing one Ziyad (known as "the son of his father," *i.e.,* he was a bastard), whom he adopted as a brother, as independent viceroy over the eastern half of the realm, Mu'awiya proclaimed, before his death, his son Yazid as his successor, and when he died (April 680) Yazid was actually acknowledged in the west and partially in Iraq, too. Opposition immediately arose, however: both a secular opposition of Ali's supporters in Iraq and a theocratic reaction from the Hijaz. Both factions, though otherwise disunited, had a common interest in getting the center of the empire shifted again, in one case to Iraq, in the other to Medina.

There is no doubt of this in the case of Iraq, since the great tribes of Kufa and Basra, mindful of their great past as masters of the realm under Ali, had been pushed back by the Syrian regime of the Umayyads. Since Ali was the center of all their ambitions, they longed for a restoration of the golden age in Kufa. Their enthusiasm for Ali was as a parochial glorification of the one caliph that Iraq had hitherto had.

The Ali party (known as the Shi'a, whence the term "Shi'ites" to this day) intended to achieve its goal by electing Ali's second son, Husayn, as caliph; but though he yielded to the pressure of the Kufites, the latter themselves suddenly had a change of heart at the realization that Yazid was still far too strong in Syria for them to risk an open movement against him. Husayn was killed in battle at Kerbela in October 680; the Shi'a gained a martyr.

Though Husayn's martyred death in itself had no particular effect, it was to stimulate still further the evolution of the Shi'a as the party of the Alids. The Shi'a movement was to become a focal point for all tendencies in Islam directed at the Arab ascendancy; to this day Kerbela is the holiest shrine and place of pilgrimage for all Shi'ites, especially the Persians, who were ultimately to become a Shi'ite community *en masse* and thus express their own national tendency within the framework of Islam.

Remorse for the death of Husayn, the prophet's grandson, added to a long list of grievances that had been making themselves felt for some time in Iraq, such as hatred of the Syrians, and above all the heterodox religious tendencies now manifesting themselves, all prepared the terrain for a great revolt that was to take place in a few years. By now the purely political and particularistic coloring of the Shi'ite reaction against Damascus was supplemented by religious ardor. Ali became not merely the companion and son-in-law of the prophet but the heir of his prophetic spirit itself; this was then conceived of as living on in Ali's sons. According to the newly evolving legitimists, only one of the Alids could become an authentic caliph. The motto of the Alid opposition, which after its political destruction in Iraq extended its influence to Persia, became more and more a struggle on behalf of the prophet's house, for the Banu Hashim, the prophet's clan. Once it arrived in Persia, to be sure, this purely Arab drive became entangled with Persian notions of all kinds. It became a vehicle of Persian chauvinism, and in succeeding generations the struggle for the Banu Hashim served to mobilize the Persians against the Arabs. It was as a struggle against the other authentically Arab house of the Umayyads that the Persian Abbasid regime was to win a victory that profoundly altered the composition and flavor of Islamic society.

The opposition of Medina, which meant the reaction of the old elective theocracy to the pretensions of the new secular Arab dynasty in Syria, gave the Umayyads far more trouble than the Alid opposition in Iraq, which had been so swiftly put an end to by the easy victory over Husayn at Kerbela. Yazid was impelled to undertake a campaign against the holy cities; Medina was taken in August 683. Yazid's army then besieged the countercaliph, Zubayr's son Abdallah, in Mecca, but just at this time Yazid died, to be succeeded by a young son who also died a few months later. This blurred the chances of any particular candidate and thus improved Abdallah ibn Zubayr's chances. Abdallah ibn Zubayr was backed even by the great tribe of the Qays, which had moved into Syria some time before. Another great tribe, the Kalb, which had long since been settled in Syria and whose fortunes were now identified with the country through Mu'awiya's intermarriage with them, all became zealous partisans of the Umayyads, since for them this meant hegemony over Syria. A new Umayyad candidate, Marwan ibn al-Hakam, was elected caliph on the basis of seniority; the battle was soon joined.

The countercaliph, the candidate of the Zubayrids, was decisively defeated in the beginning of 684 in a bloody battle at Marj Rahit; it was a sweeping victory for the Umayyads, and Marwan was proclaimed caliph in Syria.

But though this seemed to be an unblemished triumph for the Umayya cause, it in fact was to mean the rapid dissolution of the Umayyads' supremacy, and with their elimination the final end of Arab dominion in Islam. The battle had been so bitter, the losses were so great, and the hatred inspired by the contest of the factions and tribes was so intense that the desire for vengeance and the spirit of vendetta proved irresistible even for the rapidly growing religiosity of the Islamic community.

Long before Marj Rahit the Arabs had been split up into contending tribes. Only the enthusiastic desire for booty underlying the slogans of Islam could overcome their bickering and weld them together for a short time. Now the great tribes of the Qays and the Kalb were set against each other eternally by the bloodletting at Marj Rahit. The rivalry between the two great tribes proved to have a polarizing influence, and most tribal friction was absorbed into the overriding contest between the Qays and the Kalb.

The Qays were scattered throughout the empire, and tribes that had been opposed to them for other reasons now found themselves driven into the camp of their principal adversary, the Kalb. What in other communities would have been political formations or factional groups were construed, in accordance with the ancient Arab obsession with lineage, in genealogical terms. It was in fact probably around this time, in the aftermath of Marj Rahit, that the celebrated distinction mentioned above between north and south Arabs acquired its generality. As indicated above, this had little to do with real genealogy and was in fact simply a mythical conception.

The slogan "Qays or Kalb" served to split up the Arabs throughout the vast new realm of Islam. It is more than likely that this fratricidal hatred between the Arab tribes did as much to undermine the hegemony of the Arabs in Islam as the religious opposition to their preemption of state power. It was ultimately, in fact, to undermine that state power itself, since it proved impossible for the governors and ultimately even the caliphs to withstand the tug of this intertribal strife.

For the time being, however, this lay in the future. From an external point of view the Umayyad dynasty was on the threshold of its efflorescence.

Marwan himself had no difficulty in reasserting control over Egypt, but upon his death, his son Abd-al-Malik (692–705) found himself in growing difficulties. The flaring up of the contest with Byzantium, which had succeeded in inciting a mountain tribe on the Amanus against the Umayyad regime, made it impossible to control Iraq, where the Shi'ites had managed to work up an effective opposition that broke out in an actual revolt. An army sent by Abd-al-Malik was defeated by the Shi'ites, who in their turn succumbed to Abdalla ibn Zubayr's brother Mus'ab. The latter, however, was hampered in his struggle against both Abd-al-Malik and the Syrians by the presence of the Secessionists, who had now spread throughout the country under the primordial Arab slogan of resistance to every form of centralized control. Eventually this sealed Mus'ab's fate; in a battle on the Tigris River against Abd-al-Malik that was to prove decisive, he was defeated in 690. Abd-al-Malik had managed to demonstrate the superiority, both material and spiritual, of the Umayyad clan.

Abdalla ibn Zubayr himself, however, was still in Mecca. Abd-al-Malik dispatched his best general, Hajjaj, who put an end both to the countercaliphate and to Abdalla ibn Zubayr himself in 692.

Later, this same Hajjaj was to become, like Mu'awiya's Ziyad, the practically uncontrolled viceroy of the eastern half of the caliphate. Throughout his half of the realm he succeeded in effectively centralizing the state power, but by doing so he aroused the hatred of all those whose power he was infringing on and in consequence has come down in history with an image somewhat distorted. Looked at from a long-range point of view, Hajjaj's principal handiwork was the consolidation of the state in Iraq along the lines of Abd-al-Malik's efforts in Syria.

Under Abd-al-Malik the actual administration of the state, as well as its executive summit, became Arab; thus his reign set its stamp on the first, or Arab, phase of the Islamic state. This marked the consolidation, or perhaps sedentarization, of Arab rule and was a turning away from the purely external attitude characteristic of the original nomads, signalizing their integration with conventional, settled society.

The Arabs, either through insight or through a common-sense acceptance of the state of things as they were, had never made the slightest attempt to get rid of the administrative apparatus of the countries they had conquered so quickly. They would, to be sure, have been quite incapable of running an administration during the years immediately following their emergence from the desert. Illiterate and unused to any sedentary occupation at all, they would surely have found the chores of administration beyond them.

In any case they never attempted it. Their basic constitutional attitude was, after all, simply a desire to sit on top of an existing society, benefiting economically by all its activities. It was no more than the better part of wisdom to leave everything in the administration as it had always been, merely exercising as efficient a control of it as possible. The Arabs' main concern was simply the securing of the annual tribute, and they were perfectly satisfied as long as the local authorities, with their knowledge of local conditions, kept on transmitting it to them.

Hence there had been Arabs only on the topmost summits of the big administrative entities. All the intermediate and lower grades remained local down into the eighth century and afterward. It was not until the reigns of Abd-al-Malik and his successor, Walid, that an attempt was made to interfere with the inevitably complex system of local administration, varying from country to country and from province to province. The local administration was not, to be sure, arabized outright, but at least Arabic was introduced as one of the two official languages. A number of Greco-Arabic documents about this time have come down to us from Egypt. In other points as well, Abd-al-Malik seems to have made a systematic attempt to arabize matters. He is credited with having issued the first Arabic currency —at least he arabized the coins, retaining the old gold currency for the former Byzantine and the old silver currency for the former Persian territories.

But perhaps the most important insight that appeared under his rule was that the old fiscal standard introduced by Umar in the long run was untenable; it had to be abandoned formally, in practice and as a matter of principle.

The standard, referred to above, consisted very simply of exempting the Muslims from taxation while supplying the needs of the state by revenues derived from the taxation of the subject peoples. In the very beginning no thought had been given to the likelihood that the subject peoples would come over to Islam and that the very success of Islam in the warfare of the opening years of the Arab age would entail a shrinking in the number of taxpayers through a mass conversion to the new religion. From this purely fiscal point of view, in fact, it was to become obvious that Islam, which had come out of Arabia as the hallmark and emblem of Arabdom, was in fact going to undermine the hegemony of the Arabs and ultimately lead to their dissolution in a much larger community.

With the rapid development of the great Arab military encampments into great cities, it was far more lucrative for the indigenous peoples to look for a living in them rather than to remain farming the land, where as mere colonials their chief function was to apply themselves to furnishing the annual tribute demanded by their conquerors.

This initiated an unprecedented flight from the land, while at the same time the number of conversions to Islam began multiplying. Since the new convert immediately ceased being liable to the tax on non-Muslims, the consequences of this for the central treasury are easily imagined. Moreover, the actual form of the Umar administration was evidently misconceived. In a situation in which so many people were leaving the land, that is, altering the demographic composition of the country, it was just the details neglected by the Arab conquerors at first that were going to be vital, since an individual handling of all the territories subject to tribute became indispensable. This entailed a systematic immersion of the Arabs into the affairs of their subordinates and thus immediately into the complex web of administration.

It was this process that was initiated under Abd-al-Malik. His governor Hajjaj attempted to make up for the deleterious effects of the former taxation system by instituting measures to make the newly converted Muslims subject to tax tribute as well as the non-Muslims.

The growing number of conversions to Islam was complemented by the expanding settlement of the former Bedouin on the rich farming lands that when owned by non-Muslims would have been subject to tribute. Umar II, a later Umayyad (717–20), made an attempt to forestall this by prohibiting the sale of such lands, but it was not until later that a gradual process was begun of deviating from the entire principle in a way that Muslim tradition was later to veil as much as it could. The tribute had consisted mainly of a tax on land to begin with; what happened now was that an explicit land tax was levied from all landowners quite independently of religious status. The humiliating aspect of the tribute, which had functioned as a method of signalizing the hegemony of the Arabs, was transformed into an individual head tax, linked to already existing institutions, that only non-Muslims were liable to and that evaporated upon conversion.

This process, which may be called the de-arabizing of agriculture, was largely accomplished under the rule of a later Umayyad, Hisham (724–43). It was to consummated by the de-arabizing of politics that was to take place with the advent of the Abbasids. The whole development took a few generations to accomplish.

Abd-al-Malik and his two viceroys, his brother Abd-al-Aziz in Egypt and Hajjaj in Iraq, managed to overcome the various rebellions and mutinies, and his son and successor, Walid (705–15), could carry on with the expansion of the frontiers. It was under Walid that the Arab kingdom reached its greatest extent; the Arabs spearheaded the conquest of Spain and pressed forward eastward too as far as the interior of the Punjab and deep through central Asia as far as the borders of China.

Under Walid's successor, Sulayman (715–17), the Arabs made their final, abortive attempt to take Constantinople. The financial plight resulting from the unsuccessful campaign exacerbated the difficulties the Umayyads had already been having with their taxation and, by heightening the oppression of their subjects, increased the domestic friction. The whole of the Syrian fleet and army was completely destroyed outside Constantinople. Thus the Umayyad regime lost its principal lever, and Sulayman's successor, Umar II, was to devote most of his reign to coping with a problem that with our hindsight we can see to have been insoluble.

This problem involved the actual composition of Muslim society, in which the Arabs, whose early predominance in Islam had been symbolized by the rule of the Umayyad house, were rapidly shouldered aside by the upsurge of ethnic groups that though non-Arab were nevertheless Muslim.

For while, as has been pointed out, the tribal structure of primitive Arabia had been superimposed on Islamic society as a whole during the period of Arab dominion, that structure could always be manipulated to a certain extent by means of various sociofictive devices. It had always been possible to join a given tribe as a "Client" (*Mawla*), which was a special category devised for just this purpose. The tribe as a structure was so fundamental in Arab thought, at the beginning, that it lingered on for generations even after the ethnic composition of Muslim society had radically changed. The Clients of the old Arabian tribes eventually came to outnumber the "original" Arabs, so that the traditional articulation of society into tribes became a mere mythical or traditional hang-over.

Thus non-Arabs first went over to Islam by being assimilated into the structure of the theocracy laid down by the Arabs during the first phase of Islam. They were integrated with the Arab tribal system, and since they were far more cultivated and proficient in the sedentary arts, their conversion was naturally a great help to the Arabs against the resistance of those parts of the population that had not yet been islamized.

The state founded by Umar, which was responsible for the distinction between Arabs and Clients, was undone by it. As the Clients grew in numbers and hence in social weight, and as they infiltrated the Arab tribes, which in their turn were settling down in large numbers in the newly conquered areas, the universalist tendency of Islam, always implicit, to be sure, but not before so systematically expressed, came more and more to the fore. In its very nature it implied a democratizing of society between the Arabs and their subjects. In short, the leveling tendencies of Islam had become unavoidable, and the Arabs were ultimately reduced to the level of their fellow Muslims.

Contrariwise, the unflagging unruliness of the Arab tribes with respect to the central authority and against each other led inevitably to a dissolution of the political and racial premises that had been a precondition of Arab privilege.

Both tendencies resulted in the leveling of Arabs and non-Arabs in Islam. The whole idea of both categories was simply dissolved within the broader notion of being a Muslim, which to this day has been a far more potent source of personal and social identity throughout Islam than any other idea, and only lately, in the past generation or so, has it been yielding to the newer idea of nationality, which for most of Islam is still a novelty.

Thus the development of the Clients endangered the unity of the Arabs and of the Arab kingdom; Umar II's initial problem was how to reconcile the Clients with Umayyad rule.

The main administrative problem represented by the Clients was that the mass conversion to Islam of the hordes of non-Muslims now under Arab rule, plus the fairly rapid increase in the number of Arab-Muslim landowners, simply resulted in a growing number of people who were liable only to the lowest rate of Muslim taxation. The governor of Iraq, Hajjaj, had conceived the notion of driving the Clients back to their own lands and then demanding the full tax rate from all Muslim landowners. This device had produced nothing but resentment; in addition, it was manifestly unfeasible. Umar II tried to institute an arrangement to stop all transfers to Muslims of land subject to tribute after the date of 719 (*i.e.*, a century after the Hijra), while continuing to exempt Muslim landowners from the higher rate of taxation. After that date the idea was that Muslims would merely rent such land, and so would have to pay the higher tax on it. To pacify the Clients he allowed them to live in the great garrison cities and exempted them from both the poll tax (*jizya*) and the land tax (*kharaj*). On the other hand, they were still to receive lower wages as soldiers than the Arabs, except in Khorasan. The Arabs themselves were granted lower rates of taxation, while rates of pay were equalized at the Syrian level. Also, pensions were given the wives and children of the fighting men. This was all balanced by a severer attitude toward non-Muslim subjects, who were now to be kept out of the administration where they had hitherto been vital and who were more severely treated by Muslim law.

Umar II's reforms were only partially successful: essentially they increased the costs of administration while cutting down the revenues of the state, while his exclusion of the non-Muslims from the administrative apparatus made the running of the state much more cumbersome. A new system was introduced by his successors

Yazid II (720–24) and Hisham (724–43) that remained in effect well into the Abbasid period. It was based on a convenient fiction, to the effect that it was not the landowner that paid the tax, but the land itself. Hence the land itself had to pay the full land tax regardless of the identity of its owner. The "tithe land" established by the early caliphate was to go on, but could not be added to, while the non-Muslim went on paying the head tax. The administration of this new system was streamlined and made far more effective.

After Hisham's death in 743, the Umayyad regime rapidly succumbed to the various internal and external pressures that had long been menacing it. There was a heightening of tribal strife, and the opposition both of the Shi'a and of the Secessionists made itself more and more manifest. By 744 the central government was no longer recognized outside Syria; occasionally it was questioned even there.

Marwan II (744–50), the last of the Umayyad rulers, proved incapable, despite his great abilities, of coping with the assortment of problems he had inherited.

An extremist Shi'ite sect extensively supported by newly converted Clients had appeared in Khorasan, where Arab colonies from Basra and Kufa had settled around 670. These Arabs were a small minority among a large Persian population, which was both martially minded and irritated by its inferior socioeconomic status in the Muslim Arab state. Muhammad ibn Ali ibn al-Abbas, a descendant of one of Muhammad's uncles, had been nominated by Abu Hashim, the founder of the sect, upon the latter's death and assumed control of its propaganda activities. The party of the Hashimiyya, as it was called, began operating in earnest around 720. A revolt that was finally embarked on about eighteen years later was unsuccessful, and Ibn al-Abbas, in order to conciliate the moderates among the Shi'a movement, gave control of the Hashimite propaganda to a southern Arab by the name of Sulayman ibn Kathir, together with a council consisting of eight Arabs and four Clients. The movement then seemed to dwindle away, until Ibn al-Abbas' death, when his son Ibrahim sent Abu Muslim, a Persian Client from Iraq, to the Persian Clients as his confidential agent and propaganda chief.

Abu Muslim, after achieving considerable success among the Persians, including some of the Persian rural nobility, in 746 managed to launch an all-out *coup d'état* against the Umayyad regime. The black banners he raised his putsch under, which were to become celebrated as the banners of the house of Abbas, in reality corresponded to some of the requirements of the eschatological prophecies concerning the representatives of the Abbasid movement, which like all other political movements in Islam had a religious coloring. Though other rebels before the Abbasids had also used black banners, the success of this particular Abbasid rebellion was to associate the black banners with them; as far away as China and Byzantium they were to go down in history as the "black-robed ones."

As usual the Arab tribes in Khorasan were too disunited to withstand the new revolutionary movement. Once it had taken firm root in the east, it rapidly ranged westward under Abu Muslim, undoing the last armies of the Umayyads at the battle of the Great Zab. Marwan II himself was killed at a final battle in lower Egypt, in August 750.

The Umayyad house, and the Arab kingdom with it, had receded into history. Their place was taken by the new Abbasid caliph, Abu-l-Abbas, who was given the title of *Saffah,* the "Butcher."

With the advent of the Abbasid dynasty Islam was to become radically different. It was transformed into an international, cosmopolitan society whose refulgence even in the West was to become legendary—but the Arabs no longer ruled it.

They had been ousted by a singular combination of circumstances that made the replacement of the Umayyads by the Abbasids a revolutionary upheaval whose effects were rapidly transmitted throughout the vast realm of Islam. It was far more than a mere putsch, a commonplace of the age; it represented a long-drawn-out and systematic organization of revolutionary propaganda, welding together the irritations and discontents of many different elements of the now quite heterogeneous population. It was thus a coalition of various interests linked together by the general desire to overthrow the Arab regime, but necessarily breaking up again, of course, once the immediate goal was achieved.

This revolutionary movement took in a vast number of different elements. Though the nineteenth-century view that it represented a victory of "Persianism" over the "Semitism" of the original

Arabs is doubtless exaggerated, since the revolutionary anti-Umayyad movement also included a great many Arabs who did not happen to be members of the Arabian tribal aristocracy, there is no doubt that the originally patriarchal Umayyad kingdom, which had imposed its rule on so vast an empire, was quite liquidated. It had yielded to a cosmopolitan Oriental empire in which the question of Arabian aristocratic origins no longer played any formal role, though many individual Arabs could still, to be sure, make their way in the new society unhindered.

What had happened may best be put into sociological terms. During the wars of conquest, which had been conducted largely by the great tribes originally stemming from the Arabian desert, the Arabian aristocracy had been an indispensable class, but once the conquests had been consolidated and a new society began growing up and cementing itself within the newly acquired territories the Arabs as a class became superfluous. The way was opened for the unfettered proliferation of a new class of functionaries, merchants, bankers, and landowners, as well as the category of learned persons —scholars, religious authorities, and teachers—who corresponded socially, though not religiously, to the priesthood of Christendom. The town populations had been disfavored under the Umayyads, and the accumulated discontents of the Client traders and craftsmen who had infiltrated the great Arab encampment cities finally poured into the anti-Umayyad revolutionary movement.

The Arabs themselves facilitated this whole process by not grasping its nature, and especially by continuing to wage the internal strife based on tribal and factional allegiances that made cohesiveness as a community unattainable.

It may be said that the influx of the Persians into Islam made it more religious, since the Persians had more of a bent for the religious attitude toward life. When they flowed into the Shi'ite opposition, which may have had no more than a religious tinge to begin with, they made it genuinely religious, and it was perhaps the religiosity of the movement that gave it the strength to sweep away the secular rule of the Umayyad house once and for all.

In this way the national Arab kingdom of the Umayyads was replaced by the international society of the Abbasid empire. The Arab ruling stratum simply disappeared or individual members married out of the group. The upshot was that it was simply ousted by a mongrelized aristocratic bureaucracy that no longer had anything to do with either religious piety or nobility of descent, but quite simply represented a power delegated by the prince, who was to become more and more despotic.

In this way the secular kingdom of the Umayyad House, a patriarchal development of ancient Arab tribalism somewhat sketchily adapted to the new circumstances of rule over masses of foreigners, was transformed into the absolutist state of the Abbasids.

And with this the core of Persian civilization, now clad in the garments of Islam, was transported in bulk into the new community. What to many had seemed and still seems to have been an original entity had in fact been absorbed into the traditional patterns of the ancient East.

The victory of the Abbasids over the Umayyads was the culmination of a process that had begun being adumbrated toward the end of the Umayyad regime and that had its roots actually in the very essence of Islam. For even under the Umayyad regime, which in its beginnings was purely Arab and in its practical aspects, indeed, purely secular, the expansive force of the religious element in Islam had been held in check for only a short time. Despite the proprietary attitude of the Arabs toward Islam in the beginning, it had such unchallengeable prestige as a religion that it served as a cloak of authority for all rulers. Yet since at the same time it was universal in all its implications—revolutionary and ecumenical with respect to all other religions and sociopolitical structures—it could be appealed to by all oppositionist elements; it gave all opposition to any existing ruler an endless variety of sanctions and a great impetus.

Thus in the Abbasid victory there was no question of a threat to Islam as such; it was merely the triumph of what was basically a Persian movement over the Arab hegemony represented by the Umayyad House. What had taken place was a fundamental reshuffling of the various elements of the population as Islam had become rooted in the new society that had evolved after the initial military successes of the Arabs. The subject classes of the population, slowly working their way up through the evolving Islamic society to a footing of equality with the Arabs, came at last to constitute the new society themselves.

• • •

The most dramatic symbol of the meaning entailed by the dynastic change was the transfer of the capital, which took place under the second Abbasid caliph, Mansur (754–75), from Damascus to Baghdad, on the west bank of the Tigris, quite near the ruins of the old Sassanid capital of Ctesiphon, whose actual stones were used to build the new capital.

Baghdad—the name of the ancient Persian village on this site, generally used instead of the official title, "The City of Peace"—was chosen because of its remarkably favorable strategic location near a navigable canal connecting the Tigris and the Euphrates, in a key position at the junction of routes in all conceivable directions—and more especially to India. Mansur is supposed to have called it a "marketplace for the world," with ships coming up the Tigris from all over the Arabian Peninsula and going back down again on their way to Syria, Egypt, and North Africa.

The center of Baghdad was laid down as a circular town about two miles in diameter, a sort of fortress that constituted the caliph's residence, functionaries' quarters, and the guards of the regime, who at first were brought in from the east. This was to serve as the core of a vast business metropolis that evolved very rapidly and was to make Baghdad legendary.

The core of the Islamic Empire thus moved from the Mediterranean to Mesopotamia, a lush, irrigated valley intersecting countless trading routes. The new Islamic Empire had ceased being what could be regarded as a succession state of the Byzantine Empire and took its place as an Oriental empire of a traditional pattern in which the original Arab admixture was both diluted and overlaid by ancient Oriental institutions, especially those of Persia.

This change of dynasty also signalized a process, begun under the Umayyads, in which the Islamic state was transformed from the pattern of a tribal Shaykh whose rule was based on the consent, however reluctantly given, of a ruling caste that essentially remained independent of the Shaykh to an autocracy in which the person of the caliph became the source of all authority. An official hierarchy, dependent for all purposes on the central office of the caliph, replaced the headstrong Arab aristocracy that had regarded itself as completely self-sufficient.

Thus from the very beginning the tone of the new capital was quite different from what it had been when the Islamic state had been centered in Damascus. The Arabs could no longer look upon the caliph as simply another Arab prince or Shaykh, whom they could approach with free-and-easy manners as simply as though he were merely the First among Peers, which had been the general atmosphere of the Umayyad court. In Baghdad there was no longer a tribal Shaykh, but an Oriental despot, a successor in the flesh of the Great Kings of Persia.

Ceremonial procedures at the court of the Sassanids acquired great interest and were eagerly imitated by the parvenu universal state. Rank and status were no longer hereditary privileges, as they had been when the nobility was independent; status depended exclusively on the caliph's favor. This was paralleled in clothing, in which an honorary garment—the *khal'a* (whence our "gala")—which had been unknown under the Umayyads became customary. Under the Umayyads the caliph could be seen after a superficial screening procedure managed by one official; in Baghdad there was a dense web of functionaries, flunkeys, and chamberlains of all kinds that barred the public altogether from the caliph's person. This in its turn entailed a certain devolution of authority; actual administration was wielded very largely by the caliph's ministers, the *Wazirs,* whose office rapidly grew in importance. But the caliph's power over the life and death of his subjects was exercised very directly. His powers were externally signalized by the presence of the official executioner made so familiar to the West by *The Arabian Nights.* The executioner, a novelty among the Arabs, was always in immediate attendance on the caliph. The leather pouch destined for the heads of the culprits lay constantly near the throne.

The caliph's new elevation was naturally expressed in his titles. He was no longer a mere Deputy of the Prophet of God, like the first caliphs—he was now the Deputy of God himself; his authority was claimed as deriving from God directly. This was reflected, for instance, in the sonorous title "Shadow of God on Earth." In theory, to be sure, the supreme authority in the Islamic community remained the Holy Law, but since no institution had been established to enforce this theory what happened in practice was that the caliph could simply do as he pleased. The only curb on him was insurrection.

Hence the Abbasid regime was a general despotism in which the despotic summit was elevated above all subjects equally. It thus represented a heightening of the coercive element in the purely Arab kingdom where the Arabs had constituted an oligarchy perched on the shoulders of many different nationalities. As these nationalities became fused together within Islam they turned into a mass of subjects, and as the Arabs, except for those who continued leading their nomadic life in the desert, lost their collective identity in the mass of islamicized subjects of the despotic regime, the regime was boundlessly magnified into a classic Oriental despotism.

When the Arabs had ruled their own kingdoms as Arabs, they were naturally compelled to use diplomacy and persuasion, since they were after all no more than a small ruling minority with an ethnic solidarity that did not extend beyond their own tribes. But as the state summit became elevated endlessly above the mass of the population as a whole, it could, because of the concentration of the executive power in its hands, rule in a despotic way, consulting no one outside the immediate circle of the caliph. Sociologically, on the other hand, the Abbasid despotism was weaker than the Oriental despotisms preceding it, since it had grown up without an established feudal caste to support it and without an established priesthood, which Islam lacks.

The influence of old Persia became stronger and stronger, partly through the influx of countless Persian functionaries into the state structure and partly through the rapid assimilation of Persian tradition from books, and above all, perhaps, by virtue of the dynamics involved in the leveling tendencies of Islam plus the needed executive concentration for the administration of such a vast area. The racial discrimination and aristocratic exclusiveness characteristic of Arab rule vanished under the Abbasids; in a sense the leveling of Islam had eliminated them.

An immense scribal class was required to carry on the business of the state, and this class was recruited very largely from the Clients and organized in a whole series of bureaucratic divisions (Chancery, Finance, Army, Posts and Intelligence, etc.).

The office of Wazir, which headed the entire administrative apparatus and was subject only to the caliph, was probably itself a Persian hangover introduced by the Abbasids. Provincial authority was exercised by both the governor and the financial comptroller; each had his own staff and armed forces and a certain degree of autonomy. It was the Postmaster's duty to report directly on events to the Ministry of Posts and Intelligence in Baghdad.

The military arm of the regime was the Khorasanian guards, vital since the Arab militia was no longer of any importance, while pensions to the Arabs had come to an end except for such Arabs as were enrolled in a standing army, which now consisted entirely of paid troops who might be either regular troops or volunteers for one campaign. Though for a short time under the new regime there were some loyal Arabs organized as a unit, ultimately the armed forces of the caliphate came to depend on specially trained slaves (Mamluks), many of whom were Turks. Ultimately, indeed, the Turks were to infiltrate Islam *en masse* and become its executive power for centuries, in the strongest political formation ever engendered by Islam.

A concomitant of the ousting of the Arabs as a collectively authoritative group was the parallel elevation of the purely religious principle at the core of Islam. The very elimination of the Arabs as a ruling oligarchy led the new regime to turn to the doctors of the Islamic law for support. It was now that experts in the Holy Law and in the Tradition, who while the Umayyads had been running the empire had constituted a sort of built-in anti-Umayyad cabal, were now mollified by the fact that the new regime did not base its claims on aristocratic lineage and Arabdom, but simply on the body of Islam as a whole, whence its despotic position. It was the second Abbasid caliph, Mansur, who made an effort to attract the doctors of the law to his court. This was relatively simple since now, in accordance with the theocratic ideals that had always inspired the religious milieu in Medina, power over all Islam was being exercised by a member of the prophet's family—genealogically, after all, the Abbasids were largely of Arab descent personally, except through the mother, who in Islam is irrelevant in this connection.

It was the religious notion underlying Islam, as well as the religious organization that had grown up within it in lieu of a priesthood, that filled the vacuum in the state summit left by the departure of the Arab aristocrats, or rather by the dissolution of Arab racial solidarity within the melting pot of Islam.

Perhaps the most profound, far-reaching, and comprehensive effects of the leveling of nationalities within the Islamic Empire and of the elimination of the Arabs as the dominant nationality was the creation of a new cosmopolitan society under the cloak of the Arabic language and on the foundations of the religion initiated by Muhammad. As an object lesson in the manner in which social movements interact with traditional authority, the movement known in history as the *Shu'ubiyya*—a movement for the equality of nations—is very striking.

Though the Arabs as a collectivity had vanished from the helm of the state, the Abbasid dynasty itself was Arab, closer indeed to the prophet than the Umayyads—and above all the language of the empire for both state affairs and culture, as well as religion, was Arabic. The religion, especially, could be claimed to have had Arab beginnings. Hence the theoretical superiority of the Arabs could, as a cultural matter, still be maintained, while the rulers took pride in their Arabdom.

This combination—an actual decline in the power and authority within the state of the old Arab tribal aristocracy coupled with the claims of individual Arabs to superior prestige because of the services of the Arabs in introducing a new language and a new religion to the areas now united under the Islamic Empire—led to the emergence of the countermovement aimed at the establishment of the equal status of all Muslims independently of racial origins. The actual name of the movement is taken from a celebrated passage in the Quran (49:13) mentioned above (p. 39), in which the word "nations" (or "races") is used to refer to the creation of all mankind by God as equals.

The "Nations" party, accordingly, was based on a desire to realize the equality of the nations as preached by Muhammad and amplified by the Tradition based on it; *i.e.,* it was aimed specifically at the Arab propaganda claiming superiority for the Arab people.

This movement was in no sense a social upheaval since the masses of the people were quite uninvolved. The Nations movement was made up exclusively of scholars and writers and sought its effects within the realm of literature, in works designed to captivate the rather restricted reading public. The movement blossomed during the second and third centuries after the Hijra (the eighth and ninth centuries A.D.), and in its most moderate version simply preached the equality of the Arabs and all other nations, within, of course, the bosom of Islam. In its bolder formulations it went so far as to say that it was actually the Arabs who were inferior, the Persians much superior.

The Persians, in fact, had come to such positions of influence and authority under the Abbasids and wielded so much power within the Islamic Empire that they were emboldened to speak up openly against the arrogance that had long been associated with the Arab aristocrats. It is doubtless likely, moreover, that though the caliphs were proud of their Arab descent they allowed free expression to all these egalitarian, anti-Arab views. The ninth-century Arabic essayist Jahiz—a Negro—put the contrast in a lapidary form: He simply called the Umayyad regime an Arab kingdom in contrast with the "Khorasanian" (Persian) regime of the Abbasids.

Of the numerous Wazirs during the efflorescence of the Abbasid regime scarcely a single one of Arab origin is to be found; the great majority are Persians and Clients. Nor was this situation ever regarded as the least bit strange. In court circles the atmosphere with respect to the Arab claims of glory was quite unmistakable. On hearing a poet compare the caliph with some glorious Arab heroes, a Wazir upbraided him indignantly for his arrogance in "comparing the Commander of the Faithful with these Arab barbarians!" By the time of the Abbasids the point of view of Arab society proper, according to which even an obscure woman in the lineage of a leader was regarded as shameful, had been completely superseded by the leveling tendencies within Islam and by the elevation of all non-Arab Muslim elements in society to a footing of equality with or even superiority to the Arabs.

One of the Abbasid caliphs, Mamun, made no secret of his having a much higher regard for the Persians than for the Arabs, whom he regarded as voracious and quarrelsome.

An instance of the way Persians might make fun not only of Arabs but of Islam itself can be seen in the career of one of the most distinguished of the Abbasid field marshals, Haydar ibn Kawus, who jeered at Islam, read the religious books of his own people, dreamed of the restoration of the Persian Empire, and while carrying on his campaigns against the enemies of Islam mocked at Arabs, Moroccans, and Muslim Turks.

Although Persians were the principal exponents of the egalitarian ideals of the Nations movement, since they were by far the most massive national bloc in the Islamic world as well as the most cultivated, many non-Persian Muslims also took advantage of the decline of the Arabs to campaign for ethnic equality and for the preeminence of the non-Arabs. Syrians, Nabateans, Copts, and others all took part in a general movement among cultivated circles to denigrate the Arab barbarians in the light of the glorious history of their own civilizations. In this general movement, which was directed at the Arabs, it was not uncommon for writers to vaunt not only their own non-Arab nationality but also some other non-Arab group simply in order to attack the pretensions of the Arab minority. Copts could point to the splendors of ancient Egypt, and Arameans to the splendors of Nabatea and for that matter to the colossal achievements of the Arabs' predecessors in Mesopotamia, the Assyrians and Babylonians. While the pretense or indeed the reality of Quranic piety was kept up, a very good case could be made out demonstrating the preposterousness of any special Arab prestige.

The frankness of expression of these Nations-movement writings is remarkable. Under the Umayyads it appears to have been a little dangerous for anyone to vaunt the glories of his own non-Arab people and to sneer at the barbarism of the ancient Arabs, but by the time of the Abbasids it was perfectly possible for an egalitarian to make a point not merely of the abstract principles of equality sponsored by the Quran, but also of his own non-Arab ethnic origins.

The polemics against the Arabs could, of course, find an immense variety of instances proving that the Arabs were parvenus and barbarians in comparison with what had gone before.

The Chosroes and the Caesars, Solomon and Alexander the Great, the great Indian emperors, all the great prophets since the beginning of the world except for the handful allocated to the Arabs and headed by Muhammad were, after all, non-Arab to a man—to say nothing of the very ancestors of all mankind, Adam and Noah. Nor did the Nations-movement partisans forget to enumerate the various sciences and branches of scholarship in which Arabs had played no role; philosophy, astronomy, and even lacework embroidery had been cultivated by non-Arabs while the Arabs were sunk in the deepest ignorance. As for the poetry that the Arabs were so proud of, even there they had been outclassed by foreigners such as the Greeks. The Arabs had not even invented chess! What could the Arabs point to as proof of their superiority, after all? As a poet put it, "Compared with all this culture the Arabs were no more than howling wolves and roving wild beasts, mutually devouring each other and in constant mutual warfare."

On the positive shortcomings of the Arabs, much was made of

their various repellent customs from before the adoption of Islam, some of which had been incorporated in Islam. Some of what might seem to us to be the superficial mannerisms of the Arabs were also openly mocked: the use, for instance, of the staff and the bow in public speaking, apparently for the theatrical effect. The exponents of the egalitarian point of view maintained that since a staff was for keeping time and the bow for shooting arrows and there was no connection between speaking and either one, it was a serious weakness on the part of the Arab orators to use them. It looked to them as though a camel were being brought to a halt while on the march. For that matter, said the anti-Arab egalitarians, the Arabs' braggadocio with respect to their well-known talent for oratory was completely misplaced. The fact was that a talent for talking is commonplace among all peoples and that barbarous peoples in particular often excel in it, even if the content of their speech is often coarse and shallow. But it was well known that the most perfect of all mankind were the Persians, especially those who lived in Fars, and of those the finest talkers were those from Merv. In short, if one took into account the remarkable achievements of the Persians, Greeks, and Indians, it was evident that the Arabs amounted to zero!

The shaft about the Arabs not even being good orators seems to have been the most painful, since this was one of the most systematic vanities of the Arabs, largely because of the vaunted beauties of the Arabic language, which Arabic speakers have always regarded as unattainable in any other language. A defense of them was made by the same ninth-century essayist, Jahiz, who praised the native Arab gift for spontaneous discourse and poetizing as a complete contrast to the intricate sophistications of the Greeks, Indians, and Persians. The Arabs, he said, needed no preparation and no cerebration; once engaged by the object of their inspiration, sounds and thoughts would simply gush forth like a fountain, without the slightest effort or the slightest study, without the use of the conscious mind or any help from anyone. The Arabs, after all, he pointed out, could not read or write, nor was that necessary; every one had the gift so deeply implanted within him that there was no reason to hoard it up by writing it down, nor any point in remembering what others had said before.

One of the oddities in this whole complex polemic was, of

course, that it was carried on in Arabic. The subject races had learned enough Arabic only a generation or two after the Arab conquests to carry on their whole spiritual life in an Arabic that was as good as or better than the so-called pure Arabic of the tribes. Indeed, it was Persians and other Clients who in fact made distinguished contributions to Arabic prose and poetry and even claimed to have surpassed their original teachers.

Thus, at a time when the actual Arabs had been shouldered out of state authority by the rise of the subject races within the democratic structure of Islam, Arabic itself was cultivated as never before. I shall discuss the importance of the language in the next chapter; here I must digress for a moment to make a preliminary outline of the definition this book is partly designed to provide—what is an "Arab"?

The above-mentioned developments involved the ousting of the Arabs from their monopoly of the state, the elevation of non-Arab Muslims to equality in Islam, and a proliferation of false Arab genealogies to cover these shifts during the generations following the conquests. This complicated rescrambling took place against a general background of biological miscegenation, stimulated by polygamy, in the Muslim melting pot and meant a *de facto* mongrelization of the population of the Islamic Empire—and hence a total transformation in the content of the word "Arab."

With the ending of the social superiority of the Arabs as a caste superimposed on society, with the universal miscegenation, and with the spread of the Arabic language as a vernacular—with the arabization, in short, of the whole society—the word "Arab" in one sense lost its significance. It became coextensive with the word "Muslim" or "Saracen," at least in the minds of foreigners, while within Islamic society itself the word reverted to its initial significance—*i.e.,* a member of one of the nomadic tribes stemming from Arabia, though many of these tribes, to be sure, were by now leading nomadic lives outside the Arabian Peninsula. When the "Arabs" ceased being an exclusive hereditary caste of conquerors and became a sedentary Muslim people, the leveling tendencies in Islam became ineluctable. Any Muslim who spoke Arabic as his native language became, in a way, an "Arab."

But in the society of that time this was a meaningless differentiation, and it would be misleading to look at this method of ethnic classification from our own point of view.

Our own criteria have been formed by the perspective of the modern nation-state based, very largely, on language, and by the growth of nationalism following the formation of the French nation and the spread of nationalist ideas in the wake of the French Revolution. But for the inhabitants of the Islamic Empire, and indeed for the whole of medieval Christendom before the growth of nationalism, the basic criteria for distinguishing people were religious. A person would be classified according to religion; the community would be understood as based on one religion or another; a man's civic position was a reflection of his religious affiliation.

Thus a Muslim would—until our own generation—have thought of himself as *essentially* a Muslim, in the world at large and in contradistinction to believers in other religions. Then, within the Muslim community he would think of himself as coming from a certain locality, say Basra. Further, if you asked him what language he spoke, he would say, "Arabic, of course," and he would be aware of coming in addition, perhaps, from some larger locality, such as the Hijaz, or the Delta, etc., but this larger locality would be a vague geographical definition with no emotional or other meaning. If you were to ask him, in his own Arabic language, whether he was an "Arab," it would be an altogether meaningless question, since in Arabic the word would simply have referred to a Bedouin, a member of one of the nomadic tribes, who were all lumped together as the only "Arabs."

There was also a phrase current among the Arabic-speaking Muslim population of the Middle East that meant something like "Sons of the Arabs" to refer to the speakers of Arabic who were Muslims. This was merely a broad synonym for Arabic-speaking Muslim and meant nothing beyond that. The word "Arab" as understood in our own day would have been literally devoid of meaning. "Sons of the Arabs" is merely an Arabic idiom reflecting a historic fact, the spread of the Bedouin tribes, and is in any case quite outmoded.

Down to our very own day, indeed, the great masses of the Muslim world are unaware of such a national reference in everyday life. Today, too, if you were to ask an Egyptian peasant whether he is an "Arab," he could, in Arabic, understand the question only in the sense of whether he was a Bedouin and would, accordingly, say no. It is only very recently that the modern contemporary meaning of, say, the Arab national movement has been made meaningful to broadening circles of contemporary Muslims, and then only as part of the spread of just that national movement that requires the word for its self-definition. Even today the process is far from having made any substantial inroads on the prenational consciousness of the Arabic-speaking Muslim masses.

Thus, under the Abbasid empire, the word "Arab" lost its previous significance as the Arabs were diluted by blood and by the spread of their language to include the Arabic-speaking Muslim masses of the empire, and the word itself was once again restricted in its use to a member of the Bedouin tribes, as it had always been, indeed, when understood in the context of the great conquests and the spread of Islam.

The social emancipation of the Clients was bound by definition, after all, to take the form of integration with the Arab tribes. Even the caliph's Khorasanian guards became arabized in the linguistic sense as they became islamized in the religious sense. West of Persia the process of arabization was still easier, since Arabic became an actual vernacular there, as it is to this day. As the Bedouin scattered throughout the Middle East, with so many of them settling down to sedentary pursuits, and as the language spread from what had originally been the Arab centers of conquest to the countryside and hinterland beyond the great towns, the population became rapidly homogenized linguistically. In Iraq, Syria, Egypt, and North Africa, Arabic became the common parlance of Christians and Jews as well as Muslims. In North Africa the process was held up for a long time by the presence of the Berbers, who had retained their own dialects very substantially, at least in Morocco, though even here the immense importance of cities in the modern era has given a great impetus to the spread of Arabic.

In this sense, it is clearly most misleading to use the word "Arab" in connection with the Islamic Empire after the disappearance of the Umayyad regime. Even though the Abbasid dynasty might have prided itself on its pure Arab descent, and even though the Arabs of the peninsula and the Arab aristocrats of the Bedouin tribes might have retained a certain personal arrogance or snobbishness as belonging to the people that had produced the prophet, the

Quran, and Islam itself, the very success of the Arabic language had, within its prenational religious context, meant the shunting aside of the "real Arabs" as a minority within the cosmopolitan society of the Islamic Empire.

Curiously enough, with the homogenizing of Islamic society by the dual process of arabization and islamization, the expansion of the language to the point of generality made it of no use in distinguishing one group from another. It became impossible to single out the "Arabs" on the basis of their speech and far easier to single out, in the flux of the Islamic Empire, precisely the non-Arab nationalities, like the Persians, Turks, Jews, Greeks, and so on.

In short, the national content of the word "Arab" as we are accustomed to accepting it today was not formed until the nineteenth century, and then only under the direct influence of ideas emanating from Europe affecting initially only the Arabic-speaking Christians of Syria and Lebanon and only gradually penetrating the consciousness of the Muslim elite. I shall revert to this phenomenon, of cardinal consequence for the world of today, in Chapter VII.

• • •

Economically the Islamic Empire under the Abbasids flowered far more luxuriantly than the comparatively provincial regime of the Umayyads. Its apogee was doubtless reached under Harun ar-Rashid and his son Mamun. The empire bustled with industry and trade; Baghdad was the center of an immense and ramified network of commerce pouring up and down the Tigris and down the Euphrates from Syria. Great trains of pack animals carried goods from Baghdad up to Persia and back.

The rise of the Islamic Empire entailed the blocking off of Europe from the rest of the known world. This meant, of course, that the empire itself had relative freedom of the seas. By the middle of the ninth century, Saracen ships were making regular trips to Canton and were in constant business relations with Malacca, Java, and Sumatra, as well as India and Ceylon. A big colony of Saracen merchants had settled near Bombay, and the east coast of Africa, down to Madagascar, had long been known to Saracen shippers. Silks from China, spices from India, as well as tropical woods, coconuts, and tin all came through to the big trading establishments in Baghdad. Merchants from Tunisia and the Maghrib got plentiful supplies of gold from the "Gold Coast," present-day Ghana.

The Abbasid regime saw a remarkable abundance of gold, at a time when it was almost unobtainable in Western Europe. The Muslims used it not only for coins but for ornament and for eating and drinking utensils.

The conflict between Islam and Christendom had led to a practical cessation of trade between the Islamic Empire and Europe; the Mediterranean was now plied only by war fleets or by pirates. An exception to this seems to have been a very brisk trade between the Islamic Empire and Byzantium via the Black Sea, handled in the main by a Mongol people called the Khazars.

The wealth of the empire was reflected in huge crops of wheat, barley, and rice produced in the great irrigated river valleys, with dates and olives also grown in abundance. There were great metal resources, with silver from the east, especially the Hindu Kush; gold from the west, especially Nubia and the Sudan; copper from around Ispahan; and iron from as far afield as central Asia and Sicily. Pearls abounded in the Persian Gulf; jewels were found abundantly throughout the empire. From the east there came a good deal of timber, too; considerable quantities were regularly imported from India and still farther east.

Irrigation was greatly extended, and great areas of swampland were drained, increasing the general agricultural yield and enabling the taxation of the peasantry to be lightened somewhat.

The combination of the resources of the empire and its strategic location across great commerical crossroads and highways, especially between Europe and the Far East, laid the foundations of an immense commercial society, fortified by the central government's ability, for quite a long time, to maintain law and order and to exploit the peaceful relations that followed the unflagging bellicosity of the Umayyads. Trade was practically boundless. Saracen merchants would range far and wide throughout the known world, from Aden and the Red Sea ports to India, the East Indies, and China, bringing home an immense variety of goods such as silks, spices, woods, and metals, both for local use and for reexport. Some alternative routes to the Far East ran through central Asia; goods from China such as silks, paper, peacocks, horses, gold coins, slave girls, hydraulic engineers, marble workers, and eunuchs would be exchanged for tigers, elephants, ebony, and coconuts from India. The Arabs had established trading posts in China by the 700s, and under the Islamic Empire Saracen ships plied the Eastern seas with great familiarity.

There was an intimate connection between the Vikings and the Islamic Abbasid regime. Countless thousands of Saracen coins have been found in Scandinavia generally, especially Sweden, from between the late seventh to the early eleventh centuries, indicating the vigor of the trade relations between points beginning at the center of the Abbasid empire and going from the Black Sea and the Caspian along the Volga routes as far as the Baltic Sea. Endless numbers of commodities—chiefly skins, furs, amber, and, above all, slaves (the word itself is derived, in fact, from "Slav")—were transported along this great trading route. Though the Saracens may not have gotten as far as Scandinavia themselves, they made use of intermediaries, like the Bulgars and the Khazars (whose leaders were at one time converted to Judaism) to make contact with the peoples of northern Russia. The earliest known Swedish coinage, oddly enough, is based on the weight of the Abbasid monetary unit. In Old Icelandic there are even some Arabic words.

There was a lively overland trade with Africa, too, consisting mostly of gold and—again—people. When the Arab conquests interrupted business relations with Western Europe, the Jews, at home in both worlds, helped bridge the gap. A ninth-century geographer described the remarkable liveliness shown by parties of Jewish traders from southern France, speaking many languages, from Arabic and Spanish to Russian, and plying the routes from east to west and back. These merchants would bring all sorts of slaves from the west, as well as furs and swords, embark in the Mediterranean, change at the eastern end, go by land to the port of Qulzum (Suez), where they would reembark for China. They would then load themselves up with the characteristic goods of China and make their way back, to sell their wares in Constantinople, back in France, or in many other ports.

But trade was not the only aspect of the Saracen economy. There was a great deal of industry, in which textiles of all kinds were doubtless the most thriving branch. The Abbasid state was probably the greatest producer of silk fabrics, despite Muhammad's prohibition of silk as a luxury. Fustian comes from Fustat, near the site of present-day Cairo; muslin comes from Mosul, damask from Damascus. "Taffeta" is derived from a Persian word; the French *"jupe"*—"skirt"—comes from the Arabic *"jubba."* Throughout the Islamic Empire rugs and carpets were in common use, though it was to be centuries before they were to be found on the floors of European houses.

Industry in the Islamic Empire appears to have been largely state-controlled, though trade was always carried on by private persons. Industry was generally subsidized by the central government, though in commerce great fortunes were often built by the immense far-flung trade with the Far East, Russia, and Africa. Before the Turco-Mongol invasions in the thirteenth century destroyed, at least for a time, the trade and industry of the Middle East, the numerous craftsmen were widely organized in guilds.

The paper that tradition records the Chinese as having been making since the first century B.C. finally came to the West via Islam when an Arab force defeated some Chinese in 751 A.D. and captured some papermakers. Under Harun ar-Rashid paper finally came to Iraq; its use rapidly spread throughout Islam, though it took more than a hundred years for it to reach Spain. The manufacture of it also spread, though more slowly; by the tenth century paper was definitely being made in Iraq and even Arabia, and somewhat later in North Africa and Spain.

The state was rather lax about helping trade, in distinction to industry, and merchants often had to contend not only with the general absence of good roads, etc., but with the encroachments of the ubiquitous bureaucracy. Yet in spite of the great obstacles to be overcome, the vitality of trade throughout this enormous area was such that during the ninth century there was a rapid evolution of banking, rooted perhaps in the dual currency system that had been derived by the Abbasids from the Persian Empire on the one hand and Byzantium on the other.

The Persians had used silver and the Byzantines gold. Since the caliphate maintained both coinages based on a standard weight and since there was an uncontrollable fluctuation between the standard values of the coins and the price of the metals they were made of, the money-changing profession ultimately developed into a sort of banking system; the money changer was a standard feature of every Saracen town.

By the ninth century money changers, doubtless acting as agents for rich merchants looking for investment outlets, had evolved into bankers. There were banks with branches all over the empire, making use of checks (from the Arabic *sek*), letters of credit, and so on, so that credit arrangements could in fact be made throughout this vast realm, and a check drawn in Baghdad could be cashed in Morocco. Basra is reported to have had personal bank accounts for every merchant; bazaar transactions were via checks, never cash. By the tenth century the government, too, had a system of banks in the capital, utilized by the regime as sources of the substantial sums of liquid money needed for administration and advanced against mortgages on uncollected tax revenues. Since the Muslims banned usury and since interest was considered usurious, the bankers were generally Christians and Jews.

The lively commerce characteristic of the Islamic Empire was naturally reflected in social attitudes—the type of the "honest merchant" was held up as a social ideal. In accordance with the process mentioned above—the retrojection of contemporary situations into the life of Muhammad—traditions grew up attributing to the prophet all sorts of laudatory remarks about the merchant class. Caliph Umar is attributed a most curious remark: "There is no place where I would be more gladly overtaken by death than in the marketplace, buying and selling for my family." Contemporary literature makes much of the honest merchant; for good measure it is full of advice about the wisdom of investing money in trade.

The emphasis on business and trade is itself a reflection of the degree to which society had changed. The Arab warrior was no longer a meaningful social type. Indeed, the real Arab warriors had by and large vanished from the public eye. The Arabs themselves, that is, the Arabs proper, were now to be found largely in the deserts, outside the towns in any case. Where Arabs were in evidence it was simply as individuals; they no longer had a collective role to play. The Bedouin tribes had lost all their privileges with respect to the state, and their treasury grants, too. Arabic chronicles, beginning around this time under the Abbasids, no longer pay much attention to the great feuds of the Bedouin, which has nothing to do with the actual existence of such feuds—many of which, among the great Arabian tribes, have come down to our own day—but simply implies that there was no longer a place in contemporary society for the Bedouin as real people. They had vanished from the government sphere that in an earlier generation, under preceding regimes, they had helped create and grown great in; now their feuds were their own and no longer concerned society as a whole.

It was around this time, when the Arab aristocracy had been ousted from the public authority, that the Bedouin began abandoning the great encampment cities that had been theirs during the early expansion and either lapsed back into the nomadism they had never entirely abandoned or began adopting sedentary farming lives. Once on the land they also lost their character as nomads and simply fused more or less with the peasant population of the country they were in, with, perhaps, a slight source of family pride in the recollection of their origins. The Saracen town was no longer a garrison city left in the wake of an army of occupation in a subject country, but had become a marketplace and an exchange point; that is, it was now performing the classic functions of city life, and merchants and craftsmen began forming guilds to defend their mutual interests.

The Arab aristocracy had been replaced by a new ruling class, consisting of the wealthy and educated. Immense fortunes had been built up, both in money and in real property, very often through the holding of government jobs, which gave great opportunities via trade and banking operations, and through business speculation and the exploitation of the land.

The non-Muslim subjects of the Islamic Empire were treated with a degree of tolerance that in comparison with the official church in Western Europe at the same time must be considered remarkable. It is true that they paid taxes at a higher rate than Muslims and also suffered from some social disabilities; occasionally they would be subjected to outright persecution. On the other hand, they could exercise their religion with perfect freedom, could own property and engage in business in a normal way, and could and did make careers in state service that brought them to the top of the social hierarchy. They could become members of the various artisans' guilds, and they even controlled some of them. They were never martyred or exiled because of their religious beliefs. The Muslim government indeed was celebrated for its tolerance; in comparison with its record, that of Christian Europe is of almost unrelieved black.

During the Middle Ages the idea of Muslim "racism" would have been an absurdity, in view of the immense mongrelization brought about by the conquests and by the spread of Islam and Arabic. It is true that the ancient Arabs had been aristocratically haughty, proud of the purity of their blood—understood, of course, as coming from the paternal line. Yet the vast number of unions with slaves, in a polygamous society, had provoked such a fantastic mingling of all sorts of stocks during the Abbasid period that from then on it was quite impossible even for the caliph to make a point of racial purity. Though individual groups persisted and there were individual instances of discrimination, by and large there was no such thing as racial segregation, even for those of a different color such as the Negroes, many of whom were in control of the state at various times.

The upward-thrusting pressure of the nationalities that during the period of Arab ascendancy had been underprivileged in Islam kept growing from one caliph to the next. Ultimately it was to upset all Islam and leave it wide open to various forces of disintegration. Incidentally, as indicated, it meant the eclipse of the Arab element.

Of these nationalities the most important was the Turks, who had made their appearance in the Islamic realm during the ninth century, under the Caliph Mutawakkil (847–61), and whose influence on the Baghdad regime grew steadily. The Turks in one branch or another were soon to be in control of the whole of the Islamic realm, and in a branch that was ultimately to become by far the most important—the Osmanlis, or Ottomans—they managed to establish the most powerful Muslim, and indeed world, empire in history.

From the time of Caliph Mutawakkil the most important offices at court in the national administration and in the army were all in their hands, in spite of their poor knowledge even of Arabic. Turkish generals were sent out against the headstrong tribes in the Arabian Peninsula. The chronicles of the period are full of the atrocities perpetrated against the Arabs and against all Alid pretenders. The palace intrigues of the Turks dominated court policy. By the time of Caliph al-Musta'in (862–866), two Turkish court functionaries were given a free hand with the state treasury. Ultimately it was the Turks and other adventurers who were to make the office of the caliph, at one time overwhelmingly powerful, a mere emblem of power that was exercised by the caliph's adjutants, who were theoretically under his orders but practically were the rulers.

The degradation of the Arabs was completed by the degradation of the caliphate itself, an institution rooted in the early history of the Arabs as the bearers of Islam. By the time of the fourth century after the Hijra the descendants of the Abbasid caliphs were living on as obsequious poets, roaming from one parvenu court to another.

But this lay in the future; at the height of the Abbasid caliphate a new civilization unfolded. Before looking at it, a word as to the physical extent of Islam and its relationship to Europe may be illuminating.

Around the middle of the tenth century the inhabited world was dominated by Islam, which even though its political unity had already been shattered nevertheless constituted a cultural and mercantile entity that had Mecca as a religious center and Baghdad as a cultural and political hub.

On the west this empire took in Egypt plus the entire northern coast of Africa, including the Atlantic coast as far as the Anti-Atlas and nearly all Spain except for Asturia and the islands of Sicily and Crete. Sardinia and Cyprus were under more or less constant Muslim attack, as was the southern Italian coast. Some towns, like Bari, were under Muslim rule, and others, like Amalfi, were part of its sphere of influence.

North of Arabia, Syria, together with Armenia and the southeast of the Caucasus, were integral parts of Islamic society, as, in the east, were Mesopotamia and Iraq and the whole of present-day Persia, together with Afghanistan. Going north, Transoxania was in Islam, including the delta area of Khwarizm, in the west, and the valley and mountains of Farghana in the east. The Indus had been crossed as early as the eighth century; the territories along its lower course were part of the Islamic Empire, together with Sind.

Looking at this relatively concentrated political and cultural bloc, which from the vantage point of Europe constituted a strong central power, we can see how dependent Christendom of that age was on the Islamic realm. In the south the Mediterranean was an insuperable obstacle; in the east the Byzantine Empire was confronted by Islam in Armenia and Syria; the northern Caucasus and eastern Europe were inhabited by barbarous peoples who were to come under Muslim far more than under Christian influence. It was, in fact, only the northwest of Europe that was untouched by Islam, except for the purposes of its own trade. There the still-pagan Scandinavians were about to launch an expansion that in the twelfth century was to play a substantial role in undermining Muslim hegemony in the world.

The far-flung areas of the Muslim world led to an immense expansion of geographical information that was passed on to Europe, especially since the fundamental Muslim religious obligation of the Meccan pilgrimage gave rise to an interest in all the new lands that had come under Islam. This led to a fairly comprehensive interest in geography, travel, and exotic customs that was ultimately to benefit Europe during the Middle Ages and also to prove an invaluable adjunct in exploration in general and in the spread of world trade.

At this time, in short, the cultural horizons of Europe were more or less confined in all relevant directions by Islam. It was partially the desire to burst through this containment that led Western Europe to seek new trade routes to the Far East, and thus the discovery of America was in a way a consequence of the Muslim impact on Christendom.

IV

THE FLOWERING OF A CIVILIZATION: THE ISLAMIC WORLD EMPIRE

IT was the impulse of the Arab folk migration, channeled through Islam, that laid the foundations for the Islamic Empire that evolved with such remarkable rapidity out of the secular Arab kingdom of the Umayyads, but the final structure of the world empire was very different from what had been in the minds of Muhammad, his entourage, and his first followers.

As I have indicated before, Muhammad's basic idea had been the substitution of a religious community for the concept of tribal or national solidarity. This was of course clearly implied by the very nature of Islam, but when Islam was carried abroad by the Arabian tribes i. was, despite its implications, still regarded as an Arab appendage. Universalism *belonged,* so to speak, to the Arabs.

Thus the Umayyad house, while not utterly impious—or rather, pious in the somewhat cavalier manner of the desert—could still regard itself as the exponent of a universal religion, interpreted, to be sure, as meaning the secular dominion of the Arab nation.

With the advent of the Abbasid regime, however, and the rapid transformation of the Arab secular caliphate into the executive organ of a cosmopolitan and essentially non- or even anti-Arab state, the universalism implicit in Islam revealed itself for the first time in a systematic body of thought and institutions, and the unitary civilization that has come down to us lustrous with the prestige of accumulated tradition can be seen as an entity in which only the medium of expression—Arabic—and the rudiments of the religion—Islam—can be ascribed to the actual Arabs whose name it sometimes bears.

But if the structure of the Islamic Empire owed so little to the Arabs proper, how can its genesis be explained? What was responsible for the unitary civilization that arose on the basis of the Arabic language and the new world religion?

For this a radical shift in perspective is needed. I shall try to sketch a sociocultural profile of the Islamic Empire as it was formed and as it has formed our own view of the world. The role in all this of the Arabs proper was, as I have indicated, subsidiary, though seminal; yet the Arabic-speaking peoples of the present day were also formed by Islam. To see them, too, in perspective a look at this whole development is needed.

• • •

The folk migration and spread of the Arabs in the seventh century shaped the beginning of the Middle Ages. If it was folk migrations that laid the foundations of the development of the West into potential state formations, the expansion of the Arabs created the traditional and indeed still valid division of the world into East and West. It was as a direct result of the promotion of the new Arab religion that the split between Christian Europe and the Islamic Middle East, Africa, and for that matter India and Indonesia, was given a shape that remains to this day. The later Spanish adherence to Islam and the resistance for some time to come of eastern Europe and Asia to the advance of Islam can be seen now to have had a merely episodic significance. The contrast as such was established in its broad outlines within a couple of generations after Muhammad's death.

The reason we understand this phenomenon in purely theological, or for that matter ecclesiastical terms, is because the Middle Ages, deeply imbued with piety in all forms, regarded the incursion of the Arab Muslims as an outrage against the church. This view is still very widespread, even among scholars. It may be summed up as the theory of the "Quran plus the sword"—the notion that the Arabs became so inflamed by their enthusiasm for Muhammad that they flew off the handle and stormed the bastions of the known world in a mad desire to convert everyone to the One True Faith.

The thread of classical evolution is conceived of as having been snapped; an alien civilization created by the Arabs in the grip of a new fanaticism is thought to have obliterated the evolution of ancient Christian society and to have replaced it with completely novel ideas. It was not until the Crusades, it is thought, that any reciprocal interaction took place.

The oddity is, as I have indicated, that when scholars began devoting themselves to the Arabic sources they found the identical attitude in reverse. For here too, in the minds of the Muslims, everything was thought of as having started only with Muhammad and the eruption of the Arabs. Muhammad was naturally thought of as having laid the foundations of both Islam and of Islamic civilization, a work that the first four caliphs—the "orthodox" caliphs—carried forward and consolidated.

Modern scholarship, however, has clarified this oversimplified and above all tendentious picture. Islam can be seen now not as a startlingly novel phenomenon, but as a link in an altogether different chain of events.

It is, in fact, the last link in a lengthy chain of historic evolution going back, ultimately, to the time of Alexander the Great. For it was after the incursion of the Greeks into Asia under Alexander the Great, and after Greek ideas had made their way as far as the heart of Asia and India that the stage was set for the establishment of a culture that could be regarded as essentially unitary.

This process is veiled by the great division of the Middle East into the Roman and the Parthian empires, succeeded in roughly the same proportions by the Byzantine and the Persian (Sassanid) empires. Yet beginning with the third century A.D. and even before, there was a convergence of Asiatic and European elements in both the Byzantine Empire and the Persian.

And it was this interaction between Asiastic culture and Hellenism that gave the Middle East a basically similar intellectual and social texture. It created a homogeneous social framework over which the new Muslim religion flung a state structure, cementing together an already unitary society under a new set of slogans and through a new language, which thereby became a world language.

What the eruption of the Arabs accomplished, then, was not the introduction of a completely novel element; on the contrary, it established a unitary society on the basis of something that had long been present. The remarkable parallelism between medieval Christianity and Islam, which I shall revert to later, is ultimately founded on the simple fact that both societies had their roots deep in the Hellenistic civilization of Christian antiquity. It is true that the Arabs conquered the entire area, but though they imposed a new language and apparently a new religion on it, the cultural content of the new civilization, though called "Islamic," was in reality a sequel of Christian antiquity, shifted farther and farther eastward by fortuitous circumstances in the fortunes of the caliphate. Thus, while carrying on the tradition of the ancient Orient, the caliphate merged with it in a manner that Alexander the Great's conquests had made possible and indeed inevitable. In this way the Islamic society, which was at bottom quite Hellenistic, became more and more Oriental, while at the same time on the terrain of Western Europe the great folk migrations of the Teutonic peoples created a bastion of resistance to the influences of that civilization and thus created the contrast, still valid, between the East of Hellenism-plus-Orientalism and the West of the past thousand years.

When Islam is seen in its true aspect, as a unitary civilization overspanning vast areas and no longer as a mere appanage of an Arab ruling caste, the great question of its genesis can be more clearly put.

Taking for granted that Islam as a religion may originally have been rooted in the mystical experiences of one man, Muhammad, however the actual content of that experience was formed by the scraps of information he had derived from Jewish and Christian doctrines, how was it that the immense civilization of Islam, as represented in the Abbasid regime, came about altogether? What were the prerequisites for its homogeneity? And to what extent did religion play a role in it?

Now, there can be no doubt that when Muhammad was still in Mecca the germs of Islam were still predominantly religious. It is difficult to imagine, as some hostile scholars have done, that Muhammad was a mere political opportunist looking for an occasion to become powerful by balancing between Christianity and paganism. In any case, however, the debate about what went on in Muhammad's soul is futile; whatever the answer, there would still be the further and more essential question, after all, of how Muhammad's personal experience was translated into a vast social structure.

For whatever Muhammad's spiritual disposition was in Mecca,

the sociopolitical process that was to take shape with such amazing rapidity after his death had its inception when he moved to Medina, where the religious impulse he had started with was instantly associated with a *Realpolitik*. After Mecca the slogan that came into effect, and remained so throughout the first phase at least of the nascent Islamic community, was no longer mere conversion to the religion of Allah, but subjugation by the prophet of Allah, that is, subjugation to Islam as a community. In this phase, even if given individuals may have gone over to Islam out of religious conviction, when whole tribes went over it was obviously a political affair. Thus the spread of Islam in its first phase was intimately bound up with the fortunes of the Medinese community considered as a political center. Even before Islam had overflowed the borders of Arabia it had already become a sociopolitical as well as a religious community. On the other hand, the acceptance of the Medinese Umma did imply, automatically, the acceptance of the religion, too.

This situation changed completely the moment the infant Islamic state found itself conquering the ancient civilizations of the Middle East and northern Africa. Here there was a sharp and instantaneous differentiation between the spread of Islam as a religion and its spread as a state.

The widespread tradition that the early Muslims came pounding out of the desert with the Quran in one hand and the sword in the other, converting the infidel by force, is a manifest superstition, an adjunct of traditional Christian polemics. As has been indicated above, the last thing the Arabs were thinking about during their conquests was the actual conversion of the infidels; it was the taxes paid by infidels, after all, that sustained the Islamic state. In turn the subjects of the new state had complete religious freedom provided they paid those taxes; this fact alone would be quite enough to demonstrate that Islam had come a long way from the propaganda of belief that had been carried on in Mecca by the prophet. Even though the religious freedom of its countless new subjects may have been acceded to out of political necessity, it is nevertheless a testimonial to the vanquishing of the religious impulse by the material interests of the Arab ascendancy and to the predominance within Islam of the vested interests of the Arab minority over the universal pretensions of Islam as a religion.

The only full citizens of the new Islamic state were the Arabs, who in the fashion of nineteenth-century European imperialists were quite content to remain the overlords of a mass of taxpaying serfs.

There is thus a gap of some centuries—from one to three—between the political conquest of the Middle East and northeast Africa by the Arab tribes and the religious conversion of the whole area. In consequence a dual historical process must be considered.

The basic concept to be retained in this consideration of the genesis of the unitary civilization of Islam is that of its having been initiated by the Arab folk migration. As indicated above, the Arab migration out of Arabia was doubtless due to some long-drawn-out socioeconomic process—whether the desiccation of the peninsula or something else is of academic interest. Though some scholars have been doubtful about the proof of desiccation as a source of the ethnic fermentation in the peninsula, it must have been that or something similar, since that seems to be the only explanation for the pre-Islamic and Islamic overflow from the peninsula into the fertile areas lying to the north, northeast, and northwest.

As I have indicated, all Arabia had been in a state of upheaval for centuries before Muhammad. The remains of ancient constructions, as well as classical literary sources, indicate that for centuries, perhaps for tens of thousands of years, Arabia had been receding economically, an economic recession that might have been accelerated by the destruction of the woodlands, by floods, and so on. Nor need there be a direct connection between the progressive decline in the peninsular economy and any specific folk movement. Indeed, had it not been for the belated effect of monotheism on Muhammad and the singular enfeeblement of the Persian and Byzantine empires, an enfeeblement that simply clamored for conquest by outsiders, the Arabian tribes might still be milling about today without having made any more impact on world history than they had before Islam.

Of course the mere peregrinations of the Arabian tribes, without the unifying influence of Islam, would have been quite meaningless and above all futile as against the overwhelming military power of the great cultures on their borders, however enfeebled at the moment they might have been. The mutual envy and unflagging contentiousness of the tribes would have isolated a particular tribe in any merely tribal enterprise. It was at this crucial point that the function of Islam can be most clearly perceived; by uniting the tribes within its bosom, though perhaps for only a short space of time, it overcame their bickering or at least subordinated the classical intertribal envy to the larger perspectives offered by the Muslim-Arab expansion.

Here again, however, it was not the religious impulse *as such* that unified those tribes. On the contrary, it was to be precisely within the bosom of Islam that the ancient rivalry between the south and the north Arabs, for instance, acquired its legendary venom: in the opinion of some scholars the rivalry was actually generated within Islam! The aspect of Islam that united the tribes was again the political formation; the religion, to be sure, had engendered the infant Islamic community that produced the infant Islamic state, but it was the state in turn that then transformed the Arabian folk migration already in existence into an instrument of its own.

Thus the generals that were made use of by Islam, the great conquerors of the first heroic period of the Arab expansion, were not in the least interested in religion. They were, in fact, quite indifferent to it except from a purely utilitarian, indeed Machiavellian, point of view. The movement may have been organized by the Medina regime together with its generals, but it is obvious that there it soon acquired a spontaneous momentum, partially through the dynamics of the migration itself and even more decisively through the unexpected weakness of the great states on the borders of the peninsula. The central government was completely disconcerted by the scope of its own initial successes. Its skill was displayed only later when it very adroitly gave the cupidity of the tribes a particular goal and gradually created the effective administrative forms for containing the vast areas that had fallen into its lap.

Islam thus still remained the unifying slogan of the whole movement, but it was conceived of as meaning the secular dominion of the Arab tribes. This national concept may have had a religious tinge, a natural and perhaps inevitable phenomenon for the ideas of the period and place, but, as I have indicated, the predominance of the national factor precisely in the question of conversion was demonstrated by the fact that with all the universalism, both implicit and explicit in Islam as a religious system, there was no way for any non-Arab to become a Muslim except as the Client of some Arab tribe.

It was, accordingly, not the proselytizing zeal of the Arabs newly converted to monotheism that drove out the tribes on a mission that quickly became a world mission, but the economic pinch and the concomitant restiveness of the great tribes.

There are thus three factors in the remarkable success of Islam: the timeliness of the slogan-cum-institution that could unite the headstrong tribes of the peninsula; the political drive of a youthful state entity; and the corresponding weakness of the surrounding empires that made military and political success so easy.

At first glance, to be sure, it is difficult to see how Islam, as a religion, could even begin to spread, since the Arabs themselves regarded it as a chattel of their own and in fact discouraged conversions. Yet in spite of this exclusiveness the subjugated populations did, after all, go over to Islam in a short period in substantial numbers and with a rapidity that makes the early spread of Christianity seem positively sluggish.

The expansion of the Muslim religion was tantamount to the growth of the ruling class and the shrinkage of the taxpaying elements. This ran counter to the interests of the Arab conquerors and of the government itself, regardless of the zeal it might have aroused in some authentic idealists. Those to whom state affairs were a matter of indifference must have been completely overshadowed by the overriding needs of a state that was built up on this contrast between Muslims and non-Muslims. The utter obliviousness of the early Muslim Arabs to the problems arising out of mass conversion can be seen in the simple fact that the whole of the state's financial structure was built up on this economic foundation. When the conversions began to take place *en masse,* the state order had to be transformed from top to bottom.

At the same time, the Arab-Muslim state was obviously doomed to destruction as long as it did not perceive the necessity, from this point of view, of actually *forbidding* the conversion to Islam. If anyone could slip into the ruling class and benefit substantially in an economic and social way from the mere religious conversion that made this possible, it is obvious that the social cleavage depending on this religious split would not have a long life ahead of it.

But it is equally obvious that a conversion to the religion of Muhammad could not actually be forbidden. The universal factor in Islam is quite undeniable; no one on earth could simply be forbidden to believe in the God of the prophet. In this way the idea of the universal religion actually shattered the principle of nationality, according to which the religion underlying the state had originally been coextensive with that state. The nationalist force of the early Arab-Muslim state is attested to by the lengthy delay before this took place. So far from promoting the Muslim religion, the early Arab Muslims did everything they could to prevent it from realizing itself. Without the resistance, perhaps unconscious, of the Arab conquerors to the whole idea of the spread of Islam to non-Arabs there would doubtless have been mass conversions within the first decade of the eruption out of Arabia. By the time the state-destroying influence of the religion became evident, it was already too late. The universalism of Islam had created a new state and a new society.

On the arrival of the Arabs, to be sure, a few thousand of their new subjects were doubtless converted at once—those few thousands of the population who came in from the countryside to ensure their own futures by assuming the religion of their conquerors. This would have had no particular effect on finances and was probably welcomed by the Arabs, since it helped them out by providing them at once with the administrative personnel they lacked. As long as the many millions throughout the country went on paying the taxes imposed on non-Muslims all was well.

The elite, of course, must have seen the advantage in having as close a connection as possible with the newcomers; there are records of debates that took place between Muslim and Christian elites. The activities of elite circles in the capital and other cities meant little, however, with respect to the general diffusion of Islam. Missionary work was soon taken over by the newly converted Arameans, whose point of view was altogether different from that of the secular-minded Arabs.

But however effective the missionary work came to be, the major incentive in adhering to Islam was bound to be the economic factor. The moment a convert became a Client of some Arab tribe, thus simultaneously a Muslim, he was freed of the heavy tax burden imposed on non-Muslims. He could also take advantage of the pleasures of the city as well as of some of the social privileges of the Arab ruling caste. Even from a purely religious point of view, for that matter, it was not particularly difficult for a Christian subject of the nascent Islamic society to be converted, since before Islam evolved a dogmatic system of its own it was not very different from Christianity; it gave the impression of being simply another sect. In a way it might even have been welcomed, since the Monophysite heresy in some ways implied a turning aside from the polytheistic element felt to be inherent in the notion of the dual nature of the Christ, of the Trinity, and so on. Some scholars have seen in the receptivity to Islam, with its extreme simplicity of doctrine, a reaction of the monotheistic spirit from the thoroughgoing hellenization of Christianity that had become characteristic of the Middle East.

Besides, it had to be admitted that there must be something to be said for the new religion, since it was that of the victors and hence a sign of divine favor.

Thus there were not many spiritual obstacles inhibiting the acceptance of the material advantages of Islam, which were undeniable, immediate, and substantial. The oddity is really in the other direction—that *in spite of* all these factors half a century seems to have gone by before the mass conversions to Islam began throwing the state budget out of kilter. The final decades of the Umayyad regime were afflicted by the necessity of doing something to regularize the relationship between the growing islamization and the foundations of the state. Ultimately this was to lead to a general tax reform, which from then on no longer meant freedom from an onerous tax burden, but at least retained the social advantages attendant on becoming a Muslim.

Although this material factor was at first very influential, the groundwork for a really large-scale movement of islamization was not laid until the first century of the Abbasid regime, by which time the notion of Arab paramountcy as a state principle was completely liquidated. Perhaps the most important of the many reasons behind this massive movement of social interpenetration was the decisive and overwhelming superiority, both material and spiritual, to the Bedouin of the cultivated nations they had conquered.

This superiority was not socially effective as long as the Arabs had not mixed intimately with the subject populations. While the Bedouin warriors were quartered in the great army encampments, keeping aloof from their subjects and simply playing the princely role of someone whose sword is his shield, it was quite simple for them to be persuaded of their own superiority as warriors who had conquered great masses of people and imposed on them a new religion and a new language.

This situation was bound to change, however, as the massive migration of more Arabs from the peninsula continued, as the wars of conquest came to an end, as the Arabs eventually stopped being pensioners of their own private state and started earning a living in a conventional way, and, more especially, as the very Arab caste itself began being diluted by the massive infiltration of the Clients and finally exploded altogether.

When this happened it was inevitable that the material and spiritual superiority of the ancient civilization of the Persians, Arameans, and Egyptians came to be organically implanted within the bosom of the new community. Once the countless cultivated and trained individuals of the subject nationalities could express their cultural superiority freely through their conversion to the simple slogans of Islam, the way was cleared for those simple slogans to be elaborated in the most complex and subtle ways by the gifted or in any case highly trained minds that had been formed in a more complex culture. The Arabs had no cultural reservoir, outside their language itself and their religion in its simple form, that could enable them to withstand the manifest superiority of their subjects. For that matter in language, too, they were soon to be equaled, if not outclassed, after a mere generation or two, when the Clients came to know Arabic as well as the Arabs and could moreover codify and regulate it in a complicated and authoritative way.

Thus the Arabs came to adapt themselves to the new society in which the Clients had come to form the majority and ultimately became quite dependent on them.

This happened in the countryside as well as in the cities. The moment the Arabs became farmers, landowners, and petty bourgeois just like the surrounding population of former subjects, now placed on more or less the same level as the Arabs themselves by the process of islamization, there was no longer any question of the Arabs conserving their ancient privileges.

Spiritually the Arameans, Greeks, and Persians were so much more cultivated, in both education and tradition, that the ordinary

Arabs were looked down upon as coarse ruffians and uncouth barbarians. Nor did the Arabs have anything special to point to in self-defense against such sneers, except their priority within the Muslim religion. In this way many Arabs gradually became more religious, partly through adapting themselves to the far more religious atmosphere of the conquered subjects and partly to take advantage of one of the few spiritual points in which they could claim any prestige. The credit for Islam was the only spiritual superiority they could pretend to.

It might have been conceivable for the Arabs to have gone on conducting themselves as a superior caste if the state summit had been able to put up an energetic defense of the aristocratic principle underlying the Arab state of the first four caliphs and the succeeding Umayyads. But in order to keep functioning with any effectiveness the Arab state had to make concessions to the overwhelming non-Arab majority of its subjects. Even under the Umayyads we see the beginnings of what was to become, under the cosmopolitan Abbasids, a flowering of all the characteristics of the ancient Oriental despotisms—the magnification of the prince, the exclusive ceremonial that barred the public from the sovereign's presence, the bureaucracy as an instrument of public pillage, and the weapon of the slave guards. As this complex of despotic institutions evolved, the prerogatives of the Arabs too, as a favored group within the community, were bound to become more and more unendurable for the state summit. The state that had been launched as a chattel of the Arab aristocrats was, in short, dissolved by the general despotism of the ancient East.

From then on it was no longer a question of a master race ruling its subjects, but of the general enserfment of the population under one single ruler. This accomplished the leveling of all classes in society vis-à-vis the despot. The masses of serfs naturally hastened to take on the religion of the ruling house; with this the language, too, spread out rapidly, accompanying the swift expansion of the religion.

From now on, the missionizing of the subject populations was carried on at a much more rapid tempo, far more than under the Arabs, who lacked both the institutional drive to do so and for that matter the requisite religious zeal. Missionary work was carried on now by the converts themselves or their descendants, and when these started in on their religious drive they did so from a quite different starting point.

The former Christians among the newly converted started out from well-remembered traditions of the clericalism that had played such a role among the Arameans. If they were Persians, their starting point was that of a state church and the ubiquitous diffusion of religiosity. By the time the despotic state of the Persian Chosroes had been given a new envelope to bloom in, the foundations were laid once again for a blossoming of the notion of a state church, which would have been quite alien to any Arab no matter how much he plumed himself on his religious superiority.

With the blossoming of this idea of a state church the conversion of the infidel now lay in the interests of the state summit, *i.e.,* exactly the opposite of what it had been under the rule of the Arab Umayyads and before. And now the rulers found themselves propped up on a completely new class of people that had been quite absent during the beginnings of the Arab era—the theologians, legalists, and dogmaticians, in short, the scholarly classes that in Islam replaced the clergy of Christendom. Since these people were on a footing of social equality with the bulk of the population, they could operate in a religious sense with perfectly uninhibited zeal, quite different from the psychic stance of the previous Arab seigneurs, who accepted the presence of foreigners with the greatest reluctance. During the Abbasid epoch it became highly meritorious to win converts for Islam, so that islamization now took on a far more massive scope than it had under the Arab conquerors. In fact very rapidly, by the third and fourth centuries after the Hijra, it had spread to roughly the boundaries in the Middle East it has retained to this day.

Briefly, there was a convergence in this respect between the very early period of Muhammad's activity in Mecca and the later evolution of the Islamic Empire under the Abbasids. Between these two eras the motives for conversion had economic and political roots far more than mere proselytizing zeal.

In this way the modern East was to come under the influence of Islam as a religion as well as a political system. Yet this does not imply that it was the religion of Islam that created a unitary civilization out of the Islamic Empire. To see the reasons for the unitariness we must look far further back. It was not the Muslim faith that created a homogeneous culture; it was the homogeneity of the ancient East, expressed in another language under the caliphate, that laid the groundwork for the expansion of the Muslim religion down to the present day.

This is, perhaps, the nub of the traditional and persistent confusion between the Arab Empire and the Muslim world. Just as the theological explanation of the success of Islam, pandered to by both Christian and Muslim historiographers and scholars, was a source of great confusion, so the linguistic misunderstanding of the nature of the Muslim advance has been highly misleading.

Since the Arabs were traditionally supposed to have created the civilization of the caliphate, they are also held to be responsible for everything in it, from the Alhambra in Spain to the buildings of the Mamluks. And because the Islamic era was triggered by an Arab folk migration, because the Middle East has spoken vernacular Arabic ever since the caliphate, and because its oldest literary monuments are written in Arabic, its civilization as such is taken to be a creation of the Arabs.

There was, in fact, practically nothing at all in the caliphate that can be called Arab. It is true that the very beginnings of the Islamic state, the Umma constructed by Muhammad, the regime of the first four caliphs, and perhaps that of the Umayyads were Arab in origin, but that state lasted scarcely three generations; it was obliterated by the Abbasid caliphate. Nor was the administration of the Islamic Empire the handiwork of Arab wisdom, as later Muslim tradition for its own motives has sometimes put it, but a creation of the ancient Byzantine and Persian bureaucracies.

The differences are even more marked in the spheres of material culture and of ideas. Indeed, the Muslim religion itself was molded by the dogmatic struggles that were taking place within Christianity and by neo-Platonic and Indian mysticism. The natural sciences and philosophy were taken over from the Greek heritage and transmitted further—back to Europe, in fact, perhaps the greatest contribution of the cosmopolitan civilization of the Islamic Empire. Architecture was taken from the Byzantines and Persians, and historiography itself, on which Muslims were to pride themselves, from the Persians. In Islamic civilization there was a strong Arab motif in poetry and in some areas of the law, such as inheritance and marriage laws, but even in law as a whole most of the debates originated outside the material referred to in the Quran and outside the practices of the Arab upper caste that ruled only a hundred years. It is characteristic, after all, that even in basic Muslim jurisprudence, which is divided up into "sources and principles," it is only the sources that are in Arabic, while the principles come from the civilizations the Arabs took over.

There can be, in short, no serious claim that there is anything more than a tinge of Arabdom in the Islamic civilization. Even in the great works of literature and tradition often considered typically Arab, such as the Hadith and belles lettres (*Adab*), the bulk of this is simply Middle Eastern, and at best Arab *too,* but very often quite non-Arab in all respects. This is sometimes obscured, but no more than obscured, by the Muslim habit of wrapping up all such references in a literary form that links all maxims and daily actions to an example set by Muhammad. It is, in short, a mere literary-cum-religious convention.

To sum up: What the Arabs did upon their eruption from the peninsula was to adapt themselves to a culture they found waiting for them. And the genesis of that culture is to be sought in the great historical phenomenon of the spread of Greek thought, known in its international version as Hellenism.

• • •

The immensely mongrelized, variegated, mixed culture of the Middle East was expressed most consummately in Aramean Christendom. Aramaic, which developed many dialects over the vast area where it was spoken, is a most revealing reflection of the extraordinary cultural mixture it was the expression of, through the intermingling in its vocabulary, as well as in its entire structure, of Semitic, Persian, and Greek elements. Its unitary ecclesiastical organizations, too, created a natural bridge that could easily cross one border after another. For that matter, the society it was the vehicle of achieved a sort of ethnic unity precisely by virtue of the intermingling that the language and the culture made possible. I have already indicated that the Arab conquerors collided with serious resistance only where there was a strong people rooted on its own land, such as Persia and Berber North Africa.

Even in pre-Islamic times the Arabs that had come into contact with foreign civilizations were dependent primarily on the

Aramean culture. After their conquest of the Middle East, they simply fitted themselves into the local Aramaic-speaking population and in a sense simply went on living out Aramaic civilization, with a mere change of language and a different religious formulation. In this way the Arab conquests and the Aramean cultural sphere they encompassed provided the basis for the unity of the Islamic Empire; this basis was further built on to by the presence of the third and decisive factor—the existence of the Middle Eastern Great State.

Before the Arab conquests, a cultural unity had been able to evolve in spite of the political split into states and in spite of the fact that the Middle East was gravitating politically toward the West. After the Arab conquests, the partition between all states was eliminated, and the cultural unity that had already been formed could find its political expression in the unity of the Islamic Empire. Very suddenly immense territories were linked to the center of the Islamic Empire in what had been the former Persian center. The Western contributions were put a stop to for the time being, and Asia, already largely hellenized, could exercise its influence undisturbed.

Neither the Arabs nor the Arameans were in a position to see this historical process in the proper perspective. During the Umayyad period, with the Arabs still ruling as tribally minded chieftains just one step removed from the desert, it could be considered natural for the imperial center to be on the periphery of all developments, in Damascus, which it was natural to overestimate because of the purely contingent course of events and because of the initial preponderance of the Arab Bedouin element.

Even during the political preeminence of Damascus, however, the greater importance, culturally and economically, of Iraq became manifest. A proof of the inevitability of this process was the transfer of the capital of the empire to Baghdad. Once that happened, the caliphate was transformed into a sequel of the Persian Chosroes Empire, on a much enlarged basis. In this sense it was only a matter of course for the caliphate to show an increasing number of Persian and for that matter of Asiatic features in general. Later it was to be influenced still more by central Asia—bringing the Turks to the heart of Europe—and even by China.

Thus the caliphate was not Arab, and not Aramean, and not even wholly Persian. Nevertheless it constituted a unit on the basis of a unitary state structure; that state was of course Islamic, and that is, indeed, the justification for calling the whole phenomenon the Islamic civilization.

One of the hallmarks of old-fashioned Arab life, as has been noted, was its traditionalism. There was a marked tendency for everything to remain as it had been before. But under the influence of the unitary state, basic socioeconomic processes were stimulated that resulted in a vast flux of mongrelization, aided principally by the vast flow of trade made possible by the unifying of markets.

Even though the former customs stations remained in existence, trade was able to penetrate through vast territories previously accessible only with great difficulty. What had been transfer points along the previous frontiers became transit stations. Together with the trade in goods, great numbers of capitalist enterprises of enormous scope developed on the basis of great speculations launched by entrepreneurs whose transactions spread a network throughout the caliphate at the time of its efflorescence. These economic factors were of primordial importance in developing and fortifying the unitary Islamic civilization.

Once the unifying effect of economic and political factors was felt, there was an immediate reflection of it in the spiritual domain as well, where the new religion acted as a cement in binding together the previously independent elements of the population, since the religious partitions that had divided them in the past were simply obliterated by the mass adoption of Islam. Once the Muslim religion had become a force and absorbed the spiritual legacy of its predecessors, it developed autonomous traditions that were basic in the establishment of a spiritual unity within the framework of Islam. In this way there arose from the borders of China to the Atlantic Ocean a unitary religious science in which the doctrines of Aristotle, for instance, assimilated by the new class of scholars, could flow back and forth together with other intellectual commodities throughout the whole realm, and even far beyond, all the way into the African interior.

A cardinal consequence of this unitary state was the influence it exercised over great areas that previously had remained outside Aramean civilization, such as Persia, Egypt, and North Africa. Even after these territories split away from the central Islamic state again, as they did after the collapse of the caliphate, they lived on in the memory of an ideal unity. In this way a genuine intellectual interchange could go on taking place.

Thus the Aramean lake gradually, with the absorption of powerful influences from many sides, swelled into the great sea of Islamic civilization. This process had as a by-product the gradual permeation of all of life by religious thought, in a way that had been quite alien to the Arab conquerors themselves, though the general pietizing of life was also, to be sure, characteristic of Jewish post-Exilic thought, the background of Muhammad's own religious development.

But the clericalism that was to imbue Islamic civilization was not at all the outcome of Muhammad's message alone. Its roots must be sought in the much older tendencies mentioned above—Byzantine clericalism and the Persian ecclesiastical state. The victory of the cosmopolitan Abbasid caliphate over the secular Arab kingdom of the Umayyad house was, in short, an institutional succession. It was far more than the mere victory of Muhammad's purely religious idea—as distinct from his statesmanship—over the hedonistic paganism of the Meccan aristocracy. It was also the victory of the Persian and Christian ecclesiastical hierarchy, and of the ancient pietism of the East in general, over the religious apathy of the secular Arab state. This whole cultural entity was to continue under the name of Islam, whose significance was thus radically, though unconsciously, transformed.

And it was only now, with the triumph of this curious intermingling of political, cultural, and religious factors that signalized the high point of the Abbasid caliphate, that Islam became capable of becoming the instrument of a world mission. This was to be unmistakable in spite of the many individual deviations from this ideal, with the occasional formation of sects and of local orders, and with the occasional succumbing of whole sections, such as Chinese Islam, to the smothering effect of a more powerful national civilization. In spite of all this, Islam retained an unmistakable unity of civilization that even today, and especially, perhaps, among the Arabic-speaking nations, must be regarded as a political reality.

This is all the more marked, indeed, precisely since the collapse of the old unitary state. Not only did that state remain as an attitude of mind, that is, the unitary state itself became the *ideal* of a unitary state that still stirs the imagination of all Muslim leaders;

even more, what may be called the existential ideals of Islam have retained their primordial vigor, and even today, with the constant expansion of Islam throughout the primitive areas of Africa, Islam still displays the same potent combination of religion, culture, and state-making initiative that has been its hallmark ever since its inception. It is only, in fact, since the most recent period, within our own generation, that the unifying tie of religion has begun to be frayed, fairly systematically, by nationalist and liberal tendencies.

This description of the advance first of the Arabs after Muhammad, then of the Arab initial state structures—Medina and Damascus—then of the replacement of the Arab ruling summit by the cosmopolitan empire of the Abbasids, and the attendant massive spread of Islam beginning with the Islamic Empire and enduring to the present day, indeed making still more momentous advances in Africa since its opening up by European colonization (see Epilogue), presents a very different picture from old-fashioned views. The notion of Islam as a child of the wilderness or as a manifestation of the desert-inspired Semitic taste for a monotonous monotheism or as the product of "Arab culture" or for that matter the still more grotesque view that Islam was engendered by the Quran or by Muhammad's career must be totally dropped. These traditional views must be regarded, in the light of recent research and, perhaps, of a still more recent objectivity, as the consequence of one form of bias or another, of a sort of deception or self-deception that has been indulged in by both Christian and Muslim scholars.

• • •

It was, essentially, Hellenism that Islam served as a vehicle for, as indicated, plus various admixtures from Persia, itself partially hellenized, from India, and from Egypt. The channels that conveyed the culture of Hellenism into the reservoir of Islam present a revealing instance of cultural diffusion.

As I have pointed out above, the transformation of the Greek heritage into the content of Islamic civilization was the continuation of a much older current of cultural infiltration—through Aramaic—of the Middle East by the heritage of the Greeks. When the task of translating Greek thought was resumed by Arabic, however, the consequences were limitlessly greater, since it was through Arabic that Greek culture, after spreading throughout the vast world of

Islam, was to make its reappearance in Europe and thus more than make up for its previous decline in Europe itself. It is interesting to observe, also, that it was Hellenism, not Latinism, that found its way into Arabic, which also, as I have indicated, took in many elements of Hindu thought via Persian translation.

This complex process took a little time to get started.

Under the Arab Umayyads the only intellectual product was poetry, to a large extent of the old-fashioned traditional Arab type. The culture and science associated with the Greek heritage, which were to acquire such importance in the cosmopolitan civilization of the Abbasid caliphate, were a matter of indifference to the poets, who were the only intellectuals in Umayyad society. The poetry was in fact a continuation of the times of the *Jahiliyya,* the "Ignorance" that preceded Islam. The Umayyad poets would improvise eulogies of their sponsors, lampoon their enemies, sing lyrically of the perils of the desert by now left far behind, and echo the ancient tribal feuds of the Arabian wilderness.

The Arab gift for poetizing and the immense concentration of the desert Arabs on all the arts of rhetoric, especially poetry, lived on in Islam even after the Umayyads in the most diversified form, which ultimately had a direct influence on the evolution of literature in Europe. The great memories developed by illiteracy ensured an immediacy in the evocation of poetry that made it an integral part of the lives of the ordinary people. The old Arabs seem to have been justly famous for their powers of improvisation and in any case the convention of putting long poems into ordinary narrative corresponded to the tastes of Arabic-speaking audiences long after the Arabs proper had retreated to their deserts. Histories are full of ordinary people, as well as caliphs and so on, rising to some little occasion with a burst of poetic improvisation; even slave girls were required to spout an impromptu verse to amuse their owners.

Poetry is perhaps of unique importance in the history of the Arabs if only because of its role in shaping what has been the Arabs' greatest pride—their language.

The most striking single element in the unfolding of the complex civilization that came to be known as Islamic may be the remarkable evolution of this language, the richest and most complicated of all Semitic languages, though at the same time seemingly the most primitive in its structure. Embodied in one of its forms in the Quran itself, it has set its stamp on Arabic poetry down to the present day. Arabic has always held a quite matchless position in the minds of its speakers; it is regarded as being itself one of the wonders of the world, and the Quran is for this reason alone a divine revelation. Not only was it thought to outrank all other languages simply because of its spiritual rank, as being the selected medium for the expression of God's conclusive revelation, but its objective features, too, bear out its unique distinction, especially the endless range of its vocabulary. It is, in fact, quite true to say that the Arabic vocabulary is scarcely to be matched by any other language except possibly English today, and even then only if the countless "side languages," or specialized technical vocabularies, of English are included. In classical Arabic the actual body of the language, more or less accessible to all cultivated readers, is practically boundless.

As the defenders of Arabic uniqueness would point out, where Greek often has only one word for several objects, Arabic has many words for one object. The stunning phonetic beauty of the language is matched, they say, by its staggering wealth of synonyms. The possibilities in Arabic for the use of figurative language are endless; its allusiveness, tropes, and figures of speech place it far beyond the reach of any other language. Arabic has numerous stylistic and grammatical peculiarities that are quite unique; hence nothing can be translated from Arabic satisfactorily. The Arabic version of something foreign is always shorter than the original. Arabic loses on translation, but all other languages gain on being translated into Arabic; thus it is quite understandable, says a well-known writer, that upon being expelled from Paradise Adam was naturally forbidden to speak Arabic and had to talk Syriac instead, and when he repented God let him go back to Arabic!

Because of this, of course, Arabic is so stupendously difficult that only a prophet can master it; hence the Quran must be studied night and day for it to come within the reach of the understanding.

The fact that the Quran, the very Word of God, was in Arabic hallowed forever the literary paramountcy of the language within Islam. Later, Arabic spread as the language of the conquering believers from the peninsula to the Mediterranean and to hither Asia. Less than a century after Muhammad's death it was the official and dominant, though not exclusive language of the state as well as of literature from Spain to Persia. Verses modeled very precisely on the old desert poets of the peninsula, with the same metrics, diction, and style, were being composed at Córdoba, Qayrawan, Fustat, Damascus, Kufa, Marw, and Bukhara. Ancient cultures simply withered away or utterly vanished before the new synthesis effected by the conquests. Latin, Greek, Coptic, Syriac, Armenian, and Old Persian weakened and tended to vanish as vernaculars before the spread of Arabic. By the time the Abbasids eventually substituted their cosmopolitan supranational theocratic state for the Arab national kingdom, Arabic had already become the lingua franca of this cosmopolitan society; detached completely from its ethnic origins, it could be used even by those who were violently opposed to what had been the cultural and sociopolitical primacy of the Arabs.

Thus Arabic reached its actual pinnacle of cultivation during the great Abbasid culture of the ninth and tenth centuries, precisely at a time when the Arabs proper had already receded far into the distance and the society was dominated by non-Arabs of all kinds, chiefly Persians. The heart and mold of classical Arabic literature, the period in which it became the vehicle of an immensely complex and ramified civilization, was thus a cosmopolitan, non-Arab society. It was the zenith of the Muslim effort, expressed in an Arabic that dominated the whole of the Afro-Asian and south Mediterranean world from Spain to Transoxania.

It was during these two centuries that the literature expanded to create new art forms and flung itself open to the influences of preceding cultures, beginning with the Greek and including the Persian and the Indian culture that had already influenced the Persian. Thus the most brilliant period of Muslim civilization was achieved under the inspiration of thoroughly non-Arab elements.

Poetry itself had a curious fate under Islam. Theoretically, the developing orthodoxy of Islam should have condemned poetry out of hand as the inherent archfoe of revelation, a frivolous and perhaps impious enemy of the new religion and a living hangover of the paganism that was so detested by the zealous new believers. The fact that pre-Islamic Arab poetry survived into Islam to serve as a literary model for generations to come was not simply because of its fascination—of the kind that got it banished for this very reason from Plato's *Republic*—but because it represented a specific Arab achievement that it never even occurred to the proud aristocrats who were the first wave of Muslims to disregard or abandon. For them it was the paramount demonstration both of tribal pride and of personal self-assertion. Bedouin poetry had been the sole means of spiritual expression, as well as a record of ancient pageantry and the living testimonial to a past they revered in the traditional nomadic manner.

Because of this, the ancient poetry survived the transformation brought about by Islam; it was piously recorded, indeed, hoarded in collections and zealously studied. Though there may be some truth in the notion that the poetry was conserved in order to facilitate the understanding of the Quran, parts of which have been obscure from the very earliest times, there is no doubt that the poetic tradition had a tenacity and charm all its own. It also, of course, served as an axis for the struggle between the admirers of the pagan way of life and those who believed in the austere elements of the new religion—in short, the ancient contrast between *Muruwwa* and *Din*.

During the first two centuries of Islam all literature was in Arabic; then the neo-Persian literature began to appear, vital not only for the history of Persia, which thus reasserted its ethnic uniqueness, but also for all Islam. The rapid growth of and renascence of neo-Persian literature broke for the first time the indissoluble fusion hitherto prevailing between "Arabism"—surviving in the language, at least—and Islam; thus new possibilities for spiritual expression were opened up for non-Arab Muslims. In Persia, accordingly, all the vital media of expression were switched out of Arabic, which retained merely technical idioms; religious, juridical, and philosophical disciplines continued to be dealt with in Persia for quite a long time in Arabic. Yet by the time Persian made a linguistic comeback it was already heavily permeated by Arabic, not merely in vocabulary but in actual phraseology. By the eleventh century the Arabic sector of Persian expanded enormously and encompassed literary rules, stylistic themes and models, metrics and rhetoric, and almost all terminology in the sciences and arts. The Persian influence in literature was ultimately to be concentrated on the heroic and romantic epic. It was in mysticism, indeed, that the Persian genius was to express itself in an incomparably inventive and moving manner.

Though far from being a language suited, one would have

thought, for the expression of abstract ideas, Arabic was to prove an incredibly adaptable medium for the expression of the most complex aspects of philosophy and all the natural sciences. When the conquests placed the handful of conquerors at the pinnacle of a rapidly expanding state spanning several ancient cultures, the language had to be instantly amplified and extended in two different directions at once—to serve as the governmental language for the new state, and to encompass the entire heritage of the ancient world that had fallen into the Bedouin's laps.

A great many foreign words were added to the vocabulary, but the nature of Arabic—with its vast structure built up out of relatively few root formations—enabled it to meet all new linguistic requirements by using its own resources in a remarkably plastic and limitlessly applicable way. There was thus no need for the creation of an immense specialized language, such as has encumbered English. The speakers of Arabic, both native and foreign, could assimilate the immense stores of new knowledge in an idiom that was self-sufficient and thus constitute a new universe of linguistic expression on a unitary base.

It was this Arabic language, basically the poetic, artificial lingua franca of the peninsular tribes, enriched by the new cultural impact, that was to become a world language that far transcended even the Islamic Empire itself and became a cultural language, somewhat like Latin, for all the nations that came to accept Islam. It was in fact the remarkable and almost unprecedented expansion of the language—reminiscent of the spread of Mandarin Chinese, Spanish, and English—that was the true marvel of the Arab conquests, for it created a new cultural universe within the space of a few centuries. By the eleventh century Arabic not only was the principal everyday vernacular all the way from Persia to Spain, it also had completely ousted as a cultural vehicle ancient cultural languages like Coptic, Aramaic, Greek, and Latin from areas where they had had undisputed sway for centuries or millennia. It was the spread of the language that most potently wiped out the distinctions between the ethnic groups that constituted the empire and led to the dissolution within Islam of the original Arab newcomers, so that the term "Arab" itself was restricted, as I have indicated, to the tribesmen who had originally borne it exclusively or else retained a merely honorific ring as the basis for a snobbish claim of lineage,

The Caliphate at Its Height

0 Miles 500

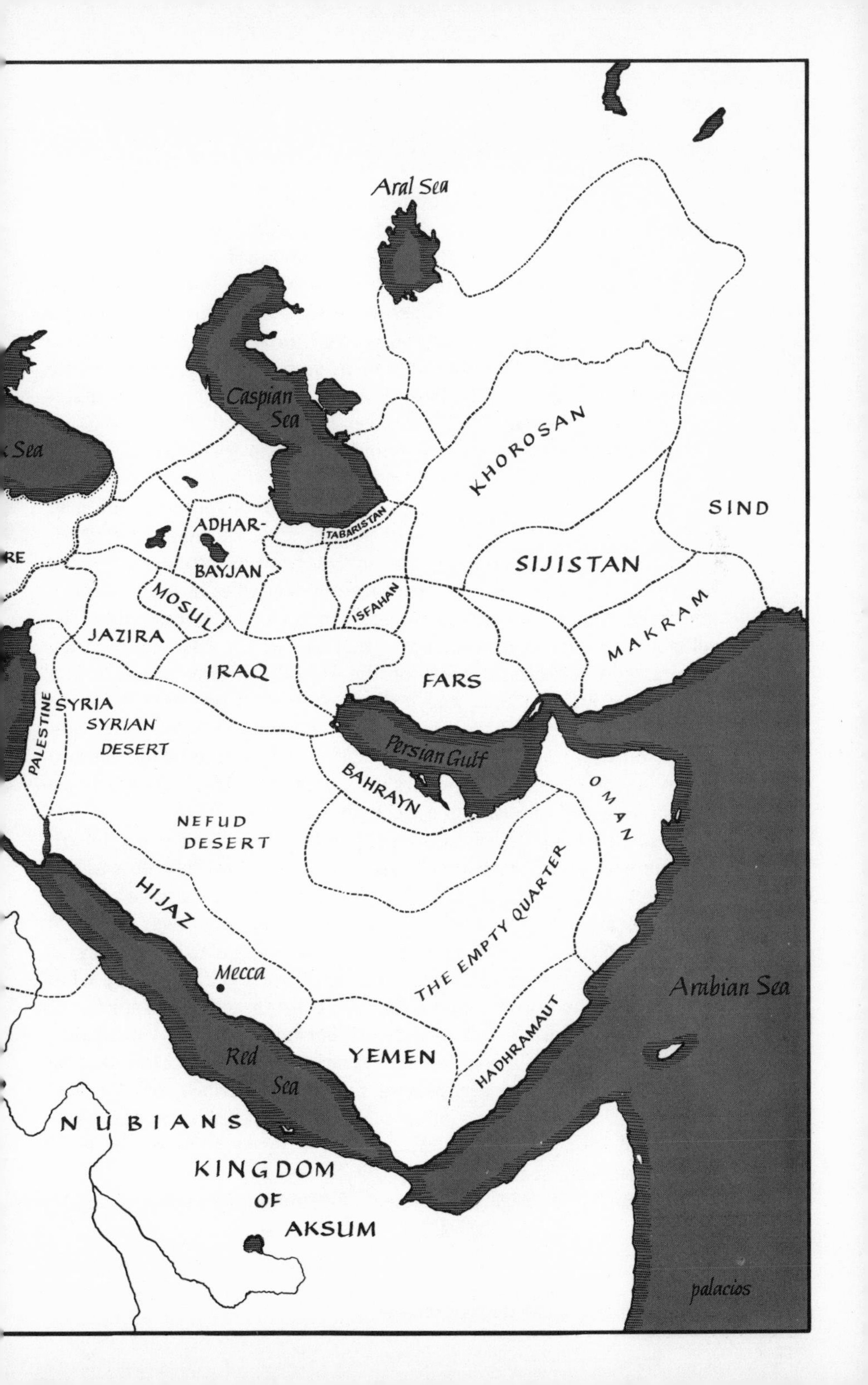
Aral Sea
Caspian Sea
KHOROSAN
SIND
ADHAR-BAYJAN
TABARISTAN
SIJISTAN
MOSUL
ISFAHAN
MAKRAM
JAZIRA
IRAQ
FARS
PALESTINE
SYRIA
SYRIAN DESERT
Persian Gulf
BAHRAYN
OMAN
NEFUD DESERT
HIJAZ
THE EMPTY QUARTER
Mecca
Arabian Sea
HADHRAMAUT
YEMEN
Red Sea
NUBIANS
KINGDOM OF AKSUM
palacios

itself rather diffused and in any case devoid of any particular social or economic meaning.

In addition to its development as a vernacular, Arabic was to swamp many languages on its borders or within the Islamic world community. Persian, Turkish, Urdu, Malay, and Swahili were not merely written in the Arabic script but had an immense bloc of Arabic vocabulary, *i.e.,* Arabic ways of looking at things, grafted on to them to this day, in some cases even more than the Latin and Greek components of modern English, and extending over a whole intellectual universe. Thus, though Arabic itself evolved novel material out of its own resources to meet the new cultural demands, it was to become itself a learned mandarin idiom for those languages it came to infuse with its own world view.

In the early Islamic world, religion, with its special position in society, gave rise to all forms of science and learning in general. Grammar and lexicography, for instance, were produced by the necessity of interpreting the Quran authoritatively, in a situation in which so many converts were pouring into the community. The religious sciences proper were concentrated in Medina—Quran, dogma, and the classification of the Hadith. It was this last that engendered jurisprudence and history, elaborated on the basis of the legal and biographical aspects of the Hadith, itself based—theoretically—on the practice (Sunna) of the prophet. Ultimately this last discipline produced the remarkably elaborate legal code of the Shari'a, ramified to cover all conceivable aspects of life.

History among the Arabs proper had begun with the life of Muhammad, appropriately enough, since for Islam that life was the beginning of understandable history as distinct from a mere chronicle of morally neutral events. Muhammad's biography was added to by the material drawn from the pre-Islamic Arab tribal history as recorded by oral tradition, and later, far more significantly, by what the new Persian converts put into Arabic of the court chronicles of the Sassanid rulers of Persia. History became one of the most diligently cultivated pursuits of the Arabic-speaking world, ranging from purely parochial accounts of families and tribes, set down in the primitive style of eyewitness accounts, to the encyclopedic work of Ibn Khaldun (1332–1406), considered by many to be the most remarkable historical mind of the Middle Ages.

Though the original message of Muhammad would seem so

simple as to defy ornamentation, the plunging of the Arabs into the intellectual universe of Hellenism, with its endless debates about the most abstruse theological themes in Christianity, soon forced the nascent Islamic caste of scholars to begin coping with the elaboration of their own religious tradition. In the course of this a great deal of Christian apocalyptic as well as Jewish talmudic material was grafted onto the youthful plant of the new religion. A serious application to theology was begun under the direct influence of Aramaic Christianity with a huge later admixture of Greek thought. The ancient heritage of classical Athens, transmuted through the Aramaic-speaking society, was to have a quite decisive influence on all the sciences, as well as on philosophy. It has been rightly said that Islam shared with medieval Christendom the transmission to the modern world of all the basic content of Greek thought.

In the ninth and tenth centuries the vast enterprise of translating Greek into Arabic, either directly or via intermediate Aramaic translations, produced a renaissance within Islam, superimposed on the Greek schools that had survived in Alexandria, Antioch, and elsewhere; there was also a Persian college founded by Nestorian refugees from orthodox Byzantium.

The enterprise of translation—basic in cultural osmosis—had already made a beginning under the regime of the Umayyads with the translation of some works on chemistry from the Greek and Coptic. The groundwork of Muslim medicine was laid by some translations of Aramaic medical books, generally done by Jews and Christians in Syria. But the sporadic translations that had been begun under the Umayyads were systematized and officially stimulated under the Abbasids. Its height was probably reached around the ninth century, under Mamun, when an official school for translators was set up in Baghdad, equipped with a permanent staff and a library. Scholars were sent out by the government to all sorts of places in quest of manuscripts, going as far as Byzantium. All the sciences, mathematics, astronomy, geography, chemistry, physics, and natural history, as well as medicine, were translated quite systematically.

The work of these early translators was soon followed by native schools of thought, generally Persian. Though the fundamental medical theory of the Greeks was not replaced, the Muslims added a great deal of clinical observation. In mathematics, chemistry, and physics, however, the contribution of the Muslims was to have far-reaching consequences. The Indian inventions of the zero and simplified numerals (mistakenly called "Arabic") were transmitted by Muslims from India to Europe, while algebra, geometry, and particularly trigonometry were very largely Muslim developments.

Not all branches of Hellenism were equally cultivated. Literature as such was scarcely touched at all. Scraps of Homer came in through odd elements of popular recitals or storytelling, rather than by real translations. Oddly enough, too, Greek history was of little interest to either Arabs or Persians, except, of course, for the overwhelmingly mythicized figure of Alexander the Great. The only thing taken from Greece was its philosophy, minus a few elements too indigestible for pious Muslims, and its sciences, to some extent for their utility and to some extent for the polemical reinforcement they might give Muslim argumentation. Of course, as the various Christian communities gradually adopted the Arabic language, they eventually translated into Arabic texts of service to them, independently of any Muslim demand.

What the Abbasid milieux got from the Persians, on the other hand, was not so much their science, which in any case had been derived in its turn from the Greeks, but their history, more or less mixed with mythology. In this way Islamic historiography ultimately became a composite of two quite different currents, more or less artificially made to flow together: on the one hand, the pre-Islamic old Arab tribal traditions plus the Biblical material that came into Arabic via the Quran; and on the other, Persian, not Greco-Roman, history. Persia was also turned to for a whole series of manuals of etiquette, especially for the use of princes and well-behaved people, and at the same time folktales and morality stories, themselves often taken from a Hindu source. It is difficult to say just how much the Arabs took from the Persians, since though most of the works translated from the Greek are known, it is, on the other hand, only through the translations into Arabic that we know the Persian works at all. Nevertheless it is clear that though the Greeks contributed the cerebral, reflective element to Islam, it was to Persia that the Muslim "ideal man" must be traced.

Coptic influence scarcely existed culturally; as for the influence of the Jews, though there was a certain amount of vulgar Judaism that influenced Islam at its very beginnings, on the superior levels

Jewish literature was too specialized and of interest to too small a number of people to warrant the assumption of a large element of Jewish influence in the constitution of Muslim civilization. On the contrary, it was the broad dissemination of Greek culture, as digested by the expanding Muslim society, that brought the Jews into closer contact with Greek antiquity than they had been before and thus enabled them to play an important role in Islam itself.

The Greek writings that were translated were an important part of Plato's works (*The Republic, Laws,* a number of *Dialogues,* including *The Apology of Socrates,* etc.), very often accompanied by the characteristic commentaries of the Alexandrian mystical neo-Platonists such as Proclus, Porphyrus, Jamblicus, Plotinus, John Philoponus. Practically all of Aristotle, with some gaps at first, was studied, especially his *Logic;* he was also studied for the *Physics,* the *Metaphysics, Nicomachean Ethics,* etc.—these too with Alexandrian commentaries tending to reconcile him with Plato. The figure of Aristotle, regarded as Alexander the Great's Wazir, became a sort of magician or superman in Muslim tradition. His real works were added to by some apocryphal ones, of which one claiming to deal with theology gave the Muslim theologians a great deal of trouble in their attempts, all of them hopeless, to reconcile him with Islam. Some neo-Pythagorean, Stoic, and other Greek elements also came into the orbit of Islam via translations.

Science accompanied philosophy into the Muslim domain, with medicine (Hippocrates, Gallien, and their successors); botany, as related primarily to pharmacy; then mathematics, astronomy, mechanics, geography (as part of astronomy, with Euclid, Archimedes, and Ptolemy, to mention only the best known). There were also, of course, astrology and alchemy, economic treatises, and some astronomic tables translated from the Pehlevi (ancient Persian), themselves translated from Hindu originals. On the whole a very considerable mass of work was translated, of an unusual variety.

Nor was the work all mere translation, since many of the actual translators, in the first place, made their own adaptations as they went along, and very soon there were original commentators springing up. Nevertheless the first Abbasid century may be characterized as essentially an era of translations and of not very original adaptations. More personal philosophy, and original work in science, came later, during the flourishing of the Islamic Empire and its decay.

The transplanting of Greek philosophy was to have fundamental importance; translations of Aristotle permeated the whole world outlook of Islam in philosophy and theology—beginning in the reign of Mamun—and stimulated numerous works by a whole series of original Muslim thinkers, of whom the best known in the West are Ibn Sina (Avicenna) (d.1037) and Ibn Rushd (Averroës) (d. 1198). Curiously enough, this list contains only one specifically Arab thinker, Ibn al-Kindi (d. *ca.* 850).

When the Arabs came out of the desert, the very idea of a book was unknown to them. Since time immemorial the spoken word, in oral transmission and in recitation, was the only recognized type of publication. But as they came into contact with the older cultures they came upon the idea of a *book*—a physical object, a cluster of pages bound together with a title and subject, a beginning and an ending, later supplemented by ornamentation of various kinds and bindings on which great ingenuity and artistry were exercised. The process that quickly began among the Muslims and, as the scope and extent of literary productions increased, culminated in a book is based on the classical idea; this process was accelerated still further when paper, a Chinese invention, was brought in via central Asia in the eighth century. In capsule form this anticipated the later effects of the invention of printing in the West, since paper made it possible to produce more books far more cheaply, and fitted in with the expansion of learning in the Islamic Empire.

Perhaps the most noteworthy influence exerted on European literature by the various literary modes processed through Islam, most of them distinguished by a sort of romantic floridity of form in contradistinction to the classical emphasis on austerity, beauty, and simplicity that was inherited by Europe, was in the new poetry, new social psychology, and new technique that abruptly appeared in southern France at the end of the eleventh century and that may have been influenced by developments in contemporary poetry in Muslim Spain. Arabic poetry, all the way back to its origins in the Arabian desert, had celebrated love as one of its major themes; bold, daring, and sensual imagination was poured out in the description of earthly love. The mystical poetry of the Arabs and all the numerous types of love lyric developed by them, and even more by the Persians, were to find their way into European literature.

It has been proved beyond question that the "Moors" of Andalusia were overwhelmingly Spanish by blood and were completely familiar with the Romance dialect that was to become Castilian. Thus there was a constant stream of fertilization and cross-fertilization between Spain and Western Europe, a process that was duplicated in Sicily.

The apologues, fables, and tales that constitute most of belles lettres in Arabic were transmitted fairly early to European literature. The most famous of these is doubtless the compilation known as *The Arabian Nights,* which arose as an Arabic translation of a Persian version of some Indian tales. In the eighteenth century it had thirty editions in English and French, and since then it has been published more than three hundred times in Western Europe.

In the arts, too, both major and minor, Islam effected a universal synthesis.

The homogenizing effects of the one-state society based on one language and one religion were seen in the remarkable eclecticism that enabled the Muslims to borrow from cultures as far afield as Persia and China. The Arabs had begun, very naturally, by taking over the actual works of art, and for that matter the artists, of the cultures they engulfed; then they gradually began imitating them and ultimately began to create something original of their own through the fusion of old and new. The process can be graphically demonstrated by a study of the designs on the walls of the Umayyad castles of Syria, for instance, and in the tools and other artifacts dug up in Iraq and Egypt. In the archeological explorations that have unearthed ninth-century pottery handiwork in Iraq, there is the usual crop of ordinary Byzantine and Persian craftsmanship, then artifacts imported from China, together with indigenous imitations of these Chinese models, and, alongside all these, original developments based on both types of work.

Pottery was one of the principal and typical achievements of Islamic culture, spreading from Persia all the way to Spain. Similarly, Muslim artisans developed all the crafts involved in the working of metal, wood, stone, ivory, and glass, in addition to the textiles and rugs that they have become famous for and that constitute specific Islamic creations based on the work of their predecessors. Glazed colored tiles had always been a speciality of the Middle East, but the vast expansion after Islam gave this and related arts and crafts a tremendous stimulus. Porcelain was imported from China under the Abbasids, and there were great pottery works from north Persia to Spain and throughout the Islamic Empire. Industries that had once been rooted in one particular country were often transferred throughout the cultural area of Islam, in all the large cities and towns of the empire from India to Spain. The political upheavals and separations did not affect the cultural unity of Islam, based as it very largely was at this time on an identity of religion and of language, even where Arabic never became the actual vernacular of the people. In painted and enameled glass, the Syrian and Iraqi centers were to transmit the craft later to Venice. Though Muslims changed their artistic style from one epoch to another and from one country to another, they never gave up a nonhuman representation of the ideal of beauty. This doubtless illustrates the curiously close connection between Muslim and Jewish law, which developed even after the early period of Islam, when the Muslims had not yet begun to occupy themselves with the problem of artistic representation. It was after the first period in Islam that the Muslims took over from the Jews a repugnance to graven images—based on a misunderstanding of an Old Testament interdiction—with the result that in all Arabic-speaking countries it became impossible to represent plastically the human body. Though in painting such representations were not entirely unknown, they were rather rare. To make up for this, the Muslim Arabs devoted themselves to abstract decoration, in the celebrated arabesques (whence the word) and very often in a remarkably elaborate development of the ornamental possibilities of the Arabic script.

The Muslims borrowed wholesale from Byzantium, especially in art and architecture; here too, accordingly, they carried on the Greek heritage in an amplified and modulated form. The prejudice against the plastic reproduction of the human body led the Muslims to heighten still further the abstract and formal elements in Byzantine art.

Islamic art as such, that is, painting, had no influence on the work of any particular individual artist in Europe, nor was there any great movement in painting that received any stimulus from Muslim influences, beyond, perhaps, the extensive use of Eastern motifs for ornamental purposes and more especially the use of the graceful, sinuous Arabic script for decoration. There is no denying that in the minor arts, as well as in architecture, Islam transmitted a great many elements that while perhaps not native to the genius of the first Muslim Arab conquerors themselves were in any case transmuted into a fusion that may now be thought of as characteristically Islamic.

Christianity had substantially transformed the non-Christian art that was prevalent in Syria and Egypt. Reanimated by the new spirit of Christianity, a new fusion of many factors was effected, producing a coherent and impressive series of works of art. In Persia, on the other hand, the native Persian regime of the Sassanids that had been dominant for centuries had engendered an extraordinary artistic revival, in which Hellenistic elements current since the invasion of the country by Alexander the Great had combined with various imports from central Asia into a uniquely Persian culture of striking magnificence.

These two cultures, Byzantine and Persian, were what received the Muslim Arabs; though both cultures were mutually hostile, they were both equally offensive to the austerity of primitive Islam.

What seemed to the Christians to be deeply religious symbolic exposition seemed to the Muslims mere idol worship. Overextending the Jewish prohibition of graven images, they regarded the iconography of Byzantium as both blasphemous and quasi-magical. In Persia, too, the very splendor characteristic of Persian art seemed to the primitive Muslims somehow effete and offensive.

Beginning with barren mosques as an architectural norm, the Muslims soon assimilated the cultures of the peoples they had conquered and became great builders. Since their religious prohibition of human form inhibited the development of statuary, they turned to carvings of stone, wood, and other materials, in which they displayed great skill.

In the fine arts in general, except for architecture, the Muslims could not compete with Europe, but as the direct heirs to many ancient crafts that were still unknown in Western Europe, they took over, developed, and transmitted the traditional "workshop practice" of arts current in the East. Design became predominant in the treatment of all sorts of objects as such, whether of ordinary everyday utility or for ceremonial usage. Patterns of an endless variety were so integrated with the shapes of the objects that they seemed inherent parts of them rather than external, man-made ornamentation. The recurrences of intricate patterns seem to have impressed the eye of the Muslims in much the same way as the Western ear may take pleasure in melodic rhythms. In fact, decorative design may be thought of as the most eminent minor art developed by Islam.

Even the absolute religious prohibition on the use of the human form was in fact contradicted in objects made for secular utility. They were never allowed in the mosques and were not exactly tolerated in a principled way by any particular sect, but they were in common use for purposes of utility and simply winked at by the more broad-minded.

The sole specifically Arab contribution to Islamic arts may be the Arabic script itself, which was early developed into a remarkably beautiful creation whose pietistic justification was its having been used for the writing down of the Holy Quran. The script was early imported into Europe; in the first few centuries after Islam coins from Muslim mints were widely current in Europe, in use by Christian rulers who were evidently unaware of the meaning of the words and regarded the script as merely ornamental. Snippets of Arabic lettering, sometimes quite illegible, as well as decorative details imported from Muslim sources, became more and more common in Christian European craftsmanship.

The astrolabe, an ancient Greek astronomical invention perfected by the Saracens, was one of the objects brought back by wandering scholars from Islamic seats of learning. Metalwork in gold and silver was a great speciality of the Saracens; the extensive use of inlay, enameling, pottery, especially the celebrated "lustered pottery" ceramic and tilework, elaborate glasswork, and perhaps European heraldry, at least as a systematized science with its own nomenclature, which seems to have evolved during the Crusades, may be traced to Islam. In Persia, Syria, and Egypt the textile arts, which the Saracens were to develop so efficiently, had already been highly evolved when these countries were conquered by the Arabs. The European demand for rich textiles, especially silk, developed rapidly with the growth of the commerce with the East. The Saracens also served as transmitters of Chinese art, especially after the conquest of China by the same Mongol house that overthrew the

Abbasids. Thus Europe received Chinese influences through Islam as well as the characteristic Islamic fusions of Indian, Persian, and Byzantine work. The elaborate working of ivory was a great Saracen speciality. Carpets came into Europe from the East primarily as a luxury commodity monopolized by rich connoisseurs, though in the East they were an ancient commodity regarded simply as an indispensable necessity for daily living. They reached Europe as early as the fourteenth century; by the sixteenth they were current commodities. It was the Persians who developed the art of carpet weaving to unprecedented heights, in the sixteenth century, when the Arabs had long since been steeped in stagnation.

Curiously enough the production of books, generally considered a uniquely European device, owes a great deal to the Islamic Empire, for it was the Saracens who first introduced Europe to the use of paper, an ancient Chinese invention that the Muslims learned about when in 704 they captured Samarqand and some Chinese craftsmen, who taught the craft to the Muslims. Its westward spread from that date was uninterrupted; it was brought into Christian Europe in the twelfth century, becoming common there after the thirteenth. Paper was of course to become essential for the manufacture of books in the industrial quantities made possible by the invention of printing. The East also contributed the actual design of bookbindings during the fifteenth century, when Venice acted as a transmitting chamber for the diffusion of Islamic art styles. Books bound in Italy during this period had a very Oriental look; and a peculiarity common to Muslim bindings, the flap folding over on the front to safeguard the edges, still persists today in certain special accountants' bindings.

The common contacts between Christians and Saracens had already begun very substantially in Spain and Sicily and throughout the Mediterranean, where Muslim ships ranged freely from one end to the other. The legends of Saracen magnificence that had become current throughout Christendom were suddenly confirmed by the ocular evidence brought about by the Crusades, when a vast host of Christians, from every corner in Europe, abruptly came into intimate contact with a society that surpassed their own parochial experience in every respect. The arts of Islam became familiar, and as Italian traders laid down direct lines of communication with the ports of Syria, commerce with the East was systematized and an immense variety of Saracen products began arriving in Europe. Since the West was in the throes of its extrication from the Middle Ages, the Islamic pursuits had a directly fructifying effect on the sumptuousness and the lucrative arts attendant on the Renaissance. Technical procedures in Renaissance Europe were broadened and extended; Saracen designs were studied with great interest and care and were adapted to European tastes. Even outstanding figures like Leonardo da Vinci immersed themselves in Saracen patternwork, a rich source for the exploration of many potentialities in the development of design.

With respect to architecture, the strange thing is that although the original Arab Muslims, most of them nomad in origin and disposition, had no knowledge whatever of any elaborate form of building and thus had to prompt the characteristic Islamic fusion of disparate cultural elements, the resulting blend became a unique illustration of the characteristic Islamic art form. Thus in spite of the Arabs' ignorance of architecture, the fact remains that at all times and in every country that turned Muslim, architecture developed and retained an unmistakable singularity despite the diversity of its constituent elements. Though various local schools of craftsmanship and design had been technically vital in giving rise to Islamic architecture, they were all fused into a new style.

All the nations conquered by the Arab Muslims had various styles of building already in being, from Persia to Spain. It now seems clear that the original monopoly of Rome, taken for granted with respect to Western medieval architecture, has been shaken. It is necessary to look farther east, to Armenia, Mesopotamia, and Turkestan, for further influences on European architecture.

Indeed, the reaction of even the first Bedouin out of the desert to the architectural splendors they came in contact with must have been remarkably lively, since as early as the reign of the Umayyad caliph Abd-al-Malik (692–705) a whole series of splendid castles, palaces, and mosques was already under construction. It was in this—purely Arab—reign that the Dome of the Rock in Jerusalem, considered by many a most remarkable work, was built. Though the very earliest mosques leaned almost exclusively on architectural models found in the societies they were governing, such as the mosque built in Qayrawan by Uqba ibn Nafi and the celebrated Mosque of Córdoba, which made use of Roman columns and capitals, Saracen artists later developed a characteristic style of their own. There is an incredible variety of minarets, for instance, throughout Islam, including the Arabic-speaking world, made of all sorts of materials and in all sorts of shapes. Some of the hallmarks of this characteristic Islamic art are horseshoe arches, pierced stone windows, intricate tracery in stucco, and the immensely elaborate geometrical designs and arabesques used to cover large flat surfaces.

Domestic as well as military architecture was also developed; the patio, for instance, was evolved in Islam and disseminated wherever the climate allowed for it. It seems to have had the purpose of giving freedom in the open air to the substantial female component of the large households, and so the living rooms were built around a central patio while showing a dead wall to the public streets. Trees, flowers, pergolas, and fountains were a natural accompaniment of this idea of a house.

In military architecture the medieval castles in Europe owed their battlements and machicolations to the Muslims.

A splendid example of the flexibility of Islam in its formative period may be seen precisely in the field where one might have expected the most orthodox single-mindedness—the formation of the religious law.

Here too the Muslims, beginning with the Muslim Arabs themselves, rapidly ingested the culture of their subjects; the first stages in the evolution of Muslim law were characterized by a very comprehensive receptivity. Not only is the substratum of Muslim law not at all original with Islam, it has still less to do with the Quran. Islam merely provided the formal structure into which elements borrowed from other civilizations were integrated. During the first two centuries of the existence of Islam, a central complex of ideas and institutions came into being that went very far beyond the Quran, both in content and in implication, and the Muslims, because of the central position in their intellectual life of the Quran and its unquestionable authority, regarded them all as Muslim. The foreign elements were admitted in a flood at first, later being rejected because they were then held to be incompatible with this focal complex, though the focal complex itself was due to unavowed foreign influences. That is to say, the declared authenticity of the borrowings as being Islamic in origin was held out as a criterion for the rejection or acceptance of other borrowings; it was in fact a mere fiction. Whatever the provenance of a given element, however, this mythified attitude constituted a powerful homogenizing element. The focal complex of ideas and institutions was permeated by what was declared and of course felt to be the authentic Muslim attitude. Ultimately all foreign elements were completely digested and colored over to such an extent by this Muslim tint that only a vigorous process of historical analysis and investigation—quite alien, of course, to believing Muslims—could even discover what the origin had been.

Thus the complex of ideas and institutions itself became the assimilating factor with respect to foreign elements in general. In a way it adumbrates the assimilating power and the spiritual paramountcy of the Islamic sacred law as the ideal to be looked up to over and above the actual practice of the Muslim community, once the two became separated with the growth of state structures.

This whole cultural process can be seen as a unit. To the eye of an outsider it looks as though the positive content of Muslim religious law were being molded by external influences; for the insider, unaware of being molded by historical factors, it looks as though the central complex of Muslim ideas and institutions were merely expanding. Thus there was achieved a certain equilibrium between the religious ideal and the actual practice of society, an equilibrium that lasted for many centuries until the impact of the West in our own era practically shattered the whole society and in any case had a decisive effect on the intellectual superstructure, so that in the modern period Islam once again was to be reduced to the wholesale borrowing of ideas and institutions from outside.

A striking instance of the way in which ancient and authentic ideas were molded to the new demands of Islam may be seen in the very institution of Islamic law that is regarded as basic by the religion itself: the notion of the Sunna of the prophet—his life style—as being binding religiously.

This concept of Sunna is a primordial Bedouin idea. The Bedouin tribes were completely bound by tradition and precedent, doubtless a natural thing in the circumstances imposed on them by nomadism. This old Bedouin idea of Sunna was a major obstacle, practically insurmountable, to every novelty. Islam, the most remarkable novelty ever seen in Arabia, had to overcome the traditionalism of the tribes, and it did so, as has been indicated, only after a severe struggle, and then only because the opportunities for material expansion and aggrandizement presented themselves at a favorable conjuncture. But after the victory of Islam over the Bedouin, the novelty itself was encased in the ancient mold of traditionalism. It was Islam that now was the right thing, something made sacred by tradition and custom, in short, a Sunna.

The highly educated new converts naturally brought their inherited ideas, including legal ideas, into their new religion, though of course the early Muslim specialists in religious law never *consciously* adopted any foreign legal principles.

Thus ideas originating from Byzantine law, the canon law of the Orthodox church, from the Talmud, and from Persian law permeated the evolving religious law of Islam during the first century after the Hijra, the period of incubation, so to speak, of the new society. These comprised, for instance, methods of legal disputation and reasoning, including the "consensus of the scholars," a device for imposing authority.

All this permeation took place during the first or early in the second century of Islam. It is curious to remark that Muslim religious law seems to have been unaffected by foreign influences that the pre-Islamic Arabs had surely been in touch with, since they had, after all, come in contact with Byzantine administration, if only superficially, before the conquests.

In the general transosmosis that took place throughout the Islamic realm, the Arabs, while busily assimilating the substance of the Hellenized East, set a stamp of their own, of course, on society as a whole, quite apart from their language and the rudiments of Islam. In family life, for instance, the polygamous clan life of the Arabian Desert became a very general pattern throughout the areas homogenized by Islam. Family life was a far larger and more diffuse unit than the narrowly monogamous circle both Judaism and Christianity have made familiar. A typical feature of Eastern houses came to be a huge conclave of any number of individuals from the clan as a whole, all related to each other in varying gradations. The family itself, in fact, was conceived of as a mere unit of the more significant larger unit, the clan, and, beyond that, the tribe. Family kinship, understood in this broad sense, may be said to have been a decisive factor in sociopolitical life under both the Arab Umayyads and the cosmopolitan Abbasids.

At the same time the Arabs assimilated a good deal even in this field of relations between the sexes. The primitive heroic tradition of the early Muslim Arabs tended to exclude women from public life; this tendency, reinforced by Muslim piety as such, was given physical expression by still another tradition, ultimately based on Persian and to some extent on Greek habits. This is the tradition, rather contrary to the relations between men and women among the Bedouin, in which friendship and, for that matter, sexual relations between men are considered the height of refinement. This tradition has survived, of course, to our own day, and in the Middle East is most firmly rooted in Persia and Egypt.

Summing up the cultural achievements of the Islamic Empire, we can see them as based on two remarkable facts:

For the first time in history, the vast territories extending from the borders of India and China to Greece, Italy, and France were brought together by one language and one religion. Thus a single society was set up that encompassed the ancient, lush, and ramified Mediterranean culture of the Middle East—Greece, Rome, Israel, and the ancient Near East—and the opulent culture of Persia, in its turn linked to the impressive cultures of countries still farther east. This made Islam a great melting pot in which peoples of many previous faiths, cultures, and languages were able to live together in the bosom of the neophyte Islamic society, a new civilization that set its stamp on the fusion of these various elements.

The second and perhaps the most striking feature in the atmosphere, so to speak, of medieval Islam was its extraordinary tolerance. Though Muslims might have been just as self-assured about the advantages of their religion as medieval Christians, they saw no reason to anticipate the issues of divine punishment and reward in this world by persecuting those who disagreed with them. Muslims were perfectly content to rule communities of unbelievers provided the unbelievers paid up. As long as Islam was politically dominant there was no reason, according to its own theory, why it should not remain at peace with lesser faiths, which were subject to certain social and legal disadvantages but otherwise were quite free to enjoy the economic and spiritual benefits, including religious freedom, that the Islamic Empire granted all its subjects.

The Muslim theory of history was designed to create an intellectual edifice in which Islam organically was situated at the apex, since Muhammad, by claiming that his revelation merely consummated and thus superseded the prior revelations of Judaism and Christianity, thereby assimilated all past history into the history of the Islamic community. Thus the Muslims inherited ready-made, so to speak, a philosophy of history comprehending all previous epochs and giving them all an enduring rationale. In this way the Muslims could accept, in a sense, both "Peoples of the Book," regarding them as the bearers of a revelation that was valid but outdistanced. The progress of Islam, after all, had been a striking contrast to that of Christianity, which had plodded steadily along for a few centuries as the faith very largely of the socially underprivileged before it became the state religion, whereas Islam had had a bewilderingly rapid triumphal march during the lifetime of its founder and a still more kaleidoscopic career in the generation or two after his death.

V

A MEDIEVAL CONFRONTATION: ISLAM AND CHRISTENDOM

An analysis of the confrontation between Islam and Christendom on an intellectual level, paralleling the historical confrontation that took place with the massive incursion of the Muslims around the southern borders of Christendom—and carried by the Ottoman Turks into the heart of Europe—would be too vast an undertaking for a history of the Arabs.

Yet it may be sensible to make a broad comparison between the two systems as they faced each other at the zenith of Islam and on the eve of the European Renaissance, which ultimately led to the domination of the world by Western institutions and ideas.

To do so I shall go back to the roots of Islam considered as an ensemble, for though in Muhammad's mind Islam came into being very largely derived from Jewish sources, it quickly grew into a complicated edifice under the shaping influences of Hellenism and Christianity. Thus the ultimate parallel was to be found between Islam and Christendom, itself, to be sure, the repository of numerous Jewish elements.

• • •

A basic difference between Islam and Christianity, considered as religions, is, of course, that while Muhammad was in time magnified beyond the mortality he acknowledged in the Quran, his personal cult as such never became the actual basis of his religion. It is true that tradition transformed him, a man who expressly disclaimed miraculous powers, into the greatest wonder-worker in history and from a mere mortal into a potent intercessor with God, but faith in these qualities of Muhammad's performed no redemptive function in the framework of the Muslim system.

Contrariwise, though there is unmistakable evidence in the Gospels that Jesus had no intention of founding a new religion, and in his own mind was merely treading one of the traditional paths of Judaism, the magnification of Jesus went altogether beyond the bounds of mortality. His transformation into an actual God, the Light of the World, the Savior of Mankind and the Lord of the Universe, made Christainity a religion essentially different from either Islam or Judaism.

Nevertheless, if we keep this difference in the kernel of the matter clearly in mind, it is illuminating to consider the immense structural similarities between the two systems.

Nothing can be more misleading than the assumption, still widely held, that there was something inherently alien to Europe, and to Christendom, in the Islamic cultural complex that emerged and took shape with such speed. I should like to phrase the opposite contention as concisely as possible: For Western Europe and for Islam the Middle Ages are essentially identical.

This basic fact has been veiled over by the historic conflict between the two religions and the societies they represented, so that the differences between them were systematically exaggerated at all times, and by the articulation of Islam in a new and difficult language.

Nevertheless, in the Middle Ages, when Western Europe was securely fixed under the dominion of a rigid ecclesiastical hierarchy that had exercised the most pervasive effect on effervescent Islam and in return received in the domain of philosophy priceless material by way of repayment from Islamic scholars, there was an overriding identity in both the religion itself—with the above-mentioned basic exception—and the concomitant view of the world that overlaid it.

As indicated above, there is only a thin thread connecting the vast edifice of medieval Islam with the preaching of Muhammad. Granted that Islam was launched by Muhammad's ideas and political career, it was enriched so substantially by the introduction of the vast reservoir of ideas in the two great civilizations it collided with during the first few decades after Muhammad that a totally different entity came into being.

Even in Muhammad's own life, to be sure, we quickly become aware of the subordinate relationship even his own religious experience put him into with respect to Islam. We have the convenience of learning this, even though in a fragmentary and obscure way, from his own sayings in the Quran. This makes Muhammad's religious inspiration infinitely easier to follow that the thinking of Jesus, distorted by the labors of the first few generations of Christians that produced the present text of the Gospels, the product of a long-drawn-out, contentious travail whose orientation, in the perspective of the Crucifixion and Resurrection, was bound to be altogether different from Jesus' own point of view.

Muhammad's ideas, borrowed almost wholly from perhaps vague and nebulous communications from various Jews and Christians, were nevertheless in acute contrast with the prevailing views of his pagan countrymen. On the other hand, there is no doubt that there were countless christianizing currents flowing vigorously throughout the Arabian Peninsula. Many scholars incline to the view that if there had been no Arab folk migration and if Muhammad had not had his inspiration around this time, the whole of the peninsula would nevertheless have been more or less christianized within a short period of time.

Christianity's chief contender at this time was Judaism, which was spread out both in the south and in the north of the peninsula and had already made numerous converts, though it may be doubted, on the whole, whether the ritual demands of Judaism could ever have been accepted by the Arabs themselves in any numbers, since Christianity of the purely formal and superficial kind that was much practiced throughout the peninsula in the many places where it had found a foothold laid far fewer burdens on its believers than Judaism.

In addition to the Christian, Jewish, and ancient Semitic cultic elements, there was also a certain admixture, as it seems, of Zoroastrian notions, attendant on the nearby presence of the great and prestigious Persian Empire.

All these cultural fragments floating about, being carried back and forth by all sorts of wandering merchants, partially and wholly converted Arabs, in different kinds of settlements and so on, worked together to form a fairly confused picture in Muhammad's mind, aggravated perhaps by his never having actually read any of the scriptures these ideas had found full expression in. As I have indicated, it is clear that Muhammad never read anything either in the Old or the New Testament. Everything he says in the Quran indicates mere hearsay, based, moreover, on slightly heterodox excrescences. It may in fact well be this that explains the extreme simplicity of his own message: He may have been looking for the lowest common denominator of all the various ideas he heard references to, which, indeed, was what made up the content of the Quran.

Perhaps the thing that struck Muhammad most weightily concerning Judaism and Christianity was the earnestness with which life was taken, surrounded as he was by the pagan indifference and hedonism of his countrymen. The actual *idea* of a supreme god was not unknown, after all, even among the pagan Arabs. In addition to the three goddesses worshiped in Mecca, there was their father, known even before Muhammad as Allah, a name he simply took over and adapted to his own purposes. But the notion of Allah remained a mere idea; there appears to have been no desire to enter into a direct personal connection with him—there was no need to get anything from him. The idea of a mutually binding relationship was quite alien to the pagan Arabs.

It was at this point that the influence of Judaism and Christianity first made itself felt. The idea of a reckoning, of a Day of Judgment, in which certain conduct would be rewarded and other conduct punished, in which the worthy would go to Paradise and the unworthy to a fiery abyss, was the basic idea that suddenly overwhelmed Muhammad around his fortieth year; he became appalled by the triviality of mere everyday life.

This amplified conception of God as the paramount, just, yet compassionate Creator entailed the annihilation of all lesser gods. Indeed, once this idea of a single all-powerful god occupies the mind, emotional as well as cerebral logic would seem to entail the utter elimination of lesser gods as being not merely weaker but as being simply nonexistent, just as in the course of the Hebrew Scriptures we can see as though on a palimpsest the various stages in the attainment of the idea of the One God.

In the case of Muhammad, too, the idea of monotheism was

accepted without question, so much so that in the beginning of the Quran, reflecting Muhammad's Meccan period, it is simply laid down without even the polemical emphasis it was to acquire in the course of Muhammad's differences with the pagans and later, also, with the Christians.

From this vision of God as One and the sole Creator of the Universe, there was still a big jump to be made. The Jews and the Christians had sacred books, the word of God sent by him to the Jews through Moses and to the Christians, as Muhammad thought, through Jesus. Who was going to do the same for the Arabs? The jump was perhaps not so great in ancient Arabia as it might be today, since there was a deeply rooted tradition among the pagan Arabs of seers and fortune-tellers. Muhammad's vehemence in rejecting such comparisons may imply a certain original affinity, something like the early Christian indignation at any comparison between Christianity and the pagan mysteries.

Muhammad's primitive message, in short, was a duplication of a Jewish and Christian formula: Just as Jesus and John the Baptist came saying, "Repent, for the Kingdom of God is at hand," so Muhammad originally said, "Repent, for the Day of Judgment is at hand." He then went on to say that this had been revealed to him by God as God had done for Moses and Jesus, and that salvation could be achieved only by surrendering to the will of God as revealed by Muhammad (whence the word "Islam," or surrender).

Thus even in the very beginning, in the shaping of the kernel of Islam, at the very core of what was to become a gigantic sociopolitical and religious edifice, Christianity played a cardinal role.

For Muhammad Judaism and Christianity were perfectly valid revelations of God's word, which was, of course, changeless and timeless. It was only in the revelations to man that that word had hitherto differed in its exposition. Muhammad had also heard of the Jewish Messiah and of the Christian idea of the Paraclete, though he never identified the latter with the Holy Spirit. He made great play of references to the notion of someone coming after Moses and after Jesus and took them to refer to himself, as in Sura 61:6, where the coming of an "Ahmad" (*i.e.,* Muhammad in another form) is predicted by Jesus, "son of Mary" to the "Children of Israel" after —curiously enough!—"confirming the [Jewish] Torah."

Muhammad's religious ideas surely had a most profound effect, perhaps more far-reaching than the religious development of any other individual, including Jesus, since it is by now, I think, clear and accepted by most noncommitted opinion that while the figure of Jesus of the Cross generated a new religion, nothing of the kind had been in Jesus' mind itself.

Perhaps the most obvious point about Muhammad's own evolution was that as far as he was concerned, Judaism and Christianity were identical with respect to the idea of a single God. Indeed, since he rejected the Trinity, the divinity of Jesus, and hence the Redemptive Crucifixion, this was in fact so. He thus assumed both an identity between these two religions and between both and his own message; then to justify his own appearance and make it essential, he laid down a relationship of sequence. In this way he set up a linear series in the realization of the divine determination to save the human race, beginning with Adam, going through Abraham, Moses, and Jesus, and coming to an end with himself—the "Seal of the Prophets"—after whom all further prophecy was superfluous.

Muhammad was not at all disturbed by the fact that the previous prophets were sent to different peoples. Their careers had, he thought, the same pattern: Though sent to disbelievers and forced to go elsewhere to find their following, they are ultimately successful. It was this rather curious train of thought that made him reject Jesus' death on the cross as a malicious invention of the Jews. Thus, although influenced by Christianity in the perhaps primitive form in which it was making the rounds of the peninsula, Muhammad seems in fact to have missed the central point and rationale of the whole religion. According to him, the Jews crucified (sic!) someone else, presumably for purposes of their own, and Jesus ascended in glory to God.

Quite unaccountably, accordingly, Muhammad did not understand the meaning of the Redemptive Crucifixion, the cornerstone of Christianity and of the Christian community of his own day. As he with experience came into closer contact with both Jews and Christians, he fell into the habit of simply declaring out of hand that any discrepancies between his own ideas and Judaism and Christianity were mere inventions, naturally pernicious. In the beginning, before knowing anything in detail of these two religions, he simply referred doubters to the basic facts as expressed by them, as a sort of warrant of his own authority. The theory was that for him to have hit on such tremendous truths he must obviously have been in contact with God and had enough divine inspiration to quell all doubts. Then, as he came to know more about the other religions and came up against differences that were, after all, quite important, he summarily dismissed them as falsifications. He could only have maintained this seriously, to be sure, in a society almost totally unacquainted with any form of scholarship, so that the question "How do you know that?" would have been unthinkable. By the time Islam had acquired solidity, on the other hand, it was already strong enough to put forth its own polemical claims without bothering much about intellectual cogency.

An oddity is that though he rejected all the basic ideas of contemporary Christendom, he accepted the story of Jesus' supernatural birth, which must have seemed to him an acceptable miracle for a prophet; in any case, it may have appealed to his primitive listeners.

Muhammad's knowledge of Christianity, accordingly, is quickly summed up: He thought it revolved around the miraculous birth of a child to Mary, the sister of Aaron (evidently an echo of Miriam in the Old Testament); the child is dedicated by a vow of her mother's to God and lives in the temple under the protection of Zacharias, who in due time is to father John, the forerunner of the Holy Spirit. Jesus' birth is announced to Mary; she gives birth to him under a palm tree, whose dates she eats, next to a fountain. On being reproached on her homecoming, she merely points to the child in the cradle, who suddenly speaks and says he is the Prophet of God. Later Jesus performs all sorts of miracles; he makes birds out of lime and has them fly about, heals the blind and lepers, resurrects the dead, and even brings down a covered table from Heaven. The Jews do not believe him, but his disciples, of course, do. He is not killed, but is simply taken to God. The Christians differ as to his death; the Jews, however, have invented his death on the cross.

It is clear that Muhammad must have gathered these scraps from hearsay; he could hardly have heard them from any sort of Christian, however ignorant. Some scholars have thought it likely that he was in contact with a particular sect with heterodox beliefs, but the scrappiness of Muhammad's information, combining a few apocryphal with some canonical fragments isolated from the basic dogmatic ideas, makes it seem unlikely that it was in any sense organized even by a heterodox sect. Hence Christianity did not influence him in any direct way; he simply gathered together a few of its general traits and assumed that they constituted the religion itself.

Indeed, the only thing Muhammad accepted as Christian was simply the fact of its existence as a revealed religion with an actual founder. In addition, a number of features common to both Christianity and Judaism—prayer, ablutions, chief days of prayer, a sacred book, angels, and prophets, etc.—were also thought by him to be inherent in any really religious community. He took them over as a matter of course.

While in Medina Muhammad worked loose from his original idea that he was simply preaching the same message as Jesus and Moses. By that time he was aware of the great differences between what he was saying and the actual elaboration of that simple message in the formal structures of Judaism and Christianity. He had come to the conclusion that the only way to bypass their contradictory claims was to go back to a predecessor of both Moses and Jesus—Abraham himself, who since he was revered in both religions could be taken as his own predecessor *par excellence*. He then placed Abraham in a direct connection with the ancient Arabian cult of the Ka'ba, a sacred shrine in which the "Black Stone" was walled up (this stone had been worshiped by the Arabian pagans and was to be revered by the Muslims in their turn). Thus Islam evolved into a religion that became more and more Arabian, while simultaneously, however, retaining the universalism that was to prove decisive after the Arabs achieved their military successes and Muhammad ascended to his paramount status as "Seal of the Prophets."

He made one vital concession, however, that was to prove very important to the believers in the two religions Muhammad regarded himself as having outgrown. The new Muslim community was to fight Jews and Christians only until they paid a tax; otherwise they were to worship freely. Thus the motto of the new movement was not "Islam or death!" Islam required of Jews and Christians, as the "Holders of the Scriptures" or "Peoples of the Book," that they accept the political dominion of the Muslims—no more.

There was at first not the smallest question of fanaticism with respect to Christianity. Indeed, for the first few decades after the establishment of Islam no fuss was made at all about worshiping in the same building together with Christians. The disadvantages Christians were vexed by were due not to their religion but to their status as tolerated subjects of a vanquished state. This was indistinguishable, to be sure, from the Muslim point of view, for which religious affiliation and political status were part of the same entity. In any case, the difference in religion was merely ancillary; it was not until later that the absolute contrast between the two religions was gradually built up, perhaps during the first century of the eruption of Islam.

Strangely enough, it seems to have been Christianity itself that played up the contrast between Islam and Christianity onto the religious level. This is paradoxical, but when one thinks of the relative indifference to religion on the part of the Muslim Arab conquerors, aside from the immediate entourage of Muhammad, it is an irresistible conclusion. Just as the Muslim conquerors learned everything they knew from their subjects, so they were to learn intolerance, which at this period in Christendom had reached unprecedented heights. But that was to happen well after the germination of Islam.

Though Christians as well as Jews were considered second-class citizens, they were not prevented from achieving the highest positions in the country, including the Wazirate, especially during the first few centuries of Islam. Even during the long-drawn-out period of the Crusades, which again represented a Christian initiative in the renewal of hostilities with the world of Islam on a religious basis, Christian high state functionaries were commonplace, as was demonstrated by the voluminous Muslim polemicizing against them. Despite isolated or sporadic cases of religious zeal among Muslims, and despite an occasional instance of actual persecution, the general attitude of Islam toward Christians and Jews was one of tolerance. Even in the eleventh century it was possible for Christian funerals to move through the streets of Baghdad in all the trappings and emblems of Christian faith; chroniclers mention disturbances as exceptions. In Egypt Christian holidays were enjoyed to some extent by Muslims too, in sharp contrast with the situation in medieval Christendom, where such a state of affairs would obviously have been unthinkable.

For that matter the Christians of the Middle East, who had

fallen out with the Byzantine religious authorities and for a long time had been persecuted, regarded Islam even from their own point of view as a lesser evil than the Byzantine state church, which, indeed, I have pointed out as one of the principal causes for the Muslim successes at arms. In addition, Islam as a mixture of state and church organization naturally recognized the Christian community as a state-within-a-state and allowed it its own jurisdiction and, in the beginning, even its own administration. The bishops were turned to as representatives of the community; the tax offices were set up in the churches. All this was bound to appeal to the clergy as a vested interest; indeed, in this somewhat contracted form it realized an ancient claim of the church itself.

This relatively harmonious state of affairs naturally worsened in the course of time. The Crusades, the bitter wars against the Ottoman Turks, followed by the dynamic expansion of Europe itself later, widened the gap very substantially between Islam and Christendom. As the East itself grew more religiously minded and less secular, it too began to develop what had originally been the Christian excess of zeal in religion and accepted a more and more religiously minded view of the contrast between Islam and Christendom.

Nevertheless the notion of a fanatical hatred of Christianity among the Muslim conquerors and their successors is a fiction constructed out of whole cloth by the fanatical Christians of the Middle Ages and later. It has come down to us today as a legend believed in even by scholars.

The Quran is to Islam what the Gospels are to Roman Catholicism. Just as Christianity made its way by fusing with Hellenism—which indeed definitively shaped it as a religious system—so Islam was bound to collide with Hellenistic Christianity, since its own intellectual structure was also rooted in Hellenism. This is the ultimate explanation of why the religious culture of the Middle Ages is the same in Islam as in Christianity; the deepest roots of both are organically linked.

But as a glance will indicate, the Quran was a book of preachment; it had no doctrine. It laid down a few laws, but had no system. Islam began as a piercing battle cry—it meant no more and no less than the recognition of the Arabs' dominion, the oneness of God, and the focal importance of Muhammad's mission.

It is out of the question that the untrained companions of the prophet and their immediate successors elaborated the structure of Islam. It was the new converts in the conquered countries, as I have pointed out, who accomplished the immense intellectual feat of harmonizing Muhammad's sermons and his few positive requirements with the religious culture Islam ran into on its triumphal procession. The rapidity of this evolution is remarkable; only a few centuries went by before Islam had become a vast intellectual edifice, Greek philosophy and Roman law had rooted themselves firmly throughout the structure, and all the details of life, from ideal ethical conduct to the prescribed hairdo, came under a complex system of regulations. Here, to be sure, Islam merely retraced the steps of all the great religions of the world, which began with something essentially very simple and then added countless doctrinal and behavioral layers. Religious innovators may act on religious impulse, but when translated into a credo for whole communities that impulse quickly becomes, if not atrophied, at any rate encapsulated in a sociointellectual edifice encompassing both the impulse itself and the dense cultural web it finds lying in wait to ensnare it. Just as Christianity evolved in the Hellenism of the old Middle East and would be unthinkable without it, so Islam found waiting for it the great complex of Christianized Hellenistic cultural and social institutions it simply adapted to its own purposes.

If we imagine the situation of nascent Islam, we see a desert people barely unified by a rather simple slogan and instantly placed as rulers in direct contact with vast, densely populated areas with very ancient cultures. While still only partially united —particularism, after all, instantly began eroding the Arab political community—it is called upon to interpolate itself into the complicated social structure of ancient countries like Babylonia, Persia, Egypt, and Syria, whose complex administrative systems, set up over a period of a millennium, would have surely been quite impossible for desert-dwellers even to grasp at first, to say nothing of manipulating plastically.

Despite the obvious impossibility of this, many scholars have believed that the primitive desert Arabs were capable of introducing a wholly new sociopolitical structure to these ancient communities. This was, to be sure, a natural consequence of studying the sources closest to the events, the Arabic chronicles themselves, which naturally take as their starting point the total originality of Islam as the beginning of everything. Since the conduct of the prophet and his companions was regarded by them as an article of faith and a model for all conduct, so they naturally conceived of the state structure they were living under as created by their initiative. And in a way there was something to this; the organization of the ruling caste was so thoroughly, indeed so parochially, Arabian that at first the institution of the Clienthood had to be created as a method of integrating rulers and subjects and of allowing the subjects to become inducted into a religious-cum-state community whose claim on them was, after all, universalistic.

Nevertheless this was merely external and formal. Inwardly all essential administration was kept quite intact; otherwise the chaos would have been indescribable. This was demonstrated even in such a basic thing as customs duties. The united Islamic Empire kept the ancient customs stations at the borders, long since wiped out, of the older countries overwhelmed by Islam. For the Arabic chronicles, also, the only legitimate forms of taxation were the Islamic legal taxes; everything else was considered to be an abuse. What is odd here is that such "abuses" were identical with the forms of taxation inherited from Byzantium and Persia, which lived on into Islamic society.

From this point of view material culture presented largely the same picture as administration. The same economic and cultural problems that had beset declining antiquity kept on besetting the Arab conquerors, who simply carried them forward. Indeed, these problems were bound to go on demanding a solution unless a cataclysmic upheaval in social relations had taken place, such as in fact did take place when the Teutonic tribes overran and shattered the classical world they had irrupted into. That is just what did not happen under the Muslims, who simply went on living the life of the Middle East in a new language.

At first sight it may seem that socioeconomic problems are inherently less malleable than spiritual problems; nevertheless, what happened in the spiritual sphere was largely the same as what happened in the socioeconomic sphere.

Islam, a simplistic, unelaborated slogan or two, collided, as the religion of the ruling caste, with the immense intellectual entity of Christianity, heavy with the thought of Greece and Rome. Obviously, the purely material military accomplishment of the Arab conquerors was going to settle nothing in the spiritual tussle that was bound to ensue. Once the Islamic state was abroad, the collision took place primarily with Christianity, in spite of substantial Jewish admixtures. The Jewish influence on Islam was exercised primarily at its source, on Muhammad himself; Jewish ideas laid their stamp not only on the Quran itself in large measure, but on the oral tradition that was later fixed in writing. A good deal of Jewish influence was of course already quite discernible in Christianity, and a certain number of Jews came over into Islam bearing their own culture and ideas into the new milieu. Curiously, it was the Middle East Christian communities above all that had a special regard for many of the prescriptions of the Hebrew Scriptures, which they regarded as binding. In any case there can be no doubt that Jewish thought very largely spawned the contest between Islam and Christendom. The whole attempt to imbue the tiniest details of life with the religious spirit was another aspect of the parallelism between Islam and Christianity that may illustrate the debt of both to Judaism.

Christian thinking naturally included not merely the whole of Hellenistic thought, but also the ideas current in Persia and elsewhere throughout the ancient East. Thus an immense variety of traditions and ideas, all more or less predigested by Christianity, was transplanted *en masse* to the new universe of Islam.

The transplanting of this immense fund of new religious notions was facilitated by the fact that it had already been assimilated into another and related language, Aramaic, which not only is quite close to Arabic but had already served as an agent for the transmission of different cultural concepts from both Greek and Persian into Arabic long before the rise of Islam. Even before Muhammad, many Aramaic words for cultural concepts and for things had penetrated into Arabic; by the time the Arabs pressed collectively into the cultivated societies of Byzantium and Persia, the process of translation and retranslation into and from Aramaic took on enormous dimensions. The mere fact that it was natural for Arabic to lean directly on Aramaic, which was a fully privileged cultural language in both Persia and Byzantium, in and for itself implied a direct Christian influence.

The process of cultural transmission was intimately bound up with the composition of the Quran itself, with its interpretation as a standard of life and thought for coming generations, and with the Arab ruling caste's intermingling with and assimilation to Aramaic-speaking Christians and Jews.

Since in the Quran itself constant reference is made to Christians and Jews as holders of previous authentic divine revelations, when it became a question of discovering what countless completely obscure passages in the Quran actually meant, it was a matter of course to appeal to Christian and Jewish scholars. This in its turn was immensely accelerated when the Christians and Jews, mostly the former, converted to Islam *en masse* since they were vastly superior in learning to the primitive Muslims who were the initial believers in Islam. They thus became the natural teachers of the whole community once an intellectual upper class came into being that, though Christian a little while before, was now converted and thus in a position to attract the ablest of the Arabs themselves.

Now, once these former Christians became Muslims they did not, of course, simply forget everything they had been thinking beforehand. Indeed, the Muslim message had been so simple that it had to be fitted out with an apparatus of ideas, so to speak, in order to lend it the weight necessary to serve as the consolidating element for a superstate. It was inevitable for them simply to take along their supercargo of traditional attitudes and ideas and once having accepted the simple formula of Muslim allegiance to deck it out with a body of notions that were in fact the product of centuries of Christian thought. It was thus the recently islamicized Christians who accomplished the major task of adapting the new religion imported from the desert—that is, from a society with only a few fragments of culture to begin with and those largely inappropriate for its new milieu—to the needs of a highly complex and ramified society.

This process of adaptation absorbed the Christian elements of the society in two different ways; the subject population was partly the raw material and partly the teaching staff. From the point of view of the newcomers from the wilderness, Christian culture was accepted as being inherently superior, both spiritually and materially.

What this implied, concretely speaking, was that the Muslims accepted from a Christian milieu the most fundamental element in any philosophical approach—*the questions that had to be answered.* This alone entails an identity between the roots of the two cultures.

The asking of questions does not, to be sure, imply that the answers will be the same. There were some situations in which the Quran, did, after all, have an answer that went against Christian belief; the differences between the religions were substantial. Indeed, with respect to the one cluster of questions that had been ignored by Muhammad himself—the divinity of Christ and the Redemptive Crucifixion—there was an absolute and violent contrast.

Yet despite the importance of this basic cleavage between the two religions, it constitutes, in one way, merely the apex of an intellectual structure; countless practical questions are not affected by it. Thus Christian ideas came into play even in situations where in a purely theoretical way the Quran seemed to be laying down some categorical attitude. There was, of course, very often a lively polemical accompaniment to the whole question of transmission. In the case of a weekly paramount day of prayer, for instance, the notion of a Sabbath was taken over, ultimately from the Jews but more immediately from the Christian Sunday. Yet it was slightly transposed. First it was made a Friday, then the character of the Friday itself was changed to make it *only* a day of prayer, but not a day of leisure; business was to go on as usual once prayers were finished.

But even this was exceptional. Whenever the Quran gave the slightest encouragement by its wording, a Christian interpretation both of practical details and of the whole world outlook had a decisive effect.

There was indeed the groundwork for this development in the very nature of the situation, since Muhammad, who had begun as a visionary in Mecca, had become a prince of this world in Medina, but without taking such a distinction seriously. Indeed, very consistently, from his point of view, his attitude was the same both before and after: If God had spoken to him and conveyed certain instructions, what could be more natural than conducting the whole of life directly under the instructions of the Creator himself? The Envoy of God was also, quite simply, the head of a state. This basically simple, indeed absolute, concept immediately led by implication into treating the whole of life as a religious exercise. Here, too, of course, Islam coincided both with the general Jewish outlook, especially as elaborated by rabbinical Judaism after the destruction of the Jewish temple in 70 A.D., and also with the ecclesiastical Christian view of the whole of life and the whole of the world as being bound together in the perspective of God. The whole attitude was, in short, what we think of as medieval.

Thus, although pious circles in Medina may have had the time to think out the structure of Islam as a theocracy during the period when they were shunted into a backwater by the transfer of the Islamic capital from Medina to Damascus, in reality it is adequately explained by nothing more than the logic of the intellectual development due to the political fortunes of the Islamic state, as well as by the incontestable preponderance of former Christians among the new converts to Islam.

In details, as well as in the basic principles of jurisprudence, dogmatics, and mysticism, there was an unmistakable Christian inspiration. The fittingness of the whole process may also be judged as a realization, longed for from the beginning, of a specific Christian desire for exactly the same kind of state on earth as Muhammad and his immediate entourage and followers merely implemented consistently. The very evolution of the Islamic theocracy was in reality a Chirstian ideal; it was a society in which religion governed all life and all its manifestations, from the state to the individual.

It was in just the unfolding of this question, of the total encapsulation of life within religion, that the growth of Islam showed such an unmistakable Christian stamp.

Christianity, as it had evolved under the initial impact of the idea of the kingdom of God, supplemented very quickly by the parallel notion of the second coming of Christ and by the wave of asceticism of the first few centuries of the Christian era, was essentially an otherworldly religion. Its hopes and aspirations were linked to the idea of personal salvation in a real Heaven and hence were rooted in a fundamental denigration of the life of this world.

This is in striking and irreconcilable contrast with Judaism, the other component in the genesis of Islam. Devoid of any religious doctrine concerning personal salvation and indifferent to the question of Heaven, Judaism could concentrate all its energies on the Here and Now. Islam took over most of its basic ideas from both Judaism and Christianity, but in respect to otherworldliness, mysticism, and asceticism, under the influence of the great Christian masses during the first few centuries of Islam, it very obviously elected Christian otherworldliness.

Christianity had, however, been driven to compromise through becoming one more current, though a dominant one, in the complex play of forces in declining antiquity. It had succeeded in almost suppressing the joy of life of the classical world, pleasure, the arts and music, and secular education. These were all converted into mere ornaments of religion, with no other sanction or justification; in the era of Islam's emergence the Christian world was completely enthralled by the denial of the world.

Yet Christianity could not utterly annihilate the joy of life. While denying the value or enjoyment of sexuality, it could not destroy the impulse itself. It could shackle but not eliminate economic activities. It had, in short, been driven to a compromise with the powers of this world, and it was, of course, perhaps the most important of the temporal powers of the age despite its negative and otherworldly aims.

Islam entered into this spiritual atmosphere of early medieval Christianity with two faces. One was ascetic, the other was a completely joyful acceptance of this life as it is here, partly because of the original hedonism of the early Muslim Arabs, and partly, perhaps, because of the Jewish strand in it that emphasized the charms of this world. Even from a religious point of view, after all, the world, too, is God's handiwork. There was something basically unascetic about Islam in one of its incarnations: "There is no monkdom in Islam" is a traditional summing up of this basic tendency in early Islam. In Muhammad's own life, after all, the compromise reached so arduously by early Christianity was present as it were full-blown: Muhammad was both a religious visionary and a prince, indeed a very hedonistic prince of this world. But when Islam penetrated the Christian milieu of the Byzantine Empire, taking over millions of Christian subjects so many of whom became so quickly converted to Islam, it had to go through the same compromise with this world on a much loftier and systematically developed intellectual plane.

The compromise worked itself out in stages, so to speak. At first Islam was permeated by the ideas of Christian asceticism; then a tendency rose to counter this, summed up in the above phrase aimed at monkdom. This tendency in its turn, however, was suppressed, if only because in Muhammad's actual preaching—as distinct, perhaps, from his life—the real world was sneered at in favor of the Other Side. This, together with the continuing pressure of a still largely Christian milieu, produced a major current of asceticism within at least the intellectual structure of Islam, and at least in the pious sector of the population.

In this way, despite obvious differences in form, a certain parallelism between the two religions grew up. The Christian clergy came to be paralleled by a class of scholars of texts and traditions that, even though it lacked the magical powers of the clergy as sacred figures, buttressed by the magical potency of the sacraments, nevertheless enjoyed a venerated status as interpreters of the sacred texts. This class was largely modeled on the Jewish rabbis. It was, after all, the unanimous opinion of the scriptural authorities in Islam that set the norm for the community, and in fact orthodoxy was quickly established within Islam as a counterpart to what it was in Christendom. Everything tacitly agreed to by the class of scholars was obviously approved of by God himself and was, accordingly, valid for all time. This is obviously almost a copy of the Roman Catholic Church, more especially of the attitude of the Oriental Christian churches, which even though incapable of creating an actual clerical cult against the practice of early Islam nevertheless created a clerical class as tutor for all religious thought and hence—in that age—for all thought *tout court*.

Christianity had a very direct effect, also, in worsening the status of women in evolving Islam. Muhammad himself, to be sure, had thought of sexuality with so much enthusiasm that it would have been impossible to take an attitude toward marriage that was clearly hostile; the Quran is full of indications that the married state is blessed as such. Though Christianity had originally been rather hostile to marriage and indeed sex itself, it had been bound to accept both as part of its compromise with the world. A persistent and pervasive Christian influence, however, may be discerned in the overemphasis given by Muslim tradition, as distinct from the Quran itself, to warnings against the female sex. The position of women was made so much worse by the elaboration of the Tradition, as against the general attitude of the Quran, that the development of the Tradition in an antifeminist way, in the direction of denigrating the entire sex, must be traced back to the cultural milieu in which Islam developed. It may be true that this notion of feminine inferiority coincided with the generally inferior status of women in the ancient East—quite distinct from the relatively high prestige and freedom of women in Bedouin society—but as that notion permeated Islam it did so in the garb of Christianity, with all the religious prestige of the hostility to marriage that had been a strand of Christian thought since Saint Paul himself.

It is doubtless in connection with this Christian hatred of marriage that a prohibition of nudity crept into Islam. The prohibition of exposing anything more in the ancient Christian church than the face, hands, and feet probably hung together both with the disapproval of sexuality generally and with the opposition to the far more open and joyful life of the ancient pagan world. This was paralleled very directly by numerous Muslim statements against nudity, but though these can be regarded, rather plausibly, as being derived from the Quran, it seems more reasonable to consider their articulation as being built up on Christian views; they occur very often in connection with warnings against the public baths.

Differences between the two religions are of course undeniable, yet in comparison with the over-all similarity of the cosmic stance, what is most striking is the convergence, especially since the convergence often takes place from diametrically opposed starting points.

The basic points are these: This world is ephemeral; we are only transients on our way elsewhere; there is hardly any point in making ourselves more comfortable in a mere way station. This was the justification of the modesty and simplicity, indeed, the barrenness of private houses in the Middle Ages, in both East and West. The churches and mosques on the other hand could be decked out with appropriate magnificence; they were in the service of God.

This is supplemented by the condemnation of every pleasure, even in necessary things when taken to excess. Eating is necessary, but eating twice a day is sinful. The same goes for clothing and other pleasures. It is extraordinarily significant that later Islam could portray the earliest caliphs—who lived after all perfectly comfortably, a large part of their lives being devoted to pleasure—only in the guise of Christian saints.

Death is supposed to be dwelled on day and night; when the

Bible and Quran are read aloud, at every mention of the Day of Judgment an outburst of tears is indicated. From this point of view the whole age was in fact an age of weeping. Tears as a gift of grace were characteristic of the whole attitude toward life in this vale of tears. The tears were directed, of course, not at mere misfortune, but at one's own irremediable sinfulness. When it came to misfortune, the indicated attitude was one of patient resignation to the will of God, of endurance and stoicism. If a loved one is lost to death, tears are not indicated at all; that would be like the pagans who mourn vociferously. For the God-fearing, the proper stance is the dignified acceptance of a good thing: "We belong to God and it is God we go back to," is what a pious Muslim is supposed to say on the news of an unexpected loss. In this way as in others, something originally adumbrated in the Quran was articulated in ways closely similar to the habits of contemporary Christendom.

This fundamental and irreconcilable contrast between God and the world, identical for both cultures, is all the more markedly of Christian origin since philosophically, after all, Islamic thought was dominated, in theory, by God as the unique Creator of everything. In which case, of course, there was no reason not to revel in his handiwork, not to enjoy oneself in the contemplation and exercise of all his gifts, the pleasures and functions bestowed on us by him, and so on, which would still be the attitude, say, of devout Jews. Islam was influenced, that is, by the corpus of Christian thought even against its own theoretical formulations to such a degree that the very concentration on modeling one's own life after that of Muhammad, the ultimate paragon, was a precise imitation of the Christian practice of the Middle Ages, when for the devout Christian the only justifiable goal in life was to produce as close a copy as possible of the life of the Savior, down to the very stigmata of the cross.

In this way, even the boundless authority in Islam of the Sunna —Muhammad's style of life—is probably to be explained as a parallel to the exemplariness of the life of Christ, just as Muhammad himself, despite his own claims, was elevated far above mortality by the development of Muslim tradition, though, as I have indicated, never so far as the transcendency of Christ.

This is reflected in another way in the comparison of the ideal of poverty that was taken over into Islam from Christian thought.

The imitation of the Christ is demonstrated by a life of poverty and destitution. This corresponds with the actual life of Jesus, at least with what the earliest tradition said of him and with the humiliation of his death on the cross. In the case of Muhammad, however, it does not fit at all, since after undergoing his religious experience Muhammad ended up as a temporal prince who thought possessions a sign of divine favor.

Nevertheless Muhammad's followers were to learn to praise poverty as an ideal for the community; consequently this must be taken as a sign that what was being thought of was not Muhammad's own Sunna, but something taken over *in toto* from a Christian or Christian-minded milieu. Islam is revealingly full of contradictory statements that show the contending influences of Christianity and what may be thought of as "pure" Islamic ideas. Muslim tradition is full of praise of poverty and of warnings against the temptations of riches; at the same time there are many sayings pointed in the opposite direction, doubtless arising out of Muslim anti-Christian ideas. Scholarship has found practically the whole of the Lord's Prayer in traditional Islam. Even the notion of loving one's enemy, which surely would have seemed rather absurd to Muhammad, made its way into Muslim tradition, as did the celebrated Gospel remark, of Jewish origin, to do unto one's neighbor as one would have him do unto oneself (Matthew 7:12 and Luke 6:31), as well as many similar ideas. By "neighbor," of course, only one's own fellow believers were meant, by Muslims as well as Christians.

Thus the whole field of Muslim ethics was permeated by ideas stemming from within the Christian community.

There is an organic similarity, too, between Islam and Christianity with respect to the state.

In antiquity the state was not singled out for disdain—quite the contrary—but beginning with Christianity there arose a hatred of the state insofar as it lay outside the sphere of religiosity. In its beginnings Christianity had to contend with the state for recognition, later on for dominion. Islam began quite differently, as a mixture of state and religion combined in one entity that soon became no more than a theocratic ideal. An ideal theocracy was developed by Muslim thinkers down to the most minute detail, and although it was never in fact realized on earth, the sanction of religion was always required if a ruler was not to feel like a usurper. In a way, the lip service of later Muslim rulers who maintained a purely temporal power sanctioned by the rubber stamp of some shadow caliph, for instance, was in complete harmony with the Christian view of the state. For this reason the cosmopolitan, universalistic Abbasid caliphate benefited enormously from the ferocious hatred developed by later Muslim theoreticians against the purely Arab secular rule (the "kingdom") of the Umayyad house, and, though it is quite possible to develop this theme in a purely logical way on the basis of Muslim theory, the revulsion of later generations for the Umayyads is best explained as a reflection here, too, of the Christian hatred of the state as such.

Islam and Christendom had a similar attitude toward many basic economic questions, though in Islam a certain respect for an "honest merchant" was more in evidence. In any case, both religions show a sharp opposition to the taking of interest and to any speculation in goods, which for the Middle Ages came under the heading of usury. This was taken in a very broad sense in both religions and polemicized against with great vigor. A characteristic and decisive point involved in all definitions of usury was that one of the elements in it was an absence of work done by oneself, so that in both religions trade was in sharp contrast with manual labor, which was highly praised as ideal in both the East and the West.

The enormous elaboration of public charities in both Christendom and Islam had an identical motivation—the care of the poor, needy, disabled, and underprivileged not for their own sakes but as a form of self-castigation, to serve one's own selfish purposes by lightening the paupers' burdens in this world in order to improve one's own claims on the benefits of the next. The same may be said of the similarity between both religions with respect to the regulation even of everyday table manners, in which Islam actually outdid Christianity, though by building on Christian models.

It may be said that society, the individual, economic life, and ethical behavior were uniformly under the influence of Christianity in early Islam. This is also so with respect to magic, which, though proscribed, was so only as long as it meant pagan magic. Once it was sanctified by association with religious purposes, it lived on in both Islam and Christendom in appropriately changed forms that very often conserved ancient Babylonian ideas. Both religions also believed in the validity of dreams insofar as they coincided with religion: They were considered either divine revelations or those made by deceased notables. The very having of dreams was taken as a sign of divine favor, as was the appearing to others in their dreams. These folkish attitudes were doubtless common to the general milieu of the Middle East in the broadest sense, but the manner in which these folk notions were elaborated seems to have been largely due to Christian influence, as was the idea that the intercession of pious celebrities through prayer had a peculiar efficacy.

A peculiarly striking illustration of the manner in which an idea can be developed on the basis of a borrowed model is the celebrated Muslim interdiction on reproducing the human body, which was a problem that the Muslims found awaiting them when they came into the Byzantine cultural milieu.

Byzantine society had had a lengthy debate about the legitimacy of reproducing images of the body. Constantinople was subjected to immense pressure to forbid the worship of images, though the pro-image party in the church succeeded in securing its authorization. The Muslims, encountering the same problem, that is, taking the problem seriously, perhaps under the influence of Jewish ideas based on what seems to be a suggested, though not a complete, interdiction in the Book of Genesis, decided the question in the opposite sense. Countless sayings were then attributed to Muhammad in the traditional manner. The interdiction made its way into canonic law; indeed it is still binding today, though to be sure its force has been substantially weakened.

Thus Islam and Christianity regarded the same problem as paramount and simply gave it different solutions, each one, however, shaped by the same intellectual attitude. In the case of Christendom a certain advance was made, or at least a loosening; in Islam the same stage of thought was clung to. The differences for the evolution of art need no comment here.

The same is true for the development of the ritual obligations, which had originally been left in a quite shapeless state. Since religion was held to govern all acts of life, however, it was bound to dominate all duties and obligations, toward God as well as toward one's fellowmen.

The pervasive code of ethics underlay to a large measure the elaboration of a Muslim cult, which in the lifetime of Muhammad had been quite unknown. The mosque as a place for general worship had not been known in Muhammad's lifetime, nor had any ritual been worked out for fixed ecclesiastical functions, including public ritual and the sermon. There had been hesitant impulses, but nothing came under regulation until the Muslims left Arabia and came into intimate contact with foreign cultures in which Christians as well as Jews had fixed forms of general worship. There was, in fact, no social grouping that had a vested interest in developing such cultic activities. It was not until a social grouping developed under the influence of Christianity that a complex system of public worship was actually worked out. In the beginning, for instance, public prayer was simply led, that is, participated in, by the commander of a unit or the governor of a province or even the caliph. Eventually, however, a whole complex of ritual prescriptions was created that served the interests of the social grouping in charge of religious affairs. Ecclesiastics attempted to overspread all life not merely with a churchly but with a cultic coloration, and even without the presence in Islam of priestly intercession or the potency of sacraments there was a gradual development of quasi-cultic customs in weddings, for instance, and funerals.

Still more important was the working up of an official form of divine worship, forms for the regulation of the passage of time, and the introduction of a sermon, all of which gradually took on the characteristics of a cult. Something that originally, during Muhammad's lifetime and far into the Umayyad age, had been done impromptu or *ad hoc* became congealed in a cult. An instance of this was the introduction of a prayer for the caliph, which was to become an emblem of or indeed the acknowledgment of the caliph's sovereignty and which was doubtless borrowed from the notion of praying for the emperor.

The gradual equipping of the mosque evolved so that it was no longer merely an enclosed space but was articulated into functional sections such as the pulpit, borrowed from the Christian church. Before mosques were even built, long after Muhammad, prayers were held behind a lance thrust into the ground. Later, praying corners were arranged in mosques, borrowed wholesale from the Christian milieu that lay in wait for the Muslim conquerors. Despite the many obscurities in the evolution of the Muslim cult, there can be no doubt that it was largely dependent on the various elements of Christian custom that it was destined to absorb so much of.

A revealing instance of the cultural byplay between Christianity and Islam can be seen in the evolution of mysticism.

In its nature, of course, mysticism, as an emotional bridge between the individual and what is experienced as a direct, oceanic union with the divine principle, contradicts all forms of positive religion. The ultimate mystical attitude leads directly to a fusion, or at least a blurring of the distinction between the personal ego and the divine. It annihilates the very foundations of any religion ramified into dogmatics and hairsplitting intellectual analysis and speculation—seen most luxuriantly in Christian theology—as well as all doctrines of good works and obligations.

In Islam the outstanding rationalism and ritualism of the Holy Law produced a mystical countermovement that in spite of rationalist hostility rooted itself in Islam for centuries and in the modern period set its stamp on the entire culture.

The Holy Law made access to God difficult for emotional spirits, if not impossible. Those hankering after communion with the divine could not be satisfied by the arid speculations of dogmatics, which were just as rationalistic as the law itself. In both cerebral speculation and legalism the chasm between man and his Creator was unbridgeable. Thus a new way was sought to establish an inward personal relationship between man and the divine. This way was the direct, emotional sensation experienced by the individual soul of the nearness of God, indeed, of the very permeation of the soul with the intoxication of God, of ecstasy.

Islamic mysticism provides a striking parallel to Christian mysticism, for Islam proved to be elastic enough to incorporate all strands of mysticism, without the smallest warrant for the process to be found throughout the Quran or in the development of Muslim dogmatics. To be sure, Islamic mysticism was not influenced by Christianity exclusively; it parallels Christian mysticism by going back, though via Christianity, to roots common to both, doubtless to the neo-Platonic, pantheistic circle of Dionysius Areopagita, the source of the fruitful notion of the mystical love of God. It also, perhaps, goes back to influences stemming directly from central Asia, Persia, and India, though a more specific point of departure, to be sure, might be found in the Quran too, in the Quranic preaching of the Day of Judgment with all its ascetic implications.

The concept of Nirvana, for instance—Arabic *Fana*—liquidates monotheism altogether, yet Muslim orthodoxy, though theoretically opposed to any form of mysticism, in practice was very tolerant. Everything in the circle of pantheism was absorbed into the practice of Islam and tacitly allowed to coexist peaceably with the rather rigid monotheism of the Quran and with the later development of Muslim dogmatics. Islam proved to be just as tolerant in this way, in fact, as it was with respect to other faiths. At the expense, perhaps, of logic, it allowed for complete freedom of belief by the negative device of a refusal to insist on a formal creed in the domain of emotion or philosophy.

Since ecstasy enables the believer to achive union with God, it also leads, most naturally, to enthusiasm. In Islam this led to an immense proliferation of sects and orders divided according to the means chosen for the attaining of ecstasy, such as the various Dervishes and Faqirs (Persian and Arabic respectively for "Beggar"; another sign of the asceticism inherent in mysticism, like Sufi, the "Woolwearer").

With obvious differences these Muslim orders somewhat resemble the monkish orders in Christendom. The goal of ecstasy, achieved by dance or recitation—as in the dancing, twirling, or howling Dervishes—led to a severe spiritual discipline. The beginners, mere putty in the hands of the initiates, at first merely lose consciousness; then they gradually ascend to a higher degree of initiation into knowledge until finally an awareness of absolute fusion with the Godhead is attained. The goal is to achieve closer and closer communion with God, with fewer and fewer interruptions. Ultimately the howling Dervishes, for instance, after beginning by yelling over and over again "Hu! Hu!" ("He," *i.e.,* God), then going through a phase of yelling "Thou! Thou!" arrive at a point of yelling "I! I!" At this point, of course, the notion of the One God is seriously dented. The "spiritual exercises" devised by Ignatius Loyola may be regarded as an aftereffect of the immense heritage left by Islam in Spain during the fourteenth and fifteenth centuries.

This sort of mystical emotionality was bound to be combated by the legalism of orthodox Islam and has been to this day, though with no decisive effect. The religious internalization and the growing feeling of religious responsibility made the whole mystical attitude very attractive to masses of Muslims, though it was Persian mysticism especially that gave the movement its most fruitful expression.

The cult of saints arose as a stage of intercession for anyone prevented for one reason or another from participating in the mystic cults. In their essence, saints are just as alien to the basic principles of Islam as pantheistic mysticism; but once the person of Muhammad was projected beyond the human scale by the magnifying labors of later generations, the incorporation of saints into the Muslim system became perfectly feasible.

The magnification of Muhammad was itself doubtless the result of the competition with Jesus, an unprecedented wonder-worker, after all, if only through being identical with God. The founder of Islam could not simply be outdistanced by Jesus as an object of veneration for primitive minds. Islam could not hope to match the basic tension of the Christian drama, with the crucifixion of a divine being as the central act in the cosmic struggle of good and evil, but on the level of appealing to a formerly Christian milieu already accustomed to unprecedented claims being made on behalf of the figure regarded as the author of the religion, it was possible and perhaps inevitable for Muhammad, too, to be elevated beyond mankind.

This process of magnifying Muhammad took place very rapidly, within the first century of the new faith. He was decked out with all the various categories of miracles encountered in the Gospels—healings, resurrections, multiplying of food, and so on. This transmission took place both in the form of the direct borrowing of specific features and in the paralleling of the process itself that had already been gone through by Christianity only a few centuries before.

The above sketch of the religious parallels between Islam and its Christian predecessors and contemporaries has omitted dogmatic thought, which might seem to be the one area in which the intellectual differences between the two religions would emerge with unmistakable sharpness.

Nevertheless, despite the fundamental disagreement between the two religions, considered in terms of their cardinal postulates, the actual working out of the dogmatic edifice that served as the underpinning of those postulates also displays some striking parallels.

Muslim dogmatic preoccupations revolved around three basic

questions: free will, the attributes of God, and the timelessness of the divine word.

Clearly, the very notion of posing such questions is itself a direct reflection of an intellectual debate that had been going on in Christendom ever since its inception. The contest between Christians concerning free will and the attributes of God reached a probably unprecedented degree of heat in the ferocious struggle around Christology. In the Quran, which was bound to serve as the starting point even of such abstruse matters, there is any amount of support for both views, since for Muhammad it was child's play to believe both in divine omnipotence and in personal responsibility.

The feeling that the problem *was* a problem was simply taken over from Christianity; for that matter the solution, too, was found in an imitation of Christian hairsplitting and casuistry. The absolute all-power of God was naturally acknowledged, while human responsibility was salvaged by the claim that the human being had been given the freedom to assent to or dissent from the possibilities God had implanted within him. In this way two things were accomplished: The ideal justice longed for by reflective natures was reconciled with the more or less blind fatalism of the masses, that in its turn was not particularly Muslim, but was simply the outgrowth of ancient Eastern piety.

The question of the attributes of God, by definition doubtlessly completely irreconcilable with the very idea of his absolute oneness, also became a Muslim preoccupation. The problem itself surely reflects the intellectual desperation undergone by so many generations of Christian philosophers in their attempts to reconcile the Trinity with monotheism, a reconciliation that was entailed by the necessity of somehow squeezing Jesus, elevated to the status of a deity in accordance with the heritage of antique paganism, into the totally insulated concept of the One God, the heritage of Jewish monotheism.

The problem was solved in a way that while ingeniously casuistic is not, perhaps, wholly satisfactory philosophically. It was maintained that the only attributes to be predicated of God are negative—he has no beginning or end, no limitations and so on. Yet the Quran does apply qualifying adjectives to God. Orthodox opinion defended these by saying that such adjectives can be applied to God because they *are* applied to God, but they do not mean the same thing as they would if applied to men, and for that matter we have no idea what they do mean. Thus both problem and solution seem to have been borrowed by the Muslims from Plotinus and other neo-Platonists.

The third problem that preoccupied Muslims—Was the Quran created in space-time or not?—is a manifest reflection of the Christian struggle concerning the acknowledgment of the eternity and absoluteness of the Logos as well as of God. The solution contrived by Muslim thought is a plausible, though essentially self-contradictory idea. The conclusion was that there were two Qurans, one the eternal and uncreated Quran existing together with God, the other Quran as created by God and revealed through Muhammad. The notion of an eternal and uncreated Quran in existence since the beginning of time together with God clashes, of course, with the strict simplistic monotheism characteristic of Islam; however, it was convenient to disregard this. The contradiction does not seem to have bothered too many people. Indeed, this curious doctrinal tangle may be thought of as an ultimate triumph of Christian dogmatic speculativeness over the simplicity of the original Muslim idea. In a sense Christian speculation shattered the basic principle of Islam, somehow all unbeknownst to the believers.

This adoption by Islam of conceptual speculation, what the Greeks had called dialectic, was due not to the world of antiquity as such but to that world as transmitted through the Christian universe that young and unformed Islam was enveloped by when it first left its native deserts. Islam took up dialectic initially in order to make use of the same weapon its intellectual opponents used so skillfully. Once it had taken over the weapon, however, it found it handy for all relevant contexts. In practice this meant all human activities, because of the overriding need to contain all of life in a web of piety.

It was this that led directly to the creation of an edifice that reflected the influence of medieval Christian scholasticism, which perhaps did more than any other institution to make medieval Islam and Christendom such twins. This remarkable institution, which with all its utter sterility displayed such intellectual adroitness within the rigid framework of the premises accepted by the medieval church as sacrosanct, was an inevitable outgrowth of the adoption by the Muslims of the Greek dialectic and all it entailed.

On both sides, in short, a systematic philosophy was produced by the common adoption of the legacy of antiquity. At bottom both systems were ecclesiastical, though on each side the philosophical system was responsible for some breaches in the partitioning of life that had been set up by religious institutions. It was just on this terrain, in fact, that the Muslims were to pay Christianity back some of what they owed it, since the Saracens may legitimately be considered to have been the intellectual leaders of the Middle Ages.

The intimate intellectual symbiosis of Islam and Christianity during the first centuries of the Islamic efflorescence is explicable only on the basis of an inherent identity of attitudes. The function of religion in life, as well as the actual philosophical questions regarded as essential, made it possible for the further elaboration of Christian ideas and inspirations that was to be accepted by the Christian West without difficulty. The Christian roots of Islam, in all its intellectual manifestations, are what explains the very possibility that the West could accept the philosophical and theological ideas worked out in Islam and that a vital intellectual exchange between the two cultures could take place at all.

Just as primitive Islam found no difficulty in absorbing so much of Christian thought just because Muhammad in his basic ideas had already been formed by Christianity as well as by Judaism, so it was possible for Western Europe to digest so much Muslim thought just because it had roots in Christian soil. In the last analysis, both systems were rooted in the Middle East and in the intellectual universe of the Middle East.

It may be said in passing that the Jews played a peculiarly seminal role throughout this mutually fecundating interchange between the sister cultures. The Spanish Jews especially not merely transmitted cultural commodities back and forth between Arabic and Latin but also helped create part of the edifice. They were also fundamental in facilitating the exchange of ideas that was constantly taking place through countless translations and orally, too, through the symbiosis of Christians and Saracens in southern Italy, Sicily, Spain and along the far-flung highways of commerce.

Another question of general interest may be asked: How was it that medieval Islam so quickly, in only a few centuries, was on so much higher a level than medieval Christendom, from which it had, after all, learned its major lessons?

From the seventh to the thirteenth century it may be maintained that Western Europe had suffered a profound disruption of culture as a result of the Teutonic irruptions into the former Roman Empire. In the East, by contrast, Islam proved so adaptable that without destroying anything it simply created a framework for an organic fusion between various peoples and various cultural elements that went on functioning without interruption. The whole of the Middle East changed no more than a few religious dogmas; its whole general attitude as well as its social structure remained unimpaired.

It is true that from the thirteenth and fourteenth centuries on, after the Teutonic peoples had calmed down and had been absorbed into a newly evolving sedentary society, cultural progress was resumed once again and this time rather quickly outpaced the Middle East, at this time beginning to decline, but till that happened it was only natural for youthful Islam to come on the scene as the heir of the Hellenistic, Orientalized mongrel culture of the Middle East. Because of this it easily gained the upper hand, intellectually and in other ways, over Western Europe, in which the Oriental Christianity that also had its roots in the ancient East only very slowly gave shape to the society that had been thrown into chaos by the Teutonic invasions.

The superiority of Islam was heightened still further, in comparison with Western Europe, by the singular fusion of ancient Eastern cultural elements—especially those stemming from Greece and Persia—the terrain for which had already been prepared by what had been happening for centuries during the constantly increasing Asiatic influence on Hellenisms. Now, ever since the Sassanid regime at the latest, Persia had been the principal source of culture for the whole of the East; the Byzantine debt to Persia is notorious. Even before Islam the material culture of Persia had made its way westward directly; after Islam the same process went on indirectly. The same may be said for spiritual culture without even going into the question of the effect of Persian ideas on the Christian schools of Persia, which gave the Muslims their first contacts with Greek as well as Persian literature.

This lush spiritual background, which Islam was able to benefit by because of the factors referred to above, may explain the enormous cultural influence exercised by the Islamic world on Christendom. A very minor though unmistakable illustration of this is to be seen in the countless loan words made to Europe from Islam via the Arabic language that so quickly became its lingua franca.

Not only words for material objects came from Arabic. Basic economic concepts and ideal expressions of even such a characteristically European institution as romantic love and chivalry, as well as the foundations of our entire natural history and even influential ideas in philosophy and theology, swiftly seeped into practically all European languages and became an integral part of Western culture.

Indeed, the use of the phrase "Muslim philosophy" is misleading; what is meant is actually an extension of the philosophy of late antiquity. The interaction between Christian culture and Islamic culture is in reality a case only of the interaction of two more or less parallel branches of the same mongrelized culture of declining antiquity, which first worked in a Christian form on Islam and then in an Islamic form on Christendom.

Christian scholasticism had at first based itself on mere fragments of Aristotle and had lived on neo-Platonic ideas. With the Muslim conquest of the East almost the whole of Aristotle was rediscovered and the Saracens began exercising an important influence on Western Europe, doubtless through the wealth of material they discovered. The achievements of Hellenism in natural history and in logic led to an extension of the dialectic and also to an intellectualistic metaphysics. This harmonizing of church dogma and the Greek knowledge of natural history was woven into a system such as we encounter in Thomas Aquinas' Summa. Thus, since philosophy was a mere handmaiden of religion, the primary influence of the Saracens at first lay in the elaboration of an ecclesiastical view of the world.

As time went on, however, the specifically Muslim view of the world began exercising an influence independent of the Saracen role in the transmission of Greek knowledge. Muslim tradition had always been very strong in its emphasis on reasonable information. Knowledge among the Saracens, too, was originally praised only for its utility with respect to religion, but gradually reason as such came to acquire an independent role. This had not been rejected by orthodox thinkers as long as it coincided with the tradition itself, but now, under the influence of Aristotelianism, especially as developed by Ibn Rushd (Averroës), reason was transformed into a force that was felt to be hostile to faith.

The doctrine developed by Ibn Rushd out of Aristotelianism was quite simple. As a method of bypassing faith, without simply contradicting it, the point was made that there was a dual system of truth: one based on faith, the other on reason. By acknowledging both criteria simultaneously it was possible, of course, to stay orthodox, but the danger was obvious; the Church grasped it immediately.

In the course of this diffuse, complex intellectual struggle many Islamic ideas were absorbed into the religious life of Christendom. These ideas were later intertwined with the roots of the Renaissance, which freed the Western world from the ecclesiastical fetters of antiquity and ultimately eroded the traditional view of the world as it had been formed by the Eastern church. The new world that came into being, with the creative contributions of the peoples in the north and west of Europe, was finally able to develop the ideas of classical antiquity without the tincture of an Eastern tradition.

At this stage Islam and Christendom were still more or less on the same level, but as the West gradually put the twilight of the church-ridden Middle Ages behind it, the greater grew its superiority over the East. The churchly garments woven in the East came to be thought of as asphyxiating, and by the time a new world came to be constructed it retained no more than fragments of the traditional Eastern point of view.

As for the East, it is still in the process of self-transformation. Even today it is still shackled by the Middle Ages, despite the recent and increasingly energetic struggle of so many Muslin communities to reform themselves and assimilate the heritage of Western Europe without losing their own communal identity. Yet it remains a struggle. Modern Muslims, no matter how thoroughly imbued with a European education, still seem to operate, even in journalism, in medieval scholastic style filled with respect for proofs based on a combination of traditions and reason.

There is, of course, no reason to think this will go on indefinitely. Christendom also took centuries to shake loose its chains and become to some degree master of its own intellect. The medieval Christian attitude was ultimately broken up by quite un-Christian ideas that eventually assimilated and fused with Christianity as a whole.

It must be emphasized again that in spite of individual dogmatic differences, which if this comparison had been limited to Islam alone would have stood out in sharper relief, the two communities constituted essentially a single entity during the Middle Ages. Even today, with the increasing divergence since that time, if we keep in mind the world outside both Islam and Christendom taken together, we see the striking basic similarity between the two. With all the strangeness Westerners feel inherent in Islam, if they make a point of comparing pagan Africa, say, or India or China, with Western Europe, they at once become aware of how much closer they are to Islam than they had thought. That is because despite the exotic encrustations that Islam has taken on, from the Western point of view, the cultural roots are somehow closely intertwined and in many areas identical.

Islam was also shaped, of course, by Zoroastrian and Jewish ideas, but the same thing might well be said of Christianity, too. The more one penetrates into the arcane areas of religious history, the more obvious it is that everything is dependent on something prior. The religious experience that might have been undergone by the founder of a religion is bound to come to terms with the cultural elements that it finds ready-made in a given culture and that it finds itself wrestling with in the course of its expansion. The ultimate secular triumph of any religion is perforce no more than a compromise, since no matter how important religion is, it is, after all, merely one among many conditions of the human spirit.

Today the ecclesiastical tradition of the Middle Ages and for that matter religion as such are being battered to bits; in Islam the break-up is only just beginning.

All these factors are relevant to the Arabic-speaking peoples of today insofar as they too have in their great majority been formed by medieval Islam and by the lengthy period of social and intellectual stagnation that followed it. I shall make an attempt in later chapters to discuss the rise of the modern Arabic-speaking peoples, the genesis of Arab nationalism and the changing sense of identity of these peoples, and their stance in the modern world.

VI

THE EMPIRE CRUMBLES: THE TURKS COME IN: THE LONG STAGNATION

THE Abbasid dynasty was to have a very long life—some five hundred years, from the eclipse of the Umayyads in the middle of the eighth century until the Mongols' destruction of Baghdad in the middle of the thirteenth century. From a technical point of view it lasted still longer, since the glamour of the Abbasid caliphate sustained a long line of mock-caliphs under the protection of the Mamluks in Egypt for another three centuries, until the Ottoman Turks conquered Egypt in the beginning of the sixteenth century.

Yet even while the Abbasid caliphs were still ruling in their own name, their power had become a shadow. Their authentic sovereignty had vanished by the middle of the tenth century, with the transfer of all real power in Baghdad first to a Persian dynasty, then to one of the countless Turkish dynasties that had by then infiltrated Islam to such an extent that the Arabs, eclipsed initially by the Persians through the rise of the Abbasids, were now obliterated as a self-conscious grouping beneath the political and social weight of these Turkish newcomers.

In one dynasty or another the Turks were to become the overlords of the Islamic realm. This is not meant to imply any unity, which was not established until the rise of the Ottoman Empire. It simply indicates that whatever the political currents and crosscurrents in Islam, the effective political leadership was in the hands of another non-Arab people.

The bypassing of the Arab element in Islamic society, signalized most dramatically by the flowering of the largely Persianized Abbasid regime, became absolute with the emergence of the Turks. For centuries, as I have indicated, the very word "Arab," after it shrank back upon the Arabic-speaking nomads of the various wildernesses encompassed by Islam, was to have no political and scarcely any cultural significance.

The explanation is doubtless to be sought in the heterogeneity of the areas that had come under the Arab Muslims in the beginning and had become "Arabized" without becoming "Arabs."

The Arabs upon their eruption throughout the Fertile Crescent had not encountered a unified, vigorous nation but merely denationalized and subjugated populations without arms. Moreover, the state structures were completely debilitated, which made it possible for small numbers of mounted tribesmen to pulverize them.

The Arabs' decline and retreat from the great state they had been the chief architects of seems to have been due to many causes, though of course certainty is elusive. Despite their initial warlike qualities, they may have been inherently more disposed to civil pursuits such as literature, art, science, and religion than toward the army and the state, which were to become the speciality of their Persian and Turkish successors; or they may, in the classic phrase, have been corrupted by a life of pleasure seeking.

The former Arabs, that is, the descendants of Arabs, altogether diluted by the blood of the subject populations they had conquered, were themselves absorbed in the large, still-denationalized subjugated population of the Middle East and were no longer admitted to the regular army that came to be composed mostly of slave soldiers drawn from various barbarian peoples in central Asia, North Africa or elsewhere; they were no longer even in the administration. In addition, no new nation emerged out of the Arab conquests that in the event proved able to defend or rule itself or to exercise any control at all over its socioeconomic life.

Because of this and because of the concomitant decline in the fortunes of the caliphate, the Middle East succumbed to successive barbarian invasions. From the thirteenth to the eighteenth century, it was ruled by various castes of foreign slave soldiers. Long before the arrival of the Osmanlis, or Ottoman Turks, the Arabic-speaking countries were ruled by other Turks. Indeed, the Mamluks who held Egypt, Palestine, and Syria for almost three centuries before the Osmanlis (1250–1517) were called in Arabic the "Turkish government." These soldiers, originally slaves, were constantly being infused with new blood from Turkish-speaking countries, and even before the Mamluks a similar method of government had been applied, from *circa* 900 on, by foreign soldier castes, mostly from central Asia and the Caucasus.

Thus, up to the beginning of the nineteenth century the Arabic-speaking countries were governed by corps of slave guards who invariably came from abroad. The ability of these slave corps is celebrated: it was doubtless the victory of the Egyptian Mamluks over the Mongols in September 1260—a decisive victory in the history of the East—that kept the Mongols out of the Nile Valley and accounts for the swinging of the socioeconomic balance in Egypt's favor over Iraq and Syria, despite the great fertility of these two.

The inability of the subject populations of the Middle East to defend themselves gave rise to a vicious circle. The rule of the slave guards was not merely ruthlessly parasitic, it was also honeycombed with dissension; the various cliques and castes were in a state of more or less constant civil war, and there was a general tendency to sociopolitical deterioration. Thus the way was thrown open to a renewal of the Bedouin depredations that tend to recur whenever the central government of a sedentary society is debilitated. Since the farming population could not protect itself or be protected against the general rapacity of its numerous oppressors, it tended to restrict agricultural productivity to the barest minimum. As this kept going down, society as a whole soon reached that stage of malnutrition that is still endemic in so many areas throughout the Middle East.

• • •

After the death of Harun ar-Rashid (786-829), whose reign may be taken as the zenith of Abbasid power and has been traditionally regarded in the West as the absolute paradigm of Islamic splendor, the conflicts that had been smoldering for years exploded in the form of a civil war between his sons, Amin and Mamun, or between Iraq, plus the capital, and Persia, which was where the strength of the two contenders was respectively located. Though the struggle between these two princes has been widely interpreted as an overt struggle between Arabs and Persians, pointing up the largely Persian influence that had been embodied in the Abbasid regime to begin with, it seems more sensible to understand it as an extension of the social and economic struggles that had preceded it, combined, possibly, with a regional though not an ethnic conflict between Persia and Iraq.

Mamun, as the representative of the eastern or Persian provinces, considered transferring the capital to Khorasan, at Merv, and the possibility of this acted as an immense stimulant to the people of Baghdad, who saw their own ruin if Baghdad lost its strategic position as the hub of a great concourse of commercial routes. Mamun won the struggle against Amin, but failed to dislodge Baghdad from its favored position.

The central regime was shaken beyond recall. In the west, even before the civil war in the heart of the empire, local dynasties had long since replaced any form of central power. Shortly after the decay of the Umayyad house and the removal of the Islamic capital from Damascus to Baghdad, the western dependencies had struck out for themselves under various contenders for power. The caliph's power dwindled rapidly and was soon limited to an occasional payment of tribute, a mention in the Friday prayer in the mosque, and in coin inscriptions. This weakening of political power did not have an immediate effect on the social life or economy of the realm; it actually may have stimulated it, for the time being, at least as long as Baghdad remained in control of the great trade routes. But soon the caliph's power began shrinking in Baghdad itself. The top-heaviness of the bureaucracy, exacerbated by the remarkable extravagances of the court, created financial difficulties that were soon aggravated by losing the actual sources of the precious metals to invaders who were encouraged by the general contraction of political power.

The caliphs were driven to an extreme solution, which proved to be rather short-term; they began farming out the state revenues to various authoritative persons, *i.e.*, governors or army commanders, who were supposed to transfer an agreed-on sum to the central government and to keep up the local forces needed to get it. This process of tax-farming in turn led at once, by a sort of organic logic, to the replacement of civil by military power, since providing a given governor or tax-gatherer with the effectiveness he needed meant furnishing him armed units. Thus the civil appointments were ultimately transformed into military posts in which the commander of an armed unit could be responsible for the sums promised the central regime. This meant the elevation over the civil structure of armed pretorians whose sole source of real power was the allegiance of their guards.

In such a situation those in charge of military forces were obviously favored, and from the reigns of Mu'tasim (833–42) and Wathiq (842–47) on, the caliphs became figureheads in their own capital. Their own army commanders were in *de facto* control of the country and merely required the caliphs to rubber-stamp their decisions. The commanders and the actual bodyguards of the caliphs used them as mere pawns; they would juggle them about at will, and only the title of caliph remained as an emblem of a state power that had in fact evaporated.

More and more these commanders and guards came to be Turkish Mamluks, as military slaves were called to distinguish them from the slaves assigned to mere menial and household tasks.

Even before mounting the throne Mu'tasim had assembled a major force of Turkish Mamluks; he was later to make provision for an annual tribute to be paid in Turkish slaves from the East. This was partly a reflection of the social molding that had taken place when the former Khorasanian guards of the Abbasid caliphs merged with the local Arabic-speaking population, while the Persians had managed to set up local dynasties all over Persia. Because of this, the caliphs remaining in Baghdad needed a new point of support. The Turkish Mamluks, totally uprooted individuals, had no ties of any kind with the other elements of the indigenous population and so could be depended on, at least for a time, by the central regime.

The Turks had always been distinguished for their military prowess, apparently based on their combination of cavalry and archers, and as the central regime became militarized in accordance with the process referred to above, the Turks became more and more prominent as the prop of the central regime.

In 945 the special office of "Commander of the Commanders" (*"Amir al-Umara"*) was formed to show that the officer who was commander in the capital was paramount in the country. Ten years later the Buwayhids, a Persian house that had already managed to make itself practically sovereign in western Persia, entered the capital and completely subjugated the caliph. From this point on the caliphs were totally at the mercy of a whole series of palace mayors, generally Persian or Turkish, whose authority was derived from their own personal armed forces.

In the century following the Buwayhid seizure of power in Baghdad, the decay that had set in throughout the Islamic Empire made rapid strides. The Buwayhids were the *de facto* rulers and assumed a new title—sultan—to denote political sovereignty as distinct from the notion of political-plus-religious sovereignty implied by "caliph." Though technically the Buwayhids were Shi'ites—the major schismatic party in Islam—they clung to the mantle of the Abbasid caliphs as a purely exterior symbol of power and the theoretical source of sovereignty of the central regime over the outlying parts of the empire.

Though the Buwayhids managed to restore a measure of prosperity to the heart of the empire, they failed to arrest its general deterioration.

By the eleventh century the Middle East was foundering in a state of irremediable decay. The empire of the caliphs had been shredded into oblivion. The trade with China and Russia had dwindled away, while the short supply of precious metals, manifest beforehand, kept declining, contributing to the smothering of the economic vitality that had once characterized a bustling empire based on trade.

The empire, weakened throughout its structure and more than ever a prey to internal dissension, was ringed by barbarians of all kinds who ultimately accomplished its undoing. Christendom in Sicily and Spain was advancing by leaps and bounds, forcing back the borders of Islam all through southern Europe and ultimately manifesting itself in the Crusades, which for a time implanted Christian rule in the Middle East itself. A new religious upheaval took place at about the same time among the Berbers of North Africa, who, based in southern Morocco and in the area of the Senegal-Niger, welded together a new empire encompassing most of northwest Africa and the areas of Spain still under Muslim control. In the east two great Bedouin tribes, the Hilal and the Sulaym, erupted out of upper Egypt, where they had been settled for some time, and poured across Libya and Tunisia, broadcasting a general catastrophe; they sacked Qayrawan in 1056–57. The career of these Bedouin tribes, in its singular destructiveness, is in striking contrast to a movement of some centuries before—*i.e.,* just after Muhammad—when similar Bedouin tribes swept out of the peninsula only to found an empire, Islam, on the ruins of the Byzantine and Persian states. Now the same sort of Bedouin, with nothing positive to accomplish in the way of state building, simply spent all their time pillaging and ravaging in the way rendered classical for us by the literary reactions of sedentary societies to such events. The irruption into the Islamic Empire of these three kinds of barbarian served as an inspiration to the greatest of Arab historians, Ibn Khaldun, to meditate on the nature of the genesis and decline of civilizations; by the time Khaldun lived (1332–1406) the Hilal and the Sulaym had been ravaging all northwest Africa for three and a half centuries, reducing what had been a densely settled area to a wilderness.

But however destructive the Bedouin were in this second and historically pointless outburst of theirs, the real power for social change was the previously mentioned eruption of the Turks out of central Asia. Of all the barbarian invasions, this was incomparably the most far-reaching in its consequences. For though some of the local dynasties in Syria and Mesopotamia were still "Arab" in lineage, the whole of the vast realm formerly under the caliphate had come more and more under the control of this new people. It was now that the Turks, whom the Arabs on their initial thrust forward into central Asia had collided with and enslaved as "Mamluks," to make use of them to some degree even under the Umayyads and very substantially under the early Abbasids, began entering into history on a majestic scale. In a variety of clans and subclans, they were now to take into their own hands, as warriors and administrators, the destinies of the Middle East and, even farther afield, of India and ultimately of Asia Minor and the Balkans.

The plains of southern Siberia and the great steppelands between the Caspian Sea and the Altai Mountains have been an inexhaustible reservoir of manpower since the earliest known times. The Turks, who for generations had been pushing their way into the central Asiatic steppes, seem to have emerged out of a racial and/or linguistic community that at one time must have included the Mongols.

In any case, by the time they appeared along the borders of Islam they already bore a number of well-marked traits some anthropologists have called Turanian. Some of the northerly groups had a Mongolian look, but the southerly branches were distinguished by a moderately large and graceful body, a medium long face, a strong straight nose, a steep forehead, and a good deal of hair.

At the very beginning of the eleventh century a Persian dynasty (the Samanids) in Khorasan and Transoxiana had been succeeded by a Turkish dynasty, the Ghaznevids, who were the first Turks to found a great Muslim state and who moved east in their islamization of India. By the middle of the century, with the formerly flourishing Islamic Empire in full decay, the Turks had begun to infiltrate into the cosmopolitan world of Islam not merely as captured individuals, but as whole tribes of free Turkish nomads, traditionally organized as tribal entities and migrating *en masse* from their steppelands. China had been closed to them by the development of a self-sufficient Chinese culture that had learned to defend itself for a time against further incursions by the nomads, and so the central Asiatic tribesmen turned their faces to the west. These Turks who now invaded Islam were a branch known as the Seljuqs (a name taken from the leading clan).

The Seljuqs were part of the tribe of the Kinik, one of the chief families of the entourage of the Oghuz king whose capital was at Jand and who accepted a sort of vague suzerainty of the Khazars of southeastern Russia. It seems to have been the propagation of Islam that led to a break between the Seljuqs and the Oghuz king, who remained a pagan while the Seljuqs, toward the end of the tenth century, became Muslims. The Seljuqs were forced to leave the Oghuz kingdom and were welcomed by the last of the Samanids in connection with the latter's struggle against some local rivals.

The progress of these central Asian peoples meant the beginning of the process of Turkification of the ancient Persian lands in the north, a process that has continued down to our own day. Around that time the islamized Oghuz nomads began to be called Turcomans; they may have arisen from mingling with the ancient Indo-European nomads.

The Seljuq empire was relatively short-lived, but it had the decisive effect of introducing the Turks into the heart of Islam, as rulers and to some extent as settlers. In addition, the Seljuq espousal of orthodox Islam, as distinct from any of the sectarian movements that were to have such a lacerating effect, had very long-range consequences.

With the advent of the Seljuqs the sociopolitical history of the Middle East and North Africa became the handiwork of Turks, who were all, to be sure, ultimately assimilated into Islam and into the orthodox sector at that. The Turks' only competitors as Muslim rulers were the Persians who had preceded them as *de facto* masters of the caliphate after the Arabs had been dislodged through the Abbasid dynasty. It was because the Turks had come into Islam via the Persians that their approach to the cultural life of Islam was to be made through the immensely cultivated and elegant culture of the Persians, and though Arabic as a language retained its traditional prestige in religious affairs because of the Quran, as far as the Turks were concerned the actual speakers of Arabic throughout the provinces they came to administer were merely a subject rabble of no special consequence. When the Turks finally evolved a specific cultural tradition of their own, it was on the basis of Persian models, and in this sense they are to be regarded as an outgrowth of Persian culture.

From this time on, also, the Abbasids, massively Persianized themselves, were the only dynasty to retain even a claim on Arab origins throughout the eastern lands of the caliphate; everywhere else some Turkish dynasty was in control of one or another of the fragments the caliphate broke up into.

The dominant military aristocracy, as well as the army officers surrounding the Abbasid sovereign, were largely Turkish in organization and language. The opponents the Crusaders came up against were not Arabs but various Turks. It was the Turks who ultimately repulsed the Crusaders, and with the exception of the short-lived though brilliant regime of Saladin and his Ayyubid successors—neither Turks nor Arabs, but Kurds, *i.e.,* Persians—it was the Mamluk Turks who defended Islam and the Middle East against both the menace of Christendom and for that matter their own cousins the Mongols.

It was, finally, another branch of Turkdom, the Ottoman Turks, that pushed the boundaries of Islam into the heart of Europe, while at the same time coming to absorb every Arabic-speaking country with the exception of half-Berber Morocco.

The progress of Turkish infiltration was remarkably rapid and enduring. Around the middle of the eleventh century the regime that had been put together in the east by a Seljuq Turk, Tughril Beg, at the expense of the Persian Buwayhids and the Turkish Ghaznevids, ingested Iraq with no difficulty. In 1055 it ousted the Buwayhids altogether from their position as "protectors" of the caliphate. A few years later the Seljuqs conquered Syria and Palestine, as well as an Egyptian dynasty (the Fatimids) and soon managed to do something the Arabs had never managed: They seized a substantial portion of the Anatolian plateau from the Byzantines and settled it with a Muslim Turkish population, which is still there.

Tughril Beg was granted the titles of sultan and "King of the East and West" by the Abbasid mock-caliph al-Qaim. The Seljuq state expanded still farther in the west under Tughril's successors, Alp Arslan and Malikshah (all three the "Great Seljuqs"), took Syria away from the heterodox Fatimids in Egypt, and then forcibly installed Islam in Asia Minor for the first time through the victory over the Byzantines in 1071 at Manzikert.

This marked the beginning of the period in which the real power in Iraq was invested in a sultan, with the caliph as spiritual and traditional warrant for it, in the form of a nominal diarchy, occasionally solemnized by marriages.

Although these conquests were carried out by a specific people, there was no question at this time of merely ethnic factors. As orthodox (Sunni) Muslims, the Turks were hailed by many as a counterweight to the detested influence of the Shi'ite Buwayhids. As before, the caliphs in Baghdad were allowed to retain their emblematic status, but the real rulers of the Islamic Empire were now once again united under a single house, the Seljuqs, known as Grand Sultans, who had duplicated the feats of primitive Islam by defeating the chief powers in the eastern Mediterranean, the Byzantines, and another—schismatic—Muslim dynasty, the Fatimids.

Under the Seljuqs, too, who after all had far less to contribute to the culture than the original Muslim Arabs, the Persians remained the keystone of the state as the principal functionaries both throughout the administration and in the higher posts. Perhaps the most distinguished figure of the period was the Persian state functionary, Nizam al-Mulk, who regularized the previous tax-farming abuses, which had led to the downfall of the preceding regime. His reform served as underpinning for a new feudal system in which the parceling out of the land was the pillar of a new socioadministrative order. This streamlined and reinforced the tendency toward feudalism that had already been encouraged by the tax-farming device itself.

Land grants to officers, peaceably allocated or taken by force, entailed the furnishing by the grantee of a certain number of fighting men. The land grants gave the grantee a right not only to a commission on the taxes to be collected, but to the actual revenues themselves. The grants sometimes became hereditary as a result of the intervention of force, but legally they were generally revoked after a certain period and in theory were always revocable. The transition from a money economy to a feudal economy came about not merely through administrative acumen, but as a natural consequence of the disorder in the country that was rooted in the presence of vast numbers of unruly Turkish nomads with no interest in the countryside beside that of pillage. Nizam al-Mulk, perceiving that the country was failing because of the widespread anarchy to produce the monies expected from it, simply took the path of lesser resistance and allocated the actual land itself to the troops as fiefs; they were granted both the land and the actual revenue. This had the effect of involving them in the fortunes of the countryside and thus transformed them from "outs" to "ins," from exterior invaders to a settled sedentary population with a vested interest in the agriculture of the country.

Social turmoil gradually brought commerce to a halt. After Nizam al-Mulk's death (1092), the atomizing of the former Islamic Empire that he had succeeded in arresting for a time resumed its course. The empire established by the Seljuqs was fragmented into a congeries of successor states headed by various Seljuq notables, the most important of which was the "Seljuqs of Rum" (*i.e.,* Byzantium) in Asia Minor. From the eleventh to the thirteenth centuries it degenerated still further into the local dynasties of the "Atabegs," which set up small states around the borders of the disintegrating caliphate at the beginning of the twelfth century. Though theoretically dependents of the Great Seljuqs, they were quite independent; the unity of the empire was long since gone. It was primarily these statelets that the Crusaders came up against in Syria and Mesopotamia and that put up the most effective Muslim resistance.

It is curious and illuminating that the administration of the Seljuq state, like the histories and poems commemorating it, was conducted far more in Persian than in Arabic, for Persian had already asserted itself as at least the second Muslim language. More particularly, Persian had been absorbed by the Seljuqs, as it was by the other Turks who entered Islam from the Eurasian steppelands.

The actual military and social structure of the Seljuq state remained wholly Turkish. It was based on a characteristic Turkish notion, that of a military fief, that is, a nonhereditary allotment of land to a feudal lord who had the prerogative of collecting taxes and the duty of providing the central government's forces with a corresponding military unit. For many centuries this Seljuq system of military feudalism was to remain the groundwork of the socioeconomic structure in western Asia. The Seljuqs passed it on to the Atabegs, the various Mongol states, and the Mamluks later; it even influenced the Christian statelets created by the Crusaders.

• • •

The modalities, so to speak, of disintegration are of primary historical interest. Like so much else in historical causation, they too are bound to remain elusive, yet in broad outline one or two agencies may be distinguished in the general transformation of Islamic society. These lie primarily in the field of organization and economics, or, to put it another way, in the army and in the state.

The eastern Islamic army went through three phases: an Arab draft army, a Khorasanian semiprofessional army, and a semiservile army, mainly Turkish. In the beginning the armies that carried out the Arab conquests were made up solely of Arabs, fighters in the Holy War, who were entitled to a pension and part of the war booty; these armies cost scarcely anything to maintain partly because of the victories and partly because the warriors remained attached to their tribes. These armies' primary incentive was enthusiasm, both for spiritual and for material reasons; mobility, essentially, was their sole form of superiority, often combined with a gusto for the performance of individual feats of heroism.

But from the time of the first Umayyad caliphs on, these armies quickly came apart, by virtue of the very victories they had won. The expansion itself put a great space between the Arab fighters and their tribes, and the conquests became more difficult as the peoples they were threatening began arming more efficiently. The conquests began, in short, to cost more. Heavy combat equipment was needed, and the profits of the military operations became less assured as the expense of the armies went up, which added to the general imbalance of the finances that at bottom had brought down the Umayyad regime. In some cases, reinforcements had been found among the subject peoples, superficially converted to Islam in the hope of getting in on the booty themselves. North African Berbers, for instance, were launched against Spain; eastern Persians were used against the central Asiatic Turks, their hereditary enemies; even nonconverted Armenians were led by their chieftains, vassals of an Islamic power, in specific anti-Byzantine campaigns, etc.

The Abbasids introduced the second phase: They recruited an army mostly made up of Khorasanian natives, which had manifold significance. Ethnically this meant that from now on it was no longer Arabs who were in the military forefront but Persians. In and for itself, perhaps, this might not have meant any radical change, for in any case the Arabs did not simply vanish from the armies overnight, and the Abbasids had no intention of abandoning the Arabs as such, since they not only still considered themselves of Arab "blood" but also had Arab allies. Thus for a time there was an Arab army alongside a Khorasanian army, the Arabs being used more outside the borders of the Islamic realm proper, as against the Byzantines, while the Khorasanians were the bodyguards of the caliphs.

Nevertheless this duality in the armed forces reflected the duality being realized between the Arab and Persian elements of the empire. When Mamun conquered Baghdad and the Semitic parts of his brother Amin's territories, it was a further step in the de-arabizing of the realm, since from then on the non-Persian element tended to be suspect *a priori*. Mu'tasim put the seal on this process by systemically forbidding the army recruitment of Arabs in Egypt and *de facto* abandoning it elsewhere.

Thus from a conquering army with major claims on the state and a seedbed of the artisocracy, the nomadic Arab world lapsed into its primordial state of nomadism and once again became, except for some individual chiefs, as destitute as it had always been.

Not merely politics was behind this abandoning of Arab recruitment; one of its prime causes was the obsolescence of Arab military techniques, which no longer suited the new conditions of warfare. What was happening everywhere was that heavy as well as light cavalry was being made use of; siege techniques the Arabs had never even heard of were becoming routine.

Military training had become necessary. The Persians, for whom the new requirements were the least novel, were best prepared for them. For a long time they had been familiar with the bows and crossbows that seem to have been required, especially against the Turks of central Asia. Also, they were practically alone in being able to furnish mines, siege machines, "artillery," and the highly effective Greek fire, and thus to compete with the Byzantine techniques. In any case the necessity of maintaining a technically fairly advanced army was more apparent to the Abbasids than it had been to the Umayyads, who had clung to the life of the Arabian tribes they had originated from.

From this period on, the army had two distinct elements: on the one hand there was the professional army proper, made up of soldiers who were inscribed in the army ministry by name and so made up a sort of collective body, recognized as such, with carefully hierarchized pay (there was a systematic and extraordinarily detailed control of the whole institution down to the horses used); then there were volunteers mobilized for some specific campaign, paid at a lower rate and then only for the duration of the campaign. Only the first category was regarded as the real army. In addition, there were special formations used along the endless borders of the Islamic realm, as well as in the war fleets of the state.

It was a demarche of the Caliph Mu'tasim that was to accelerate a process already adumbrated by the logic of the standing army. In order to keep a large guard devoted exclusively to his own interests, he began to recruit for their personal qualities young soldiers from the most backward parts of his empire, which were not necessarily any more than superficially islamized. He began recruiting soldiers, for instance, among the Daylamites of the south Caspian Mountains and Kurds everywhere, and also, especially, among the Turks, who became particularly popular because of their physical abilities, their sobriety, and their military discipline. There were a great many of these along the outlying parts of the empire in Asia, more or less islamized; some of their chiefs had already made great careers fighting for Islam. This Turkish recruitment was added to now by the purchase, in central Asia or in the steppelands of southern Russia, of young Turks bought specially for this purpose from slave traders. They were taken to the caliph's palace and trained there in arms, in the rudiments of Islam, and in devotion to the caliph as the primate of Islam.

In this way a tailor-made bodyguard could be put together that was quite dependable. Even when some were freed on promotion to the status of officer, it was still thought that they would remain faithful to their vows to the caliph and go on displaying an *esprit de corps* that would guarantee their military value.

Mu'tasim made another fateful decision: In order to avoid the constant turbulence of the Baghdad population and to preserve his bodyguard from contamination by it, he decided to leave Baghdad altogether and set up a new capital a little upriver in a place called Samarra. For fifty years the Abbasid capital was outside the periphery of the metropolis. But he never succeeded in finding an absolutely homogeneous source of army recruits; the Abbasid regime generally was characterized by constant disputes and rivalries between the various elements that composed the elite armed forces —Persians, occasionally Arabs, the old free Turks who had been assimilated into Islam, and the new Turkish slave recruits. These rivalries existed even between Turkish chiefs, whom the recruits, gathered together from all quarters and with no other attachment but allegiance to their army chiefs, followed faithfully in the unflagging jockeying for power and the caliph's favor.

Thus Mu'tasim's decision to recruit an army that was alien to his subjects resulted in alienating the regime itself; the particularistic oppositions were strengthened in consequence.

In addition, finally, Mu'tasim's basic objective was just what he achieved least—the army units whose fidelity he had been taking for granted, on the theory that he was their only resource in the state, soon realized that if they needed him he needed them still more and was in fact completely dependent on them. A situation parallel to that of the Roman pretorians, whose recruitment had been similar, soon evolved. Up to the time of the Caliph Mutawakkil (847–61) it was possible to keep up appearances, but when he was assassinated, on the insistence of his own son, by one of the Turkish commanders, there could no longer be any doubt about the army's control of the caliphate. It was now the army chiefs who when a caliph died made up their own minds which successor of his to favor, simply in their own immediate interests, based on the promises he made them or, if he was too young, on their view of who would prove to be the most docile on growing up.

Thus the army commanders' awareness of being indispensable just because of the dangers that were generally increasing through the frictions within the state made them increase their demands on the state budget just at a time when the demands could be met only with the greatest inconvenience. In fact a vast proportion of the state budget was allocated to the army; this in turn aggravated the very evils the army was needed to cope with.

One of the ways the central government sought to meet its chronically mounting expenses was to provide army commanders with land in one form or another. Because of this a segment of the landed gentry became military, and often foreign, so that the social composition of Abbasid society was rapidly transformed.

Thus the Abbasid regime was transformed into the above-mentioned regime of the "Commander of the Commanders" around the middle of the tenth century. The first to bear the title was the eunuch general Mu'nis, who had saved the Caliph Muqtadir in 908 from a revolt led by a relative, and from then on, for twenty-five years, was complete master of the government both in domestic and in foreign affairs, making and unmaking Wazirs and even replacing one caliph with another.

Nor was it merely the armies of the caliph that kept contending for privileges and power. The moment the principle of recruiting mercenaries and slaves for the army was laid down, there was nothing to stop a powerful captain or for that matter a mere adventurer favored by fortune at the outset of his career from recruiting his own personal armies in the style of the *condottieri* that became notorious in Italy. This was how a number of small local dynasties made their appearance in the tenth century on the ruins of the caliphate.

Moreover, this state of affairs produced a sort of chain reaction in the provinces where the local populations were warlike by nature, such as the Bedouin of upper Mesopotamia, the Syrian interior, and the borders of the peninsula, and the Berbers of North Africa and

Spain, who constituted elements of resistance to any central authority. Many dynasties were in fact based on the mere recruitment of local personnel for private ambitions.

In the east, however, it was most exceptional for a dynasty based merely on indigenous manpower to have any durability without calling in Turkish slaves. The same thing took place in the Islamic west; the difference was only that the Turks were replaced by Negroes or Slavs. In the Islamic west, also, there was always a substantial segment of indigenous personnel in the armed forces, whereas in the east they came to be progressively excluded. Finally, the foreign element was absorbed in the west with relative rapidity, whereas the east came to be characterized more and more by a radical split between a foreign military aristocracy and the civilian population.

Strangely enough, it was during this gradual decomposition of the caliphs' power that Abbasid governmental and administrative institutions reached their greatest efficiency. The very fact of having to make some sort of attempt to withstand the forces of decomposition, indeed, the very shrinking of the central power led to a ramification of the government structure.

The first Abbasids had still governed in a highly personal manner, merely delegating functions as they thought best at the moment. But the requirements of the regime became so complicated that a bureaucracy gradually came to be in demand, and a caste of bureaucrats quickly evolved. Roles were worked out and became fixed, traditions and administrative styles were established, and a hereditary caste of "scribes" (*kuttab*) came into being that embodied the corpus of traditions and functions. It was during this period that the image of the Wazir achieved its classical outlines.

In the beginning the Wazirate had been not a function but a general participation in the behavior of the sovereign, because of the very difficulty of the tasks to be performed and/or because of the incapacities of some of the caliphs. Just because of this the Wazir could not interpose himself between the caliph and any one of the caliph's other agents; still less could he nominate them. By the end of the ninth century, however, the situation had become quite different. The Wazir, who generally emerged from the ranks of the hereditary scribes and who had made himself rich in one way or another in the government, through bribes, etc., was altogether his own man. He was the natural summit of all the administrative services that had been removed by their complexity from the caliph's scope if not from his rights. It was natural for the Wazir to nominate his own agents from among the clientele he had brought with him from the scribal caste. The Wazir would be the head of a clan with ties to one military or religious coterie or another; there was no point in retaining the personnel of his predecessor, who was doubtless tied to some other coterie. He was sometimes forced on the caliph by such a victorious coterie, and since he had its confidence, more than the caliph, his own prestige vis-à-vis the caliph was naturally bound to grow proportionately. In this way it was precisely during the period of the most serious decay of the Abbasid caliphate that its two most remarkable Wazirs made their appearance: Ali ibn Isa and Ibn al-Furat, who kept relaying each other in power for twenty-five years.

This power of the Wazir's, however formidable, clearly had a feeble base, since in order to govern, the Wazir in spite of everything had to keep the favor of the caliph, who kept asking for money, as well as the favor of the army chiefs, who kept asking him for even more, against the intrigues of all sorts of careerists and of hostile groupings. On top of this, one of the ways in which a financial crisis came to be met was by making some bloated Wazir disgorge his wealth. The caliph may not have ruled, but he still reigned; he still had the power of putting his preceding Wazir to the torture and had enough army commanders around to make him do so. As long as Mu'nis was alive the Wazirate was still kept in order, as was its administrative authority, but after him the Wazirs were no longer able to resist the daily pressures of anarchic parties. The institution practically expired, with the army chiefs meddling in every aspect of administration until the Buwayhids occupied Baghdad.

Thus the bureaucratic administration of the Abbasid empire was characterized by a minute devolution of function, with a whole series of offices and services each one with a chief under the Wazir, and a remarkably elaborate system of mutual controls based on an immense amount of red tape, made possible by the recently preceding diffusion of paper from China. The provinces reproduced this system in miniature. The efforts of the first Abbasids were directed at bringing the provincial administrations into as close dependence as possible on the central regime, not only by controlling them, but by appointing, in contrast with the Umayyads, the commander, especially the army commander, and the tax collector, as well as the chief magistrate. This rule had still been considered imperative around 900, but it too was breached by the growth of the military aristocracy. The army chiefs who managed to get the provincial commands did so in order to get into their own hands the tax collection, too, or in any case to have the right to put their own nominee, not the caliph's, in charge. This was just another way, obviously a very important one, of cutting into the power of the caliph still further. There was nothing to prevent the governor from exercising unrestricted authority in his own province and eventually from establishing his own autonomy, in this way undermining the very principle of centralization that had engendered the relationship to begin with and restoring an anarchic situation when the central edifice of the state became debilitated.

The early Abbasid dynasty rapidly evolved into a sociopolitical system based on a tripartite division: at the summit the military power, which had control of political areas of commands handed out for political reasons; then the administration, with the scribes headed by the Wazir, quite indifferent to the religious law; justice became a specialty of a third category.

The political and military functions of the regime were reserved for the ethnic groups, more or less foreign, that made up the armed forces; the indigenous population, barred from the military, retained the functions of administration and of justice, with their natural dependence on local expertise.

• • •

The remarkable economic activity typical of the Middle East during the centuries following the establishment of the Abbasid caliphate created an immense amount of socioeconomic friction that led to open movements of dissidence and hostility to the central authorities. In Islam almost all such movements were expressed in the form of religious schisms. Whatever the motivation, social or economic, the movement found its expression as an aspect of the interpretation of the Holy Law of Islam, which meant that opposition would be embodied in a sect or in a religious leader.

It would be naïve to regard this religious form of expression as a disguise for the "real" reasons. On the contrary, in a society conceived of, not merely theoretically, as a dense mélange of social and religious themes in which the orthodox faith of Islam was merely the official religion of the orthodox society and of law and order as officially interpreted, the religious cult was the tangible emblem of the cohesiveness of the orthodox community. Loyalty to the cult was thus social conformism. The established order rested on the orthodox view of religion; opposition to it entailed a pronouncement of apostasy. Since church and state were indistinguishably intertwined, religious controversy was the medium in which all controversy was expressed, including social conflict. Thus what every movement of opposition sought in expressing itself in religious terms was a functional and organic formulation of its wishes in such a way as to be publicly effective.

Religiously formulated threats with some social or economic motivation had beset the Abbasid dynasty from the moment of its establishment. The Abbasids themselves, brought to power by a coalition that was united by opposition to the Arab Umayyad house and that was composed of various Muslim dissidents, including both Arab Muslims and Persians of all strata, soon fell out. Abu Muslim, the Persian general and popular leader who had put them in power, was killed by Mansur, the second Abbasid caliph, who consolidated the new regime. The caliphs found their support as before in Persia, especially in Khorasan, from the aristocratic clan of the Barmecides, who survived under many reigns as the chiefs of administration and as the warrant of the support of the Persian upper classes.

The Persian peasant population had been subjugated together with the rest of the country by the Abbasid regime, but it still kept flaring up in revolts expressed in religious terms. Curiously enough, in the case of the Persian peasants these revolts still echoed the situation *before* the Muslim conquests. They were not revolts based on the national religion, Zoroastrianism, but schismatic movements that before the Muslims had been directed at the indigenous monarchy, the Sassanids, and its old state Zoroastrian religion. For the time being, the Persian upper classes allied themselves with the new Muslim regime of the Abbasids; hence the peasant rebellions, though indigenously Persian, were directed both at the Abbasids, still regarded as an Arab regime, and at the Persian ruling class allied with them. The principal dissident movement was inspired by the memory of Mazdak, a revolutionary of centuries before, whose own movement had almost overthrown the Sassanid regime. The social doctrines of Mazdak were still fermenting among the lower classes under the new and consolidated Arab-Persian regime of the Abbasids. Now the memory of Abu Muslim himself was made much of by Persian insurrectionaries who claimed to be avenging his betrayal by the caliphs he had put in power.

These dissident movements were generally Persian in character, though later they came to constitute a mixture of Mazdakite and extreme Shi'ite ideas, with orthodox Zoroastrians remaining neutral or hostile.

Perhaps the most serious of these movements was the insurrection of Babak (816–37), based on the peasantry and remarkable for its comprehensiveness and dynamism. Babak advocated the break-up of the big estates and their distribution among the peasants and seems to have been supported by the Persian squires (*Dihqans*), who by this time had shrunken to the level of peasants themselves, though with some airs of nobility. The movement, centered in Adharbayjan, spread to southwest Persia, where it received some support from the Kurdish mountain people, then moved to the Caspian districts of the north and westward into Armenia. Babak, an open heretic and a man of remarkable gifts as a leader, seems to have been allied with the Byzantine emperor against the common Muslim foe; for seven years he held out against four of the Caliph Mamun's generals. After Mu'tasim ascended the throne in 833 the Islamic Empire consolidated its forces enough to move against Babak more efficiently. The movement was confined to Adharbayjan and finally crushed.

A most important and quite different revolt was the upheaval of the *Zanj,* the Negro slaves, between 869 and 883. Islam has always been a slave-holding society as it still is in Arabia and elsewhere, but the slaves were not the principal factor in production, as they had been in the Roman Empire. In the Islamic Empire production was assured by peasants, free or semifree, and by artisans; the slaves were generally used either for domestic or for military purposes. The latter, known as Mamluks, actually constituted a military caste based on extensive privileges. (I have described the process by which they later came to take over the state structure.)

Yet there were major exceptions in which great business enterprises led to the gathering together of huge numbers of slaves in specific agricultural enterprises based on substantial investments of the liquid capital arising out of large-scale business speculations. Such slaves would be thrown together in single colonies, with many thousands belonging to a single landowner or businessman. These slaves had generally been procured in East Africa by capture or purchase, or as tribute from states subject to the Abbasid regime.

The salt marshes east of Basra constituted one such large-scale business enterprise. Tens of thousands were employed in draining the salt marshes to ready the land for farming and to extract the salt for sale. Their conditions appear to have been unusually disagreeable, and the slaves themselves, as newcomers without even a knowledge of Arabic, were complete outsiders in Islam. A Persian who called himself Ali ibn Muhammad, who may have had some Arab blood, succeeded in inciting them against their masters not by preaching a general reform—including, for instance, the abolition of slavery—but simply by promising these particular slaves a more favorable position after their revolt.

The movement was thus unrefined by any broad concepts, but even so was necessarily expressed in religious terms too. The Zanj leader, though claiming descent from Ali, Muhammad's son-in-law and the fourth of the "orthodox caliphs" immediately following Muhammad, did not join with the Shi'a, the major schismatic movement in Islam, but with the Secessionists, who had become essentially egalitarian anarchists opposing all forms of hereditary distinction and favoring the idea of personal merit as a sole qualification for leadership. The Secessionists thought all other Muslims the same as infidels, and the Zanj followed them. From this point of view all Muslims, like everyone else, were subject on capture to slavery or death.

The movement was remarkably successful; it spread very rapidly and was joined by one slave gang after another, attracting to its ranks black troops sent out against it by the imperial armies and also Bedouin tribes hoping for loot. Some free peasants also joined it, doubtless because of their opposition to the landowning class. By 870, after capturing the important seaport of Ubullah and then expanding into southwest Persia, the Zanj had become a major threat to the Islamic Empire. A year later they captured Basra, though after sacking it they left it immediately. By 879 they were carrying out major raids only some seventeen miles outside of Baghdad.

This, however, marked the zenith of the movement; by 881 a vast expeditionary force prepared by Muwaffaq, brother of the caliph, had forced the Zanj out of all their conquests and successfully ended the siege of a capital they had established on a dry spot in the salt flats called al-Mukhtara, which fell to assault in 883. The leader, Ali, was killed and his head brought to Baghdad on a pole some months later.

These movements of social upheaval were generally sporadic and without general objectives, and they left no lasting imprint on Islamic society. But there was one movement, a branching out of the Shi'a, that expressed the discontent of the oppressed classes far more comprehensively. Toward the end of the ninth century, it shook the empire.

The Shi'a, which had started out as an Arab party claiming to represent the rights of Ali, Muhammad's son-in-law, had quickly developed into a religious sect based on the non-Arab Clients; its major success was the launching of the Abbasid caliphate.

But there was another line of Shi'ites who claimed descent from Ali through his wife, Fatima, Muhammad's daughter. These Shi'ite pretenders, called Imams by their followers, put forth claims of a far more transcendental nature than those of mere caliphs. Their Imam was practically divine; in any case he claimed complete infallibility and consequently demanded blind obedience.

There was a widespread doctrine among the Shi'ites to the effect that all injustice in the world would be eliminated when the last of the Imams, who was still in hiding, came to the earth as the *Mahdi*—the "(rightly) Guided One." All were waiting for the end of the world, but one group expected their Mahdi to be the twelfth descendant of Ali, who did, in fact, vanish under mysterious circumstances and is still being waited for to this day by the "Twelver Shi'a," a generally moderate group not very different from Sunni (orthodox) Islam.

The other party thought the Mahdi would be the seventh descendant of Ali, one Isma'il, who had died in 762. The magical virtue of the number seven might of course have had something to do with this. In any case the "Seveners," or Isma'ilis, rapidly turned extremist and revolutionary, carrying on the original character of the Shi'ite movement at its inception.

During the eighth and ninth centuries Isma'il, his son Muhammad, and their immediate followers seem to have spent most of their time thinking out the organization and propaganda of the sect. They evolved a doctrine combining Persian elements of divine grace, Gnostic speculations of hermetic origin, and some strands of Greek philosophy and the Manichean religion of the elite into an esoteric doctrine that was facilitated by the tendency to the formation of secret societies, which were prevalent throughout the Orient as part of its ancient heritage and were utilized for the promotion of various political enterprises.

The initiates ascended in the sect via seven, later nine, degrees, which won over the novice, through an intense study of his religious faith, first to the conviction that the whole beauty of the faith was not yet clear to him, then to a doubt of its foundations. He then became bound to the authority of the Hidden Imam and his representatives, whose identity never was revealed to him. He was shown that all previous religious revelations and precepts were simply a veil for an esoteric meaning that could not be communicated except through allegories. The novice who had been prepared this way was finally bound over to unconditional obedience to the society and its officers. He was liberated from all constraint of dogma and also from all legal fetters. This doctrinal elaboration was articulated on the basis of a method of Quranic interpretation that assigned dual series of meanings to every verse in the Quran: One was literal, which anyone might grasp; the other was esoteric, known only to the inner few. The doctrines of the sect were thus basically secret and were diffused down through the sect in a sort of graduated hierarchy; only on the highest level did the convert get the ultimate message. The device of dual interpretation also made it possible for all sorts of social or philosophical innovations to be introduced into Islamic doctrine without seeming to disturb its foundations. Isma'ilism contained the seeds of a rationalist revolution that, had it been successful, might have changed Muslim thinking and so the destinies of Islam.

By the beginning of the tenth century the empire was passing through an acute social crisis. The peasants and slaves were defeated and harbored resentment, and an immense urban proletariat was exacerbated by the increasing concentration of labor and capital. The Isma'ili sect seems to have elaborated its doctrines in such a way as to attract a great part of the social discontent into its own channels and to have had immense appeal for the common people who were suffering so much from the social afflictions of the period. Beginning with substantial peasant support and gradually infiltrating the urban workers, especially the craftsmen, with their revolutionary ideas, the Isma'ilis seem to have created some of the Islamic craft guilds; in any case, they incorporated them into their sect. The sect was accused of communism and also, curiously enough, of collective ownership of women, *i.e.,* licentiousness, all of which may mean no more than that they had some sort of social program for ameliorating the conditions of the lower classes and for granting women a higher status than they enjoyed in orthodox Islam of the time.

With the outset of the tenth century the movement engaged in open rebellion, and its secrecy enabled it to prosper despite the imperial police system. The Qarmathians, an affiliated group based on the gulf coast of Arabia (present-day Bahrayn), where the Zanj rebellion had been suppressed only a short while before the sect's emergence in 890, sent ravaging bands through Syria and Palestine and as far as northern Mesopotamia. The Qarmathians, named after their founder, Hamdan Qarmat (perhaps an Aramaic word meaning the "secret teacher"), were bound together on the basis of complete community of property and communal love feasts with paradisaical bread, doubtless patterned after a Mandean Gnostic sect that had long been rooted in the region. The movement was immensely ferocious; only Damascus could withstand it. It succeeded in taking the province it had started in away from the agents of the central government and in establishing a republic, apparently oligarchical in character, that lasted well into the eleventh century. It seems to have been governed on principles of equity.

In the Yemen, too, Isma'ilis had succeeded in gaining control of the regime, after a missionary arrived there in 901 and rapidly assumed power, to use the Yemen as a base for dispatching envoys to North Africa and India, and doubtless elsewhere.

In Tunisia the Isma'ili mission was singularly successful. In 908 the first Imam Ubaydallah was installed as the first caliph in a new dynasty, the Fatimids, whose rise to power was curiously like that of the Abbasids themselves; that is, they had created an apparatus based on heterodox propaganda aimed at the exploitation of existing social friction and had managed to win power in an outlying district of the empire. Yet they never became an all-encompassing dynasty, nor did they, on the other hand, ever turn away from the sect their ascension was due to.

The first four Fatimid caliphs established themselves only in the west of Egypt. They encountered major difficulties in translating their doctrinal intransigeance into state forms; indeed, they instantly fell foul of the fanatical idealists among them who thought their concessions to the needs of administration involved a betrayal of true Isma'ilism.

Having covered Egypt with a network of secret envoys and propagandists, the fourth Fatimid caliph, Mu'izz (952–75), after a number of abortive attempts managed to conquer it in 969 and thus took away from the Abbasid realm a major province.

Mu'izz constructed Cairo as the capital of the Fatimid faith and also built a great mosque, Al-Azhar, as its intellectual center. Al-Azhar, one of the oldest universities in the world, was converted to orthodox Islam centuries later and is still today a major spiritual center of Islam. Mu'izz's two ablest men were Jawhar, a European Mamluk, and Ya'qub ibn Killis, a Baghdadi Jewish convert to Islam and a remarkable financial wizard and organizer.

The Fatimids quickly developed into a serious rival to the orthodox caliphate based in Baghdad. They spread their dominion through Palestine, Syria, and Arabia; and at one time, under the reign of the Fatimid caliph Mustansir (1036–94), the Fatimid realm encompassed all North Africa, Sicily, Egypt, Syria, and western Arabia. The zenith of Isma'ili Fatimid power was reached in 1056–57, when a general in the service of the Fatimids even occupied Baghdad and proclaimed the paramountcy of the Fatimid caliph in the very capital of the Abbasids. This, however, was the high point from which Fatimid power immediately began ebbing away, eroded at home by the rise of military commanders who soon overshadowed their theoretical superiors. Thus the Fatimid caliphs were swiftly divested of their boundless authority and became the pawns of the army commanders in a process that, as I have indicated, was endemic throughout Islam. In the case of the Fatimids this classical process entailed the loss of the religious support of their own sect. Ultimately they were simply dislodged by a man whose name has become famous in the west as the paragon of Islamic chivalry—the celebrated Kurd Saladin (Salah ad-Din), who was to liquidate the Fatimid caliphate once and for all and reinstall an orthodox regime in Egypt.

The great power of the Fatimid caliphs lay in their acceptance as divinely infallible the Imams, in accordance with their Shi'ite origins; the idea of absolute monarchs ruling by heredity divinely transmitted through a divinely authorized family proved effective for a long time. The government, highly centralized, was divided into three sections; religious, military, and administrative. The religious section consisted of an immense group of missionaries, in graduated order, in charge of all the higher schools of learning and of a remarkably well-developed propaganda organization, which controlled an immense apparatus of agents scattered throughout the eastern half of the Islamic Empire, still nominally under the Abbasids. Their activity seems to have been highly effective, as is indicated by the repeated outbreaks throughout the countryside, from Iraq to India, that these Isma'ili agents seem to have been behind. Isma'ili social and religious ideas seem to have been very attractive to all sorts of somewhat unorthodox or radical intellectuals. Two of the greatest poets in Arabic, Mutanabbi (d. 965) and Abu-l-Ala al-Ma'arri (d. 1057), were under the spell of Isma'ili ideas. In Iraq an Isma'ili group known as the Sincere Brethren of Basra published a series of fifty-one epistles, constituting a sort of encyclopedia that contained all contemporary knowledge. This encyclopedia, with a marked Isma'ili bent, was read by Muslims from India to Spain and greatly influenced later writers. The Sincere Brethren were not merely publishers and writers; they organized a network of semisecret reading groups under their own centralized direction that helped spread Isma'ili doctrines.

The Fatimid age was one of great prosperity, with a thorough awareness of the vital importance of commerce, both economically and politically, for the extension of Fatimid political influence. Egyptian trade before the Fatimids had been quite limited in scope, but under the impulse of the financial administration founded by Ibn Killis whole plantations and industries were developed in the countryside and Egyptian products began being exported in quantity, while at the same time an extensive network of trade relations evolved both with Europe and with India. The Fatimids, while still based in Tunisia, had had lively trade relations with southern Europe, and when they got to Egypt their business connections with Italy, especially Pisa, Amalfi, and Venice, were resumed and extended. Egyptian ships and traders, based at two great harbors, Alexandria in Egypt and Tripoli in Syria, went as far west as Spain. Indeed, the whole of the eastern Mediterranean was dominated by the ships of the Fatimid regime.

In the East the Fatimids managed to swing the trade with India out of the Persian Gulf into the Red Sea; there was also extensive trade with Byzantium and with other Muslim states. Throughout all this commericial activity there was parallel activity of an intellectual nature, since the Isma'ili missionaries followed wherever the Fatimid traders led; and wherever the missionaries brought their ideas a similar intellectual effervescence developed in the Muslim world, from Spain to India.

The Isma'ilis reemerged as an extreme opposition party in a splinter movement that became addicted to systematic terrorism. Hasan-i-Sabbah, a Persian Isma'ili, paid a visit to the Fatimid capital in Cairo in 1078, by which time the formerly all-powerful Fatimid Imams had long since transferred the real power in the country to the military captains, who paid them merely nominal allegiance; and on the death of the Fatimid caliph Mustansir in 1094 Hasan-i-Sabbah, who had fallen out years before with the army autocrat in control of Egypt, refused to acknowledge Mustansir's successor, who had been nominated only because of his pliability by the real military ruler of the country. Hasan-i-Sabbah, with his Persian following, cut off all ties to the greatly enfeebled sect in Egypt. The Persian branch now launched a campaign of revolutionary activity throughout the eastern half of the realm, now under the Seljuqs. The followers of Hasan-i-Sabbah and his "New Preaching" were called Assassins, from their sectaries' alleged habit of taking hashish to bring about ecstatic states of mind. The meaning of the word "assassin" in European languages refers to their tactic of systematic political terrorism; it began with Hasan-i-Sabbah's seizure of the mountain fortress of Alamut in northern Persia in 1094. Beginning in 1094, from this base and from similar strongpoints in Syria during the following century, the "Old Man of the Mountain"—the title for the chiefs of the sect—sent out gangs of devoted fanatics against all the leaders of Islam in the interests of an unknown, mysterious Imam. The Old Men of the Mountain arranged for very bold assassinations of various Muslim notables, statesmen, and generals; they assassinated Nizam al-Mulk, too, in 1092. The Assassins throve until the thirteenth century, when the Mongol invasions put a stop to the movement in any serious form. From then on, Isma'ilism shrank to the dimensions of a negligible heresy, though it took on a certain importance in the eastern half of what had been the Islamic Empire.

It was during the general debilitation of the Islamic center that the Crusaders made their first appearance in the Middle East. They came under the theoretical aegis of a religious quest for the Holy Sepulcher, to wrest it from the infidel; in reality, the Crusade was a large-scale enterprise of imperialism in an early version. Its basic motivation may be considered to have been largely materialistic, though from the point of view of the organization of the masses who participated in the movement, religion was undoubtedly a catalytic unifying force, providing the movement with an exciting slogan. Italian traders, enterprising young noblemen, younger sons looking for dominion, and sinners, perhaps, on the lookout for penance combined with profit, were the personalities that made a characteristic impact on the Islamic world.

For a generation the lack of cohesiveness of contemporary Islam made the progress of these European adventurers rather easy. A series of Latin feudal statelets was set up along the Syrian coastline and in Palestine, based in Antioch, Edessa, Tripoli, and Jerusalem. This was the first phase of the Crusader period, when the newcomers from Europe settled down in Syria and mingled with the local Christian communities that had survived the wave of the Muslim conquests. These Crusaders were quickly assimilated, both in culture and customs, though their zone of settlement remained the coastal strips on the Mediterranean, in intimate contact with Europe. But the Islamic world was still vigorous enough to evolve a reaction to this thrust from Europe. By 1154, with the capture of Damascus, a single Muslim state was established in Syria on the ruins of previous Muslim rivalries and frictions, and the Crusaders found themselves faced by a state that was powerful enough to contest the total Crusader enterprise.

A basic issue was the control of Egypt, where the Fatimid caliphate that had been in control of the country for so long was now in its death throes. Saladin, who had been acting as Wazir to the last of the Fatimids though really representing the interests of Nur ad-Din, the son of Zanji, the Seljuq officer who had consolidated the Muslim state based on Damascus, announced the demise of the Fatimid caliphate in 1171 and made himself ruler of Egypt, only nominally subject to Nur ad-Din. On the latter's death (1174) Saladin consolidated his own rule by ingesting Syria. By 1187 he was strong enough to attack the Crusaders, and at his death (1193) Jerusalem had been recaptured by the Muslims and the Crusaders thrown back on a thin strip of land based on the towns of Acre, Tyre, Tripoli, and Antioch.

Saladin's handiwork did not last long. The Syro-Egyptian Empire he had consolidated soon broke up, though Egypt itself remained fairly strong, the strongest Muslim state in the Middle East, repeatedly repelling all the attempts of the later Crusaders to get a serious foothold in Palestine again.

The chief effect the Crusaders had on the Middle East was in the field of business. Under the Crusaders there had been numerous colonies of European merchants, who lived on and were encouraged by the Muslim authorities after the defeat of the Crusaders. A very important and thriving business of both export and import passed through their hands, in spite of all the church's irritation with this frustration of the religious inspiration of the Crusades and in spite of the various decrees of excommunication against the businessmen engaged in it.

The Crusaders proved to be a mere episode in the life of Islam. They had little or no effect on thought, and outside the purely administrative conveniences they provided through the business network of the merchants who had come with them, there were no aftereffects.

It was in the East that a far more serious menace was evolving. Chingis Khan had succeeded in unifying various nomadic tribes of Mongols and Turks and, using their remarkable powers of horsemanship and their qualities of discipline and endurance, he created in the space of a few years a vast empire that extended across Asia into the heart of Europe, putting its stamp on Europe and Asia for centuries.

By 1220 the Mongols and Turks had taken all Transoxania; and by the next year Chingis himself had crossed the Oxus into

Persia. He died a few years later, and his empire remained relatively quiescent for a while, but by the middle of the thirteenth century the Mongol march was resumed on a grand scale.

By 1258 the Mongol prince Hulagu, with instructions to occupy all Islam as far as Egypt, marched into Baghdad, sacked the imperial city, killed the puppet caliph, and simply wiped out the Abbasid caliphate once and for all, terminating the shadowy existence it had led for so long. This was a turning point in Muslim history, since in spite of its *de facto* impotence the Abbasid caliphate had been the legal focus of Islam and the outward emblem of at least its ideal unity. From the purely material point of view, of course, the Mongols were doing no more than wiping out an institutional fiction, the symbol of a reality that had been dead for centuries.

The Mongol invasion, though executed by the same tribes, roughly, that had produced the Seljuq regime, was different in that this wave of conquerors, unlike the Seljuqs, had not had time to become assimilated by Islam. The destruction they wrought throughout the country, much exaggerated in the conventional manner by their victims, seems to have been based on a strategy and was not at all as wanton as has been maintained. In any case it came to an end with the success of their campaign of conquest, and under Mongol rule a new era was initiated in Persia, characterized by both cultural and economic development.

In Iraq itself, however, the Mongols had much more pernicious effects. Civil government broke down completely and the great irrigation works, the source of the country's prosperity, were shattered, leaving the country wide open to the incursions of the Bedouin, whose unruliness had been curbed by the sedentary society that was now ruined. Moreover, Iraq was now detached from the East-West trade that had contributed so much to its prosperity. The great international trade routes now lay north and east, to Turkey and Persia, and westward to Egypt and the Red Sea. Iraq and its fallen capital, Baghdad, were now a mere appendage of the Mongol state in Persia and were doomed to centuries of stagnation.

The rest of the Arabic-speaking world was not much affected by these new Mongol invaders. Egypt and Syria were shielded against the Mongols by some of their predecessors—the Kurdish regime (Ayyubids) that had succeeded Saladin and was organized along the lines of the Mongols' predecessors, the Seljuq Turks, who continued making up the personnel of the (Ayyubid) sultan's entourage and were in fact an autocracy of the same kind as that of the Mongols.

These Turkish Mamluks that ruled Egypt, beginning in the middle of the thirteenth century, created another Turkish institution whose dominion over Egypt and Syria lasted until 1517, when another group, the Ottoman Turks, or Osmanlis, who remained the most powerful force in Islam until World War I, ousted them and took over the entire Middle East.

The Kurdish Ayyubid dynasty founded by Saladin came to an end in 1260, when a Qipchaq Turk by the name of Baybars made himself sultan and, very much like Saladin, managed to unite Syria and Egypt in a single state, far more enduringly than had Saladin. He stood off his Mongol cousins in the East and wiped out nearly all remnants of Crusader rule in Syria. Baybars was pliable enough, or had enough insight into the magnetic power of myths, to invite a member of the Abbasid clan to come to Egypt and to be installed there as caliph, though he was even more powerless than the Abbasid caliphs had been in Baghdad during the decline of their dynasty. Thus the Abbasid caliphs in Cairo were mere mythological ornaments of the Mamluk sultans, spending all their time amusing themselves and thanking the givers of banquets for inviting them.

Baybars introduced into Egypt a feudal system brought over by the Kurdish house of the Ayyubids from the Seljuq Turks. A land grant would be made to an officer on condition of his providing a certain number of Mamluk soldiers, according to his rank. Generally two-thirds of his income went for the soldiery.

Perhaps the most interesting point about this feudal system of the Mamluk Turks in Egypt was that it was carefully prevented from becoming hereditary. The descendants of any given Mamluks soon adopted Arabic as their speech and were assimilated into the countryside; their places as officers were taken by Mamluk newcomers from the outside, and thus it was impossible for a hereditary landed gentry to come into existence since the land grants would normally be for life or less.

The Mamluk officers, not rooted in the land at all, generally lived either in the capital or the chief town of whatever district their fiefs were located in, and hence they were interested in income rather than in the possession of more land. Thus the system had no tendency to develop strongpoints of a military nature, or strong dukedoms or counties as in Western Europe. Indeed, the division of the land itself into fiefs was not a permanent one, but kept shifting in accordance with a periodical reallocation.

Perhaps the most unusual thing about the Mamluks, sociologically speaking, was that the whole institution, the actual ruling class of a large state, was composed of slaves bought abroad and trained for their roles in Egypt. In the beginning they had been chiefly Qipchaq Turks, born along the north shores of the Black Sea; later they included other kinds of Mongols and Turks, Circassians, and occasionally some Europeans. The Mamluk state power had an intricate dual administration, for civil and for military affairs, both sides being in charge of Mamluk officers assisted by civilian staffs.

The Mamluks were successful in holding their state together against its various Christian and Mongol enemies. They maintained the fabric of Muslim society against both forces until the fifteenth century, when they were undone by a new power, again composed of Turks, this time of the Ottoman Turks who had emerged on the ruins of the Seljuq regime in Anatolia. By this time the Ottoman Turks, with remarkable military and administrative ability, had penetrated into Europe; on a firm basis they turned toward the East again and their relations with the Mamluks, which had been friendly at first, turned hostile.

The Ottoman Turks were ultimately to wipe out the Mamluk power, as a result of circumstances that had led irremediably to its debilitation. Egypt had always depended on the trade with Europe, especially the trade between Europe and the Far East that passed through the Middle East. But this was shattered once again by the Turco-Mongol troops of Tamerlane (ruled 1369–1405), which devastated Syria, put Damascus to the sack, and opened the countryside to the further devastations of the Bedouin and for that matter to plague and locusts as well.

The Mamluks were hard pressed and resorted to desperate economic measures to squeeze as much profit as possible out of the transit trade, with the result that rising prices led to retaliation from Europe and thus dislocated the whole of the Egyptian economy. Meanwhile the recruitment of other Mamluk slaves began encountering difficulties in the countries they came from, while the Mamluk rulers at home became increasingly tyrannical, wasteful, and oppressive.

By the end of the fifteenth century, the catastrophic situation of the Mamluk regime in Egypt was consummated by a major calamity: The whole country was completely bypassed in world trade by the opening up of an alternative sea route—around the Cape of Good Hope—that enabled European traders to disregard Egypt completely. On Portuguese initiative another overseas route to India was established. The Mamluks, together with the Venetian traders who were in the same plight for the same reason, desperately tried to cope with the Portuguese peril, but found themselves outmatched by Portuguese navigational and naval superiority. Portuguese fleets, better built, better armed, and better sailed than the Egyptian, soon did away with the Saracen merchant shipping in the Indian Ocean and even got into the Persian Gulf and the Red Sea.

In a word, the Middle East, so strategic a locality for so long, had as last been bypassed; for another four centuries international trade was to go on neglecting it.

This long period of decay in the Islamic realm was characterized by three basic changes:

The Muslim Middle East was transformed from a trading economy based on money to a regime that was basically feudal, with its roots in subsistence agriculture. The great cosmopolitan market economy in which the chief sources of business activity were business speculations based on money investment was replaced by great peasant populations living on their land and enveloped in a complex political structure based on feudal property holdings.

The second change was the assumption of all political authority by the Turks, who in various forms—that is, various tribal confederations—ousted both the Arabs and the Persians and eventually, after passing through Persian cultural influence, came to exercise dominion over nearly the whole of Islam, with the exception of far-off Morocco. The sedentary Arabic-speaking populations lost all trace of political independence and remained in thrall to the Turks until World War I.

The Arabs proper, by whom I now mean the desert tribes, did, it is true, recover the independence they had once lost at the height of the Umayyad and the Abbasid caliphates, but they simply receded into their vast and thinly populated wildernesses and no longer exercised a discernible influence over anything in Islam. They could never be subjugated more than nominally; they held out against the Turks quite successfully until they managed to shake off even the nominal allegiance they had occasionally been forced to show the central Turkish power. There were also a few mountain outposts where Arabic-speaking communities still held out against the Turks.

But with these minor exceptions the speakers of Arabic—not, that is, Arabs in the sense we give the word today—were to be deprived of political authority for more than a millennium. In the cultivated areas of the great centers of Arabic speech—Iraq, Syria, and Egypt—there was not the smallest question of the Arabic-speaking peoples' governing themselves.

Thus, in spite of the unique role that had been played by the Arabic language in the genesis of Islam and in its cultural accomplishments, Arabic as a vernacular gradually sank to such a level of contempt in the minds of the populations of these areas that it was considered a sign of something inherently unworthy; it was widely taken for granted that only Turks could govern. Even at the beginning of the nineteenth century Napoleon was forced to use only Turks to enforce order, since speaking Arabic as a mother tongue automatically lost face for anyone in a position of authority.

The third change was perhaps only a shift of emphasis; when Iraq was shattered for so many centuries in the wake of the Mongol invasions it was only natural for the center of the Arabic-speaking world to be transferred to Egypt. Iraq was so disorganized and now so remote from the Mediterranean centers that it was bound to be replaced by Egypt, which, as the country athwart a major trade route and consisting of a single valley-country along a single river whose powers of irrigation imposed a degree of centralization on the country, was bound to become the only powerful centralized state in the Arabic-speaking Middle East. It is true that the Egyptians never regarded themselves as Arabs, as I have pointed out and shall point out again, and indeed did not until the 1950s, under the leadership of Nasser (Jamal Abd-an-Nasir), but in the middle of the twentieth century the fact of their speaking Arabic was to prove of cardinal importance.

Arabic culture itself was not impaired, in a sense, since it was thrown back more and more on the centers where Arabic had become the actual vernacular of the people, but it lost its status as the cultivated language par excellence of the Islamic society. First the Persians and then the Turks, who in succession had inherited the state structure from the Arabs themselves, rapidly developed cultural languages and milieux of their own. The Persians especially, who had never been entirely submerged ethnically or linguistically by the Arabs, had never forgotten their ancient culture or language. Now these both came back for a vigorous efflorescence, though the Persian language was revived, to be sure, with a very substantial admixture of Arabic terms and idioms.

Even the Turks, though they were only to begin their cultural career through conversion to Islam, once they assumed control over its political destinies soon evolved a cultural milieu of their own, initially based on the Persian culture they took as their model but soon developing literary styles and media of their own. Thus both Persian and Turkish became the cultivated languages of Islam and took over the cultural as well as the political leadership of Islam.

After the Seljuqs, in fact, Arabic shrank back to the use of the Arabic-speaking countries, where indeed it was to fall into a period of almost total stagnation until modern times, except for a rather dwarfed output of theological and scientific works, the latter of which had no particular significance at all as the intellectual centers of Islam in general began rapidly contracting with the decay in its political fortunes and all serious scientific work began to be accomplished in Western Europe alone.

As the political center of gravity of Islam came under the control of Persians and then of Turks (of all kinds), and as the center of gravity of the Arabic-speaking world itself naturally moved westward to Egypt and to some extent to Syria, both these countries became the principal centers of culture insofar as it was expressed in the Arabic language.

The independence in both speculation and research that had characterized Islamic society at its height now became a thing of the past as the society became static intellectually, however much it was still subject to political and economic turbulence; it also developed a congealed and formal theology that became completely authoritative. As conformism became the mode in public life, so literature too became passive and dependent on accepted models. In addition, there was a general decline in the actual numbers of writers and readers, and a moving away from an interest in real life. The combined phenomenon led to a substantial loss of liveliness and spirit. Perhaps the most striking characteristic of the time was the increase in emphasis on mere form in the arts and on the development of mere memory in scholarship.

Still, some distinguished men wrote in Arabic during this period of decline, including Ghazali (1058–1111), a Persian who was a major exponent of a blend between the new scholasticism and the Sufis' mystical religiosity, an energetic opponent of Isma'ilism, and a reformer of Muslim orthodoxy; Hariri (1054–1122), traditionally regarded by students of Arabic as supreme in formal elegance; Yaqut (1179–1229), the celebrated biographer and geographer; and of course Ibn Khaldun (1332–1406), whom I have already mentioned as a brilliantly original philosophic historian and sociologist.

A word must be said about the fate of the western half of the Islamic realm, whose most brilliant creations were the mixed civilizations of Spain and Sicily. These have, of course, vanished and strictly speaking were not "Arab" at all, as I have indicated, yet they had a profound effect on the imagination of Western Europe and so played a part in shaping reciprocal attitudes between West and East.

The Maghrib—*i.e.,* the west of the caliphate, consisting of North Africa and Spain—had had a series of satraps ever since the conquest of Spain (thoroughly islamized for a long time except for the small state of León in the northeastern corner) all based in Qayrawan. The Spanish vice-governors, however, often had a special and almost independent position. A permanent government seat was finally established in Córdoba that for centuries was to remain the chief residence of the western caliphate. The Berbers in consequence were established on both sides of the Strait of Gibraltar, and even after the splitting up of the Muslim caliphate into an eastern and a western half, it was they who were to control the fortunes of Spain for several centuries. Spain was to be part and parcel of North Africa because of the Berber presence.

In Africa the Berbers had been a subject people, aiming at equality with the Arabs only through conversion to Islam, but in Spain they and the Arabs together had undertaken a collective enterprise, the subjugation of the country, in which the Berbers might legitimately have counted on a fair division of the spoils. But the

Arab leadership made a dual error. In Africa they had treated the Berbers, even after their conversion, with irritating high-handedness, and in Spain they had given them a lesser share of the booty.

Berber restiveness began growing by leaps and bounds. Its first formal outbreak—in Spain, under a Berber chief—was put an end to by 730, but in Africa things were more serious.

The unrest was during the reign of the Caliph Hisham, under whom the transformation of the fiscal system made necessary by the mass conversions to Islam was being introduced in a systematic and energetic way, and went in tandem with the growth of the bureaucracy and the Asiatic despotism that was beginning to replace the democratic ethos of the Arab tribal patriarchs.

This economic and political process had the worst possible effects precisely on the Berbers, who had been brought to heel only by diplomacy and the hopes of loot. These sociopolitical and economic reactions were, as is usual in Islam, given a religious complexion, and the idea of the Secessionists, mentioned above, assumed unexpected proportions.

The basic idea of the Secessionists, who had abandoned Ali after the Battle of Siffin, was that the will of the people was absolute; an unjust caliph could legitimately be deposed at any time. The allegiance to Secessionism was one of the most important ways in which the opposition to the state power could be expressed precisely by the old-fashioned Arab circles that were irritated by the elevation of the state, just as among the Persians opposition to a central authority took the form of allegiance to the Shi'a.

In North Africa, as the Umayyad troops began falling foul more and more often of the Berber populace, the latter began turning more and more to the ideas of the Secessionists as a suitable vehicle for expressing Berber opposition to the caliphate in Muslim terms.

When the Arabs lost their military effectiveness as a result of the great schism between the Qays and the Kalb, the Berbers saw an opportunity to break loose of their Arab shackles. A few small revolts were followed by a really massive rebellion in the far west of North Africa; as early as 741 the whole of present-day Morocco had shaken off the Arabs' overlordship.

Hisham sent a tremendous army, the pick of his Syrian troops, to put down the opposition of this headstrong people, so similar to the Bedouin themselves. These Syrians were supposed to act in tandem with the garrison troops still stationed in North Africa, but their superior equipment was counteracted by the internal friction that was rapidly becoming endemic throughout the Arab milieu.

The whole notion of Arab preeminence, even at this early stage of Arab hegemony in Islam, was put in doubt by a greater Berber victory on the Zebu River that same year of 741. Countless fugitives made their way to Spain to add to the political turmoil there.

This particular Berber victory was compensated for by an Arab one the following year at Qayrawan, and the Berber revolt was broken; order was restored in Spain too a little while later. The Umayyad house had a breathing spell for a few years, until the upheavals that were to undo it began spreading from the Middle East throughout North Africa and Spain, in the wake of the complications that beset the central regime in the Middle East. Then, when the seat of the caliphate was taken away from the Umayyads and removed from Damascus to Baghdad, it was rather natural for the densely settled Mediterranean countries to manage their own political destinies.

After the Umayyad collapse in the eighth century, the countries overrun by the Arabs were ruled by the eastern caliphate only occasionally and superficially. In 745 Abd-ar-Rahman ibn Habib in Spain declared himself independent of the caliph's governor and was eventually recognized as having *de facto* power by the last Umayyad caliph, Marwan. In return for this, Abd-ar-Rahman had to make only a few trivial concessions, such as paying a small tribute and mentioning the caliph's name in prayer. Abd-ar-Rahman's own position was too far removed from the dynastic upheaval in the east to be effected.

When the Abbasids finally consolidated their position in Baghdad and showed signs of taking some action against Abd-ar-Rahman, he announced his formal allegiance while at the same time welcoming to Qayrawan various Umayyad princes (754–55). These Umayyad princes, however, were to create trouble for Abd-ar-Rahman himself; he and two of the Umayyad princes were ultimately killed, while a third (Abd-ar-Rahman ibn Mu'awiya) made his way to Spain, where he became the founder of the western caliphate. In Africa itself the killing of Abd-ar-Rahman ibn Habib led to general chaos; all decentralizing forces exploded. The whole country fell prey to practically unflagging warfare, with small dynasties appearing and disappearing. The whole of the Maghrib was lost for good, though the Baghdad caliphate managed to restore some semblance of order at least as far as Algeria.

From the purely ethnic point of view the result of all this turmoil was the overshadowing of the Arabs in North Africa by the Berbers. Though the Arabic language was to spread there as it did in the Middle East, it never succeeded in arabizing the Berbers any more than it did the other peoples that took on Arabic without feeling themselves to be Arabs. For that matter it was not wholly successful even in driving out the various Berber languages, many of which are still very much alive. Thus it was ultimately the Berbers and not the Arabs who in the future were to govern the territories in North Africa. Even the religious tendency of the Secessionists has survived (as Ibadites) in North Africa, as well as East Africa and southern Arabia.

One of the dynasties cast up by the unremitting turmoil in North Africa was the Aghlabids, a Tunisian ruling house that distinguished itself through the conquest of Sicily, which led to one of the most curious episodes in the cultural coexistence of Islam and Christendom.

Sicily, by virtue of its geographical position alone, was bound to become a football of politics once the Arabs had established a state strong enough to cope with Byzantium. The very earliest attacks on Sicily had been launched while Mu'awiya was still governor of Syria, and there were also constant piratical attacks on Corsica, Sardinia, and even Ischia, though nothing substantial was achieved until 827, when the Aghlabids came over on the invitation of a Christian Sicilian rebel and managed to conquer the lush island. This placed Islam in the very midst of the multicolored riot of Italian statelets in central and southern Italy. By 831 the Muslims had occupied Palermo, which was to remain the capital of the island throughout Muslim rule. The warfare between the Byzantine and the Muslim forces continued for decades, until 895–96, when the Byzantines finally gave up the island. Messina (*ca.* 843), Castrogiovanni (859), and Syracuse (878) fell into the hands of the Muslims, who also managed to plant themselves on the mainland, setting up garrisons at Bari and Taranto for a while. Muslim freebooters threatened Naples and Rome, and even northern Italy; a pope paid them tribute for two years.

At first Muslim Sicily was a province of Tunisia; when the Aghlabids were replaced by another dynasty, the Fatimids, Sicily went to the latter. When the Fatimids ultimately moved to Egypt in 972, the ties to the central regime weakened to the point where the governorship became *de facto* hereditary in the line of Hasan ibn Ali al-Kalbi, which retained power until 1040, a period that marked the highest efflorescence of Muslim power on the island. In the tenth century a traveler noted three hundred mosques in Palermo alone; though little has come down to us, there is no doubt that there was a luxuriant flowering of Arabic culture and letters.

The Muslims treated Sicily as they had the countries conquered in the East; property in land was radically altered to suit Islamic notions. A dense and systematic colonization of the island took place, rather than mere executive exploitation. This is attested to by the Arabic place-names and by the survival in the Sicilian dialect of Arabic farming words. The Muslims introduced oranges, mulberries, sugar cane, and date palms and cotton, as well as irrigation (many Sicilian fountains still have names recognizably Arabic in origin).

A curious symbiosis took place with the Normans, who came to Sicily at the end of the tenth century and stayed on until 1194. The Norman prince Roger II (1130–54) made constant use of Muslim troops and engineers in his military campaigns, as well as Muslim architects, who created a characteristic Muslim-Norman style. Even his coronation mantle bore an Arabic inscription and a Muslim date. He used court poets as eulogists in the Arabic style, and it was at Roger's court that the greatest of Arab geographers wrote a monumental geographical compendium dedicated to Roger, known as "The Book of Roger." A later Norman king, William II (1166–89), was known to read and write Arabic, a remarkable achievement. The traveler who comments on this also notes that in Palermo even the Christians dressed like Muslims and spoke Arabic. Records, including court records, were kept in Arabic, and even though Arabic was gradually replaced with Latin, Arabic culture lived on, though by the beginning of the fourteenth century it was extinct, while Islam was dead through emigration or conversion. Sicilian Islam became famous for translations from Arabic into

Latin. The last of the Sicilian translators was a Jewish doctor, Faraj ibn Salim, who introduced a great medical work of Razi (Rhases) to the West via a Latin translation.

In 1035 a civil war broke out in Sicily that put an end both to the Muslim dynasty and in general to the rule of Islam on the island. It was not a part of the constant friction between Berbers and Arabs that had already had such fateful consequences throughout North Africa and Spain, as well as in Sicily, but came about through a decision to replace the Berber troops with others who cost more money and so led to a rise in the tax rate. This inflamed the local population, which took to arms itself, and in the confusion that followed, once again every man's hand was raised against everyone else. Sicily emerged from the war no longer a single state, but split up into endless tiny principalities and city republics that remained in a state of reciprocal hostility. In the conflict between the Arab aristocracy and the islamized natives the Arabs themselves were to appeal to the Normans, who had meanwhile set up a strong state on the Italian mainland. After the Arab prince had summoned them in 1061, the Normans proceeded to conquer the whole island, accomplishing this in some thirty years.

This marked the end of Islam in Europe outside Spain. The expansion of the Arabs had reached its peak, and the Muslim flood ebbed back into Africa.

In Spain Islam lasted another few centuries, steadily falling back under the impact of the various Christian states in the Iberian Peninsula. The realm under the control of Muslim regimes was hacked away piecemeal, and the last Moors and Jews were formally expelled from the peninsula in 1492. Moorish civilization had been exceptionally brilliant, though it, too, was the handiwork of a mixed population in which the percentage of actual Arab blood was infinitesimal. Intermarriage both with Berbers and with the local, already much mixed population led to a situation in which very often the greater the proliferation of Arabic personal names the feebler was the connection with any actual Arabs.

In Spain and Sicily Islam proved to be a mere episode. Culturally the West was to benefit enormously from Muslim civilization in both places, especially in Spain; it benefited at least as much as it did from the blessings that came to it from the East during the great Crusades. The barbaric reputation earned by Moorish buccaneers—

the "Barbary pirates"—was largely due to Christian propaganda; the Moors simply did what every Christian sea-power of the period regarded as normal. Plunder and slaving were characteristic of both sides equally. Here again the ecclesiastically conditioned Middle Ages harped on the religious cleavage between the two sides, though the activities of both were much the same.

• • •

It was the Arabian nomads who created the sociopolitical and linguistic framework in which Islam could articulate its cultural unity, but it was the Turkish nomads, from the steppelands of central Asia, who gave the various state structures of Islam their substance.

Of these Turkish nomads, it was the Ottoman Turks, as I have indicated, who surely made the most extraordinary career for themselves, by founding the most powerful, durable, and efficient empire ever seen in Islam and scarcely excelled elsewhere. Since it was the Turks generally who governed all Arabic-speaking communities for the better part of a millennium, and since it was within the framework of the Ottoman Empire that the first seeds of the modern Arab nationalist movement began to germinate, a brief note on them is called for.

The Osmanlis, like all the other Turkish clans that became Islamized, made their way into Islam initially by way of the Persian subculture. By the time they were Muslims they regarded Persian culture and the Persian language as the matrix of their own civilization. The Muslim subculture of their own that they later developed is best looked on, accordingly, as an outgrowth of Persian civilization.

The Osmanlis, together with a kindred Turkish people, the Qaramanlis, were successors to the Seljuq sultanate that had been set up in Anatolia in the eleventh century by Turkish adventurers enlarging Islam at the expense of Christendom. When the Anatolian Seljuq sultanate broke up in the course of the thirteenth century, the Osmanlis were left with mere scraps.

Of all the Anatolian Seljuqs' Turkish feudatories, the Osmanlis were the latest comers; their circumstances had been singularly humble. They had been mere refugees, a nameless band of flotsam and jetsam flung out to the farthest corners of Islam by the torrential impact of the Mongol wave of conquest when it smashed onto the northeastern marshes out of the heart of the Eurasian steppe. The last of the Anatolian Seljuqs had given these refugees a wedge of territory on the northwestern edge of the Anatolian plateau, where Seljuq territory adjoined land still held by the Byzantine Empire along the Asiatic shores of the Sea of Marmara. After a trek that had brought him from the Oxus to the Sangarius, Osman, the Osmanlis' eponym, was reduced here to being a frontiersman; he set himself to enlarge his borders at the expense of his Orthodox Christian neighbors. His first objective was Brusa, an Eastern Roman city; this took him nine years (1317–26) to capture, and from then on Osman and his successors, after gaining a foothold on the European shore of the Dardanelles in thirty years, moved forward until the siege of Vienna, conquering a vast area in the Balkans. They also subdued their fellow Turks in Anatolia, and after taking Constantinople in 1453 the Osmanlis rounded off the rest of their empire in Anatolia by annexing Qaraman once and for all in 1465.

The stimulus that had been given the Osmanlis by their location on the marches of a territory was doubtless what enabled them to defeat their Qaramanli rivals, who had been stagnating in the interior.

Nomads are generally successful in conquering sedentary populations and in establishing empires, since the qualities they have developed tending herd on steppelands also enable them to cope with the problems of herding human populations. By the same token, however, once the empires are established the nomad qualities tend to vanish; thus their empires have generally been ephemeral, as was pointed out by Ibn Khaldun. After the shock of nomad conquest, inversely, the subject populations generally recover their morale, since they are on their own land and have remained economically productive, while their nomad masters have become parasitic in a sense in which they were not parasitic when tending flocks and herds.

It is because of this reversal of roles that nomadic empires dissolve so quickly—Ibn Khaldun reckoned an average duration for empires at three generations, or 120 years—since the human cattle being manipulated by the nomadic parvenus eventually reassert their independence by either ejecting or assimilating their shepherds.

Yet the Osmanlis were a brilliant exception to this generality. Part of the explanation of the Ottoman durability doubtless lies in the positive political function they were performing in welding together the main body of orthodox Christendom against its own disruptive forces, but the greater part of the explanation of the Ottoman's sociopolitical tenacity—which lasted well over four centuries, and even longer, down to World War I, if we include its period of decline—lies in their peculiar adaptation to the executive role in a sedentary society. The singular ingenuity of the Ottoman state was demonstrated by its skillful adaptation of still another nomadic institution to sedentary conditions—slaves as sheep dogs. Just as human populations were treated as cattle, *i.e.*, were milked for the produce of their lands and their toil, so another stratum of slaves was set up to ride herd on the sheep. The Osmanlis succeeded in adapting the institution of slavery to the care and tending of their subject populations, though it was not an institution they invented. In Islam, for instance, the Abbasid caliphs had, to their sorrow, trained as soldiers and administrators Turkish slaves bought in the Eurasian steppe, and in the Mamluk regime I have mentioned as ruling Egypt there was essentially the same principle at work. The institution originally used by Saladin and his successors after his destruction of the Fatimids and the launching of his own Ayyubid dynasty eventually ousted its sponsors and made itself the autonomous governor of the whole country, replenishing its ranks by slaves freshly imported from abroad. As I have pointed out, the Egyptian Mamluks maintained a political understanding with the Mongol khanate of Qipchaq and with the maritime state of Venice. The Qipchaq khans made periodic slave raids on the Caucasian highlanders, the Russian forest-dwellers and other Eurasian nomads outside the confines of the khanate itself, while Venetians transported the freshly captured slaves to Egypt; it was one of the most profitable businesses in Venice.

These Mamluks, while maintaining as a mere façade a shadowy representative of the Abbasid caliphate on condition that he do nothing, governed Egypt and Syria, while holding the Mongols at bay along the Euphrates, from 1250 to 1516–17, when the Osmanlis, using a more highly developed slave institution of their own—the celebrated Slave Household that ran the Turkish Empire—imposed their rule on the Mamluks, though without eliminating the Mamluk administration apparatus itself. By the eighteenth century this had reasserted itself and not until 1811 was its power broken by Muhammad Ali's massacre.

The Ottoman Slave Household, though broadly similar to the Mamluk Slave Household, was greatly its superior in discipline and in organizational efficiency.

The ruling institution of the Ottoman Empire, which included the royal family, consisted of household officers, government officers, the standing army, and a large body of young men being trained for all service in the army, the court, and the government.

The most curious thing about this executive institution was that it was almost entirely composed of Christians or their children and that almost every member of the institution entered it as the sultan's slave and remained that as long as he lived, no matter how important he became. The sultan's wives were all slaves, and he himself, for that matter, was the son of a slave. His daughters might be married to men called pashas and Wazirs, but these were merely titles granted them at the sultan's pleasure; they remained slaves all their lives.

The Ottoman Slave Household was modeled closely, in fact, on the lines of Plato's Republic, but its slave composition made it the antithesis of the aristocratic structure recommended by Plato. It is doubtless historically unique in that its executive personnel were selected exclusively among the children of those professing a hostile religion. It deliberately and systematically took slaves and turned them into state ministers. Boys were taken from farms and pasture grounds and turned into courtiers and husbands of princesses. The descendants of families immemorially Christian were made the rulers of the greatest of Muslim states and soldiers and generals in armies dedicated to the destruction of the Cross. Ancestry was utterly disregarded in the process of selection, which was made only on the basis of an assessment of personal qualities. Throughout their most active years the Ottoman trainees had no family cares, no sure title to property, no assurance of ultimate success or security, were taught a strange law and religion, and were kept conscious at all times of the sword above their heads.

Thus the essence of the Ottoman slave system was the training of the sheep dogs that ran the human cattle of the Ottoman Empire. The profession of public slave on this high level was dangerous, all-important, and glorious, indeed the most splendid profession in the empire, and the crowning oddity was that this career was open *exclusively* to children born of infidels. The sultan's Muslim coreligionists were legally ineligible for it, even though they were the children of the Ottoman feudal gentry, the equals of the sultan in all respects, and even his social peers. This rule is surprising, since it in fact debarred the ruling class from ruling; but granted the capacity of enforcing this disability, as it was enforced for at least two centuries (*ca.* 1365–1565), it was obviously an efficient device. Since the sheep dogs had such an arduous task in herding the human cattle, it was essential to have altogether atomized human particles wrenched away from all ties and background to manage it. It is obvious that just because the children of the Ottoman lords were what they were they would be far more headstrong and unruly, also with far more connections and family and clan ties, than isolated slave children. Thus the Muslims were barred from the service of the state at its very zenith.

Slaves were recruited abroad through military capture or purchase in the slave markets, by gift, or volunteering (a career in the Ottoman service was to remain attractive to Western Europeans as late as the beginning of the nineteenth century). The great Ottoman demand for slaves was met by the activities of the Barbary pirates (the Turkish colonists in North Africa), who raided the coasts of Western Europe by ship, and by the Krim Tatars, a hangover of the Mongol Qipchaq horde surviving under an Ottoman protectorate. At home slaves were obtained by periodical levies.

The recruits were subjected to a minutely regulated and strictly enforced course of training, in which punishments and the incentives of ambition and glory were evenly balanced. Every slave could become a Grand Wazir, an achievement dependent solely on his personal qualities; and the rewards and the glamour of the whole institution were such that it was ultimately pried open to the influx of free Muslims, whereupon it declined rapidly. Free Muslims, attracted by the charms of state service, forced their way into the executive institution and diluted it to such an extent that it succumbed to the conflicts of the society. The first breach was made by men who had come up through the system and were determined to secure its advantages for their sons; the breach, once made, was soon extended. It proved to be psychologically impossible to keep out the free Muslim gentry.

The state system evolved by the Osmanlis, which was to encompass all speakers of Arabic for so many centuries, took a little time to blossom. It was, in fact, only through a conflict with Persia, the culture that had set its stamp on the Osmanlis to begin with, that the Ottoman Empire took final shape.

As has been usual in Islam, this conflict too had a religious tinge: It revolved around the consolidation, on the terrain of Persia, of the major schismatic movement in Islam, the Shi'a.

Originally the Shi'a had been one of the primitive Muslim factions that had been worsted in the struggle over the spoils after the remarkably successful Arab conquests—first by the House of Umayya, then by the House of Abbas. The Shi'a survived as a stereotype of the embodiment of frustrated political ambitions and served as a rallying point for all disgruntled elements of society, largely directed, accordingly, against the successful Arab regime, that is, as the mouthpiece for the non-Arabs of the caliphate against the Arab ascendancy. These were, most importantly, the Persians in the East and the Berbers in the West.

Hence, under the Abbasid regime, beginning with the latter part of the eighth century on, Shi'ism, from its original fortress in lower Iraq, a meeting place for Aramaic, Persian, and Arab elements, kept trying to push forward into Persia and into the Maghrib.

When the Fatimids, the most successful Shi'ite dynasty, conquered Egypt in 969, after winning the devotion of the Katama Berbers, for a time it seemed as though the Abbasid caliphate might be overwhelmed by a Shi'ite coalition from all points of the compass, since the Qarmathians, who as Isma'ilis were coreligionists of the Fatimids, had been terrorizing the fringes of Syria and Iraq for a century (890–990).

Shi'ism became the religion of the Persians after they abandoned their Zoroastrianism in the ninth and tenth centuries of the Christian era. In the tenth century a Persian Shi'ite dynasty, the Buwayhids, overran all western Persia to take over the Abbasid caliphs in Baghdad.

The Buwayhids, though Shi'ites, were of the Six-Imam variety, not like the Fatimids and Qarmathians. Their political interest lay in keeping their hands on the Abbasid caliphs, which they did until overthrown by the Seljuqs in 1055–56. Thus the three Shi'ite powers—the Buwayhids (Persians), the Qarmathians, and the Fatimids—never agreed on the control of the caliphate, and having failed to consolidate the enterprise between the Fatimid entry into Cairo in 969 and the anti-Shi'ite Seljuqs' entry into Baghdad in 1055, the power of Shi'ism shrank rapidly.

Thus Shi'ism had vanished as a serious political factor between the shattering of the Abbasid caliphate by the Mongols (1275) and the emergence on the ruins of the caliphate of its nascent successors, the Arabic-speaking and Persian societies. In Tunisia Sunnism overcame Shi'ism about 1044–46, when the Sanhaja Berber chief revolted against the Fatimid overlords who had invested him with power, forswore Shi'ism, and proclaimed his allegiance to the Abbasid caliph in Baghdad. The later Berber masters of the Maghrib and Andalusia—the Murabits (*ca.* 1056–1147) and the Muwahhids (*ca.* 1130–1269)—accentuated their Berber separatism by adopting not Shi'ism, like the more cultivated Katama, but a strict form of Sunnism.

Shi'ism was finally done for when the Kurd Saladin liquidated the Fatimid caliphate in 1171 as the result of a contest for the mastery of Egypt between the Frankish kingdom of Jerusalem and the Seljuqs' successors in Syria. For a time Shi'ism survived only in various nooks and crannies in Islam.

Isma'ilis have survived as an obscure sect in Syria and as a diaspora in India, strangely transformed into shopkeepers who—as "Khwajas"—pay tribute to the Agha Khan.

During the two centuries between the collapse of the Abbasid caliphate and the emergence of the Arabic-speaking and Persian societies, and the debut of a distinguished statesman, Isma'il Shah Safawi, at the very end of the fifteenth century, Shi'ism must have seemed a lost cause.

Down to the career of this man, who ruled in Persia between 1500 and 1524, no Muslim would have thought it likely that the Islamic world, however fragmented by religious, socioeconomic, and political rivalries, could have been split by one major division along the lines of this ancient cleavage between the Sunni majority and the Shi'ite minority. Up to 1500 Shi'ism was merely a minoritarian religion; it was scattered throughout Islam but did not rule anywhere. Nor up to 1500 would anyone have thought that the Ottoman Empire was on the eve of embarking on the conquest of all those countries in which Arabic had become the vernacular speech of the population in addition to remaining a purely intellectual medium in its classical, written version largely unintelligible to ordinary people. Up to 1500 the Ottoman Empire had been expanding quite vigorously within the limits of Byzantine Christendom.

This situation was utterly transformed in a revolution accomplished by Isma'il Shah Safawi. This Shi'ite revolution, based in Persia, which restored Persia to its ancient status as a nation-state based on one language, blocked Ottoman advances in that direction and forced the Ottoman Empire to forestall any other Shi'ite advances by moving into the whole of the vast area covered by Arabic-speaking peoples, from Syria to the Yemen and from Iraq to Algeria.

The curiosity, as I have indicated, was that the Ottoman Empire, which was settled in the European provinces of Byzantine Christendom, regarded Persia as its spiritual progenitor. Even after developing Ottoman Turkish as a cultural language of its own, it did so on the model of Persian and not on the model of classical Arabic models that had already been largely discarded by the Persians after they had shaken off Arab tutelage in the Islamic Empire. There was a constant procession back and forth between the Persian center of Khorasan and the Ottoman center in Anatolia. Literary ideas and political refugees would leave Khorasan to go to Anatolia, and Turkish techniques and technicians would travel eastward from southeastern Europe to Khorasan and Transoxania. One of the most illuminating cultural borrowings, for instance, was the battle array worked out by the Ottomans and disseminated both to Hungary and to India via Khorasan; this cultural export was one of many. At the turn of the fifteenth century and during the sixteenth century of the Christian era, Turkish had not yet been developed as a literary language. Oddly enough Isma'il Shah Safawi, the political architect of modern Persia, used to write in his native Turkish idiom, whereas at the same time the Ottoman Sultan Selim wrote exclusively in Persian. Nationality in the modern sense had nothing to do with such matters.

In any case, down to 1500 the Arabic-speaking and the Persian worlds were isolated from each other, substantially, until the political career of Isma'il Shah Safawi resuscitated Shi'ism as a dynamic political force.

It was after the recrudescence of Shi'ism in Persia under Isma'il Shah Safawi's leadership that a major clash took place in the Persian cultural sphere between the Persian heartland itself and the dynamically expanding Persianized Ottoman Empire. By 1514 the head-on collision that had taken place between them resulted in a stalemate that forced these two great powers to avoid any further encroachments on each other's domains and to turn aside toward the vast areas lying beyond their borders, *i.e.,* primarily the Mamluk empire in Syria and Egypt, the then leading power in the Arabic-speaking portion of the Muslim world. Thus it was a question, once the stalemate was imposed on the two Iranic contenders, whether the Safawi Persian Empire would spread to the Mediterranean, thus boxing the Ottoman Turks into the Anatolian Peninsula, or whether the Ottoman Turks would move as far eastward as the Euphrates, thus barring the Persians from the Middle East.

In 1515 the Ottoman sultan seized Dhu-l-Qadar in the highlands of southeastern Anatolia, thus moving his Asiatic border as far as the Euphrates; this was only 122 years after the Ottoman Empire had laid down its European frontier along the Danube. He then moved against the Mamluks; by 1517 he had occupied Cairo. Sultan Selim's entry into Cairo had a fateful political effect; it established an intimate political connection between the Ottoman Turks and the Arabic-speaking provinces of Egypt, Syria, and the Hijaz that was to last for centuries.

This collision between the two halves of the Persian cultural sphere over the dead body of the Islamic Empire and athwart the Arabic-speaking world had some far-reaching consequences.

The most dramatic, immediate and enduring effect was the shattering of the former Persian cultural sphere into three fragments: (1) the Persian "colonial" area in India plus Transoxania; (2) Persia proper; (3) the Ottoman empire, considered to be another extension of the Persian domain jutting forward into orthodox Christendom.

Two new and historically important borders sequestered these three fragments from each other: one between Persia and Transoxiana, going from the northwestern face of the Hindu Kush northward to the Qara Qum desert, or to the southeastern corner of the

Caspian Sea; and a new border between Persia and the area controlled by the Osmanlis, from the southern face of the Caucasus Mountains southward to the Syrian desert, or the head of the Persian Gulf.

From a socioreligious point of view the great tussle between the Osmanlis and the Persians resulted in the segregation of the Shi'a on the terrain of Persia.

Beforehand the Shi'a, which had geographically speaking been intermingled quite generally with the Sunni (orthodox) Muslims, had been a minority almost everywhere. After the tussle the Shi'ites were still a minority in Islam generally, but they were concentrated in Persia, and after having developed from an anti-Arab party in the early phase of Islam into a mouthpiece for all forms of social opposition later on, they now became a Persian party par excellence, though admittedly without the purely ethnic overtones Westerners are accustomed to. Also, because of the ferocity and bloodshed attendant on Isma'il Shah Safawi's political career, the embitterment between the two sects became unprecedented in its extremism. Many have thought that the intransigeance developed by this embitterment took the heart out of Persian civilization, historically so lustrous, and halted its development.

This in turn had the curious effect of stopping the cultural evolution of the Ottoman society from the Persian roots that had given it birth in the first place. The enormous areas taken in charge by the Turks—in both their Seljuq and their Osmanli incarnations—were really an extension of Persian culture; the cultural scions of Persia depended for the renewal of their cultural sustenance on a steady flow from the cultural center. But these revivifying streams, blocked first by the hostile frontiers set up between the two societies and nullified later by the drying up of Persian culture at its source in the wake of Isma'il Shah Safawi's violent Shi'ite revival, eventually disappeared altogether, leaving Turkish culture high and dry, awaiting an entirely new incarnation in the twentieth century.

There could never have been any real question of Persia's replacement in the minds of the Turks by any Arabic-speaking community. In the first place, Arabic culture was quite alien to the Osmanlis, whose islamization, as I have pointed out, had originally taken place through Persia; in the second place, Arabic culture was for all practical purposes moribund.

The figure of Ibn Khaldun was no more than a flash in the pan; generally speaking, Egyptian culture, which had been insulated against Mongol destructiveness by the shield of the Mamluks and so had prevailed throughout the Arabic-speaking world, was retrogressive and bloodless. Though the Osmanlis had been compelled to ingest the Arabic-speaking world in order to forestall the Persians' doing the same thing, the Ottoman-Arab symbiosis was always highly uncomfortable and irritating for both sides. As I shall point out in the next chapter, dislike of the Turks was one of the chief sources of modern Arab nationalism.

In any case the present-day world of Islam—including all Arabic-speaking communities—is a result of the immense explosion kindled by Isma'il Shah Safawi's career, which split and segregated the Shi'a minority and the Sunni majority, propelled Ottoman Turkey on its path of conquest of the Arabic-speaking societies and created the image of a mongrel Ottoman society—half Persian and half Arab—that is the stereotype in Western minds of "Islam" today, while Persia itself has been forgotten.

The Shi'a-Sunni feud was probably the chief reason for the practically simultaneous debacle of the three Islamic great powers—the Ottoman Empire in Christendom and the Arabic-speaking world, the Safawi Persian Shi'ite Empire, and the empire established by Akbar in India—all of which collapsed at the turn of the seventeenth and eighteenth centuries. The feud was to remain unhealed until the last decade, possibly, of the nineteenth century, when the mounting pressure of the West evoked pan-Islam.

Yet Islam has not managed to defend itself as a unitary culture, in any sense; on the contrary, the individual fragments the world of Islam has been divided into for so long have embarked on their own reactions to "Westernization" not as self-conscious Muslims, but simply as general imitators of the West and all its institutions.

It is possibly the Western institution of the nation-state that has laid down the pattern now being followed by all Islamic and for that matter all countries of the world, with the Arabic-speaking states themselves in many ways well up in the forefront of establishing nation-states based on language, a process that of course cuts them off to some extent from their fellow Muslims.

• • •

A word might be added about a cultural factor that may help explain to Western readers an aspect of Islamic history that seems perennially enigmatic—its notorious decadence for almost a millennium, a decadence being overcome only in our own generation.

When Greek learning was imported en bloc into the Muslim world during the initial years of the Abbasid regime, it created a contest between two powerful tendencies: the rationalism of the Greek approach to the world; and the intuitive, mystical, and authoritative elements of Muslim thought.

This was a long-drawn-out intellectual struggle, which ended with a relative suppression of the Greek imports and elevated the authoritative and, from the rationalist point of view, regressive elements of Islam to a position of dominance. If the Greek doctrines had won, it might have been possible to make Islam more flexible by using the device of esoteric or symbolical interpretation to vanquish the authority of the Quran and also to outflank the spiritual monopoly of the Holy Law. It would have been a fairly simple matter to fling open the doors to rationalist progress by the device of emphasizing the powers of choice that were in any case implicit in the accepted notion of the authoritativeness of the general consensus of the spiritual leaders of the community.

Yet the rationalist revolution in Islam—a sensible way of describing Isma'ilism, for all its fanatical excrescences—was outdone by the ingrown conservatism of traditional Islam.

Thus the spirit of untrammeled rationalistic inquiry that was part of the early adaptation of the Greek heritage was finally contradicted and ejected by the later, more characteristic spirit of medieval Islam, in which all attempts to construct a causally interconnected system of explanations of the universe and of society were blocked and frustrated as a matter of principle.

The Arabs had come out of the desert as essentially headstrong individualists, but since those Arabs were merely illiterate tribesmen with no interest in a life of the spirit they failed to give rise to any corresponding intellectual independence in the society that grew up through their conquests. When the civilization recoagulated in its great centers, the individualism of the Bedouin had become a thing of the past; it became fashionable for writers to submerge themselves in a stream of traditionalist thought, the writer himself being merely one of a chain and, indeed, very often anonymous.

This was supplemented by a general philosophical stance in

which causality of all kinds was simply disregarded. God was himself not so much a first cause as merely the architect, free and unrestricted, of a complex system of concordances and parallels, but of no interconnected causes. There are, in short, no natural laws; the concordances are not necessary, merely customary. God creates everything at every second of time; hence no notion of sequence can be established outside the mind of God, which is naturally impenetrable.

When causality in all forms was rejected it became impossible to indulge in free speculation and inquiry. Both in philosophy and in natural science everything had to be taken on faith, as a reflection of divine law and revelation: no questions could be asked. The Islamic Empire settled down in a form of congealed feudalism for many centuries, indeed, until the modern age, when the entire structure of Islam throughout the world was suddenly flung into collision with the restless thrusting forward of Western civilization in all its forms—political, socioeconomic, and above all intellectual. Islam in our own epoch has been subjected to the most tremendous of shocks; it has not yet recovered.

• • •

If we were to sum up the foregoing from the point of view of the objective of this book—the definition of the historic profile of the Arabs as a community—we would see that for roughly a millennium they had faded out of the great society they had created a framework for.

The purely Arab dynasty of the Umayyads lasted some three generations; the Abbasid regime, despite its Arab genealogical origins, was essentially an expression of Persian society and in any case lost all effective power only a few generations after its inception.

By 1300 all the peoples of the derelict caliphate—Persians, Arabs, and civilized Berbers—were being ruled by nomad Turks and Mongols and by wild Berbers from the Sahara and the Atlas.

The decisive development of the final, or at least the premodern, phase of Islam was the emergence of the Osmanli Turks as the paramount power in Islam.

This was a process that took some five centuries; throughout this period it is simply not possible to discuss the Arabs as a cohesive entity at all. It is true that various Arabic dialects—

quite autonomous growths wholly independent of the artificial classical written language—were spoken throughout the Middle East and along the coast of North Africa, but since throughout this period the idea of nationality lacked any charismatic projection, none of the people speaking these dialects would have thought of themselves as Arabs at all. The word "Arab" was, as I have indicated and as I shall repeat later on, wholly restricted to the Bedouin tribes of the Arabian Peninsula and the deserts of North Africa.

Thus, strangely enough, as I have said, the very primacy of the Arab element in Islam, the fact that a huge area was arabized only linguistically, meant that the Arabic-speakers, except for the Bedouin, came to be *less* of a nationality in Islam than for instance the Persians or Turks. The latter, precisely because they came late to Islam, and precisely because of this had retained their own individuality and local cultural language, were more marked out as a people within the leveling structure of Islam than the non-Bedouin speakers of Arabic. The specifically Aramean nationality was assimilated into the speakers of Arabic, as were the descendants of the ancient Egyptians, but the resulting mélange consisted of Muslims who spoke Arabic and whose geographical habitat was understood in a purely physical way, without the halo of sentiment surrounding a genuine patriotic allegiance.

Thus, while the Turkish elements actively dominated the Islamic area, all those who might call themselves either Arabs or the descendants of Arabs—considered either physically or culturally—were in a state of passive subjugation. There was scarcely a political ripple over the Arabic-speaking territories of Islam throughout the whole period, except, possibly, for a rapid and successful upsurgence of a Muslim splinter movement in the heart of central Arabia, Wahhabism, which was to emerge in the eighteenth century. I shall discuss it in the next chapter.

The Arabic language was soon entrenched as the vernacular throughout the areas where it is still spoken in Africa and Asia today, except that in North Africa there was still a very large proportion of the population that, while accepting the cultural and theological hegemony of Arabic, actually still spoke one dialect or another of Berber, which even today is the spoken language of rather more than half the population in Morocco.

In this way the initial Arab expansion had a permanent effect on history despite the subsequent eclipse of the Arabs. The solid entrenchment of Arabic dialects as local vernaculars laid the foundations of a cultural situation that has become meaningful in our own era, when language has become the paramount though of course not the sole criterion of ethnic or at least cultural identity.

It must be emphasized that in speaking of the quiescence of the Arabic-speaking communities throughout their long stagnation I do not mean simply that they were passive objects manipulated by others; I mean that they lacked any awareness of themselves as a group. There was, in short, neither unity nor the social awareness that unity is rooted in.

One of Ibn Khaldun's key words in describing social organization was *"'asabiyyah,"* roughly translatable as *"esprit de corps"* or "solidarity." That feeling of social cohesiveness, of self-awareness, of solidarity, was literally nonexistent for centuries; it has been only within the past few generations, and through the impact of ideas from abroad, that the concept has been painfully striven for. To this day it is not yet a fact, but an aspiration. I shall discuss its evolution in the following chapters.

VII

STIRRINGS OF NATIONALISM: THE RESHAPING OF ARAB IDENTITY

In the early sixteenth century the Mamluk regime in Egypt, eroded by corruption, extravagance, and the general shrinkage of the economy, was overcome by its kindred Turkish regime in Anatolia. For four centuries Syria and Egypt were to be part of the Ottoman Empire; the Barbary States along the North African coastline as far as Morocco knuckled under to the Ottoman state, and when the Osmanlis finally wrested Iraq away from Persia in 1639 they were in complete control of the Arabic-speaking world.

In Egypt they did no more than maintain the Mamluk socioeconomic order, merely superimposing an Ottoman pasha and a Turkish garrison. In Syria, however, more radical changes were made. The country was turned into a number of feudal Turkish provinces in which most of the land was split up between various fief holders, generally Turks. The fiefs were semihereditary; annual dues had to be paid, and there was the obligation of rendering army service with the fief holders' own retainers. They could in return collect taxes and lord it over the peasants. The pashas holding the provinces (*pashaliks*), ultimately four in number, were *de facto* rulers, since the Turkish government, while splendidly centralized, became increasingly ineffective the farther away the province.

Ottoman rule, originally a source of stability as well as of prosperity, began to degenerate by the eighteenth century. Scholars generally agree that the regime was characterized by widespread corruption and chaos. There were local movements of opposition to Turkish rule, but nothing of any consequence. As has been conventional in Muslim society, opposition movements generally functioned as religious schisms. In the Arabic-speaking society of the Middle East the most general movement of disaffection was rooted in the religious attitude implied by Sufism, a successor of the far more aggressive and systematic dissident movement of Isma'ilism, which after the Mongol invasions had shrunken to negligibility.

In its beginnings Sufism had been linked to a quite individual mystical experience, but this experience seems to have arisen out of an attitude of mind that led to an actual social movement, which exercised widespread influence among the lower strata of society, organized in Dervish fraternities often closely linked to the craft guilds. Formally the Sufis were not heretical, unlike the Isma'ilis; politically, too, they were passive. It was only in religion that they counterposed their personal mysticism to the dominant orthodoxy. They cannot be said to have had, in sum, more than a trivial influence over the general cast of the Arabic-speaking communities that had come under the control of the Osmanlis.

Of these communities only Yemen, the southwestern corner of the peninsula, and the great Bedouin pasturing grounds in Arabia remained substantially independent of the Ottoman Empire; also, the rulers of the Hijaz and a number of petty local rulers managed to maintain some degree of independence. In Morocco especially the Moorish regime developed along quite autonomous lines, while at the eastern end of the Mediterranean, in Lebanon, which has always been a crazy quilt of local dynasties, regimes, and religious communities, the Ottoman state succeeded in imposing only a partial control over the great mountain of Lebanon, which to this day has remained an island of Christianity in the sea of Islam. Under nominal Ottoman sovereignty, different dynasties—Christian, Muslim, and Druze, the last a mysterious sect with roots in both religions—had a degree of autonomy that merely varied inversely with the degree of Turkish efficiency.

But these were exceptions. Generally the Arabic-speaking world lay supine beneath the yoke of the Osmanlis for all these centuries, the occasional movement or thrust for independence usually being headed not by Arabic-speaking leaders but by headstrong local Turkish pashas.

I have been laying emphasis on the expression "Arabic-speaking" in an attempt to delineate the background against which present-day Arab nationalism has gradually taken shape. It would be historically quite anachronistic to conceive of the Arabic-speaking portions of Asia and Africa, throughout the long centuries of stagnation under the Osmanli Turks, as constituting an ethnic entity of any kind whatever: the social axes of identity-formation were quite different.

Just as Western ideas and institutions came to encompass the planet, including Islam, so a Western view of nationality was to be decisive in the genesis of Arab ethnic identity today. For while the word "Arab" was, as I have indicated before, reserved in local parlance for the Bedouin, it came into use among Europeans during the nineteenth century as a handy and indeed inevitable way of referring to the speakers of Arabic. As I shall explain below, this European usage, arising out of the modern nation-state-language complex, proved to underlie the formation of Arab identity in our own day precisely as a result of the conquest of the world by the West. The idea of an "Arab nation" would have been quite incomprehensible until after the end of the nineteenth century. It was not until the twentieth century was well advanced that movements for regional independence gradually came to be generalized, "ideologized," and that the Western concept of a nation-state characterized, more or less, by a common idiom began to provide the population of the Middle East with a new matrix of ethnic identity.

A glance back at the political restiveness that began agitating the Middle East during the nineteenth century will indicate how laboriously the modern notion of Arab identity acquired a following, and how many obstacles the concept of an "Arab nation" we now take for granted had to overcome before maturing.

• • •

In the nineteenth century the countries of Arabic speech, together with Islam and the rest of the world, were subjected to the cataclysm of contact with a Europe that during the many centuries in which Islam had been practically moribund had been developing with remarkable dynamism. The Middle East, and North Africa especially, were the first to be buffeted by the massive invasions of Europeans and European ideas.

During the long period of sociopolitical stagnation that preceded this revolutionary impact, the only discernible agitation in the Arabic-speaking world as a whole had been in the Arab heartland itself, the peninsula. There a movement of religious reform was founded by Muhammad Abd-al-Wahhab (1703–91) in the form of a sect, named after him, that aimed at a return to "first principles" in the manner of so many religious reform movements. Abd-al-Wahhab's initiative inflamed a number of Bedouin tribes and set a stamp on life in the peninsula that even in our own day is still potent.

Abd-al-Wahhab wanted to get back to the Islam of the first generations, which he conceived of as a stripped, rigid, antimystical puritanism. Everything that did not fit in with his own conception of fundamental Islam was savagely denounced. He rejected as superstition and "innovations" all additional layers of belief or ritual that he considered deviants from authentic Islam. The worship of everything but the One God was forbidden, especially any veneration given to saints or sacred places—even to Muhammad's person. All forms of intercession between man and God were rejected; in short, it was like an ultimate Protestant reformation. Abd-al-Wahhab insisted on the same degree of puritanical austerity in personal as in religious life.

The prince ruling the Najd at the time, Muhammad ibn Sa'ud, was converted to these new views. The growing sect, with its new military and political institution, grew strong enough to take away the holy cities from the Sharifs who governed them in the name of Constantinople and even to menace the Turkish provinces of Iraq and Syria. It was not strong enough, however, to withstand a strong reaction led by the Albanian adventurer Muhammad Ali, the pasha and later the ruler of Egypt, who in 1818 led a Turco-Egyptian force against the Wahhabis and kept them restricted to their original province of Najd until the nineteenth and the twentieth centuries, when they made a strikingly effective reappearance under Abd-al-Aziz ibn Sa'ud, who became king of Sa'udi Arabia, and with the discovery of vast oil deposits in the late 1930s, a potent factor of change in the Middle East as a whole.

The very fact that this indigenous Arab activity in the Najd was a movement for a Muslim renaissance illustrates the slipperiness of the word "Arab" in our time.

It is true, of course, that the Arabian Bedouin and aristocrats are "Arabs" par excellence; it is equally true that they do not have the smallest feeling of kinship for the Arabic-speaking city-dwellers and intellectuals who are the chief proponents of present-day Arab nationalism. The austerity of Wahhabism means nothing at all to the Arabic-speaking world that has been under the pressure of European ideas and institutions for several generations now. As a return to primitive Islam it is merely akin to religious tendencies elsewhere in the world of Islam. Wahhabism illustrates in a nutshell, in fact, the contradictoriness between the basic concepts of Islamic universalism and the newer outgrowth of the Arabic-speaking world —Western-style nationalism.

This movement, which in our own day has come to absorb the attention of all students of Islam generally and of the Arabic-speaking world in particular, may be traced, in its beginnings, to a sort of aversion widely held in the Middle East for the Osmanli Turks.

It was only with the advent of the Osmanlis that a more or less unbridgeable cleavage began to yawn between the ruling summits of the Ottoman Empire and the mass of Arabic-speaking subjects, both Muslim and Christian.

By the time the original Muslim Arabs, in the society they had created a framework for, had been shouldered aside by the descendants of the peoples they had conquered, the Islamic world was still in the grip of the religion launched by the Arabs and intellectually still largely dominated by the Arabic tongue.

But the Osmanli Turks, full of the arrogance of dominion and conscious of themselves as scions of a special—Persian—culture, never dissolved into the Arabic-speaking cultural community or into the Persian either. It was in fact the overlordship of the Osmanlis, with its concomitant of utter subjection and also unselfconsciousness on the part of their Arabic-speaking subjects, that was to lead to the germination of a feeling of solidarity on the part of Arabic-speaking communities.

Until modern times the mutual aversion between Turks and their Arabic-speaking subjects was overlaid by their common religion. Arabic-speaking Christians merely hated the Turks, both as oppressive rulers and as Muslims to boot. This feeling of reciprocal dislike could work itself out in the Middle East with any effectiveness only when the bonds of religion had been loosened sufficiently for a feeling of national identity on the Western model to begin stirring.

Before Europe was solidly implanted in the area through Napoleon's campaign in Egypt at the beginning of the nineteenth century (1798–1801), the Osmanlis and the various European nations they had been at odds with had been, very roughly, on equal terms. Now, with the Ottoman Empire having been in decline for centuries, Europe had become endlessly superior both technically and, so to speak, civically. Evolving rapidly, it could cope more resourcefully with the problems of modern society.

From this time on, the Ottoman leaders, and all literate people in the Middle East generally, felt very directly in their own minds the contradiction between their own traditional Islamic or Middle Eastern culture and the new ferment of ideas imported from Western Europe.

Egypt especially, the chief Arabic-speaking country, was launched on a state life of its own. Ottoman sovereignty was to remain a mere fiction until it was finally done away with altogether.

It would be absurd to regard the founder of modern Egypt, Muhammad Ali, in any sense as an Egyptian and still less as an Arab. He was an energetic Albanian whose mother tongue was Turkish and whose principal aim was the construction of a revived and powerful Egypt that he himself and his family could run as they pleased, with his former Ottoman overlords definitely out of the picture. After having established his power in Egypt, through the slaughter of the last of the Mamluks in 1811, Muhammad Ali, essentially a Mamluk himself, simply wanted to have a strong country run on European lines to be a viable basis for his own power.

Formally Muhammad Ali never actually refused lip service to the sultans. In 1810–19, indeed, he carried on a long-drawn-out and difficult campaign against the Wahhabi revival of Muslim puritanism in the central Arabian desert, which was generally regarded as heretical by orthodox Muslims. He also put down a movement of Greek insurgence later; ultimately he moved against the forces of the Ottoman state itself.

In the decade 1830–40 Muhammad Ali and his talented son Ibrahim moved into Syria and Asia Minor, easily defeating the Ottoman troops this time, and managed to reconstitute a union of Syria and Egypt under their own rule. Though this conquest of Syria proved ephemeral, it was to have certain consequences in local affairs that were reflected in the relationship of the Arabic-speaking provinces to the Ottoman state.

There was nothing remotely "Arab" about the Egyptians. The ruling class was almost entirely Turkish in origin and in fact spoke nothing but Turkish. The masses of the peasantry, perhaps the most ancient sedentary population in the world, had a self-consciousness all their own.

To the Egyptain peasants, after all, the "Arabs" were simply members of the Bedouin tribes roving about upper Egypt, the Sudan, and of course the Arabian Peninsula. Most Egyptians, as Muslims, would simply have classified themselves as Muslims. They could not have considered themselves "Arabs" in any sense at all; indeed, it would have been impossible to put this question to them so as to make it meaningful.

As I have indicated, the situation was the same throughout all Arabic-speaking societies and has remained so very largely down to the last generation, in which the potent effects of mythologizing—and more particularly the polarizing of propaganda, emotions, and agitation around the conflict with the Turks and later on with the Jewish Zionists—have finally begun, but only just begun, to make the phrase "Arab national movement" an understandable category of politics.

The chief oppositionist activity in Egyptian life, the conflict around which the national consciousness of the Egyptians may be said, fairly legitimately, to have coagulated, was the determination to get rid of the British and the French, who during the decade 1870–80 had come completely to dominate the economy of the country. They were helped, of course, by the increasingly corrupt Egyptian government.

By 1882, after some bloody anti-European riots in Alexandria, instituted by a popular antiforeign uprising under the leadership of Colonel Arabi Pasha, the British, with the tacit agreement of France and Italy, took over the government and simply ran it, without even a legal mask, until 1914, when the *de facto* sovereignty was fleshed out in a document establishing reciprocal relations that lasted until the successful revolt of Muhammad Najib and Nasser in the 1950s.

The primary purpose of the schools founded by Muhammad

Ali, as well as of the educational missions sent out to Egypt from Europe, was technical.

In a general way it seems obvious that the first reaction of a backward state to the profound and comprehensive collision with Europe is bound to be one of self-preservation. This is reflected in the building up of the armed forces to enable them to compete on a more equal footing with European technical ability. In turn, the modernization of the army brings in technical thought on all levels and in many branches unforeseen by the innovators. Hygiene, commerce, and eventually literature are involved in the current. That is to say, the first aspects of life to be reconstructed are the mechanical, "soulless" elements of the society, which, being judged exclusively by the yardstick of efficiency and only existing in an almost entirely utilitarian way, are scrapped almost immediately; and a more or less faithful copy of Western institutions of pragmatically demonstrated efficiency is imposed on the society as a whole. But once this floodgate is opened the generalizing power of ideas pours in.

The new schools founded by Muhammad Ali became completely European in concept and performance, despite the retention of Arabic. Also, later in the century, they were paralleled by avowedly foreign schools—French, German, English, and others. The two together, aided by the increasing number of Egyptian students educated abroad, were to produce a native elite largely detached from traditional sources of behavior.

It was, however, Syria and Lebanon, with their ancient, deeply rooted, and unwaveringly Christian communities, that were to lay the foundations of the movement that in our own day is called Arab nationalism. Since most speakers of Arabic are Muslims, that movement has, to be sure, long since slipped away from its Christian moorings, a circumstance that was doubtless inevitable, but in the nineteenth century and the early part of the twentieth the Christian role was vital.

There were two basic factors that made the Arabic-speaking Christian communities of the Middle East the natural progenitors, so to speak, of the Arab national movement.

In the first place they were the closest to Europe, the original seedbed of nationalism in all forms, and so were the most immediate imitators of European fashions in all things.

Perhaps more importantly, nationalism was the only way the

Christians of the Middle East could break out of the ghetto constituted by their general status as second-class citizens in a Muslim state.

Groups in the Middle East—religious, ethnic, and linguistic—have been used to ghetto life for centuries. It is a natural condition, perhaps, of the Middle East as a whole. But once the impulses of modern-style nationalism penetrated the thinking of the Middle East, toward the middle of the last century, it was only natural for those sensitive to its promptings to look about them for an opportunity to slip into a larger universe.

In the Middle East of the last century this was possible only on the basis of language. Not merely is language a natural, though admittedly not the sole element in the formation of national consciousness, it was in the case of the Middle Eastern Christians the only channel of communication with their surrounding environment. For ever since the success of the early Muslim Arabs in spreading their language, Arabic had been a lingua franca over a huge area. The historical importance of this fact was not to be perceived until the modern era, in which language has become the qualification par excellence of nationality. Bismarck once observed that the most fateful element in the nineteenth century was the fact that England and America both spoke English; something similar may apply to the Arabic-speaking world.

Thus, during the Middlé Ages, when communal solidarity was not based on language, the early Muslim Arabs laid the foundations for a situation in which, centuries later, their much mixed descendants could follow the lead of the modern West in assigning decisive importance to the test of language. If we look back at this whole process from the vantage point of our own generation, it would seem that the cultural identity created by the Muslim Arabs through their language lay dormant for centuries until Arabic, at the height of Islam merely the learned language of a universal state, eventually contracted, with the decay of Islam, to the confines of populations that used it as a vernacular, to bloom once again in the modern era as the linguistic expression of at least a projected national solidarity.

It was inevitable for at least some of the Arabic-speaking Christians of the Middle East to use Arabic as a springboard into the Muslim world, in the hope of creating a new nation, in harmony with the nation-state-language syndrome, in which they would be fully privileged citizens on a footing of equality with others speaking the same language. This linguistic principle as the axis for the formation of a new nationality was, to be sure, bound to collide with the internationalism of Islam—which it stands in diametric contradiction to—but that internationalism is itself a somewhat attenuated attitude. Islam has been rent asunder by the forces of modern politics and economics, and it was perfectly reasonable for the small and isolated Christian communities of the Middle East, euphoric with Europeanism, to look forward to their assimilation into a larger community based on the latest ideas

Hence it was Syria, an ethnic patchwork, that during the latter half of the last century did most to form the "Arab nationalist" view of the world. At this stage of development Egypt was hampered precisely by its being mostly Muslim and moreover by its superimposing a "Pharaonic" or Egyptian national consciousness on the movement for national self-realization. Thus it was, curiously enough, the Arabic-speaking Christians of Syria who did the most to revive a secular consciousness of the world expressed in a revived Arabic tongue.

In the beginning, however, the longing of the Christian elite of the Middle East to burst out of its ghetto never went beyond the notion of creating a "new nation" based on old regional units like Syria and Lebanon. The idea of maximizing the ideal of unity to include citizens who would be defined by a purely abstract criterion —the speaking of Arabic—was scarcely even expressed until well into the twentieth century. For generations nationalist thought never went beyond the borders of the Fertile Crescent: both the Arabian Peninsula and North Africa, to say nothing of Egypt, lay far outside the wildest dreams of the early Syrian and Lebanese dissidents.

• • •

Western ideas were to come to the Middle East most directly through the foreign mission schools, a natural bridge from Europe to the East in general. The influence of Europe was to become a flood. In the nineteenth century life in the Middle East was to be radically transformed by the overwhelming, almost asphyxiating clutch of Western ideals and institutions.

In the attempt to revive the Arabic-speaking Middle East there was some convergence, for a time, between the movement of Arabic-speaking Christian modernization in Syria and Lebanon and the native Muslim Egyptian movement as a result of the flood of Syrian intellectuals into Egypt at the end of the nineteenth century. This came about because of the great prosperity in the generation following the British occupation of Egypt (1882) and because of the growing harshness of the Ottoman regime. This made Egypt a second homeland for the revival of Arabic, even though the basic material generally came from Syria. The relatively mild censorship, the growth of commerce through the Suez Canal, as well as the general economic boom, called forth streams of Syrian immigrants, often journalists and writers fleeing from Turkish political oppression. The largest papers were founded by Syrian Christians who became the ideologists of the most important public parties and groups. Other Arabic-speaking countries were largely a passively accepting element. Even Algeria contributed nothing; the process of Europeanization had taken place too quickly, proximity to Europe was too great, the attraction of French culture too irresistible, the tenacity of Arabic culture too feeble.

Syria was also to exercise an equally great control over the intellectual life of the Arab revival through the tremendous Syrian emigration to America, both North and South. In fact, it may be said that the latest period of the Arab intellectual revival, beginning with the twentieth century, was directly or indirectly bound up with the Syrian émigrés in America.

This emigration, which had a mass character, was supplemented by the many Syrian refugee intellectuals in Europe. The beginnings of the Arab movement of *political* revival were largely the work of these refugees and malcontents, with no mass following. It was not till the eve of World War I that political self-consciousness began to infiltrate masses of the population, chiefly, of course, the rising middle class.

• • •

Muhammad Ali's attempt to found an empire had been based on the possibility of establishing his rule over Egypt, Syria, and Arabia, but there was no thought in his mind that his Arabic-speaking subjects would actually run anything. He did not even speak Arabic himself; his son Ibrahim, who developed a certain romanticism with respect to Arabia and to the Arabic language, spoke it poorly. What *they* meant by an "Arab national revival" was, accordingly, the sovereignty of a Turco-Albanian regime based in Egypt. Their driving incentive was purely personal; it was merely a question of using peoples of Arabic speech to carve themselves an empire. They wanted to transform their conquests of Arabic-speaking territories into a single kingdom with themselves and their descendants as its dynasty. They also wanted the title of caliph; this alone indicates that their incentive had a religious germ. They were merely making use of the Arabic-speaking lands to realize a rather old-fashioned ambition, since in the early nineteenth century the prospects of "unifying" Islam were nil, while the notion of reviving the "Arab kingdom," whatever that might have meant, was obviously incompatible with the idea of the caliphate. Moreover, Muhammad Ali himself considered the speakers of Arabic, *i.e.,* the Egyptians and the Syrians, completely incapable of self-government to begin with. He visualized them all as subjects of an edifice of sovereignty sustained by Turks and Albanians.

At this time Arab national consciousness was wholly nonexistent. There was nothing even approaching any form of solidarity among the countries of Arabic speech. After the waning of the caliphate, so many hundreds of years before, its diverse congeries of peoples had fallen quite apart into separate entities, both regional and sectarian, and linked only to the district, clan, or confession they belonged to. In addition, religious evolution had led to the birth of new groupings among both the Muslims and Christians and to a heightened emphasis on sectarianism.

By the first third of the nineteenth century, at the time of the brief Egyptian conquest of Syria by Muhammad Ali, Syrian society was based entirely on sectarian allegiances. Muslims made up more than half the population; they were quite dominant, since they alone were full citizens, with a monopoly of privileges denied the other creeds. The Christians were about a third and were subject to the usual discriminations current in Muslim countries against non-Muslims. There were also a number of heterodox Muslim sects—Druze, Nusayri, and Mutawali—that clung tenaciously to their particularism.

There was no trace of patriotism in the conventional European sense. Indeed, such a concept would have been quite simply unthinkable in a country governed simultaneously by the universalism of Islam on the one hand and by the presence of parochial sects that were quite distinct in their consciousness of identity. The possession of a few things in common—language, customs, and above all hatred of Turkish rule—was not enough to unite them in any effective sense. Their motives in welcoming the arrival of Muhammad Ali's son Ibrahim had been completely divergent and, naturally, all egocentric.

Muslims, for instance, had welcomed Ibrahim since they thought that if the caliphate were in the hands of a sovereign based on Arabic-speaking countries the Turks would be ousted and the Arabic-speaking Muslims themselves would be favored. The Christians, on the other hand, had precisely the opposite interest: They had seen that Muhammad Ali's regime in Egypt, whatever its defects, had been enlightened at least with respect to them, since it had been based on tolerance and equality. They naturally hoped this regime would extend to them in Syria too. When Ibrahim actually realized these Christian hopes and during his short occupation of the country abolished the discriminatory laws aimed at the Christians, the immediate effect was to alienate the Syrian Muslims. The latter did not have the smallest interest in ameliorating the lot of the Christians; they were simply hoping to ameliorate their own vis-à-vis the Turks.

Hence Ibrahim's conduct did not evoke patriotism, a wholly anachronistic notion, but merely parochial jealousy.

Accordingly, the premature attempt of Muhammad Ali and his son Ibrahim to create a political domain based on the Arabic language, or rather—to put it geographically—on Egypt, Syria, and Arabia, was bound to fail. When they retreated from Syria, under the propulsion of Palmerstonian England, the idea evaporated altogether, not to reappear in a general form until World War I.

It was as a by-product of the tolerant regime established by Ibrahim that the door was opened to Christian missionaries, who were now to come in growing numbers, initially from the United States and from France.

To be sure, there had been foreign Christian missions in Syria as early as the beginning of the seventeenth century, but they had been quite restricted in scope. They had set up a few scattered schools and seminaries and had published a few devotional books. All of these early missionaries had been Roman Catholics, usually

French, of the Jesuit, Capuchin, and Carmelite orders. Because of the generally denominational nature of local society and because of its deeply ingrained prejudices, it was practically impossible for them to carry on any proselytizing activities. In consequence they revolved as a matter of course around the Christian communities linked to the Roman Catholic Church.

The Jesuits were, very naturally, the most energetic; they had in fact been at it since 1625. After tenaciously trying to carry on their labors, they were finally suppressed in 1773, when they left the country, closing down most of their installations and leaving others to their successors from a Lazarist order.

Their return in 1831 was largely inspired by a certain apprehension about the arrival in Syria of some American Protestant missionaries, who had begun arriving as early as 1820. The first were Presbyterians, who established themselves in Beirut, which was to remain their center. Their mission was hampered both by the problems they shared with the Catholics and by a difficulty peculiarly their own—they lacked the umbrella of an indigenous Protestant community. Whereas the Roman Catholics could at least take some shelter behind a bona fide sister community, the Protestants, in order not to remain a purely isolated compound of a few foreigners in an alien sea, had to convert someone, and finding it impossible to make any converts among the Muslims—historically a difficult problem for proselytizers of all kinds—turned as a matter of course to poaching on the preserves of the Roman Catholic Church. This instantly entailed, naturally, friction with the local Christian communities, but the Presbyterians generated an immense zeal that had far-reaching results.

Beirut at this time was a tiny city, some nine thousand people behind walls. This was where the Americans had been confined from the beginning, whereas the Jesuits and Lazarists, with a head-start of two centuries, had set up schools in Damascus, Aleppo, and elsewhere in Lebanon. The main effort of the Catholics, however, had been to make converts—a hopeless enterprise for them too—and to spread some theological propaganda. They showed no particular interest in cultivating the local idiom, spoken Arabic, and seem to have had no effect whatever on neutralizing the sectarian venom that made the partitions between the various communities so impenetrable.

By 1834, after Ibrahim's policy of toleration had been put into effect, foreign missions descended on Beirut in force, branching out from there to the rest of the country.

Curiously enough, the revival of spoken Arabic, the matrix of the future nationalist movement, was an adjunct in the ensuing duel between rival Christian faiths; it was an instrument in a competitive campaign to disseminate the new ideas flowing in from the West.

Periodicals in Arabic did not exist at all; there was scarcely even a printing press in Arabic. During the eighteenth century some monasteries had had a few hand presses, but they had produced practically nothing except a few devotional tracts. By the beginning of the nineteenth century, printing presses were set up in Constantinople (1816) and in Cairo (1822), both of which had a certain output in Arabic of some literary and scientific works. Between 1822 and 1830 the Bulaq press in Cairo published some fifty books, in Arabic, Persian and Turkish. By 1850 it had produced some three hundred books in these same languages, of which a substantial number were in Arabic, dealing with medicine, mathematics, and literature. Some of the books published in Cairo and Constantinople came to Syria, though in very small numbers. One of Palmerston's agents sent out to survey the situation reported in 1838 that there was so small a demand for books that in both Damascus and Aleppo—major metropolises for the area—he could not find a single bookseller.

Thus the revival of Arabic found itself hampered at the very outset by the accentuation of the split condition that had characterized it from the moment of its emergence into history. Just as the classical Arabic that became the medium of expression for the vast cosmopolitan society of the early caliphate had been sharply distinct from all the dialects actually spoken, so now the differences between the various dialects and subdialects and between all the spoken idioms and the written language that was a little familiar to the tiny cultivated classes became practically insurmountable. The "standard" language, artificial to begin with, was now scarcely in use at all. The process that had begun with the decay of the caliphate and was consummated by the emergence of the Ottoman Turks as the paramount group in Islam was sealed by the erosion of the literary idiom, which seemed on the verge of being totally swamped by the overgrowth of local dialects.

Literary Arabic in Syria, especially among the Christians who in any case had no use for the monuments of Muslim culture embodied in classical Arabic, was remarkably debased; moreover, the literary remains of the old classical language were for all practical purposes quite forgotten.

The missionaries were trying to plant alien growths in what was a very thin soil to begin with. Because of this a number of Ibrahim's reforms were to be very important; these all date from 1834.

The American mission transferred its printing press from Malta to Beirut; the Presbyterians set up a school for girls there, and a broad program of primary education was set up for boys in Syria modeled on Muhammad Ali's school system in Egypt. It was these innovations that led to the revival of Arabic as a language for the communication of modern ideas.

The secular trend in education was stimulated by all three innovations. Ibrahim's large-scale elementary education system, designed to educate young Muslims ultimately for the army, had aroused other Muslim parents and institutions to compete with them to save their children from military service, but it was the role of the American missionaries that was more profoundly seminal, since it was they who concentrated on the revival of the language *per se*. They took the view that if a nation is to be restored to an independent intellectual position its primary tool must be its written language. What was needed above all was textbooks; the Presbyterians set about providing them. For this they were, of course, obliged to begin with the study of Arabic itself, an immensely difficult task.

Within a few years the Presbyterians had managed to meet their own demand for schoolbooks, as well as that of other schools. Eli Smith, a man who dedicated his life to this enterprise, found himself compelled even to create a new design for Arabic type, since the Presbyterians' Arabic font was inadequate. Smith eventually left the Islamic sphere altogether, but before that he had designed and made an entirely new Arabic type, known as American Arabic. This was what was used for the Presbyterian publications, especially for the vast enterprise of publishing a new translation of the Bible. New manuals for a great variety of subjects were also commissioned and disseminated, meeting a demand that grew livelier by the moment.

Missionaries continued to be active all over Syria, which at this time, of course, included Lebanon and Palestine. New schools were opened in Jerusalem, Beirut, and elsewhere in Lebanon. By 1860 some thirty-three schools had been set up by American missionaries, attended by about a thousand pupils, including some two hundred girls—an achievement that while astounding in comparison with what had gone before nevertheless bears eloquent testimony to the extreme backwardness of the milieu.

In 1866 the Syrian Protestant College was founded in Beirut, with an enrollment of sixteen students. Arabic was the language of instruction; the studies were in higher secondary education and in medicine. The college had long since attained university status and was destined to play an eminent role in the creation of an intelligentsia. In the early stages of the revival of Arabic, and hence in the ultimate formation of a nationalist attitude among Arabic-speakers, its role may legitimately be thought more important than that of any other institution.

Catholics were equally active as missionaries; their influence was to be just as important as that of their Presbyterian rivals. In addition, of course, they had the support, even though often tacit, of local Catholic communities. By 1875 they had established the University of Saint Joseph, an institution altogether comparable to the American college in Beirut. But though influential as a cultural stimulant, the Catholic enterprises do not seem to have had the same direct effect on the resuscitation of Arabic as the Presbyterians'.

Significantly enough, the two overshadowing figures in this early stage of the revival of modernization of Arabic were two Christians—Nasif Yaziji and Butrus Bustani, who devoted their lives to the transformation of the classical tongue, based almost wholly on the vast reservoir of the traditional literature, for all practical purposes entombed ever since the Middle Ages.

Yaziji became a sort of linguistic fanatic in a career that because of the wealth and complexity of the Arabic language can easily be, and in his case was a lifelong one.

Bustani, the other inspirer of what was to become a nationalist movement, was a Christian from Lebanon. Unlike Yaziji he received a rather cosmopolitan education; he learned many other languages besides Arabic, notably Aramaic, Latin, Greek, Hebrew, and

Italian, as well as French. He was indispensable to Eli Smith in translating the Bible into Arabic. Bustani's life work was a compilation of a dictionary of Arabic in two volumes (1870) and an Arabic encyclopedia; both works were done by himself almost singlehandedly. He was also responsible for the first political review ever published in Syria—the weekly *Nafir Suriyya* (The Syrian Clarion). Bustani was an exponent of European humanism, of the view—somewhat naïve from our own point of view—that knowledge would lead to enlightenment, and that in turn to the extinction of fanaticism of all kinds and to the birth of common ideals.

Bustani not only preached this sweet and simpleminded doctrine in the columns of his weekly paper, but managed to get enough money together to found the National School, to give boys of all creeds an education based on religious tolerance and on "national" ideals—general ideas, that is, reflecting the common background of the Arabic language. After publishing his vast dictionary, Bustani began the publication in 1870 of a fortnightly political and literary journal to combat fanaticism and to propagate understanding and solidarity for the sake of the "national" welfare. The motto of this journal (*al-Janan*) was: "Patriotism is an article of faith," which appeared on the title page of each issue.

This notion was totally unknown throughout the Arabic-speaking world. The attitude of mind implied by it may justly be regarded as the seed of the modern Arab nationalist movement, though even here it contains an implicit confusion that was later to weigh heavily on the whole movement: What is the country patriotism should be felt for? Is it Syria? If so, why would that be attractive to, say, Egyptians, or Iraqis? Or is it Arabia? Or Arabdom? Clearly, at the very outset of the movement there was a contradiction in the very approach to this complex question—what is an Arab?

During the early period of their collaboration with the Presbyterian American Mission Yaziji and Bustani had proposed that a learned society be founded for the propagation of the new ideas of humanism; by 1847 the Society of Arts and Sciences was an accomplished fact. It included a number of influential Americans aside from Eli Smith. In two years it had fifty members, none of them Muslims or Druzes. This enterprise, under American patronage, seems to have been the first time that the dissemination of knowledge had ever been collectively launched in an Arabic-speaking milieu. It was quite alien to the traditional methods of teaching in the East, which generally revolved around the devotion of disciples to a charismatic teacher. The society was to act as a model for similar organizations in the Arabic-speaking world.

The American example set by Protestant missionaries was soon followed by the Jesuits, who founded the Oriental Society in 1850; this was also wholly Christian.

Neither society lasted more than a few years; still another, the largest of the three, was founded in 1857. It was known as the Syrian Scientific Society (*al-Jam'iyya al-'Ilmiyya as-Suriyya*) and differed from its predecessors not merely in being bigger, but in including Muslims and Druzes, which made it a significant innovation in the world of that age. The fervor of Yaziji and Bustani, in their attempt to generalize the knowledge of the Arabic language and of "Arab" tradition as the groundwork for a new spiritual magnet that would transcend the parochial partitions of the Middle East, and especially of Syria, had scored a certain success.

The Muslims had agreed to join the new society only if all missionary influence was obliterated. Thus, though the whole notion of the society was essentially both missionary and Christian, by eliminating at least formally the missionary connection a step was taken along a path to some sort of Syrian statehood.

In a way this society represented the first attempt at bridging the chasm between the numerous confessions and clans that had lacerated Syria for so many centuries. It was in any case the first time under Ottoman dominion that such a unifying factor had come into being and welded together, even in a superficial and mandarinlike way, the contending creeds within the country, giving them at least the misty outlines of a new ideal based on the European export of the nation-state-language principle.

By now Syria had long since been drawn into the maelstrom of currents and countercurrents generated by the massive involvement in the Middle East on the part of Great Britain and France and by the consequent embroiling of the Ottoman Empire with the swiftly expanding European spheres of influence all over the world.

The crazy-quilt of religious and ethnic communities of the Middle East naturally reflected all these international rivalries in a singularly complicated system of ricochets.

The Turkish government, however reluctantly, slowly, and efficiently, had been compelled to adapt itself in some measure to the changing situation. Part of the aftermath of the Crimean War was the enactment in 1856 of a decree that explicitly recognized complete equality between all religions in the Ottoman Empire with respect to taxation, justice, and the basis of citizenship. It thus equalized the Christian position in Syria too, following in this the initiative of Ibrahim Pasha; it had been responsible also for the founding of the above-mentioned Syrian Scientific Society, the first society to include Christians and Muslims.

By 1860 the frictions endemic in the countryside, between the Catholic peasantry and its Catholic overlords, between the Christian peasants and their Druze overlords in southern Lebanon, all exacerbated by the Machiavellian policy of the current Turkish governor, engendered a savage outbreak of communal riots aimed at the Christians, who were undone by the superior violence and discipline of the Druzes and by the treachery of the Turkish soldiers, who sided in effect against the Christians. The violence infected other parts of the country; in July the Damascus Muslims instituted a tremendous massacre in the Christian quarter of the city. Some eleven thousand lives seem to have been lost in Damascus and the Lebanon; the destruction of property was correspondingly immense. Of the Catholic missions the Jesuits especially were slaughtered and plundered with remarkable ferocity.

The clergy of all kinds emerged from the massacres rather discredited; the massacres had been at least partially the result of power politics on the part of ecclesiastics in all the communities, and the feudal regime of the country was discredited still further. Aside from the administrative reforms they brought about, as well as the intervention of European powers, the idea of transcending the feudal division of the country into cantons based on religious communities was stimulated still further. This had a positive effect on the creation of a Syrian movement directed against the Turks.

The difficulties attendant on the formulation of the very idea of Arab nationalism are well illustrated by what seems to have been the first organized political effort in what ultimately became a movement: the establishment in 1875 of a secret society by five Arabic-speaking Christians, all of them graduates of the Syrian Protestant College in Beirut. They saw the importance of spreading beyond the Christian communities; inspired primarily by their sponsorship of Arabic as a tongue to be revived and also by feelings of Syrian patriotism, they managed to get some twenty-two other members from the various confessions within the country, all members of the nascent intelligentsia. The small group, which remained secret, managed to secure the backing of one of the recently established Masonic lodges that had been founded shortly before in Syria; the group took to the clandestine distribution of street placards couched in general slogans.

The clearest placard that has survived was posted at the end of 1880. Its appeal was simple, and indicates the modest scope of the new movement; it "called for Syro-Lebanese independence; recognition of Arabic as an official language in the area; the elimination of the censorship and other restrictions; and the employment of local people only for military service in the area."

The very notion of "Arabs" as such was not recognized even verbally. The interest of the young Syro-Lebanese Christian intellectuals and their few fellow travelers was concentrated only on the local scene. Nothing was generalized beyond the confines of their own country; the insistence on Arabic as an official language was merely the reaction to the oppressive Ottoman ruling, from 1864 on, that Turkish be the major language of government in Syria as well as everywhere else. All the high officials were Turks; most of them knew no Arabic at all, and the business of administration, in the chief public services as well as the law courts themselves, was carried on in Turkish; the subject population had to master a foreign language. Thus Turkish was made to spread precisely at a time when the efforts of the Christian missionaries to revive literary Arabic as a cultivated medium of communication had already had some success. The censorship merely exacerbated this tendency by clamping a dead bureaucratic weight on the expression of thought at the same time that the countermovement in favor of expressing new and for the period revolutionary ideas was being molded by the attempt to revive the language itself.

The first demand of the programmatic placard, for Syro-Lebanese unity, was directed at the enactment of a special decree in 1864 detaching Lebanon from the rest of Syria. The Christian inspirers of the new ideas of nationalism were bound to feel confined to a tiny island, excluded from the relatively large hinterland provided by Syria.

The fourth point was directed at the new practice of recruiting local Syrians to carry on a fight against the Yemenite Arabs, a very long way from home, in the wake of the Turkish reconquest of the Yemen in 1872. This had renewed open hostilities between the Ottoman authorities and the local populations of the peninsula, which had been traditionally recalcitrant and evasive. It seemed to the Turkish government simpler to control the Arabians of the southern part of the peninsula with Arabic-speaking Syrians, and there had been a forcible embarkment of Syrian units in 1874 that greatly irritated the local population. On top of that, Syrian battalions were sent off a few years later to the Russo-Turkish War; with no solidarity between the Turkish Empire and so many of its subjects this was bound to inflame Syrian sentiment still further.

This modestly formulated program of 1880, concentrating as it did on Syria-Lebanon and the official use of Arabic, with no horizon that extended even to Iraq, to say nothing of Egypt or the Arabian Peninsula, was the zenith of the secret society's activities. There is some reason to think that it went on existing for another few years and that it issued some other appeals, but nothing tangible was accomplished. The whole organization can be regarded as at best an arrow pointing in the general direction of local political autonomy but as having no general ideas to animate the idea of "Arabism" that in a few generations was to become a slogan for so many emergent states.

Indeed, though the signs of restiveness were abundant, due to the general dislike of the Turks among the local Arabic-speaking populations, this restlessness did not in any way revolve around the notion of an "Arab nation," as distinct from the local Arabic-speaking populations of Syria and Lebanon. This is strikingly evident in the reports from the scene made by European travelers, in spite of the natural tendency coming into vogue for Europeans to assume that the speakers of Arabic were "Arabs" in the sense in which the speakers of French were Frenchmen.

For all practical purposes the movement for Syrian independence came to a halt; it became totally invisible, partly because of the success of the sultan's Arab policy and partly because of the advances made in the Westernizing of education and the growing influence of the clergy.

The device of holding out office to various Syrians, while keeping a suggestion of terror in the background, successfully isolated and muted the sporadic impulses that had produced a few public placards.

In addition the education movement made considerable strides, all of them unfavorable to the growth of any notion of unified Syrian sentiment, still less that of "Arab" solidarity. By this time missions had arrived from Russia, Italy, and Germany to contribute to the clash of spiritual interests already being stimulated in a lively way by the intense competition between the French, British, and American missions. This very variety of ecclesiastical interests dovetailed neatly with and was indeed a reflection of the existing diversity of communal entities that made the development of any sense of solidarity so enormously difficult—and, in fact, for that generation, quite impossible. The missions were not merely spiritual leaders; they inevitably brought with them the rivalries between their governments and thus became tools of international politics, in this period more confused and hectic than ever.

The French government, imbued with a sense of the universalism of French civilization, subsidized the French missions, which entered into a natural alliance with the Maronites and Melchites, ancient allies of the Vatican and the most important Christian group in the country. The Russians, in their turn, cultivated the Greek Orthodox population, also a very substantial element. Russia and France were influenced perhaps chiefly by their ecumenical point of view in church and cultural matters, since at that time it was premature to envisage an actual political incursion into the area. America had a purely cultural and ecclesiastical goal, while Great Britain, though rather detached politically in its missions, began playing politics in a different sense by encouraging the Druzes against the French and Russians.

The immense effort expended by the missions, while raising very substantially the cultural level of the educated population, by this very fact added to the welter of contending influences molding the intelligentsia, simply because of the diversity in aims, methods, and allegiances. Sectarianism, the hallmark of Syrian society, was reinforced still further, with a considerable increment of weapons for the cultural arsenal of each of the communities the country was split up into.

Thus the inspiration of the preceding generation, which, while

Christian in inspiration, had been aimed at jumping over the communal partitions in the name of at least the common language, was nullified by the generation of the last third of the nineteenth century. The Christian inspiration had meanwhile become effectively articulated into concrete institutions, all rivals, and checkmated all the idealists, few in number to begin with, who had been dreaming of a Europeanized, modernized Syria in which the divisions between creeds, communities, and nationalities would be obliterated by the notion of Syrian patriotism, signified by the common heritage of a revived language.

The influence of the various school systems attached to the missionary enterprises led to the cultivation of some European language in addition to Arabic, which very directly encumbered the cultivation of Arabic even as a language, since the two intertwined factors made its cultivation difficult and/or pointless.

On the one hand, the schools were determined to set a national stamp on their ecclesiastical enterprises, which meant that they made a point of instilling the cultural values of their respective countries into the students via some European language. On the other hand, the difficulties inherent in the revival of Arabic were insurmountable over a short period of time; the intense interest in modern ideas that was bound to be stimulated in the minds of a lively younger generation could be satisfied only by a European language, in which current concepts were already embedded. Arabic, though limitlessly rich in many ways, was still quite unadapted to the intellectual requirements of the age. Only a systematic campaign of linguistic adaptation, centralized by an authoritative institution and benefiting by widespread public support, could even have made the effort; of course there was no such thing available.

The upshot was that no effort was even made. The foreign educators eventually decided to dispense with Arabic altogether and simply teach straight out in a European language. Even the Americans, who had at first developed some rather romantic views about the revival of the language, finally gave up; around 1880 they made English the teaching language in the Syrian Protestant College.

Thus it was natural for a generation to grow up that could command modern ideas only in a foreign language—French, English or Russian—rather than in some native idiom. This in its way increased the atomization of the country, since if the problem of converting classical Arabic into a modern medium was very difficult, the notion of elevating to the level of a cultivated idiom any particular Arabic *dialect,* in any case radically different from the classical medium, was quite inconceivable.

The pupils in these European schools were, of course, overwhelmingly Christian in number. The Muslims were very fearful of having their children "corrupted" or converted and so preferred to send them to the old-fashioned religiously orthodox schools maintained by the state or by their own community, regardless of their efficiency (even if efficiency had been a desideratum!). Thus the Muslims naturally remained in closer contact with their own traditions, which had the fundamental effect of strengthening their relationship to Arabic and ultimately to its revival.

By the turn of the nineteenth century, accordingly, the ideas originally bound up with the Christian Arabs under the direct influence of Europe via the mission schools now began to infiltrate the Muslim milieu—itself, of course, now being battered by the West—and to exercise a growing influence over the new generation of Muslims, who in Syria became increasingly hostile to the Turkish regime.

From the point of view of the Arab nationalist ideology that was to emerge a generation later, the defect of the emphasis on the Muslim connections or background of the Arab past is that it tends to dilute the nationalism of the Arabic-speakers by the internationalism inherent in Islam.

On the other hand, the mere fact that most Arabic-speakers are in fact Muslims implies the possibility of their being organized *as such;* they are an already existing community, and their political leadership can create a range of general ideas to encompass them without bothering too much about intellectual or ideological consistency.

To be sure, the obstacles to any form of effective regional union, even on a purely intellectual plane, were insurmountable. In Egypt, for instance, the rise in education and the gradual improvement of conditions in general stimulated to some extent the consciousness of the cultural past, expressed, of course, in a revival of Arabic. But in Egypt, the most powerful of the Arabic-speaking countries, and the one with the most substantial, purely *national* past, dating from the Napoleonic expedition of 1801, the movement for revival took a purely Egyptian—*i.e.*, non- or even anti-Arab—form.

In the 1870s the troubled reign of the Khedive Isma'il led the intellectual ferment, in any case restricted to a tiny milieu in the two capitals of Cairo and Alexandria, to be channeled into the framework of an exclusively Egyptian revival aimed at the expulsion of the British. The movement took generations to develop any real force, but during its existence it diverged completely from the equally negligible Syrian movement for local autonomy.

Thus the major Arabic-speaking power in the Middle East, because of the peculiarities of its own national past, devoted itself to chiseling out its own national myth on the basis—more or less mythical, to be sure—of a "Pharaonic" past, and in any case of the singular qualities of the Egyptian people as such.

Because of this, though the cultural revival entailed by the modernization of the Arabic language created an element common to all Arabic-speaking peoples, there was a total break, politically speaking, between the Muslim Egyptian revival and the modernization of Syria.

The same may be said about Tunisia and Algeria, by this time totally immersed in the sea of French culture. Practically speaking this meant that the Tunisian and Algerian intelligentsia was Europeanized as never before, and in a purely Gallic form at that, while the older generations of intellectuals, an exiguous layer of the population at best, remained petrified in the medievalism of traditional Islam.

Thus the roots of the Arab revival were initially limited to Syria and to some extent Iraq. In the Arabian Peninsula, the one place in the world where the inhabitants might be said to be purely "Arab"—despite a very substantial admixture of Negro blood—the culture was so far outside the orbit of contemporary European ideas that there could be no question of the Bedouin's participation in any "movement" at all.

• • •

It was during the reign of Abd-al-Hamid (1876–1909) that Turkey made a more or less serious attempt to adapt itself to the storm of ideas and institutional innovations sweeping out of Europe. The regime of his predecessor, Sultan Abd-al-Aziz, had been marked by a corruption, inefficiency, and brutality that were unusual even for the decadence of the Ottoman Empire, though even under its worst excesses the Arabic-speaking provinces of the empire remained quiescent, the liveliest outbreaks against it taking place in its European possessions.

When Abd-al-Hamid came to the throne he made a number of liberal concessions, chiefly in order to steal the thunder of the European powers and to lull the apprehensions of his own subjects.

In Asia the Arabic-speaking countries controlled by the sultan consisted of Syria, Iraq, and the Arabian Peninsula; in Africa, of Egypt, the Sudan, Libya, and Tunisia. Algeria had been taken by France as far back as 1830, and in 1881 the Turks also lost Tunisia to France. In 1882 the British seized both Egypt and the Sudan, though they acknowledged the technical sovereignty of the Turks, while the French did not. The difference was trivial; in fact the Turks had simply lost the North African coast, with the negligible exception of Libya, which was snatched by the Italians in 1912.

Abd-al-Hamid's regime, founded on corruption, espionage, and oppression, was sadly unfit for a modern role, existing as it did merely on the sufferance of the great powers of Europe on all levels, especially the military level. In his attempt to fortify his position he paid some special attention to his technical status as Caliph of Islam, a title that had long since been entirely devoid of meaning but still had an honorific ring to it; theoretically, of course, it could be magnified once again into some genuine function.

This possibility naturally depended on the reform of Islam, which throughout the nineteenth century was as a whole receiving the same battering from the general advance of the West as the rest of the world.

Here the sultan's interests coincided, if only partially, with a concomitant though essentially quite independent movement for pan-Islamic reform that had some effect on the Muslim world in the last quarter of the nineteenth century.

This movement, led by Jamal-ad-Din Afghani, one of the few effective reformers produced by Islam in the modern period, aimed at the conventional modernization of the Muslim peoples of the world. He also thought that to achieve this end, based on general education and the adaptation of Islam to modern conditions, revolutionary action was indispensable.

The two movements were quite distinct. Abd-al-Hamid simply wanted to utilize the status of caliph more effectively by salvaging it from the neglect it had fallen into for centuries and from its being treated as a mere honorific appendage of his political quality of sultan. His aim was purely political; the caliphate was for him a mere element of statecraft. His theoretical justification for this was, of course, that historically and logically the notion of the caliph *implied* state power, despite the general assumption, among both Europeans and sophisticated Muslims, that the office of caliph was a threadbare traditional ornament with no real meaning.

Abd-al-Hamid's dual aim—strengthening his hold over his Muslim subjects by an appearance of Muslim piety and ultimately, perhaps, using their devotion for purposes of war, and buttressing the position of Turkey as a power among other powers—entailed some concessions to the non-Turkish elements of the realm, including the Arabic-speaking portions of his domain. He spent huge sums on institutions of learning in Arabic, lavished distinctions on Arab notables, and gave large sums for the repair and decoration of mosques in the three principal shrines of Islam—Mecca, Medina, and Jerusalem. His own personal service depended very largely on Arabic-speaking subjects, who even made up one of the battalions of his bodyguard. It was widely maintained that the palace was in their hands.

But his astuteness led him to use contrary measures as well, in order to keep control over his far-flung Arabic-speaking domain. He had agents roving throughout the Arabic-speaking world masked as preachers, whose real function was to keep the discord endemic there constantly aflame by the exploitation and incitement of already existing family disputes, tribal friction, and vendettas. These emissaries of his also acted as *agents provocateurs* in order to give the sultan a pretext for punishing some enemy. Aside from ordering assassination in extreme cases, he would also invite rivals to Constantinople, where they could be kept under close watch while living in luxury.

Of these compulsory guests perhaps the most notable was Husayn ibn Ali, of a family that traced its descent back to Muhammad through his daughter and for generations had provided the holy city of Mecca with its Grand Sharifs. Husayn, though never noted for intelligence, had a certain prestige through his office and his lineage; he had a personal reputation for being headstrong and stubborn, and in his youth, somehow, he also had a reputation for dangerous ideas. In any case, Husayn was courteously invited to come and live in Constantinople with his family, which he did in 1893, then being in his late thirties, with his wife and his three sons, who were ultimately to be drawn into the curious adventure of the British intervention in the Middle East during World War I. They were to become kings or kinglets: Ali, of the Hijaz (a very short-lived reign); Faysal, of Iraq; and Abdallah, who was to become Amir and then King of Transjordan. The family remained under what was in effect house arrest in Constantinople more than fifteen years; throughout this time Husayn seems to have led a life of indolence and pious meditation.

The axis of the newly contrived Arab policy of the Turkish sultan was provided by Izzat Pasha al-Abid, a singularly astute Syrian Muslim who became the most powerful functionary in the empire, second only to Abd-al-Hamid himself.

Izzat Pasha may have conceived the imaginative notion of building a railway through the Hijaz from Damascus to Medina and then to Mecca, with the alleged object of facilitating the pilgrimage to the holy cities, but really for strategic and political purposes. By the end of 1908 the line had been laid as far as Medina—some nine hundred miles. The enterprise, which was launched in such a way as to involve the enthusiasm of the Muslim masses, cost some 3 million pounds (or 15 million dollars at the time), of which a third was to consist of voluntary donations from all over Islam.

The project seems to have been brilliantly conceived; at very little cost it gave Abd-al-Hamid a first-class means of land transport, lessening the government's dependence on the Suez Canal; it also substantiated the sultan's claims as caliph.

The railway was to play a perhaps vital role in the Arabian revolt that was to be triggered by World War I. It quickened internal communications immeasurably; beforehand it took a fast caravan at least forty days to go from Damascus to Medina, while by sea it took at least ten to fifteen days to get to the Hijaz from Syria. The railway brought the two capitals, Damascus and Medina, within five days of each other; this shortening was to prove vital to the British in World War I.

Abd-al-Hamid began his reign roughly around the time Kaiser

Wilhelm II's government launched its policy of the "Thrust to the East" (*"Drang nach Osten"*), as part of the upsurge of Hohenzollern Germany. The Germans made a determined effort to penetrate the whole area under Ottoman sovereignty, as part of a background for the much touted Berlin-Baghdad railway, for which the kaiser himself got the concession on his 1898 trip to Constantinople.

The Baghdad railway was to extend the German-built line already in operation (between Haydar Pasha and Konia), go eastward to Mosul along the southern rim of the Anatolia—roughly the boundary between the Turks and the Arabic-speaking world—and then turn southward at Baghdad, to end somewhere on the Persian Gulf. Some branch lines were also under consideration, aimed at linking up the gulf directly with the Mediterranean.

This imaginative and sensible idea was an obvious menace to the British Empire; backed by German money, brains, and organization, it was bound to create anxiety everywhere. A huge new sphere of influence seemed about to be thrown into the Germans' lap, with immense potential markets and raw materials, shielded against British seapower, and a contender for the control of the Persian Gulf, with all the consequences this would have for India and the Middle East as a whole.

After Constantinople the kaiser made a ceremonial trip to Jerusalem and from there to Damascus. With great solemnity he stressed his benevolence toward the sultan and his endless sympathy for the great world of Islam. He returned to Germany apparently after having made a permanent dent on the mind of the Muslim world. The sultan gladly played the part of Germany's ally, though doubtless with numerous reservations; his main attitude toward the Baghdad railway was that it would enable him to keep a firmer hold over the distant, thinly settled, and fractious Arabian Peninsula.

In 1905, even before the fall of Abd-al-Hamid, a book appeared in Paris entitled *The Awakening of the Arab Nation,* published in the name of the Ligue de la Patrie Arabe, that adumbrated at least the idea of an independent Arabic-speaking state extending from Mesopotamia to Suez. It is illuminating that this first broad sketch of a movement from home rule carefully excluded Lebanon, which was granted autonomy. It also made a point of having both an Arab "sultan" as its head, as well as a caliph, who was to be an amir of the Hijaz.

Thus even at the very inception of the concept of Arab independence there was still a hangover of the universal religion that in fact contradicted the national impulse. Aside from the impudence of putting forth, even in a purely propagandistic tract, the claims of some random Hijazi prince to the paramount position in Islam, in which any number of other peoples—Indians, Muslims, Persians, Turks, Egyptians—were infinitely more advanced than the Hijazis—the work is interesting as an instance of the confusion about "Arabism" and "Islamism" that was bound to prevail in the minds of the forerunners of a nationalist movement whose ideas, freshly imported from Europe, had not yet had time to be digested. Just as the claim to Islamic leadership was extravagant, so the demands for Arab independence, though equally extravagant for the time, were in fact rather modest in terms of the criterion that was ultimately to become decisive for the Arab nationalist movement of the period after World War II—that is, language. The 1905 proposal did not even mention the extension of the "Arab nation" westward beyond Suez; it was really a variation of a number of schemes involving the Fertile Crescent in the north of the great Syro-Arabian desert.

The Ottoman regime, though profoundly enfeebled by the stresses of the modern era, was more flexible than many had thought. In July 1908, menaced by a conspiracy long being matured abroad—in Cairo and Paris—by the "Young Turks," the sultan granted a constitution that seemed to grant all liberal elements in the empire a new lease on life. The military revolution brought about by the Young Turk conspiracy was the work of the Committee of Union and Progress, a secret association created in Salonica to overthrow the Ottoman despotism. The CUP was rather representative of the welter of communities, creeds, and peoples in the Ottoman Empire—mostly Turks, with some Jews, a few Syrians and so on—and its efforts were primarily directed at doing away with Abd-al-Hamid's autocracy and at the modernization of the regime. It was specifically aimed at the administrative fusing together of all races, as envisaged in the 1876 constitution (the brainchild of the liberal Turkish statesman Midhat Pasha), which ever since then had been shelved.

All liberal elements throughout the Empire—Turks, Syrians, Iraqis, Muslims, Christians, and Jews—hailed the revived constitution with delirious joy, according to all reports. The prospect of mixing together all peoples into a single Ottoman democracy with Turkish as the national language seemed at first to delight all malcontents.

A *de facto* alliance of Turks, Syrians and Iraqis came into being. The first Arabic-speaking society to arise during this honeymoon between the Turks and their subjects took place in September 1908. Known as the *al-Ikha al-Arabi al-Uthmani* (the Ottoman Arab Brotherhood), it was aimed at uniting all races in loyalty to the sultan, protecting the new constitution, furthering the welfare on a footing of equality of the Arabic-speaking provinces of the empire, and promoting education in Arabic and the observance of Arab customs.

The very title of this society, with its stress on the word "Ottoman" and on loyalty to the sultan in conjunction with all other ethnic groups, indicates the absence of any specifically Arab political ideas behind it. This confusion in its basic conception was to be illuminated very clearly in the organ it actually launched.

The euphoria of political togetherness between the Turks and their subjects did not last long. After a determined effort by Abd-al-Hamid to annihilate the CUP, the following year—April 1909—he was deposed and an ineffectual brother put in his place. The real government continued to be, in a still more reinforced form, the CUP of the Young Turks, who had already shown their basic indifference to principles of mere democracy during the elections for a parliament that met in December 1908, in which the Turks were represented out of all proportion to their true numbers in the empire.

From now on the CUP was in absolute control of the Ottoman Empire. Though its dictatorship was different in a way from Abd-al-Hamid's, the very fact that it was more modern, self-conscious, and dynamic made it more oppressive to the various non-Turkish elements of the empire. One of its first acts was to ban all societies founded by non-Turks; the Ottoman Arab Brotherhood lasted only eight months.

The insoluble problems inherited by the CUP from Abd-al-Hamid's regime were exacerbated by a sort of intellectual confusion that made the CUP incapable of creating a mythology to attract the people they were trying to govern.

While centralizing the government, more or less on the model of France, they associated their sponsorship of democracy for all races under Ottoman leadership with open sympathy for a parallel doctrine that had sprung up a short while before—pan-Turanianism, a form of extreme Turkish nationalism. It maintained that all Turkic-speaking peoples—millions of whom were in Asia outside the Ottoman Empire, mostly under the Russian Tsarist government—were really at one with the Ottoman Turks and therefore should, obviously, be led by them.

This view of themselves led many of their subjects, especially in the Arabic-speaking districts, to feel that "Ottomanism" was a mere mask for pan-Turanianism and that in being asked to accept the former they were committing ethnic suicide by being submerged in the latter.

In reality the Young Turks, while accepting the catchwords of democracy, were rather dogmatic reformers bent on saving what they could of the old Ottoman Empire by keeping the Turks in the commanding positions they naturally assumed to be their due. Hence their natural reaction to any demands for home rule, from any quarter at all, was repression. In January 1914 all concessions that had been granted or discussed in the area of administration were wiped out, and a decision was made to Turkicize all non-Turkish elements in the empire. All Arab political groups were dissolved, and hence, when World War I broke out and the question of alignment in the gigantic struggle came up, it was natural for the struggle for autonomy in the Arabic-speaking areas to be linked to the general slogan for self-determination of peoples that was to justify the liquidation of the great supranational empires, like the Austro-Hungarian and the Ottoman Empires, and that provided the combatants with a potent myth.

In Turkey, in any case, the combination of state centralization, which was bound to inflame the separatist impulses now astir, and the general promotion of Turkish paramountcy failed to cope with the slight though unmistakable ferment that now began to take place. A number of anti-Ottoman societies were founded in the Arabic-speaking provinces and driven underground by the CUP ban on non-Turkish societies. The propaganda of the Arabic-speaking groups was not directed at the crystallization of a general program encompassing all Arabic-speaking countries under the concept of "Arab nationalism"—an idea that had still to coagulate, more than a generation later—but continued to be a form of agitation for local autonomy. The CUP, with its program of systematic centralization, was simply the chief opponent of the champions of provincial rights, or home rule, as it might be called in another context.

A realistic appraisal of the situation of the Arabic-speaking provinces within the Ottoman Empire was given by a secret society founded in 1909, *al-Qahtaniyya* (after a legendary ancestor of the Arabs). The society proposed converting the Ottoman Empire into a dual monarchy something like Austro-Hungary; the Arabic-speaking provinces would form one kingdom, with its own parliament and administration and with Arabic as the official language, whose crown would be worn by the sultan of Turkey. In this way it was hoped that the Turks would remain within the same state as the Arabic-speaking provinces, and on a more harmonious basis. Though *al-Qahtaniyya* attracted some army officers from the Arabic-speaking provinces, it expired very quickly, having lasted only a year or so.

Another secret society was *Jam'iyyat al-Arabiyya al-Fatat* (Young Arab Society), which was organized in Paris in 1911, on exclusively Muslim initiative, with some seven members; its goal, the total independence of the Arabic-speaking countries, went considerably beyond the projects of other groups that hoped to remain under the Turkish umbrella.

These two secret societies rounded out for the period the activities of two other publicly organized societies of a literary and cultural nature called *al-Muntada al-Adabi* (Literary Club), founded in 1909 by some functionaries, writers, and students, and another much more political group called the *Hizb al-Lamarkaziyya al-Idariyya al-Uthmani* (Ottoman Decentralization Party), which aimed at carrying on an extensive campaign for the devolution of administrative authority in the Arabic-speaking world. This Decentralization Party may be considered the first champion of an overt political effort on behalf of the local interests of the Arabic-speaking parts of the Ottoman Empire.

The activities of these four societies, and some other more obscure groups, were to lead to a congress in Paris in the summer of 1913.

The Committee of Reform, consisting of some eighty-six members in close contact with the Decentralization Party, had been formed in Beirut at the end of 1912, supposedly to campaign for autonomy for the Arabic-speaking provinces of the Ottoman Empire. Essentially it simply articulated the aims of the Decentralization Party.

After some skirmishing, the Committee of Reform was very quickly shut down by the CUP. After this act of suppression, the initiative was taken up by the Young Arab Society in Paris. In June 1913 the delegates convened, most of them Syrians, evenly divided between Muslims and Christians. Some two hundred listeners attended; on the last day the doors were opened to the general public and the proceedings, perhaps typically, were held in French.

• • •

Before World War I, it would be impossible to say that the movement for Arab solidarity had ever got beyond the stage of diffuse and feeble agitation for home rule in Syria and possibly Iraq. The agitation carried on by the Decentralization Party and reflected in the rhetoric of the Arab Congress in Paris in June 1913 was quite unsuccessful even on its own grounds. The CUP, by appearing to compromise with the small and scattered movement championing the rights of Arabic as the language of instruction in the Arabic-speaking areas, the rights of Syrians and Iraqis to government offices, and the restriction of Arabic-speaking units to action only on their own home grounds, had actually undone even this short-lived and moderate reform movement. The movement had, after all, always accepted the idea of working within the Ottoman Empire and had never thought of generalizing its demands beyond mere local autonomy. Manifestly it had lacked the broad intellectual horizon that might have enabled it to surmount mere political repression, which in any case was carried out rather inefficiently and with a certain moderation characteristic of the CUP's lukewarm reaction to what it doubtless regarded as a minor irritation.

At the other end of the Mediterranean, the Maghrib came under complete European dominion in the early 1900s. The Italian seizure of Libya obliterated the final vestige of Turkish influence in North Africa, even though Italy recognized the "spiritual sovereignty" of the caliph in Constantinople over the area. The Italians in this sector of the Muslim world had come up against a sort of old-fashioned religious solidarity, since the Arabic-speaking subjects of the Turks sided with them enthusiastically against the foreign invasion. The Italians had to overcome a good deal of resistance, especially from the Senussi Fraternity in Cyrenaica, a rather traditional brotherhood of devout Muslims who were the chief instigators of rebelliousness, in the name of Islamic zeal, with no tinge of anything approaching modern national consciousness.

Morocco had always been able to withstand the claims of outsiders, including even the Ottoman Turks, until the beginning of the twentieth century, when after holding off successively the Portuguese, Spaniards, and the Turks, it finally lost its independence to France in 1912 after a long-drawn-out period of skirmishing back and forth among the European powers. It was forced to accept a protectorate of Spain over the northwest coastal area and of France over the rest of its territory.

• • •

Thus, from the point of view of political articulation, the Arabic-speaking world was more prostrate than ever during the generation preceding World War I. If we view its political activities in the perspective of the Arab nationalist movement of our own day, we are bound to be astonished by the rapidity with which that movement has expanded beyond its meager beginnings.

It might be said that of the entire Arabic-speaking domain, from Iraq to Morocco, it was only in Syria, Lebanon, and Iraq that the very notion of an "Arab" revival had any meaning, and that meaning was restricted to various projects for purely local autonomy based on differing manipulations of the notion of the Fertile Crescent. The biggest Arabic-speaking power, Egypt, would have regarded the mere notion of being "Arab" as preposterous, as would all the makers of public opinion along the North African coast. As for the Arabian Peninsula, it was still steeped in an old-fashioned Muslim view of the world.

It might legitimately be said that the idea of "Arab unity," as a project embracing all the speakers of Arabic, was still to be born; World War I was to be its midwife.

VIII

MODERN TIMES

It is curious to reflect that until well into the twentieth century there was never a state formation of any kind called "Arab." The very concept of an "Arab nation" was literally non-existent, and the meaning of the contemporary word "Arab," so familiar from journalism and popular politics, is a rather recent creation, as I have emphasized so often.

Indeed, of the myriad influences exerted in our own day by the West on the East, it may be said that the most sweeping was the change in the perspective in which Arabic-speaking Muslims began to see themselves. It would be legitimate to maintain that the contemporary idea of the Arabs as a nation, enthusiastically concurred in by so many Arab leaders, represents no less than the triumph, paradoxically, of a quite Western point of view.

It was in fact the Western habit of referring to Arabic-speaking Muslims, at least in the Middle East outside of Egypt, as "Arabs" because of their language—on the analogy of German-speakers as Germans, French-speakers as French and so on—that imposed itself on an East that had never regarded language as a basic social classifier. It was natural for Europeans to use the word "Arab" about a Muslim or even a Christian whose native language was Arabic; they were quite indifferent to the principles of classification in the East. The oddity is simply that this European habit became the very germ that the contemporary Arab nationalist movement has sprung from.

For it was by accepting the Western view of the world as

composed, by and large, of peoples organized as such by a language and a state, both of which made them nations, that the Arabic-speakers of the Middle East and North Africa began to shape themselves as a nation in the modern sense. It was not simply that the contemporary Arab nationalist movement was *influenced* by the West during the nineteenth century; the actual idea of Arabs as a nation, of Arabs as an ethnic entity distinct from the Bedouin of the great deserts, was modeled on the Western view of society as rooted in a unifying common language.

What is surprising is the resistance encountered by the attempt to graft the Western rationale of society onto the Islamic East. In view of the blanketing effect of Western ideas and institutions on the Middle East it is remarkable that the Western concentration on language as a touchstone of communal solidarity did not spread more quickly than it did and took so long to change the views of the peoples that came under Western influence. It was a long-drawn-out process, which only in our own day has ripened substantially. It has paralleled, though only very roughly, the political articulation of the area into states that are now quite independent.

There are, in fact, two processes that have been at work in the recent molding of the Middle East: political articulation into states; and the growth of ethnic solidarity between Arabic-speakers, *i.e.*, of an Arab nationalist movement.

On the plane of political organization it would be fair, I think, to say that the present-day Arabic-speaking world owes its origin to wholly external factors: the revolution of the Young Turks in 1908; and, far more obviously, the liberation of Arabic-speaking Asia by the Allies, in particular by Great Britain, in World War I.

This development is quite independent of the growth of the idea of an "Arab nation." The two phenomena are, of course, linked, but neither entails the other. In our own day there are more than a dozen political entities that may call themselves "Arab" in one sense or another. While quite independent, they do not unite; on the other hand, a movement for unity goes on, with varying degrees of emphasis, quite independently of the relations between the states.

Looking backward, we can see that it was the liberation by external influences that set the inhabitants of Arabic-speaking Asia a very clear-cut aim—the establishment of autonomous national

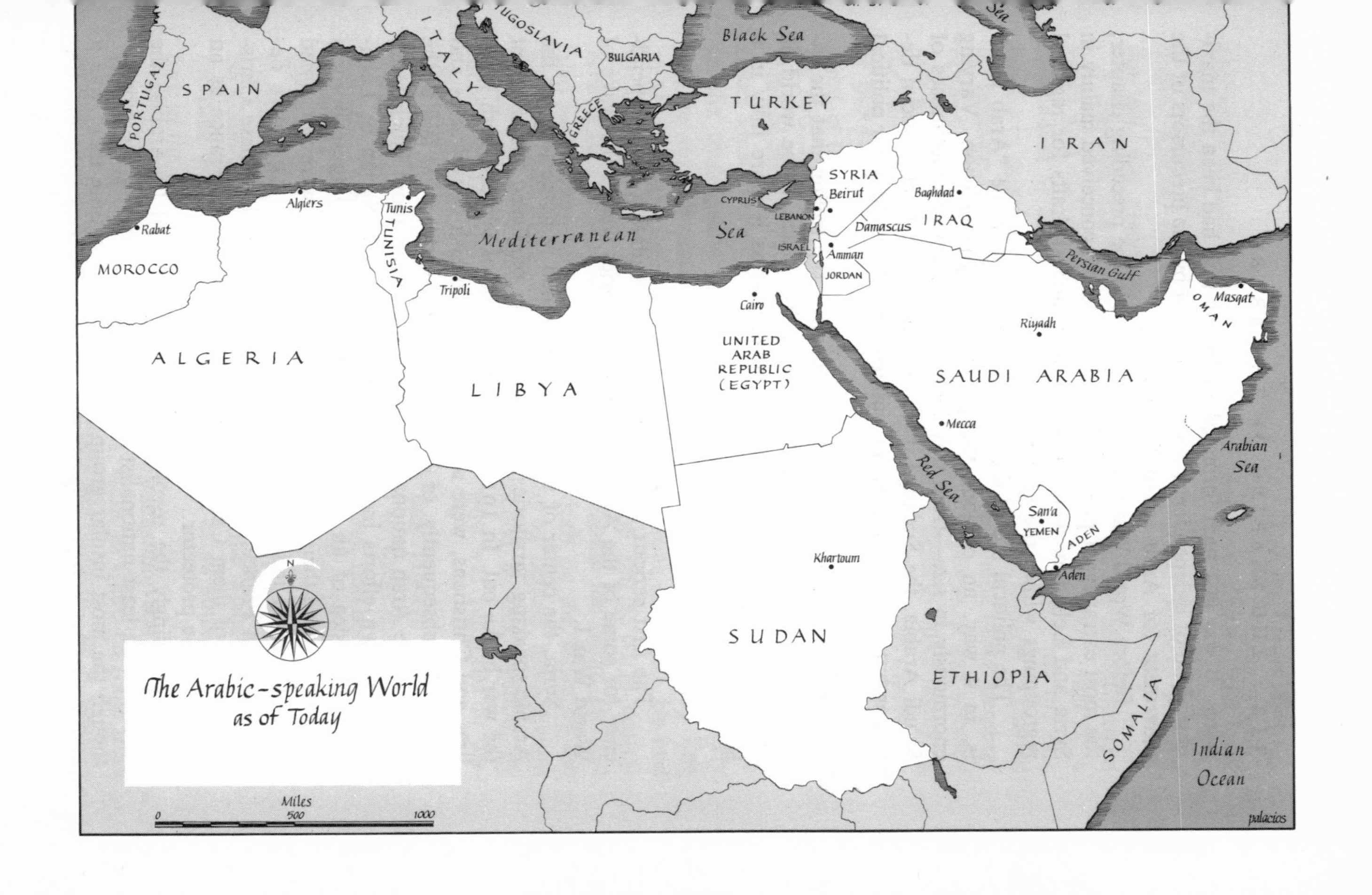
The Arabic-speaking World as of Today
PORTUGAL
SPAIN
ITALY
YUGOSLAVIA
BULGARIA
GREECE
Black Sea
TURKEY
IRAN
SYRIA
Beirut
Baghdad
CYPRUS
LEBANON
Damascus
IRAQ
Mediterranean Sea
ISRAEL
Amman
JORDAN
Persian Gulf
Masqat
OMAN
Rabat
MOROCCO
Algiers
Tunis
TUNISIA
Tripoli
Cairo
Riyadh
ALGERIA
LIBYA
UNITED ARAB REPUBLIC (EGYPT)
SAUDI ARABIA
Mecca
Red Sea
Arabian Sea
San'a
YEMEN
ADEN
Aden
Khartoum
SUDAN
ETHIOPIA
SOMALIA
Indian Ocean
N
Miles
0
500
1000
palacios

veiled way, with Ronald Storrs, then Oriental Secretary at the British Agency in Cairo headed by Lord Kitchener. The conversation was followed by others, but when Abdallah simply asked straight out whether the British could give Husayn any machine guns, Kitchener and Storrs were obliged to refuse, since theoretically Great Britain was bound by a policy of friendship with Turkey.

Thus these initial contacts proved abortive. Yet they were ultimately to produce results, since any discussion of autonomy in the Arabic-speaking Turkish provinces in the Middle East was naturally bound to dovetail with British imperial thinking with respect to the lifeline to India and the stemming of German advances throughout the area. On the basis merely of military strategy, anyone preoccupied with securing the area against a German-Turkish combination was bound to think of a number of variants for detaching various of its segments from the authority of Constantinople. This approach would automatically fall in with the thinking of those local leaders in the provinces who were aiming at autonomy. Autonomy, in short, might be the thin end of the wedge in prying loose the area between the Red Mediterranean and the Persian Gulf, or the Red Sea, from the control of Turkey and thus also of Germany. It was obvious to all British leaders, both military and civilian, that the Berlin-Baghdad project posed a direct threat to the British position in the Persian Gulf and India, and that any territorial prop against such an advance had to involve the native populations.

When the war actually broke out, in August, an obvious and indeed peremptory line of action for the British was, accordingly, to follow up the contact with Abdallah. Storrs was authorized to do so, though the situation was slightly delicate since the Turks were not to come into the war until October. Husayn replied more or less affirmatively, in a letter signed by Abdallah, to a letter sent him by secret messenger in the middle of October.

Husayn's position was particularly delicate since the scope of the war was quite beyond his imagination and he was, after all, a pious Muslim in the service of a Muslim state. However much he wanted more power, or for that matter detested the Turks, the notion of siding *de facto* with a Christian state must have given him pause.

Actually, neither Husayn nor his sons had ever envisaged Turkey's entry into a major war. Husayn's differences with the Turks had fundamentally been of a trivial, parochial nature; the prospect of action on a large scale was far beyond him. Once Turkey became involved, the alternatives were clear-cut: loyalty, to be rewarded with gratitude if Turkey and Germany won; or disaffection alongside a Christian power, to be rewarded in its turn by whatever promises could be extracted.

Faysal, Husayn's third son, had never been in any secret society and had never even considered the idea of an Arab revolt in Arabia until he went to Damascus in 1915. Hence he was rather in favor of supporting the Turks loyally. In addition, he suspected—quite sensibly—British and French designs on Iraq and Syria respectively, and he did not think anyone in Syria, Iraq, or Arabia was prepared to fight. In short, he considered a revolt unfeasible. Abdallah, on the other hand, was optimistic; he thought a call to revolt had a good chance of being heeded in Damascus and Baghdad. As for Kitchener, his message had not actually promised Husayn anything. Abdallah thought the British should be sounded out as to whether they were really offering independence, and for just what areas.

Amid the categorical disaccord of the two brothers, Husayn steered a middle course. The letter he had had Abdallah sign was just enough to keep the British interested, without committing Husayn to anything of a general nature, or even to the extension of the arena of discussion beyond the borders of the Hijaz. He merely hinted at the possibility of a revolt arranged by his own immediate entourage, if the Turks imposed a decision and if British support proved attractive.

Thus the terrain was prepared toward the end of 1914; when Turkey entered the war, Kitchener had the British Agency in Cairo inform Abdallah that Husayn would be guaranteed as Grand Sharif, that the "Arabs" would be supported in general if they allied themselves with England, and that if the Sharif were proclaimed caliph England would recognize him as such.

The combination of these terms is illuminating, more especially the vagueness about what was meant by "Arabs"—since Husayn had simply referred to the Hijaz—and the assumption that the question of the caliphate had some significance for Husayn—since that went very far beyond the Arabic-speaking peoples, quite apart from the grotesqueness of a Christian power dangling a basically religious

Muslim title before the nose of a Muslim functionary of a Muslim power.

In any case Kitchener's letter was interpreted as an invitation to instigate a revolt against Turkey; Abdallah substantially agreed to this in a reply that reached Cairo in the beginning of December. At this time the point was that nothing could be done against Turkey until things were prepared, *i.e.*, arms secured and the revolt organized.

The negotiations with the British, full of diplomatic reserve, were to culminate in documents that have become celebrated as the McMahon Correspondence. The ambiguities that characterized this correspondence were to prove particularly far-reaching with respect to the problem of Palestine, still very much with us; I shall revert to it in a moment.

In June 1916, in any case, Husayn finally came out for the British by proclaiming an "Arab revolt." He was soon in control of the entire Hijaz except for Medina, whose Turkish garrison held out for some time.

Husayn's forces were led by Faysal, with the advice of the English subaltern T. E. Lawrence, whose commentary on the two-year guerrilla campaign (*Revolt in the Desert* and *The Seven Pillars of Wisdom*) was to become famous.

The fundamental task assigned Husayn's forces was the pinning down of the Turco-German detachments in such a way as to allow the British General Allenby to move against Palestine.

This was the only front where Arabs fought as such; the Iraqi tribes never came into action. It is a little difficult to assess the military value of the campaign; like much else in this area it has been obscured by a fog of propaganda in all directions. It seems likely that it was of some help in pinning down a small segment of the Turco-German forces by the action of the Bedouin under Faysal and Lawrence. On the other hand, it is even more obvious that it had no effect on the actual outcome of the war. Later, however, it served as a justification for complaints that the British were neglecting the promises they had made via their agents, such as Lawrence, to the Arabs, especially to Husayn's family. It should perhaps be recalled that the chief criticism of the military value of the Bedouin campaign has come from Arab countries interested in making propaganda on behalf of Arabs from other parts of the Turkish Empire who had fought in Allied units, such as Egypt and Syria.

The skirmishing Bedouin campaigns led by Faysal and Lawrence simply supplemented the main advance being led by General Allenby against the Gaza-Beersheba line, strongly held by German and Turkish troops under Falkenhayn. The advance was begun in the spring of 1917, but the decisive victory did not fall to Allenby until November, when Gaza and Jaffa were taken, and December, when Allenby made his historic entry into Jerusalem. The Bedouin under Faysal and Lawrence had been advancing along the west coast of the peninsula; in July 1917 they entered Aqaba, and by surprise raids they kept disrupting the Hijaz railway supply line needed by the Turks and Germans.

The finest fruit of victory, from the point of view of the Arabs themselves, was of course Damascus, taken in October 1918 by Faysal and Lawrence.

Allenby's victory in Palestine and the Bedouin successes in the peninsula and in Syria involved the British in a tangle of claims and counterclaims even before the smoke died down.

The chief difficulty was that, whatever might have been the intentions or motives of the British, their actual promises contained an element of vagueness that made realization a very slippery question, especially when viewed against the background of British relations with France and the United States.

Husayn and his partisans always believed, or seemed to, that Great Britain had undertaken to sponsor the formation of a unified state taking in the whole zone of the Fertile Crescent and the Arabian Peninsula, that is, all of the Arabic-speaking areas of the former Ottoman Empire. The question of Egypt and North Africa did not, of course, even arise. Husayn's demands at one time had included thoroughly non-Arab areas, such as the Turkish provinces of Mersin and Adana, but McMahon had made him abandon these. McMahon had also laid down some special conditions concerning the Syrian coastline, *i.e.,* Lebanon as involving a French interest, and Iraq (the Baghdad and Basra provinces) as involving a specific British interest. Husayn, without accepting in principle any conditions at all, agreed to discuss these points later.

No mention had been made of two major areas: the central Arabian districts themselves, which were under the *de facto* control of Ibn Sa'ud, the heir of Wahhabism; and the far thornier and more important problem of Palestine, which was not mentioned by name at all. McMahon at one point—some twenty years later!—said in a letter to *The London Times* that he had "thought" of including Palestine in the areas he was discussing with Husayn. There is no doubt that it was perfectly reasonable for the Arab spokesmen to take Palestine for granted as included in the areas being dangled before them.

The agreements embodied—perhaps "hinted at" is the right phrase—in the McMahon Correspondence were essentially irreconcilable with two other sets of agreements: the notorious Franco-British (Sykes-Picot) agreements of May 1916, which, to the scandal of the public, were published in November 1917 by the new Bolshevik regime in Russia. These agreements disregarded all local interests completely and amounted to the complete splitting up of the Arabic-speaking areas of the Ottoman Empire in line with British and French interests exclusively. Thus the "great Arab realm" that seemed implied by the McMahon Correspondence had cut away from it practically all the fertile lands in the Fertile Crescent. The state promised the Arabs was to consist of the Syrian-Arabian desert, with no outlet to the sea. It took in nothing but inner Syria with Damascus in the west and Mosul in the east. The British, caught unawares by the Bolshevik disclosure of the Sykes-Picot agreements and pressed by Husayn, reassured him in vague terms; unsatisfying to begin with, these reassurances were in any case soon outdistanced by events.

The upshot of the war, in brief, was that Great Britain was left solidly in control of Iraq, Aden, Palestine, and Transjordan—where Faysal's brother, bilked of a real throne, was fobbed off with an emirate in this rather desolate piece of semiwasteland, itself truncated for the purpose from the area originally promised the Zionists as covered by the Balfour Declaration. They also retained a protectorate in Egypt and a condominium—together with Egypt—over the Anglo-Egyptian Sudan.

The French, in their turn, secured a mandate over Syria (including Lebanon), where both strategic French interests, as they thought, and French ideas about the "*rayonnement*" of civilization could be given full play.

In short, what had been put forth as a grandiose scheme for the installation of a revived "Arab" state somewhere in the Arabian heartland and extended to the Fertile Crescent was very quickly whittled down to a congeries of small administrative departments of foreign powers. Arabia itself was abandoned completely, leaving

Ibn Sa'ud in control of the domain he had carved himself out of various tribal pasturing grounds.

Husayn, who had proclaimed himself in 1916 as "King of the Arabs"—by which, to be sure, he meant no more than the inhabitants of the Fertile Crescent and Arabia—was recognized by the Allies only as King of the Hijaz; he lost that title in turn to Ibn Sa'ud some years later. Faysal, in Syria as a liberator, proclaimed himself King of Syria in 1920, whereupon the San Remo Conference in April of that year assigned Syria and Lebanon to France, and Iraq, Palestine, and Mesopotamia to Great Britain as mandates. By the summer of 1920, after a brief show of force, Faysal was out of Syria for good, to be installed later on as King of Iraq, founding a dynasty that came to a bloodstained end in the 1950s.

Thus the mandatory system sanctioned by the League of Nations between 1922 and 1924 split up the Arabic-speaking areas of the former Ottoman Empire, itself shrunk to the confines of Asia Minor as a new and essentially Turkish republic under Kemal Pasha Atatürk, into a cluster of regional establishments, some with kings, as in Iraq and Transjordan, some vaguely republican, as in Syria and Lebanon, and one, Palestine, of a highly anomalous character, but all alike in being controlled by British and French bureaucrats.

Accordingly, the Middle East, inherently divided, perhaps, if one is to judge by history, found itself more so than ever. Home rule was eventually to be achieved, but the burgeoning intelligentsia, inflamed by the nationalism acquired during the decades before and after World War II, felt itself shackled by alien rule after the intellectual ferment of the late nineteenth and early twentieth centuries.

The already complicated relationships between the victorious Allies, especially Great Britain and France, and the deep cleavage between their respective goals were confounded still further by the abrupt intrusion of a new element, Zionism, into the Middle East mishmash.

A basic ambiguity in the British position had created a peculiarly bitter international tangle in Palestine, where an entirely different and independent chain of circumstances had brought about an agreement between the British Government and various representatives of the Zionist movement.

Zionism was a movement among European Jews that had first

assumed organizational form toward the end of the nineteenth century. It was basically intended to restore the Jewish people to a state of normality—"like the Gentiles"—on their own territory and thus rectify the various extravagances that had afflicted Jews, both inside the Jewish community and in relations with their neighbors ever since the Jewish Diaspora had come into being almost two thousand years before.

Two movements had been launched with this aim: the Territorialist movement, founded in Russo-Polish Jewry and aiming at the reconstitution of independent Jewish life on any territory that might be suitable; and Zionism, which was determined to make Palestine, the Holy Land of Jewish memory and Jewish prayer, the material as well as spiritual center of a restored Jewish people.

Though there were many shadings among Zionist Jews with respect to the precise nature of the interaction between cultural and political Zionism, most Zionists agreed that in order to ensure the revival of indigenous Jewish values on Jewish terrain, including the revival and modernization as a spoken language of Hebrew, the ancient sacred tongue of the Jewish people embodied in the Hebrew Scriptures and the Talmud, some form of self-government was desirable, indeed indispensable.

Before World War I, Zionist-minded Jews were by and large in a minority in the Jewish world of Europe, though among Russian and Polish Jews the movement had been gaining in strength very rapidly and had achieved a certain prominence, perhaps even a preeminent position in the Jewish community as the one concentrated form of Jewish communal activity. On the eve of World War I, Zionists were busy in Germany, Great Britain, France, Russia, and even Turkey, doing their best to influence the policy of each state in a direction favorable to the establishment of some form of self-containment on the soil of Palestine. The movement had also struck root in America; American Jewry was to play an increasingly important and in some ways decisive role in the fortunes of world Zionism and of Palestine.

In the event it was the British branch of the Zionist movement that was initially successful, simply because of the Allied victory. The British Government, influenced by a variety of motives—imperial, humanitarian, sentimental, romantic—had issued a document that has become celebrated as the Balfour Declaration. This, in the form of a letter to a British Jewish notable, promised the "establishment of a Jewish National Home in Palestine"; it also undertook not to injure the other inhabitants of the country.

Actually, as became clear very soon after the war was won, the British had only the vaguest idea of just who or what these other inhabitants of the country were, and since they had also made promises to a number of Arab leaders, primarily the Husayn family, the Balfour Declaration and the British mandatory regime set up in Palestine by the League of Nations created a hornet's nest that plagued successive British governments for a whole generation. It lasted until well after the end of World War II, when it came to an embittered and bloodstained end with the establishment of the State of Israel in 1948.

It was in Palestine that the political situation was most inflamed. Here the peaceful development that had been hoped for both by Zionists and by their British sympathizers was frustrated by what turned into a head-on collision, or rather a tripartite collision between the Jewish community of Palestine (the Yishuv), the British mandatory administration, and the representatives of the local Arabic-speaking community. The role of this last was complicated by the ties that developed, fairly quickly, between the Palestinian Arabs and the Arabs of other countries, who were to make Palestine the emblem of Arab disgruntlement it has remained to this day.

The basic situation in Palestine was in its nature, perhaps, bound to generate friction. It is a sacred country for both Jews and Christians and contains the third most sacred city in Islam, Jerusalem. Its population had always been rather mixed, in the manner characteristic of the eastern Mediterranean littoral, and consisted of many Christian minorities in addition to the Jewish minority and the predominantly Muslim Arabic-speaking majority. The Balfour Declaration, holding out a substantial promise to the Jews, had stated that nothing was to be done to "prejudice the civil and religious rights of the existing non-Jewish communities" there. This formula, inherently vague and thus elastic, was itself to become the pawn of the sociopolitical maelstrom in the country itself and of the varying fortunes of the world Zionist movement, in its relations both with the British and American governments and with the Jewries of the world.

One of the chief complications, from the British point of view, was that the promise held out to the Jews had been due to the romanticism, sense of justice, or long-range practical views of authoritative persons in London, while the actual executors of the London policy, the British Colonial Office and the local administration in Palestine, were nearly all systematically hostile to the Zionist enterprise from its very inception. As Jewish immigration into the country increased and as political and social friction grew concomitantly with the general rise in the standard of living of the country, the anti-Zionist wing of British policy, especially on the spot, found its position strengthened. The facts seemed to and perhaps did indeed demonstrate the unviability of at least the broadest extension of the Balfour Declaration in the teeth of a growing and irreconcilable local opposition. The London government was, of course, far more susceptible to the influence of Zionism as a world political movement; thus the seeds were sown for the extremely embittered denouement the conflict was to receive shortly after the end of World War II.

Perhaps the chief element of dynamism, an element that lent a factor of desperation to the Zionist leadership, was the menace that hung unmistakably and more and more frighteningly over the Jewish people as a whole because of the dramatic success of the Nazi movement. The forebodings stirred by Hitler's racial obsession and the initial implementation of the anti-Jewish policy long before the establishment of the notorious death camps in 1942 imposed an urgency on the Zionist proposals for the solution of the "Jewish problem" that made the struggle within Palestine itself more and more intense. Jewish immigration, which had begun growing immediately after World War I, increased the Jewish population almost tenfold, from about 60,000 in 1919 to a half-million, as against a million native inhabitants, in 1939.

This was not, of course, a mere matter of numbers. The Zionist Jews, mostly from Europe, brought with them an intensity of purpose inherent in the messianic drive of Zionism itself, together with a relatively advanced Western technology. They brought, in short, the manpower, capital, and determination to embark on large-scale enterprises that provided a striking contrast with the still traditional life of the Arabic-speaking Palestinians, largely peasants and craftsmen, with a substantial Bedouin admixture and a small and, even for the Middle East remarkably backward class of lethargic, parasitic landowners. Thus the Jews acted as the spearhead for the import of the socioeconomic standards of the contemporary West, which, linked to Zionist morale, ultimately shattered the ancient Arabic-speaking community of Palestine.

Perhaps an oddity of this complex situation was the belief held by some of the most idealistic British supporters of Zionism that the country was somehow, really, quite empty—that it was a wasteland that would simply be filled by Jews sooner or later; that there was, in short, no native population to worry about. It had actually been forgotten that the local population of Palestine had roots antedating the Muslim conquests; some authorities even think a substantial segment of it may go back to the ancient Hebrews.

Though knowledgeable Jews were perfectly aware of the importance of the native population and many individuals, perhaps for romantic reasons of their own, cultivated a special interest in Arabic and in local customs, among Zionists it had always been hoped that the inhabitants of Palestine would ultimately be reconciled to the presence of a revitalized Jewish community because of the material and spiritual benefits that might then be spread throughout Palestine and even overflow into the neighboring Arabic-speaking countries. The material advantages of the Zionist presence were, to be sure, undeniable, but they not only failed to entail a change of mind among the Arab leaders, but on the contrary, infuriated them still further.

This basic conflict between the oncoming Jews and the obdurate local population was made somewhat lopsided by what gradually—especially after World War II—came to be an effective fourth party to the imbroglio: the inhabitants of the countries surrounding Palestine.

From an outsider's point of view, it seems legitimate to call this relationship lopsided because of the numbers involved: Palestine itself is no more than a "tiny notch"—as Balfour called it—in the immensities of the Arabic-speaking world. Roughly the size of New Jersey or Wales, it vanishes altogether when juxtaposed to the areas that are inhabited by people of Arabic speech and that in our own day are the target of the movement for Arab unity. If one takes into account the Arabic-speaking countries of the Muslim far west—the Maghrib, with Algeria, Morocco, and Tunisia, all now independent—the Arabic-speaking peoples cover rather more than a third as much territory as the whole of the United States, almost 4.5 million square miles, and though great stretches of this area are desert, huge stretches are not; today, of course, even the deserts hold out hopes of reclaimability.

Thus while the attention of the Zionists themselves was concentrated on the "tiny notch" of Palestine, sympathy for the Palestinian Arabs could be stirred up without much difficulty throughout a very wide range. But though it might have seemed that just because of this there might not be so much pressure on Palestine itself—only 1/430 of the total Arabic-speaking world!—in the event the clash between the two communities was to prove unavoidable and ferocious—the source, perhaps, of an enduring resentment on the part of contemporary Arab nationalists.

The question of Palestine, and the inflamed reactions of its Arabic-speaking inhabitants, followed by similar reactions throughout the Middle East and even farther afield in the Arabic-speaking world, illustrates in a peculiarly graphic way one of the chief factors in the formation of present-day Arab national sentiment.

For it may be said that it was in relation to the Jews, or rather to Zionism as the most modern of Jewish political movements, that the national feeling of the present-day Arabs has crystallized.

In this respect Zionism is simply an extreme example of European penetration. Elsewhere the inhabitants of the Middle East came into contact merely with ideas or with an upper crust of officials and administrators. But in Palestine they came into contact with substantial masses belonging to another and radically different nationality. More than that, this different nationality had a practical and philosophic program; furthermore, it kept growing in numbers and power.

It may be said that Zionism provided Arab nationalism with a core.

A principled opposition to Zionism was, to be sure, relatively late in emerging. An obvious progression can be distinguished, for instance, between the riots of 1929 and the organized quasi-revolt of 1936 on. The riots of 1929 did not have a national or social character, but were simply anti-Jewish and tinged by run-of-the-mill Muslim xenophobia. This explains the passivity of the Christian Arabs and of huge strata of the population. Not a word was said about the Balfour Declaration, about Zionism, about British imperialism, or about the establishment of the Jewish Agency, the external arm of the Zionist movement. The chief products of Zionist activity in Palestine were not touched; a few individuals in the old-fashioned Jewish communities of Hebron and Safed were hurt.

Nevertheless it would be misleading to describe the 1929 riots as pogroms exclusively. That they were such in the minds of the people is perhaps simply a reflection of the general backwardness of the masses. They were organized, however, for a national *political purpose* by self-conscious leadership that, aware of their followers' lack of political development, used nonpolitical notions ("the Jews are helpless," "the government is with us") to achieve their end.

By 1936, however, national consciousness had progressed to such a point that the disorders were accompanied by a highly developed and principled political campaign, while Zionism had become an object of concern as far off as Morocco and Yemen. It is surely significant that notables from every Arabic-speaking country without exception, to say nothing of Muslim countries in general, have associated themselves with the agitation against Zionism.

In this case the religious impulse coincided with the nationalist impulse. Muslims may not acquiesce in the loss of any territory once placed by God under the rule of Islam. It may be politic to acknowledge the suzerainty of a foreign power (of course most of Islam was recently in this condition), but this is something to be tolerated only until Islam becomes strong enough to shield itself, and in any case only if the foreign power rules without offense to the Muslim code.

But the actual surrender of land to be *inhabited* by infidels is unthinkable.

For this reason Ibn Sa'ud, not a nationalist Arab in the Western sense, made a point of categorically rejecting Zionist claims, while the old Imam of Yemen, even less modern in outlook, expressed solidarity with his Palestine "brothers." This is why Egyptians, even when indifferent, before Nasser, to Arab unity as a positive political project, have always proclaimed their support of the Palestine Arabs against Zionism.

Zionism has been an admirable target for the Arabic-speaking world in many ways, perhaps chiefly because it can enable the leaders to make positive capital out of the conflict inherent in the relations between the nationalism of given Arabic-speaking countries and the internationalism of Islam. It was natural for the numerous xenophobic prejudices fermenting in Islam for the last few generations to be expressed rather facilely at the expense of a weak power like the Jews. As early as 1931 an Islamic congress held in Jerusalem quite unexpectedly aroused echoes as far away as North Africa, at this time quite apathetic on all questions of Arab nationalism.

Zionism has in fact proved to be a potent rallying cry throughout the Arabic-speaking world. It is a bond of union among the various separatist Arab movements and has been especially popular among politicians out of office; it has great demagogic appeal. No doubt few of the anti-Zionist Arab politicians are as intransigent as they sound, but since no responsibility is implied by an anti-Zionist stand beyond a few denunciations in public, it is a cheap investment to gain prestige by exploiting a popular subject, or rather a subject that can easily be made popular because of undeniable mass feelings of resentment against the West, against imperialism, against their own hunger, against, in short, the changes brought by the West or that the West can be blamed for.

At one time, at the very beginning of the postwar calm, in 1919, when the implications both of Arab home rule and of the Zionist enterprise in Palestine had not yet clarified themselves, Faysal and the Zionist leader Chaim Weizmann, in a statement of January 1919, "recalling the racial affinity and the bonds existing of old between the Arab and the Hebrew peoples," agreed to negotiate every dispute that might arise between them. The agreement was dissolved, inevitably, by Faysal's failure to achieve realization of his own maximum demands (which he indicated marginally in the agreement with Weizmann); once that fell through, the agreement with the Zionist leader became a perhaps moving specimen of rhetoric.

In Syria and Lebanon the French poured in a huge amount of money and made a great administrative and cultural effort to reap the harvest that in this century has been usual—loathing and rebelliousness. Syria had always, after all, been in the vanguard of the movement for autonomy or independence, and to find itself under a foreign power, in the wake of a war theoretically fought to some extent at least for self-determination, envenomed all relations of the French with energetic local political activists. The specific occasions for vexation were largely territorial. Palestine and then Lebanon, historically part of the rather vague entity known as Syria, had been cut away from it soon after World War I; what remained had been split up into small administrative units that were fused into a single Syrian republic only in 1936. The administrative splitting up of the country had been due, of course, to the traditional French habit of atomizing local authorities while overarching the whole by the generalization of French culture. This French policy was peculiarly suitable in Syria and Lebanon, to be sure, precisely because throughout history the area had been broken up into a crazy-quilt of localities, communities, ethnic groups, and religions. But since the growing tide of what was to become known as "Arabism" was striving to counteract just this atomization, it was only natural for the French to suffer from it.

The French connection with Lebanon was much easier, since Lebanon was organically, so to speak, dominated by the Maronite and other Christian communities, and French was practically the cultivated language there. The Jesuit University of Saint Joseph had been the only rival of the Protestant American College in bringing the West into the country. Lebanon, too, like Syria, managed to secure a treaty of alliance in 1936, as an overture to the termination of the mandate, but both countries had to live through another world war before the French were definitively ejected.

Central Arabia has, of course, been a backwater of the Arabic-speaking world for centuries; it was to achieve importance only from the 1930s on, through the discovery of vast reservoirs of oil just beneath its surface, exploited by American enterprise from 1933 on.

British initiative was frustrated there by the quite unforeseen expansion of the Wahhabi power. Husayn, left by the final Allied partition of Turkey in rather dejected occupation of the Hijaz as king, just at a time when Ibn Sa'ud, consistently and blindly underestimated by the British because of some intrabureaucratic conflict, had substantially extended his authority in the peninsula.

Ibn Sa'ud, a traditional Muslim monarch untouched by any interest in or familiarity with such Western ideas as nationalism or political democracy, had spent the preceding two decades consolidating his power against rival chieftains. Quite alien to the ideas of Arab nationalism in any form, he had done nothing to help the

Husayn clan in the revolt it had launched for its own dynastic ambitions. Since the Husayn revolt was subsidized by a Christian power to boot, Ibn Sa'ud had had no reason whatever to help it. He had been content simply to extend his sway in the north and center of Arabia, down to the borders of the Hijaz.

In 1924, Husayn, still smarting after the collapse of his plans for large-scale independence in the area, went to the extraordinary lengths of proclaiming himself caliph of all Muslims after the Turkish caliphate, in any case an honorific fiction, was abolished by Atatürk. Ibn Sa'ud at once moved against him with armed force, and in a few months (1924–25) he simply ousted Husayn from the Hijaz altogether and took it over. Two-thirds of the Arabian Peninsula was now firmly in the hands of the Sa'udis; in 1932 the new state was named the Kingdom of Sa'udi Arabia, and there remained only Yemen, still medieval under an Imam, and the various petty sultanates of southeastern Arabia, all directly under the British.

Ibn Sa'ud's career was distinguished by its unusual combination of total backwardness, in the religious sense, and a cautious acceptance of the modern age insofar as it impinged on him. Only a century or so before, the movement of Wahhabi puritanism that had won his ancestors' allegiance had filled the Muslim world with commotion and outrage at its iconoclastic extravagance; its occupation of the Holy Places of Islam had been repelled by Muhammad Ali of Egypt, acting on orders from Constantinople, in a ferocious though fairly short war.

Ibn Sa'ud was personally unusually ignorant of the modern world: He thought the world flat, for instance, and was dumbfounded at learning that Americans spoke English, not some Red Indian language. Yet socially he was farsighted enough to realize that stability required a certain sedentary element, and he did his best to foster a program of settling the Bedouin on the land in a network of agricultural colonies. With the discovery of oil, which by now produces an annual income for the Sa'udi regime of something like 700 million dollars, in a country that may have only 5 or 6 million people, the regime is completely anchored.

Husayn's family was fobbed off with the Kingdom of Iraq, for Faysal and his descendants, and the Emirate of Transjordan, now the Hashimite Kingdom of Jordan. Iraq, formed as an individual state in 1921, was given to Faysal to compensate him for losing the

Syrian throne and by way of a token fulfillment of the promises made to Husayn and his family by Lawrence and others.

Relations with the British mandatory government were complicated by the exhausting political burden of the large minorities throughout the country—the quite non-Arab Kurds alone amounted to more than a third of the population—as well as by the relatively large proportion of city-dwellers. Friction with the British became very intense. The mandate finally came to an end in 1932; Iraq began to lead a more or less independent life as a member of the League of Nations. The active political elements in the country took up a line of implacable hostility to the British. But despite all the vicissitudes and irritations of the mandatory period and after, Iraq was launched as an independent state, leading in this respect the other Arabic-speaking successors of the Ottoman Empire. It also made a good deal of technical progress and received the benefit of the exploitation of oil deposits that while not so staggering as those of Sa'udi Arabia, Kuwayt, and Bahrayn, were nevertheless very substantial.

Elsewhere, the Egyptian independence movement, after a series of more or less constant clashes with the British occupying power and unflagging friction in the decades between the two wars, was ultimately to be successful in ousting the British by the outbreak of World War II. The declaration of Egyptian independence in 1922 and the later proclamation of the kingdom under the reign of King Fuad ushered in a complex parliamentary life, in which the three key factors were the throne, the parliamentary parties with a certain amount of popular support, and Great Britian, which stayed on in Egypt in a supremely authoritative position even after 1922.

The crown, while gripped by a conventional dynastic desire to achieve as much freedom as possible, was bound to bear in mind its relationship to the parliamentary parties. Of the political leaders, some were passive with respect to the realization of genuine independence and some were representative of a dynamic anti-British and antiroyal movement. Great Britain itself, regardless of polite fictions and forms, was evidently determined to stay on in the country in the defense of its traditional historic interests as then interpreted.

The first elections, held in 1923, gave power to the most outspoken anti-British party, the Wafd, headed by a remarkably able leader, Sa'd Zaghlul, who had played a role in the 1881 revolt of Arabi Pasha. There was a bitter struggle between the Wafd and King Fuad, which ended in 1935 with his defeat; in 1936 the Wafd, with great popular support, negotiated a new treaty with Great Britain, made more pliant by the Ethiopian crisis of Mussolini's Italy.

In this crisis Great Britain agreed to the ultimate withdrawal of all troops except for a few in the Suez Canal Zone, to be kept there until Egypt could defend itself. The Anglo-Egyptian condominium over the Sudan (which Egyptians had in fact been forced to abandon in 1924) was renewed, and the British promised to help abolish the notorious system of "capitulations" that gave foreigners a privileged position in law. The treaty was tied to a twenty-year alliance, in the conventional way; the Egyptians were obligated to place themselves at the disposal of the British in case of a conflict. Egypt was within sight of *de facto* independence, however far-off and elusive it might have seemed to critics of the treaty.

• • •

As far as the Middle East was concerned, the interval between the two world wars may be summed up, broadly, as having been characterized by the growing strength of a new creed, Bolshevism, and its consolidation of a new state structure throughout most of the old Russian Empire, the consequent outlawing in Soviet Russia of Zionism, the paralyzing success of the Nazi regime, with all it foreboded for the Jews, and a growing bitterness among both Jews and Arabs in Palestine with respect to the British Government.

These two fateful decades were filled, generally speaking, with a sort of tug-of-war between the tutelary powers that had assumed control of the Middle East—Great Britain and France—and the small, wobbly states that had emerged from the debris of the Ottoman Empire. The entire background of the relationship between great powers and territories that in another age might have been called colonial was radically altered. The propaganda of the victorious Allies had permeated the climate of opinion with all sorts of liberalism or mock-liberalism; public opinion at home and abroad had to be paid at least lip service to—there was even a public institution, the League of Nations, that in spite of its impotence constituted another shrine for public genuflection.

At the same time, as education was generalized in the Middle East the energies of many young people found a natural outlet in the political turbulence that was to become characteristic of the whole area.

The upshot was that the axis of all social life became the question of relations with the great powers—the British occupying authorities in Egypt and the mandatory regimes in the rest of the Middle East with the possible exception of Transjordan and Sa'udi Arabia, which made no pretense of representative government, and Palestine, in which the Jewish National Home imposed a special problem on the entire administration.

The European background, also, was peculiarly propitious for the proliferation of agitation of all kinds. Bolshevism in Russia, Fascism in Italy, Kemalism in Turkey, and finally Nazism in Germany were magnets for many activists in all countries. Since the immediate oppression, or at least irritation, was felt to come from the Western democracies, it was only natural to regard the insurgent regimes of effervescent Europe as inherently more seductive.

It was only natural, too, for the Fascists, and then the Nazis to devote an immense amount of propaganda to the exploitation of a situation in which the Western democracies could easily be embarrassed by the bondage of their political wards. It was in fact Fascism and Nazism that had the most dramatic effect on the molding of the Arabic-speaking political intelligentsia between the two wars. They were in one way or another the midwives of the nascent Arab nationalist movement, far more than either Kemalism or Bolshevism, since the two latter were somewhat hampered by their opposition to religion in general, in the case of the Bolsheviks, and to Islam in the case of Kemalism.

Perhaps the thorniest, most embittering, and least soluble of all the conflicts that churned up the eastern Mediterranean during these two decades was the Palestine problem. On top of the disappointment in many Arab circles with the British machinations in the Middle East after World War I, it certainly helped embitter the attitude of many Arabs toward the British and later on toward the United States, which assumed an executive role in the evolving situation in Palestine as the problem survived through World War II and considerably beyond. The possibilities of reconciliation between the Jews and Arabs, so optimistically adumbrated by the Faysal-Weizmann encounter in 1919, were utterly negated by the course of events.

• • •

From a purely material point of view, the Middle East was scarcely touched by the military operations of World War II. There was some fighting along the North African coast, but the densely settled centers of the Arabic-speaking world, Egypt and the Fertile Crescent, hardly felt any of the effects at all. It was quite unlike what had happened a quarter of a century before.

In World War II the Arabic-speaking countries of the Middle East might have been thought to be rather more than halfway beyond an intermediate point between colonial bondage and the independence they were very soon to achieve. The general reaction of the area, with the exception of the Zionists, was either lukewarm, apathetic, and cynical toward the Western democracies, or actively and venomously hostile. It was, on the whole, rather sympathetic not perhaps so much to Fascist Italy, which had after all played a positive imperialist role in Ethiopia and Libya, as to Nazi Germany, which attracted an immense amount of sympathy by the simple propagandistic device of denouncing Great Britain and the United States for their sponsorship of Zionism and promising to wipe out all Jewry and force the decadent democracies to disgorge their colonial empires. The Axis cause was on the whole favored very decisively by most of the active political elements throughout the Middle East. The humanitarian aspects of the contest, especially the loudly trumpeted Nazi racist program, were belittled or disregarded.

On the other hand, there was no way to express these quite natural feelings of animosity, since the British were physically present in force with a legal underpinning in Iraq, Transjordan, and Egypt, as well as Palestine, whereas the French were heavily present in Syria. Nor could mere animosity constitute insurrection. Hence the overwhelming bulk of the Arabic-speaking areas waited with resignation for the war to be got through, in the position of apathetic onlookers, disturbed only by an occasional local outburst, such as the attempted coup of Rashid al-Kaylani in Iraq.

This coup, the boldest measure undertaken against the Allies in the Middle East, was maneuvered by Kaylani with the open aid of the Axis powers. Kaylani was supported by Amin Husayni, the ex-Mufti of Jerusalem, who had become famous in Palestine for his intransigeance with respect both to the Zionists and to the British. Husayni had openly worked together with Hitler and Eichmann and had played a role of some consequence in the elaboration of the Nazi plan for the total extermination of the Jewish people, the notorious "Final Solution." The coup in Iraq proved abortive after only a few weeks, when troops officered by the British put an end to it; Kaylani and the ex-Mufti took refuge in Italy.

Egypt, though quite close on occasion to the North African desert tug-of-war between the German and British troops, also remained wholly outside the thick of things.

The battle of Alamayn in the autumn of 1942 was the turning point in the struggle for North Africa and in the struggle between the Axis and the Western democracies generally. It saved the Middle East from falling into the hands of the Nazis and also led to another British promise to the Arabs, this time given to one of the Senussi leaders, to the effect that Italy would never be allowed to return to Cyrenaica in Libya. With the end of the war in sight, with the Axis definitely on the road to defeat, and with the entry of the United States into the war at the end of 1941, pro-Axis sentiment among the Arab active political elements quickly dried up.

In a general way it may be said that the Arabic-speaking world came out of World War II incomparably better off than out of World War I. Its period of tutelage was in fact over; the once detested and feared Western democracies, Great Britian and France, were themselves more or less dislodged from their former primacy as two great states began to tower above all rivals—the United States and the Soviet Union. The peoples of the Middle East, no longer in a semicolonial status, had become the subjects of political activity in the newly formed United Nations; their favor was in fact being vied for by all the great powers indiscriminately. On the diplomatic level, in any case, representatives of the emergent Arab countries were on the same level in the United Nations as everyone else, including, to be sure, still more emergent states in Africa and Asia.

The emergence of the Arabic-speaking states as full-fledged national entities took place after what was a relative minimum of friction and obstruction. France had shown some reluctance to leave

Syria and Lebanon, even though its position was, politically speaking, rather weak, since their independence had been proclaimed several times over and indeed guaranteed. In May 1945 there had been some violent riots in the bazaars of Damascus and Beirut, which combined with inevitable British pressure obliged the French to resign themselves to withdrawal. By the end of 1946 both states were definitely independent of France.

The Italians, though crushed together with the Nazis, did a little diplomatic skirmishing for the right to come back at least to Tripolitania in Libya, if not Cyrenaica, which the British promise to the Senussi barred them from, but it was easy to frustrate a design that in the nature of things could scarcely be pushed with any vigor. By 1950 the United Nations had sanctioned a federal Libya (made up of Cyrenaica, Tripolitania, and Fezzan), which at the end of 1951 came into formal existence under a Senussi dynasty.

The aftermath of World War I had been characterized by the formation of small successor-states to the vanished Ottoman Empire. This had been in one way a rather organic approach to the nature of the area, which for so many centuries had been a patchwork of creeds and communities, especially in the Fertile Crescent. The hotchpotch had naturally been taken advantage of by Great Britain and France, which had hoped for the benefits of a tame administration based on the splitting up of regions with different histories, traditions, and allegiances. It was natural, from the point of view of European administrators, to allow division to go unchecked, and indeed to accentuate it if need be. For the French it was allegiance to French culture that was to be the paramount unifying factor, while the British had traditionally allowed colonial peoples to cling to their own cultures. Indeed, this was very often a source of complaint, since it implied a very slow rate of progress with respect to civilization, while it also, of course, suited the patriarchal bent of British administration.

• • •

The word "unity" has always been a potent cliché in all political discussions of parties bound together in one way but divided in another. It is a natural catchword, and it did not fail to make its appearance in the Arabic-speaking Middle East, though even after World War II the notion of unity was not extended very far beyond regional groupings of one kind or another. The initial projects for the unification of the countries in the Middle East revolved around essentially dynastic ambitions, in the first instance put forth by the house of Hashim, that is, the sons of Husayn ibn Ali.

In 1941 Abdallah, at this time still the Amir of Transjordan, put forth a suggestion, perhaps originally conceived in 1931 by Nuri Sa'id, a pro-British Iraqi politician who had dominated Iraqi politics for decades. The suggestion was based on the notion of a "Greater Syria" to consist of Syria, Lebanon, Palestine, and Transjordan—it goes without saying with Abdallah as ruler and with the Jewish National Home put under appropriate restraints. Nuri Sa'id supported this idea, originally his own, after all, and extended it to include what he referred to as an "Arab Union" with Iraq.

This project was instantly opposed, quite understandably, from three quarters at once: from Lebanon, which naturally feared for the preponderance of its Christian population if it was to be engulfed by a Muslim sea, a fear that had haunted the country ever since the rise of Islam; from Syria, which saw no reason to lose whatever individuality it had in a larger and slightly abstract entity; and from Sa'udi Arabia, whose dynasty still recalled its quite recent rivalry with the house of Hashim, which had been ejected from the Hijaz only by armed force, and saw no merit in having the Hashimite fortunes revived in a large state overshadowing the borders of Sa'udi Arabia itself.

In addition, Egypt, still quite indifferent to any notion of independence that went beyond its own borders, was opposed to this scheme for union on the general principle of preventing large and potentially hostile political organizations from arising along its borders. Egyptian nationalism, insofar as it revolved around a theory distinct from the reform of Islam, was thoroughly parochial, and was to remain so until the 1950s.

In both Egypt and the Fertile Crescent, Islam was to act as a countervailing force, since such Islamic elements as were beginning to bestir themselves on behalf of a general reform of Islam saw no reason to limit themselves, in the perspective of Muslim internationalism, to any particular country.

But though the concept of "Arab unity" was restricted in its development by the conventional dynastic, personal, and social rivalries and frictions in the Arabic-speaking world, there were many practical reasons for smaller regional groupings, since the end of the war was bound to leave any number of interlocking problems affecting the area as a whole. Thus, on the eve of the imminent Allied victory, Egypt sponsored the idea of a federation of states that would not infringe on national sovereignties while uniting the members for mutual self-interest.

This led to the Arab League, still in existence, that was supported by the British and by the other Middle eastern states, which ensured their places in the new United Nations by hastily declaring war on Germany. A preliminary conference was held in Alexandria in the autumn of 1944, and the League, called the "Society of Arab States" came into existence formally in March 1945. Its members were Egypt, Syria, Lebanon, Iraq, Sa'udi Arabia, and Transjordan; Yemen joined a little later. All members were called "sovereign and independent" and were said to have banded together for reasons of mutual advantage.

As Tunisia, Libya, Morocco, and Algeria became independent they joined the League one by one. Palestine, because of the special problem of the British mandate and the Zionist community, could not become a member, but since the Palestinian issue was felt to be vital for other states, at least in the Middle East itself, a special place was reserved for a Palestinian delegate.

The Arab League, though thought by many enthusiasts to have promoted the cause of Arab unity, in fact proved to be no more than the register of an existing situation. When the interests of the various states coincided, the League could act, though even here, as was shown in the Palestinian war of 1947–48, it was mainly on the level of rhetoric; but when their interests diverged, it lacked the capacity to reconcile them and to impose a unitary policy of its own. Since the leaders of the newly created states were delighted by their status of independence, they saw no reason to concede any aspect of it on behalf of a mere idea, however much that idea was paid lip service to. The federal ideal held out by champions of the unification of various groupings of Arabic-speaking states never got beyond the talking stage.

The chief problem of the immediate postwar period remained Palestine, where the British, after attempting more or less vainly to contain the growing pressure of the world Zionist movement and the local Jewish community, began turning more and more openly against any pro-Zionist interpretation of the mandate. From 1943 onward, the general anti-Zionist bias of the British administration was unmistakable. With the end of the war and the emergence of hostile Arabic-speaking states surrounding the whole country, it was obvious that the time for a showdown was rapidly approaching. The most embittering aspect of British policy even before the outbreak of World War II had been its decision on immigration. The British —not unreasonably, from a narrowly Palestine-oriented point of view—were adamant about letting in the flood of immigrants produced by Nazism in Europe. After the war, when news of the Nazi extermination camps came out and Jewish political leaders everywhere became aware—in 1943–44—of the remarkable success of the Nazis in wiping out more than a third of the Jewish people (the notorious figure of "6 million"), the pressure to find a haven for the surviving victims of Nazi dementia and cruelty became overwhelming, not least of all on the great powers themselves.

The great powers for their part had always turned a deaf ear to all appeals for liberalization of immigration policy. They contented themselves with at the most a token allowance of refugees that did nothing to alleviate distress while at the same time it exacerbated feelings by the curious combination of verbiage and apathy with which the most extraordinary tragedy of the Jews in all their long history was received.

The effect of the refugee problem on Palestine proved to be crucial, since the human agony originating at one end of the refugee pipeline to Palestine was transmuted into explosive violence at the other end, as the British authorities in Palestine and the government authorities outside simply evaded the problem. The upshot was the outbreak of a campaign of Jewish terrorism against the mandatory regime that seems to have completed the determination of the British Government to withdraw altogether from the scene and to allow the infant Jewish community to be destroyed, as they seem to have thought—and perhaps, as many think, to have hoped—by the indigenous Arab population reinforced by the armed strength of the newly constituted Arab states. Between 1944 and 1946 especially, the two Jewish terrorist organizations, the *Irgun Zvai Leumi* (National Military Organization) and the *Lohamei Heruth Yisrael* (Fighters for the Freedom of Israel), more vulgarly known as the Stern gang, perpetrated bold, imaginative, and atrocious acts of terrorism both inside and outside of Palestine.

The Palestine imbroglio was further entangled by the emergence of the United States as an increasingly active presence on the world political scene as well as in the Middle East.

By now United States policy was molded by two major considerations: the general question of the polarization of world power between the Soviet Union and the United States, and, in the Middle East, more particularly, by the very substantial material consideration of the vast oil deposits of the Arabian Peninsula and the Persian Gulf. A glance at a map is enough to indicate the proximity of the Soviet Union to the whole of the Arabic-speaking Middle East and the Persian Gulf. The possibility, indeed, the ease of establishing, on the basis of bona fide domestic problems, a political party that while exploiting the domestic situation would also be subservient to the Kremlin indicates further how finely drawn the balance of power in the area is bound to be. The oil deposits have proved to be even more fabulous than they had been thought when the Arabian-American Oil Company began working them in 1933; not only are they vast in extent, but their technical accessibility makes them the cheapest source of oil in the world.

For all these reasons, as well as the presence of an able and fairly influential segment of Jewish opinion in the United States that was sympathetic to the political aims of the Zionist movement, at the end of the war the United States Government inevitably and automatically moved into a position of authority with respect to the settlement of the Palestine issue.

By the time the Arab states were ready, as they thought, to cope with Jewish Palestine, for which the Arab League had actually been brought into existence, they were already outstripped by events. The British, by the end of World War II, had manifestly lessened their support of the Jewish enterprise—indeed, they had transformed it into active and principled hostility—but by this time the Jewish community itself was deeply rooted in the country, with leadership, organization, arms and, above all, morale.

In 1946–47 Great Britain found itself in the grip of two problems unrelated to each other and to Palestine, but vital to itself. The first had to do with its position in the Muslim world, now exceptionally important because the status of the Sudan had to be settled through negotiations with Egypt. The second had to do with the possibility of a massive incursion of Soviet power into the Middle East via the indigenous pro-Soviet Tudeh movement in Persia. This

Persian party, rooted in the countless abuses and miseries of modern Persia, seemed to be about to take over the whole of Persia under what were in effect Soviet auspices. This dual British problem was capped by the decision to evacuate India—an event of immense and as yet unassessed consequence.

At some point the British Government, now guided on the Palestine question by Ernest Bevin, a choleric and inexperienced statesman who was finally driven to exasperation by his inability either to patch things up or to understand the issues, decided that it could no longer cope with Palestine and submitted it to the United Nations in 1947. The solution proposed—an interim one, as events soon made it!—was for partition, which with the approval of the Jewish authorities was approved by the General Assembly of the United Nations in November 1947; the mandate was supposed to be terminated by August 1948, though it was anticipated by the British in May.

In this situation, made explosive by Jewish and Arab intransigeance, the resolutions of administrative or governing bodies outside Palestine were merely ornamental. The partition could be put into effect only by force, and on May 14, the day before the British had decided to leave the country, the Jewish National Council, a proto-governmental body, proclaimed the independence of the State of Israel; simultaneously some of the members of the Arab League—Syria, Transjordan, Iraq, and Egypt—invaded Palestine as they had threatened and pledged themselves to do.

It was immediately apparent that the Arab forces were laughably inadequate, except for the British-officered Arab Legion of Transjordan. Though the Jews too were remarkably unprepared, as it later turned out, their leadership was at least united and determined, while the morale of the troops was unusually high. The Arab forces were outmarshaled and outfought, largely because, despite the propaganda of the leadership, the troops themselves showed not the smallest inclination to fight for a cause they had no interest in.

The Arab Legion immediately thrust into Palestine from the west and seized Jerusalem, but everywhere else the Arab forces were thrust back at once. A mission was sent out by the United Nations, headed by Count Bernadotte; in the first half of 1949, after Bernadotte himself had been assassinated by some members of the Stern gang, a series of fragile and essentially indigestible armistices was worked out and signed by the now established and recognized State of Israel and the individual Arab states. These armistices still determine the borders and the relations between the countries; both are even more precarious then they are fragile.

The borders now acquired by Israel were broadly those of the UN partition plan it had accepted, but were augmented by the acquisition of all Galilee and of the Negev, zones that Israel was in possession of when the armistice was laid down. Jerusalem remains split in two, with the Old City governed by Jordan.

The failure of the Arab powers was so devastating, so dramatic in contrast with the bombastic and extravagantly bloodthirsty propaganda that all Arab spokesmen had been broadcasting, that it has left a permanent residue of embitterment in the area, not only as between the Israelis and their neighbors, but between the Arabs themselves.

The coordination of the Arabs' efforts had been practically nonexistent. The supply system was thoroughly corrupt, and above all the armies were not merely badly trained, but they lacked the smallest trace of combat spirit. The contrast with the Jews was obvious; animated by an actual ideal, the Jews displayed far greater morale, backed up by efficiency and technical skill. Most of the members of the Arab League remained violently intransigeant on the whole Palestine question. One or two, such as Jordan and lately Tunisia, which became independent after the whole thing was over, have shown some slight elasticity.

Beyond question the most serious effect of the whole Arab-Jewish conflict was the creation of a flood of refugees, relatively small in number, to be sure, for a world that had become familiar with refugees in the millions since World War II and its aftermath, but a major source of bitterness and frustration. Some 600,000 refugees seem to have left Palestine during the period of the acute conflict between the Arab and Jewish armed forces, and together with their natural increase they are now said to constitute something short of a million, still being paid for by public funds and physically located in camps outside the borders of Israel—in Syria, Lebanon, and Jordan—plus a substantial settlement of refugee colonies in that part of Palestine that was seized by Jordan and is now part of it.

It has been impossible to solve this question, since the Israelis refuse to accept any program of repatriation before peace negotiations are embarked on, while the Arab states insist on repatriation and will not commit themselves to any talk of peace at all. Nearly all Arab spokesmen, except for Habib Bourguiba of Tunisia, have repeatedly insisted on the extirpation of the State of Israel as such. About half the Israeli population came into the newly established country as refugees from various Arab countries, such as Yemen, Morocco, and Iraq, as well as Egypt and Syria, and there has been, from a purely ethnographic point of view, a sort of balancing out or sequestration on both sides of the newly established, shaky borders.

As it became clear that the refugee question was going to be a long-drawn-out one, the government of Transjordan, acting unilaterally, simply annexed the territories its Arab Legion had occupied during the fighting on the other side of the Jordan (in December 1948). A few months later it gave itself a new name—the Hashimite Kingdom of Jordan.

Since then there has been a *de facto* stalemate in the area; the Arabs have been forced to limit themselves to a policy of siege and more or less vexing economic boycott against Israel, sustaining a state of unflagging irritability along all the borders of the new state.

An incident in 1956, though minor, indicated the explosive potential of the area. Israel, backed up by Great Britain and France, made a sudden sortie into the Sinai Desert, where the Egyptian Army had been building up a huge attacking force that the Israelis and French destroyed and captured. The Israelis once again had demonstrated their striking military superiority, at the same time underlining the highly delicate condition of the area. The Israeli and Franco-British effort was put a stop to only by the ostentatious intervention of the United States and the Soviet Union, acting both together through the United Nations and independently in order to force the evacuation of Sinai and the restoration of what has been since then more or less the status quo. Egypt, despite its crushing—and embarrassing!—military defeat, proved skillful enough afterward to reap a rich diplomatic reward from its military inefficiency.

The Arabs have remained thoroughly intransigeant on the question of recognizing the *fait accompli* achieved by the youthful Israeli state, partly because of real or fancied injury to their newly sensitized *amour-propre,* and partly, too, perhaps, because it has remained a convenient rallying point and battle cry to keep together those who otherwise might be perplexed by the general failure of the Arab states to accomplish loudly touted basic domestic reforms. Many individual Arab leaders doubtless would acknowledge the necessity for a realistic compromise, but on the question of allowing the State of Israel to exist it still seems to be dangerous for public figures to express any conciliatory views. On the other hand, there seem to be signs that the present Arab leaders, with scarcely any exceptions, are sincerely uncompromising.

It may be that for a newly established would-be national elite, which has only in the past half-generation won political independence, the prospect of having even a small piece of territory lost to a people of historic pariahs, such as the Jews, is too galling for the pride that must be displayed over and over again, at least in public. After remaining in subjection to the Turks for a millennium, and then to Christian powers for another half-century, it may be just too exasperating to be borne to have a small people, for many centuries not noted for military prowess, trounce their combined forces with such ease.

The conflict with the Jews is really simply an extreme case of the general touchiness and irritability and almost pathological suspiciousness still harbored by the Arab leadership in all relations with the West. Technically independent though all the Arabic-speaking countries now are, their leaders remain obsessed by a continuing suspicion of the colonialism that in our generation has in fact been decisively dislodged from the whole of North Africa and the Middle East.

The presence of Iraq in the Baghdad Pact, for instance, an evidently defensive alliance aimed at the Soviet Union and adhered to by Turkey and Pakistan, has put Iraq in a sensitive position with respect to its fellow members of the Arab League. Nuri Sa'id, architect of many regional Arab federations, was killed together with the whole royal family, including Faysal's grandson, by a bloody *coup d'état* of July 1958 aimed at expelling the British and all British-influenced Iraqi elements altogether.

Abdallah, another fairly moderate Arab statesman, was assassinated in June 1951, apparently by an agent of the ex-Mufti of Jerusalem, Amin Husayni. Abdallah was ultimately succeeded by his grandson, Husayn, who expelled John Glubb and other British officers of the Arab Legion, and cemented ties with Iraq after the bloodstained mutiny of 1958, a rapprochement that was naturally resented by Syria and Egypt.

Egypt is, of course, the strongest of the contemporary Arabic-speaking states, with the longest national history in the modern era. It is the state that has always had the most substantial reasons for regarding itself as outside the Arab fold and as a self-contained national entity.

This is itself, to be sure, a relatively recent phenomenon. Even at the beginning of the nineteenth century and well into it the idea of an "Egyptian nation" would have seemed bizarre, to say nothing of an "Arab nation." As I have pointed out, the upper classes were largely Turkish or Circassian except for the substantial foreign colonies—French, British, Greek and Jewish, which rapidly expanded during the nineteenth century—and generally spoke Turkish among themselves. Though the long-since islamized peasants seem to be the same ethnic type as seen on the monuments of ancient Egypt, not only was there no cultural connection with the glorious Egyptian past, there was not even a living awareness that such a society had ever existed.

It was the discoveries made by French scholars that revealed the glories of the past and aroused the first feelings of national self-consciousness, though these did not bear fruit till the Arabi Pasha revolt in 1881, when the cry of "Egypt for the Egyptians" was heard for the first time. In essence this was a revolt not so much against British domination as against the dominant Turkish element, particularly the army, which provided the immediate pretext. It was a peasant movement of self-assertion against the indigenous, but ethnically exotic, aristocracy. Of course the Europeans interfered on behalf of law and order, and so the revolt, inevitably abortive, was directed against them as well. The revolt impressed them as a fanatical onslaught on authority.

This subterranean movement had a certain accompaniment in the movement for religious reform begun by Afghani throughout eastern Islam, in an attempt to harmonize the institutions of Islam with the first glimmerings of modernism that had come to the East. Afghani rejected depotism, holding forth the ideal of the people's assent and the religious law as the basis for the authority of the ruler.

The Arabi Pasha revolt was tied up, as has been the case with most nationalist movements in colonial areas, with demands for democratic reforms and the sovereignty of the people. In a way Arabi Pasha was the creator of the Egyptian nationality as a desirable thing, as opposed to the existence of Egyptians as mere pariahs in the minds of both the Europeans and the Turco-Circassian aristocracy.

This somewhat premature peasant revolt was, as we can now see, bound to fail; the Egyptian peasants of the time were far too backward. There was a hiatus of a whole generation—some thirty-five years—before another movement for independence began, under Sa'd Zaghlul, a peasant's son like Arabi himself. The significance of the later movement for independence, which came to a head on the eve of World War I and was to gather force between the two world wars, lay in the political expression it gave the new middle class now arising from the ranks of the Egyptian peasantry. It was, in short, part of the very general process attendant on the rise of a middle class in many countries, not only in the Middle East.

In Egypt these thirty-five years, passed under the stimulating, though oppressive British occupation, ushered in the European world of ideas and a gradual change in social forms. As in India, the British in effect transmitted the ideas behind the movement to all strata of the population. The economic expansion due to the occupation generated a new middle class for the first time. Previously the social order had been sharply divided in two: the Turco-Circassian upper class, the great landowners, court officials, officers, and superior government functionaries; and the peasants at the bottom. Between these two there now grew up a new bourgeoisie—lawyers, journalists, doctors, and merchants, mostly recruited from the peasantry.

But although the British disseminated European culture, they constrained education into a very narrow framework. Popular education was largely neglected, and secondary education was directed toward the career of lawyer or government bureaucrat. This tendency was reinforced by the exodus of numerous young Egyptians to Paris, Lyons, Geneva, etc. to study law while incidentally inbibing the doctrines of nationalism and bourgeois democracy. This overemphasis on the bureaucratic professions has had a lasting effect on the educated classes.

It was this new bourgeoisie that embodied the anti-British

movement for independence. It differed in composition and aims from both the peasant type of movement symbolized by the name of Arabi Pasha, and from the self-serving intrigues of the local aristocracy. It was urban and Europeanized, with a substantial sprinkling of new intellectuals, generally lawyers and journalists.

After World War I the independence movement took in some peasant elements, but the Turco-Circassian aristocracy, afraid of new ideas and in general afraid of anything that might threaten its established position, sided with the government against all purely national tendencies.

The bourgeois movement for independence was generally indifferent to religion as such, but with respect to Islam it attempted to exploit the sociopolitical magnetism of Islam as a prop for Egypt in the slowly awakening East and as a bridge to the Muslim part of the Sudan.

Before World War I this pro-Islamic tendency of the Egyptian nationalists was hindered by the presence of the Copts, who though only about a tenth of the population were disproportionately influential and who stood firmly by the British, rejecting the entire nationalist movement. After World War I, however, the nationalist movement—that is, the movement for the independence of Egypt as a self-sufficient entity—bridged the Muslim and Coptic communities. Politics in general became nationalist politics.

This was symptomatic of the extent to which social movements in Islam had become secularized. The Egyptian movement was merely a facsimile of the movements for independence and reform that were taking place not merely in Turkey and Persia, but in Russia and even to some extent in central Europe, all of them a continuation of the same wave of bourgeois emancipation that had transformed Western Europe and the United States before. Ideologically the Egyptian movement was in a favorable position, since it was easier to carry on this struggle against the occupation of the British, who at least verbally recognized the validity of democratic principles and who, of course, had incurred the odium that clings to foreigners in general.

The bourgeois movement showed such force that eventually it attracted the aristocracy, as had been the case in the other countries. This may also have occurred because of the growth of a small but truculent working class, the establishment of a Socialist party in

1920, the growth of a Communist party in 1922 with very extreme demands, and the strike movements that occurred from 1919 to 1924. When it came to the point the liberal, nationalist ministry of Sa'd Zaghlul crushed the nascent working-class movement mercilessly. The Egyptian parliament was too preoccupied with its demands for national independence to take an interest in raising the standards of working-class life.

From the point of view of the development of modern Arab nationalism, the parallel between Egypt and the Fertile Crescent is illuminating. Just as the Syrian and Lebanese Christians, in their longing to get out of their ghetto into the mainstream of a larger social grouping, had conceived the idea of "Arab unity" through the development of a national ethos based on language, so the Christian Copts of Egypt helped develop the idea of a purely Egyptian nationalism, based, to be sure, on a common language but not emphasizing the linguistic cultural nimbus as such, that would encompass them as well as their Muslim fellow countrymen in a nation-state-language synthesis revolving around the ancient culture of Egypt. This led to the development of a so-called "Pharaonic" view of Egyptian life, encouraged for some time by the British, that was to survive until present-day "Nasserism."

Shortly before the last war, so eminent a personage as Taha Husayn, the most distinguished writer and thinker produced by modern Egypt, had said over and over that Egypt would never renounce its "Egyptianism," that it was not ethnically Arab and never had been, and that "Pharaonism" was deeply implanted in the hearts of the Egyptians. He maintained that if language had been a decisive criterion of nationhood, Switzerland, Belgium, and the United States would be nonexistent as national entities. He pointed out that what he regarded as the cardinal elements constituting national unity—geographical contiguity, common history, and an affinity of interests—existed only within the borders of Egypt itself and in no larger sphere.

Although this so-called Pharaonic movement had only a brief efflorescence, the curious thing is that it was able to withstand the pull of "Arabism" as long as it did. Begun in the late 1920s under the leadership of a Coptic atheist, the well-known writer Salama Musa, it was founded on the exaltation of the permanent and unique character of "Egyptian" civilization, which Musa counterposed to Islam.

The movement met with the indifference of the masses, unaware of their uniquely Egyptian classical antecedents, and with the active hostility of the pro-Arab groups. It remained the possession of a small group of intellectuals and had, long before Nasser, substantially decomposed, perhaps because of its fundamental meaninglessness.

Before the emergence of Nasserism, accordingly—indeed, before a midpoint in the career of Nasser himself—it had been taken for granted throughout the century and a half of Egyptian self-awareness that Egypt, though of course Muslim, was Egyptian: In Egypt, "nationalism" meant "Egyptian nationalism."

But the Egyptian national movement was always burdened by the Arabic language (that is, by the absence of a distinct national tongue), by the strong hold of international Islam, and by its dubious position as a feeble state athwart the Suez Canal. It was always transported beyond its borders both by its connections with the Arabic-speaking world as a whole and by its being the center of Islam for hundreds of millions of people. These two tendencies, to be sure, conflict with each other, but both of them together weakened any chance Egypt had for genuine independence.

On the cultural level, of course, the community of interests between Egypt and the Middle East is undeniable. The vast importance of the language alone would be enough to ensure this, since in matters of culture Egypt has been the principal center of the renaissance of Arabic, the protagonist in schemes of pedagogical and linguistic coordination, and so on. The preference for the classical language among the educated classes has been tremendously strengthened by the growing emphasis on what is called Arabism (*'Urubah*). This does not prevent a certain ambivalence in the question of language, produced by Egypt's relatively extended modern national history. Egypt has been the principal Arabic-speaking country, together with Syria, to witness a systematized blossoming of the vulgar dialect, which has made a great impression on all aspects of artistic expression that are bound up with popular life (*viz.,* radio, vaudeville, comic strips, comedy in the theater, etc.). This particular reflection of national self-consciousness has thrown both religious and conservative diehards, fanatical about the classical language of Islam, and the most advanced sections of the nationalist groups, supporters of a renaissance on a supranational scale, into a bloc against the extended use of the local dialect.

• • •

Egypt emerged from World War II in a rather strong position, quite untouched by the war itself and confronting a seriously weakened British opponent. After the end of World War II, all political aims were concentrated on the liquidation of British influence, which entailed the annulment of the Anglo-Egyptian treaty of 1936 and the expulsion—or withdrawal—of the British from the Canal Zone.

This question was still hanging fire in 1952, when a revolt of army officers took place that established the present Egyptian regime. An agreement in October 1954 between the new regime, then being consolidated under its most outstanding leader, in fact its original inspirer, Nasser, actually terminated the British military occupation of the country that had lasted since September 1882.

The shattering defeat of the Egyptian armed forces by the tiny state of Israel in 1948 had had a most powerful effect in churning up political sentiment in all directions. The revelation of governmental corruption and the humiliation of the defeat kept the country in a state of ferment that had the most widespread consequences, from the savage turbulence of the Muslim Brotherhood, a group of chauvinist extremists tinged by religious fanaticism and exponents of assassination as a fixed policy, to the remarkably ferocious assaults on foreigners that resulted in a sweeping campaign of arson, looting, and destruction in January 1952. The throne had evidently not paid enough attention to the embarrassment of the defeat by Israel (the troops returning from their rout in Palestine were hailed as victors!); the upshot was the army officers' revolt of July 1952. Almost a year later the dynasty of Faruq, who had been exiled and succeeded by his son, was liquidated and Egypt proclaimed a republic.

By the end of 1954 the youthful Colonel Nasser had ousted the original figurehead of the army officers' revolt, Muhammad Najib (Neguib), liquidated the Muslim Brotherhood, and begun a comprehensive attempt to renovate the whole economy of the country by a combination of methods revolving around a vague adaptation of socialism, a one-party government system, and massive controlled propaganda. Civil and political liberties were wiped out and all movements of dissidence vigorously repressed. Europeans were systematically squeezed out of Egyptian life, while simultaneously extensive public-works programs were launched, large-scale "plans" formulated, and the regime given over to the sort of massive socio-economic overhauling characteristic of one-party dictatorships that take power in backward countries and dedicate themselves to long-range catching up with their more advanced socioeconomic models.

In foreign policy the Nasser regime has been unusually successful; after reaching an agreement with the British in 1954 for the total evacuation of the Canal Zone within twenty months, Nasser scarcely waited for the British to leave before nationalizing the canal itself. Cutting through the intricate legal tangle that had enveloped the status of the canal from earliest times, and in the teeth of very substantial Franco-British opposition on all levels—diplomatic, economic, and military, including the collaboration with the Israeli Army in the Sinai attack of October 1956—Nasser got away with an effective piece of bluff.

By the time the smoke had died down and the Sinai campaign had proved a total failure in its effects, partly because the dilatoriness of the Franco-British military operation annulled the effectiveness of the Israeli attack, France and Great Britain were obliged to accept the nationalization of the canal as well as the stability of the new regime. Nasser, though utterly defeated in the military operations and within an inch of complete collapse as a result of the defeat by the Israelis in Sinai and by the Franco-British forces in the Canal Zone proper, came out of the tussle wearing a halo. Propaganda and myth are basic for the survival of monolithic political structures; the Nasser regime was able to use the Sinai campaign as a living example of the stubbornness of colonialism.

The Egyptians kept the canal blocked for a year; in spite of all sorts of dire predictions on the part of outsiders the only result was a rise in the price of oil for everyone. By the end of 1959, when diplomatic relations between the British and French and the Egyptians were finally resumed, the only thing that had been demonstrated by the 1956 imbroglio was the division and impotence of the West in the face of any serious independent action in a backward area against, of course, the background of the Cold War.

It was doubtless as a result of these initial successes of the

Nasser regime that it embarked very soon afterward on the sponsorship of a full-fledged pan-Arab movement. Traditionally, as I have pointed out, Egypt had never regarded itself as an "Arab" country in any sense of the word. Ever since the Napoleonic expedition at the beginning of the nineteenth century, the political self-expression of Egypt as a national unit was either in the direction of developing itself as one more segment of the traditionalist, universalistic, supranational world of Islam, or as a curious Pharaonic entity, harking far back into the dead past of Ancient Egypt and looking forward into the future as a sovereign and specifically Egyptian state.

With the development of national ideals throughout the Middle East, however, the gradual revival of the Arabic language and the infusing of that revived language with current ideas originating in Europe, the possibility was manifestly always present of Egypt's simply declaring itself to be "Arab," as it were by fiat, and thus changing the conception of its national identity at least in the minds of the political elite.

The idea could always be supported by a number of objective facts that while undeniable had never been conceived of in this particular perspective, that is, the perspective of a spiritual, cultural (national) fusion between Egypt and other countries of similar background. These objective facts were of course manifest enough: a basic identity of language, or rather the same bilingual split between the classical language and the patois of the people; and a basic identity of cultural tradition, *i.e.,* Islam plus the recollection of the Islamic Empire and the spread of the Muslim faith, both going back more than a thousand years. The reason these "facts" had never led to the notion of the Egyptians' being Arabs was, as I have tried to show, that against the background of the universalism and supranational ethos of Islam the important criteria of differentiation were simultaneously both universalistic and local: One was a Muslim (or Christian, or Jew), and also stemmed from a given place, some town or village.

As the Middle East, together with the rest of the world, was immersed in the whirlpool of European ideas, and as the sole criterion of national identity increasingly came to be language itself, a tendency that had been basic in the history of all Arabic-speaking communities since their inception was tremendously reinforced. As I have emphasized, speakers of Arabic have always been singularly attached to their language, which was, indeed, almost the exclusive content of their culture for long periods. Thus it was perhaps inevitable that in Egypt, too, the view would develop that it was the speaking of Arabic that made one an "Arab." The oddity is rather that it took Nasser so long to work his way around to the proclamation of Egypt as an Arab state, since even on a superficial level the terrain had been prepared years before by the Egyptian sponsorship of the Arab League at the end of World War II. The word "Arab" in the name of the League could easily be extended, without *apparent* contradiction, to cover a new conception of Egyptian nationhood.

In this way Egyptian peasants, who for a thousand years have not even understood the word "Arab"—in their own language!—as meaning anything but a Bedouin, were asked by Nasser to work a dual violence on their traditional view of themselves—on the one hand to consider themselves "Arabs" (historically meaning only Bedouin) and on the other, and concomitantly, to ally themselves with the Arabic-speaking peoples east and west of themselves, peoples whom no one in Egypt had ever had the slightest interest in.

The advantages to Nasser of this course were clear enough: the acquisition on behalf of his political program of a hinterland covering more than 4 million square miles. At the same time his influence in what may be considered concentric circles could still be retained without difficulty. As Nasser expressed it in his book, *The Philosophy of the Revolution*—which he signed and may have written—Egypt stands at the natural focus of leadership in the Arab world, Africa, and Islam. This is, of course, perfectly consistent from a cultural-cum-geographic point of view, since Egypt is in a way at the center of these three worlds.

Yet before the Suez crisis Nasser in fact never spoke of himself as anything but Egyptian. It was only afterward, in the euphoria attendant on the transformation of his military debacle at Sinai into a diplomatic triumph, that his horizons suddenly expanded, organically, as it were, and he very abruptly projected himself as a spokesman for a united "pan-Arab" movement.

The history of Syria is perhaps even more chaotic and vacillating than that of any other Middle Eastern state. Syria has, of course, always been a hotchpotch; nothing in its postwar history gave any reason to think its course would be smooth. The broad issues that seemed to dominate Syrian politics were various projects for a "Greater Syria." A complicating factor was the advisability of accepting American aid and British suggestions for a unified Middle East defense force—in short, the question of adhering to one or another of the world blocs led by the Soviet Union and the United States. The socioeconomic structure of Syria was perhaps even more ramshackle than that of its neighbors. There was a pressing question posed by the growth of Communism to such an extent that a sort of stopgap was resorted to in the form of a political union, which in fact proved temporary, with Nasserite Egypt. It resulted in the establishment of the United Arab Republic in 1957, a flimsy and in the event short-lived political contrivance.

Lebanon has been far more peaceful. Preoccupied as usual by the determination of its dominant majority, the Christian Maronites, to remain aloof from the various expansionist schemes of its Muslim Arab neighbors while remaining somehow within the Arab camp, Lebanon has managed to maintain its own position without much more than the flurry of excitement produced by the landing of American Marines in the summer of 1958, entangled with the forward thrusting of the United Arab Republic and a small crisis between Iraq and Jordan that was going on at the same time. The integrity of Lebanon, depending as it does on the slightly fictitious numerical preponderance assigned the Maronites (actually by including the numerous Maronite and other Christian emigrants throughout the world!) is of course highly unstable, that is to say, as unstable as the rest of the political entities throughout the Middle East, all of which are sustained, perhaps, by the tension of the world balance of power between the big blocs. With this basic qualification, however, Lebanon has showed remarkable tenacity for such a tiny state, even smaller and more riven than Israel.

In January 1956 still another state was added to the Arabic-speaking bloc—the Sudan, for generations an object of the ambitions of Egypt and Great Britain and which became an independent state without much more substance than so many other newly emergent states as a consequence of the very rivalry that ultimately paralyzed the two chief contenders and enabled the tiny elite in the Sudan itself to take control of this huge country.

The Sudan, something short of a million square miles—*i.e.*, about the size of the Arabian Peninsula, or of the United States east of the Mississippi—is Arabic-speaking and Muslim only in its northern half. The southern half is inhabited by the great Nilotic tribes, still pagan in beliefs and with a great variety of languages. Thus, in addition to the basic socioeconomic conundrums that the longing for modernization and renovation has made it share with its more advanced Arabic-speaking neighbors and kindred societies, the Sudan had the perhaps insuperable problem of assimilating a very large section of the country to the customs, language, and religion of the dominant Arabic-speaking Muslim north.

The Islamic far west—the Maghrib—had been the most backward part of the Arabic-speaking world up to the beginning of the nineteenth century. Muslim for some eleven centuries, it had been untouched by Europe until the French seizure of Algeria in 1830. North Africa would doubtless have been conquered centuries earlier by the Spanish and Portuguese when it was out-flanked by the sea routes to tropical Africa and the Indian Ocean. The new areas opened up, together with the conquest of the Atlantic Ocean, deflected attention away from the Maghrib, and it was not until it was restored to its strategically focal position by the consolidation of the British Empire in India and the thoroughgoing penetration of tropical Africa by the West Europeans, after relative saturation in India and the Americas, that it became an international prize once again.

Thus the Maghrib, from having been the least Westernized portion of Islam, now fell completely under the domination of the West, partly because of geographical proximity and partly because of this very weakness of Islamic civilization.

Until shortly after World War I, a revival of Islam in North Africa seemed rather unlikely, but from then on, once again under the shattering impact of European, especially French, influences, a conventional nationalist movement began gathering strength, primarily, to be sure, among the elite.

Italy performed an immense service to Libya during the period of its occupation. The country's economy was overhauled and largely modernized, its cities were developed, and its agriculture was enormously transformed and improved. A whole Libyan upper class was created that ultimately benefited, quite without effort, by the fortunes of World War II when the Italians were completely ejected and the country became independent. In any event, Italy's fairly painless ejection from Libya, which acted as a spur to the independence movements in North Africa, helped Italy more than France was helped by its stubbornness in resisting the Algerian movement for independence.

One of the curiosities of the elite in North Africa, from Morocco to Tunisia, has been its complete molding by French culture. Many of the most outstanding leaders of the independence movements in all three countries speak and think in French far more than in Arabic, which indeed they often speak very badly or in a thoroughly uncultivated manner. They have been, in fact, completely formed by French education. In reality they are simply intellectuals educated in the French tradition, and it is this, indeed, that has turned them into champions of liberty for their own countries. French civilization is so universalist, so all-embracing, that in North Africa it was always the only counterweight, or rival, to Islam itself.

The French were determined to stay on wherever they could, partly for reasons of material advantage—in the old-fashioned imperialist sense—and partly because of an old-fashioned pride in the paramountcy of French culture—*le rayonnement français*. Not merely did they regard the present-day material culture of Algeria and Morocco as French handiwork—which, of course, it very largely is—but they thought that the very existence of the society there could not have come about if it had not been for the fructifying implantation of European colonies along the Mediterranean littoral and the subsequent development of industry, agriculture, and commerce along European lines.

In Tunisia the French were obdurate; as late as 1952 there was a peculiarly ferocious repression of independence elements in the riots that followed the arrest of Habib Bourguiba, now the president of the country. These were followed by a rather long-drawn-out period of stubborn French vacillation that was terminated only by Mendès-France's decision in 1955 to put a stop to the friction of this connection and grant Tunisia independence. By 1956 Tunisia was free; by 1957 it was a republic with Bourguiba at its head. Bourguiba's line was understandably ambivalent, on the one hand being based on friendship with France, on the other insisting on Maghrib solidarity with Algeria, then still an integral part of France, as well as with Morocco. He also took an affirmative attitude toward "Arab" union, marred only by perhaps inevitable friction with Egypt under Nasser.

In Algeria the influence of the Arabic-speaking Middle East was always hampered by the success of the French cultural policy, by the presence until recently of a large European colony, and by the growth of an enormous urban proletariat in the wake of French colonization. Up to 1930 there was scarcely even the conception of an Algerian nation, to say nothing of an interest in it. To the extent that Algerians had been Westernized, they turned their eyes toward one movement or another with its roots in Europe. The middle classes had hoped for equality with the French as French citizens; the proletariat was attracted by Communism, Socialism, or some other European importation suited to the conditions created by Europe itself. For eleven centuries before the French arrival, individual and regional rivalries, against a background of Islamic indifference to nationalism, had made Algerian unification a meaningless phrase. When the French came, they smashed the tribal and regional structure of the country and squeezed the economy into their own mold.

The movement for independence in Algeria, which even at the end of World War II would have seemed a dim and indeed altogether unrealistic prospect, remained quiescent until the late 1950s. As an independence movement, it seems more reasonable to link it not to the movements for home rule in the Middle East that had been active, at least in the minds of some minorities for many decades, and still less to the situation immediately following World War II, but to the general stirring of independence movements among the various intelligentsias of Africa and Asia.

The Algerian movement was made peculiarly bitter by the general apathy of the masses, which meant that the political leadership that was eventually victorious, that of the FLN, or National Liberal Front, became even more autocratic and terroristic than it might have if it had had some mass support. In addition, Muslim culture was lower in Algeria than in possibly any other Muslim country, so that the only educated people were those who had been educated in the French mold. This lent the struggle the ferocity of a civil war, especially since the French, totally entrenched in the country, as they thought, for more than four generations, fought with great concentration, perhaps because the pride of the military had suffered a great deal from the countless defeats of the French Army in our generations, both in World War II and in the loss of their Asiatic empire.

In any case, as a result of a complex interaction between French political public opinion—itself split, like most things in France, into extremist right- and left-wing attitudes—the French general staff, the substantial European colony in Algeria, and ultimately, as it was to turn out, the personality of Charles de Gaulle, Algeria was in 1963 relinquished by an exhausted and confused French leadership and has since then been well launched on the sociopolitical and economic modernization that is now confronting the emergent nations in Asia and Africa.

Moroccan nationalism made its appearance very late, in 1934. The country is a mosaic of tribal rivalries, in which the most important ethnic split is that between the Arabs and the Berbers. These last constitute 60 per cent of the population, distinct in language and customs though united with the Arabs by religion.

The French occupation increased the solidity of an already solid urban bourgeoisie, which was the background for the appearance of a new nationalist party in 1934, just as the last rebels against French "pacification" submitted in the Anti-Atlas.

In Morocco French policy had traditionally been rooted in the undeniable division of the country into an Arabic-speaking and a Berber part. All central Moroccan administrations had always been somewhat frustrated by the impossibility of imposing any decision on the great Berber tribes and confederations of the interior, where Berber languages, customs, traditions, and self-consciousness were very powerful. The French, under Lyautey's shrewd guidance, had always played each part of the country off against the other. These divisive efforts had been quite successful for many years, but by the end of World War II, with the formation of the Independence Party (*Hizb al-Istiqlal*) out of the two chief independence movements that preceded it (Fasi's Nationalist Party and Wazzani's Popular Party), a systematic struggle for independence was carried on that achieved its objectives some twelve years later, in 1956, about the same time as Tunisia. One of the differences between the two countries was that the Moroccan sultan, now Muhammad V, had sponsored the independence movement himself and so was in a position to benefit by its victory.

By March 1956, accordingly, the ancient Sharifian Empire of Morocco was once more restored to independence under a native dynasty. Theoretically, at least, the monarchy has been modernized; the monarch and his family seem to be abreast of contemporary Western standards. Since the protectorate long exercised by Spain over a Moroccan zone and the international status of Tangiers were ended in the same year, Morocco was definitively unified and is well launched on the road of modernization under the guidance of an enlightened ruler and of a youthful ruling class that has been formed entirely by Western Europe, especially, of course, by French education.

All these conflicts are now in the past; even so violent and bloodstained a struggle as marred the ultimately triumphant Algerian independence movement receded, with the independence of Algeria, very abruptly into history.

All the countries whose native language is Arabic are now completely independent, sovereign states. The contemporary Arabic-speaking world is divided into twelve major units: Morocco, Algeria, Tunisia, Libya, Egypt, Lebanon, Syria, Jordan, Iraq, Sa'udi Arabia, Sudan, and Yemen. There are also a number of more or less dependent statelets, some of them oil rich, like Kuwayt and Bahrayn, along the Persian Gulf coast of Arabia and in its southeastern corner, but these, even those that have money, are simply backwaters too small to exert much influence, though they have helped absorb many teachers, some of them Palestinian refugees, into the education programs made possible by their oil revenues.

• • •

Thus a cluster of new states has emerged, invested with a somewhat amorphous self-awareness that varies substantially from one country to the other. The Arabic-speaking world exists, but it would be absurd to call it homogeneous and quite impossible to encompass within a short book the endless currents, crosscurrents, factional and dynastic rivalries, and small wars that constantly beset it.

The general paramountcy of Egypt is contradicted, somewhat uncertainly, by the existence of a sort of eastern bloc, consisting roughly of Iraq and Jordan, though here too it is impossible to generalize from the kaleidoscope of detail. The vast revenues of Sa'udi Arabia enable its rulers to play a role in the Middle East and the world at large that is quite disproportionate to its population or its intellectual weight. For some years there has been a savage though veiled struggle between Sa'udi Arabia, a rich and empty country, and Egypt, a poor and crowded country, for the control of the ancient kingdom of the Yemen, one of the most medieval countries on earth. The recent ripening into sovereignty of the Maghrib—Tunisia, Algeria, and Morocco—has added another source of complexities and confusions to the evolution of the Arabic-speaking world.

Nevertheless, in the space of the epoch that began with World War I, peoples newly formed by the modern era have, with varying degrees of pervasiveness, taken on again an ancient identity. As this complex of communities evolves, and as this sense of identity is tailored and retailored, a new organism is coming into being. The Arabic-speaking world, exceptionally plastic because of its complex, ramified, and contradictory past, is being shaped by the historical process before our very eyes. It would doubtless be presumptuous to make predictions about an entity now coagulating, as it were, at different rates in different areas, under the molding influence of its revered language.

Yet it cannot be denied that the Arabic-speaking world, which may ultimately become and in some respects has already become an Arab world, still confronts a potentially seminal destiny. Formed in ancient times by its strategic location athwart the crossroads of great cultures, it is coming to life again in an area that despite all advances in modern communications remains a nodal point in world history. Arabic-speaking Islam remains focal for Africa at one end, Asia at the other, and the Mediterranean in between. If it recovers its sense of unity and develops sufficiently to give that unity a new dynamism, it may yet play a role in the future that, while perhaps never equaling the performance of the early Arab Muslims in launching Islam, will nevertheless express its real potentialities.

EPILOGUE

THE ARABS IN THE MODERN WORLD: ARAB UNIFICATION

I HAVE reserved for an epilogue some considerations of the contemporary Arabic-speaking people, or peoples, with special bearing on the modern evolution of their sense of identity and their position—very generally—in the world of today.

Since no discussion of detail is even conceivable in the case of so many different governments, so many successive and contending factions in power, so many independent sources of political activity, I shall restrict myself to dealing with the modern Arab states as an ensemble. I shall consider the political configurations of the present day, in short, insofar as they may be thought to concern the Arabs as a people.

• • •

If one takes a bird's-eye view of the emergence of the present-day Arabic-speaking peoples, it must be admitted that the rapidity with which they have taken on or been assigned a collective identity is striking. Literally nonexistent even as a concept less than two generations ago, they may be said to constitute by now a collective entity, at least insofar as their public representations are concerned.

A glance backward will outline the very sharp arc described by the Middle East and Islam since Europe, at the beginning of the nineteenth century, impinged on their consciousness through its contemporary expansion.

The most violent and immediate shock came about through the economic transformation. Egypt, Syria, and Algeria were the first to be buffeted by the full weight of the European economy. In the space of only a few decades the total economic process in each country was altogether recast, though the traditional lives of individuals were not affected so immediately.

Egypt was touched most vitally, as a direct result of the British occupation. It was made completely dependent on world trade, and its economy was wholly transformed by the British in order to convert it into a source of cotton and reduce British dependence on North America. This was done on exclusively foreign initiative, and though of course Egyptians cooperated and were enriched by this movement, the country as a whole was enfeebled by its dependence on foreign commodities, particularly food.

The absorption of the Middle East and North Africa into the European market was part of the conquest of the whole world by European economy. Colonial peoples everywhere have been made dependent to a large extent on articles of consumption produced abroad. This phenomenon is too well known for exposition.

In the case of the Islamic world specifically, what had happened is that the extravagance of the old ruling classes was excessively stimulated by the import of western articles of consumption, while the structure of society made it peculiarly difficult to build up capital reserves to participate in the new economy process. Indigenous consumption was increased and new needs were aroused, but nothing, or very little, was done to increase indigenous production. In this way the growing but sterile luxury of the small upper strata of society brought about the progressive impoverishment of the general economy of Islamic countries.

One of the reasons for this was that the parasitic nature of the great landowners, government functionaries, and the rentier class as a whole both encouraged and was supported by the dearth of an appropriately trained elite that might have been able to institute some of the changes necessitated by the West. The Islamic elite was founded on quasi-feudal patterns outmoded by the new developments; the urgency of the change made it impossible to create the necessary corps of entrepreneurs and administrators, which is one of the reasons why the state played such a decisive role in the increase of production through the increase of capital resources, instruction, and management. In Turkey and Persia, and to a lesser extent in

Egypt, state capitalism, while partially modeled on the Soviet Union, was chiefly due to the absence of organized stimulants efficient enough to arouse backward groups to economic changes. To a certain extent it was a question of tempo: The gap between backward colonial countries and the world market dominated by the great powers was so enormous and had to be bridged so rapidly that the state as an economic agent became a necessity, if only for the sake of self-preservation.

The necessary education of the population was hamstrung. Its taxable resources were too meager to permit adequate schooling. On the other hand, only education could create the personnel for a modern community. In this respect, the countries of the Middle East vary considerably. Syria in some ways is much better off than Iraq, which came into direct contact with Europe only after World War I. Syrians were trained abroad for generations and possessed a relatively abler body of intellectuals and technicians. On the other hand, Syria has been hampered by the feudal conditions among the numerous and mutually distrustful minorities and by a certain religiosity and lethargy among the masses.

Beyond all this lay the precapitalist nature of Islam. Wherever Islam is powerful it presents an obstacle to the advance of capitalist techniques, an obstacle that can, of course, be surmounted, but only with difficulty. The tempo of modernization of Islam itself has been greatly increased, to be sure, and no doubt will increase further. But the chief carriers of Western economy into the Middle East were the Arabic-speaking Christians, whose freedom from Muslim religious shackles enabled them to play a leading role in economy as well as in culture.

Aside from tempo, the development has been in a straight line. What has been emerging in the Middle East is a secular, rationalist, middle-class consciousness that is replacing the old feudal or quasi-feudal forms with immense speed and power. This secularization of thought has been going on apace throughout Islam, leaving only extremities and backwaters untouched.

The tremendous economic shock was paralleled, more profoundly and still more convulsively, by the intellectual shock.

Most Muslim and Middle Eastern communities had been stagnating for centuries, from a European point of view and for that matter from their own. They had been stewing unreflectively in the unconscious and unquestioned assumption of Muslim superiority to the world at large and the Christian world in particular. They were volcanically, ruthlessly, and impotently wrenched out of their own affairs and plunged into a vast economic and political scramble in which they had little or no control, into a game played by others—infidels at that—and in which they were not the masters but the stakes of the game.

There were two preliminary reactions, followed by a third that combined qualities of both. In any given Muslim country they all still exist, in varying degrees according to remoteness from Europe, intensity of piety, and so on.

The first two reactions were absolute rejection and absolute acceptance. The adherents of the classical tradition fanatically opposed not merely European ideas as such but every manifestation whatever of European thought or technique. This basic hostility showed itself in a hatred of machines, of new methods of communications, and of new techniques. To be sure, the opposition was chiefly ideological, not practical, since the intrusion of the machine and cognate phenomena could not be restrained by any force whatsoever, at any rate in the countries that swiftly came to be dependent on a European economy. Rejection in words accompanied acceptance in deeds. But in the field of ideas, of course, the rejection was not only more profound but considerably more effective.

The absolute acceptance of European values, on the other hand, has produced a superficially Europeanized class of people that is not limited to Islam but has become a worldwide phenomenon. What Europeanization has accomplished, at least in its initial phases, has simply been the alienation of this class from its own cultural roots. Its intellectual life is inevitably stunted; its traditional religious and social views have been disrupted without having had time to be replaced by a deeply rooted new culture. Sometimes, moreover, the Europeanism is merely a sham product; the shallowest elements of traditional culture, such as superstitions, remain quite powerful even as these superficially transformed people vociferously protest a newly modish atheism or rationalism.

These two contrary reactions have naturally produced a third reaction, a sort of obvious compromise between the two. Traditional Islamic values are "reaffirmed" in the new context. It will be maintained that modern thought contains nothing repugnant at all to Islam, "properly understood," which hence can be presented as offering a peculiarly fertile soil for modern progress.

The confusion of thought and feeling arising out of the clash between the traditional system of thought, with its more or less rigid, dogmatic basis, and the new intellectual imports from the West, ultimately rooted in the freedom of Western inquiry, has naturally created a painful situation for many in the transitional generations, and one result of this confusion has been an extreme chauvinism.

Not only was the national idea borrowed from Europe, but it was deepened and made more fanatical precisely by the European discovery of the ancient and medieval glories of the East. In this way the nationalistic impulse borrowed from Europe has naturally led to an exaggerated feeling of self-importance and an overestimation of the "national" past; this in turn has been given a more or less scholarly foundation by material also derived from Europe.

Only snatches and remnants of the great days of Islam have survived, and even these have been obscured by the triumph of Europe. It was really only through Europe, after all, that any real knowledge of the medieval and ancient East came to Eastern peoples today. A comparison of Córdoba and Paris, for instance, in the Middle Ages acted like an intoxicating drug on the imaginations of modern Arab nationalists discovering their past; it induced a feeling not merely of equality but of arrogance and disdain for the Europeans who in the past had been mere disciples of the Orient. This led to a belief that contemporary European superiority was merely a technical, material affair and that once the technical disproportion between East and West was eliminated the East would once again become the teacher of the world.

These national conceits are often nourished by European compliments paid to various Islamic institutions, a form of condescension, or ingratiation, now quite fashionable among European students of Islam and Arabic. In addition, a chauvinistic emphasis in various types of public utterance in the Middle East was greatly strengthened by World War I, which succeeded in destroying the sacrosanct character of Europeans as an upper class in the East. The two world wars have finally established the East as equal to Europe.

Of course it is understood that this equality applies only to the peoples and not to the actual instruments of Western culture. These are being borrowed wholesale and as a result of the economic transformation of the world during the past century must obviously become the basis for whatever ideological or social changes are imposed on these peoples by the increasingly urgent necessity for modernization, not in order to excel Europe but simply to avoid spiritual obliteration.

Still another tendency, one in line with modern European attitudes that I have made much of myself, lies in stressing the fundamental identity of Islam and Europe from the point of view of other civilizations and cultures. Both Islam and Europe, in this view, represent the same synthesis of Judeo-Hellenistic culture; only the Renaissance and Reformation in Europe have obscured this fundamental identity. Now that the East is learning to participate in the Machine Age, whose foundations were laid by the Renaissance and Reformation, the basic similarity will emerge clearly.

This "reasonable," moderate attitude combines the retention of the spirit of Islam plus the material and scientific accomplishments of the West. It seems the most likely to survive, perhaps by virtue of its very banality, a banality hotly contested, of course, by any school of thought that is pleased to defend one of many attitudes of willy-nilly reaction to the insistence of European penetration.

The historical parallel to this development in the history of the Arabs is crystal clear, since the whole structure of Islam was built on precisely this amalgamation of cultures that is now being repeated in the Middle East. During the efflorescence of the Abbasid caliphate, as I have indicated, the same thing occurred as a result of the Aramean-Hellenistic flood of ideas. The differences are, of course, that at that period it was an organic, voluntary, and understandable process, which took place, moreover, under the shadow of Arab Muslims who were conquerors at least in a technical, military sense. In our own days, unfortunately for education in the East, the process is incomprehensible, because of its excessive speed and compulsive character, to those on whom it exercises an elemental molding effect.

Such, roughly speaking, is the background to the emergence in our own day of the political entities that constitute the "Arab bloc." Considered as a collectivity, their problems can be summed up fairly concisely.

On the political plane alone all twelve major states have become unqualifiedly independent, insofar, at least, as weak states with backward populations may be called independent at all. The problems as they appear to the political leaders may be classed under two headings: (1) Their persistence as viable political organisms in the conditions of the Cold War, that is, of the comprehensive and ramified conflict between the Soviet Union and the United States, obscured and complicated as that conflict has now become because of the rapid emergence of China during the past few years, and, (2) As a perhaps doubtful corollary of their political existence, the question of the extent to which the ideal of unity may be realized.

The two problems are not at all the same species of problem. The existence of each state structure is not inherently dependent in any sense on a realization of the ideal of unity, which remains, after all, in the condition of a nascent myth. There has been, in fact, no political link between these various communities for an indefinite period of time stretching into the past. There is no inherent or "objective" reason why unity must be achieved at all, though there can be no doubt that it is one of the most frequently recurrent and potently hypnotical slogans that the elite has become inspired by.

Of what only a short while ago seemed the two chief obstacles to the realization of that unity—Algeria and Israel—the Algerian question has now been settled in favor of the local Algerian leadership. Algeria is in the Arab League, one of the independent group of Arab states, and a member of the United Nations. Considered purely as an aspect of the rise to self-consciousness of the Arab states as such, it must be admitted that the "Algerian question" had a very brief duration.

But in an "Arab" perspective, Algeria was simply an extreme example of the lengths that would have to be gone to if the linguistically and Islamically backward masses were to be integrated with a new community of nations based on the development and dissemination of the Arabic language and the promotion of mass welfare to a point when the indigenous population could replace the tiny

French-trained elite with a homegrown product of its own. In a way, of course, this is also the problem of all the Arabic-speaking countries, with the possible exception of the Fertile Crescent countries, which have at least certain standards of literacy.

• • •

The existence of Israel, which for the contemporary leadership of the Arab bloc constitutes, of course, a "problem," shows no signs of losing its indigestibility.

For those who like historical ironies there is something intriguing about the millennial convergence and divergence in the destinies of these two peoples connected by so many traditional links. For it is a curious fact that the Jewish people were entirely remolded by Islam at its height.

After the great Arab Bedouin conquests that followed the emergence of Islam, fusing all the countries from Persia to Spain into a single sociocultural area dominated by the new conquerors with their new religion and a few generations later by a single language, the bulk of contemporary Jewry came under the rule of Arab dynasties. There has been a good deal of sentimental exaggeration of the favorable position of the Jews under Islam, mainly by way of establishing a contrast with their sufferings under Christendom, yet there can be no denying that their situation was much better than it had been in the Byzantine Empire. Moreover, the Jews underwent a thoroughgoing socioeconomic transformation and revival, which changed the nature of Jewry completely and whose effects have lasted to the present day.

Aside from early and protracted contacts before, the Jewish-Arab symbiosis after the expansion of Islam lasted some eight hundred years, during the first half of which the Muslim religion, and the very nationhood of the Arabs themselves, were shaped under the impact of Jewish ideas and traditions, while in the second half traditional Judaism was definitively molded under the influence of Islam. From the tenth to the thirteenth centuries especially, the Jews played an important role; during this period under Islam, in fact, Judaism itself was rounded off.

Most of the Jews in the world were farmers and manual laborers during the age of the Muslim-Arab conquests. It was agriculture that suffered most under the new Arab rulers, and under Islam all the agricultural peoples of the Middle East lost their identity. The Jews too ceased to be farmers during the seventh and eighth centuries, but they retained their national identity; what Islam did was simply to turn them into a nation of merchants and artisans, a transformation due to what has been called the great "bourgeois revolution" of the ninth century. In an age when Western Europe was primarily rural, in societies dominated by knights and feudal lords, the civilization of Islam, that is, of the Middle East as a whole, was highly mercantile, characterized by trade, industry, and bureaucracy.

Through the early Arab conquests, the great majority of the Jewish people and most of the Christian communities of Western Asia, North Africa, and Spain came under Islam. These extensive wars surely caused great hardships, with substantial losses of property, life, and personal liberty.

Nevertheless the Jews were helped. They were no longer a community of pariahs persecuted by the dominant church, but one among whole classes of subjects with a special status, since the Muslims made no distinction between Jews and Christians. Obviously laws controlling a majority population could not be so oppressive as those intended to squeeze a small minority. Also, with the powerful Byzantine and Persian empires smashed, the Jews might expect perhaps a messianic restoration of the Jewish people, so that it was only natural for the Jews everywhere, especially in Palestine, Syria, and Spain, to help the Muslims, who accordingly considered them allies.

It was under the influence of Muslim thought, indeed, that Jewish thought and philosophy, and for that matter Jewish religion, were systematized. Even Hebrew developed its resources on the model of Arabic, to such an extent that the modern revival of Hebrew as a vernacular would be inconceivable without the benefits it derived from Arabic a thousand years ago. Arabic itself became a Jewish language, indeed, the major language of the Jews, and unlike Latin in Europe was used for everything except synagogue services.

As the Middle East decayed during the later Middle Ages and afterward, the Jews who went on living in Arabic-speaking countries also lost their importance for Jewry as a whole. The bulk of world Jewry transferred to Christendom, to play a full role in the remarkable expansion of the modern period, while the Jews who stayed on in the Arabic-speaking countries sank to less than 10 per cent of the Jewish population of the world.

The oddity of the Jewish revival in Palestine was, perhaps, that after the prolonged connection of the Jews with European civilization, the revival of Jewish statehood in our own generation, though engendered by the movement of ideas in Europe, was actually to be realized in the heart of an area that was itself beginning to be roused from a millennial slumber by the same leavening of European thought. The paradox is exacerbated by the hostility that has developed, but it is hard to see how things could have turned out otherwise.

One of the ways in which Israel, aside from the political conflict with its neighbors, clashes inherently with the Middle East is in the highly untraditional classlessness characteristic of the new society in Israel and also in the general position of women. Not only are women completely emancipated socially and legally in Israel, but the ideal of equality has been realized even in the unlikely domain of the army; military service is compulsory for girls as well as boys.

In the neighboring countries, on the other hand, the present-day Arabic-speaking countries have inherited two great traditions from their complex past that are bound to create a gulf between them and the Jewish society of Israel. I have mentioned them before: one is the masculine tradition of the early Muslim Arabs, which rather looked down on women in general; the other is the homosexual tradition inherited from Persia and Greece and found today in many countries of the Middle East. A slight discordance in this respect seems inevitable.

In religion, too, there are some major differences. In Israel one's attitude to religion—for, against, or indifferent—is a matter of public knowledge, whereas in Muslim countries outward forms are rigorously observed, though it is often difficult to know what the actual state of belief is. There is an incalculable but definite chasm between public profession and private belief, quite unlike the situation in Israel.

There is a remarkable coincidence between the establishment of modern nationhood for the Jews and that of the first Arabic-speaking state. The year 1922, which saw the establishment of Egypt, the first great independent Arabic-speaking—though not yet

Arab!—state, was also the year the Jewish National Home in Palestine was endorsed on an international scale. In 1925 the University of Cairo and the Hebrew University of Jerusalem were both opened. Israel became an independent state only a short while after Lebanon and Syria and was able to vote in the United Nations Assembly for the establishment of Libya.

In addition, the renaissance of Hebrew and Arabic illustrates the curious parallels that have marked the histories of both groups throughout the ages, though here there is an equally curious element of irony.

The devotion of Arabic-speakers to their language was in marked contrast to the custom of the Jews. Through the dual process of islamization and arabization the Arabs' love of their language facilitated the imposition of Arabic on many of the peoples absorbed by Islam. In the twentieth century, indeed, it was to reshape them entirely. It is a "them," to be sure, utterly transformed by history and defined in our day by precisely the emblem of ethnic identification that has become paramount—the same criterion of language, oddly enough, that served them in the cradle of their nationhood too as the essence of their collective identity.

Contrariwise, the Jews, though known as one people for millennia and regarded as unitary despite their wanderings, always spoke many languages, changing them with remarkable ease as they moved through time and space and retaining Hebrew merely as the sacred and learned language.

A consequence of this was that in the twentieth century, when language achieved this position as the basic criterion of nationality, the Arabs, despite all the profound divisions of geography, society, politics, and economics, which have to this day, in fact, prevented their achieving the unity that has become such a clarion call, were accepted without question as one of the bigger nations of the world, while Israel, after more than three and a half millennia as an identifiable collectivity, began its renewed nationhood from scratch.

The conflict over Palestine, in what may be called the fourth stage in the historical confrontation of Jews and Arabs, is a relatively short and recent episode, in which the Jews, now utterly reshaped by the West, have gone back to the original scene of their emergence into history, while the Arabs, themselves revivified by the West, are still inclined to mistrust the West, though their distrust is implemented by Western instruments, and are violently opposed to Israel as a representative of the West.

Simultaneously, the State of Israel has itself become rather Easternized by the vast influx of immigrants from Muslim and Arabic-speaking countries, making up now almost half the population of Israel.

For the time being, in any case, no political solution seems to be in the offing. The intransigeance of the contemporary Arab leaders is absolute on the acceptance of Israel as a state; Israel itself naturally insists on existing. It is difficult to see what accommodation can be possible between two such diametrically opposite attitudes; the optimistic, or sentimental can only hope that life will produce one of its surprises.

The problem of Israel is a natural introduction to another question, since, as I have indicated, it was very largely Zionism, during the period between the two world wars, that provided an axis for the formation of Arab identity.

Arab nationalism is aimed, of course, at a union of all those claimed as Arabs. It is true that some dozen states in the Arab bloc are already independent, which might seem to obviate the entire discussion, but even though the Arab states remain sovereign the Arab national movement goes on proclaiming, or demanding, unity.

In previous chapters I have indicated the difficulties in the way of the formation of a strictly Arab national consciousness. Begun in Syria and Lebanon by Arabic-speaking Christians looking for a way out of their ghetto—the way being constituted by the common Arabic language—the movement for the modernization of the Middle East was quickly joined by Muslims who in turn had come under the influence of European ideas. But the universality of Islam has exercised a deeply inhibitory effect on the coagulation of "Arab" self-consciousness. Perhaps Muslim Arabs, despite the overwhelming influence of Western views of the world, cannot wrench themselves sufficiently out of the traditional matrix of their feeling of identity and restrict themselves to a shrunken vision of themselves as merely a small nation among other nations and not full-fledged members of the universal community of Islam.

If an outsider had been told, say at the end of the nineteenth century, that there was a large body of people speaking essentially the same language, believing in the same religion, living in the same general area, and able, quite justifiably, to claim a common history, and further, that the thought of this body of people was now permeated by Western ideas, including the idea of nationality, he would surely have thought it child's play to unite these people under the banner of nationalism, in one form or another.

It is therefore surely significant that the notion did not even begin to take shape until World War I. Nasser himself had been in power for years before Egypt officially declared itself an "Arab" country. And today, as I have indicated, the Arabic-speaking world can hardly be called unified in spite of the elimination of European overlordship.

The intellectuals and politicians who have been toiling to promote the idea of Arab unity have had a hard row to hoe. The acceptance of the concept of "Arabs" as a cohesive ethnic entity, imbued with self-awareness, has had to make its way against both the pervasive factionalism of the Arabic-speaking world and the universalism of Islam. To this day the word "Arab" covers quite contradictory attitudes, splendidly contrasted, for instance, between the medievally minded, purely Muslim zeal of the present King of Sa'udi Arabia, Faysal, and the highly contemporary opportunism of Nasser, the former "Egyptian" insurgent turned "Arab nationalist" leader. Faysal, of course, while "ethnically" an Arab of the Arabs and a pure-bred scion of the Arabian heartland, is essentially an old-fashioned pious Muslim whose proclaimed goal is still Islamic unity, in our day surely a utopia. Faysal would like to see Arab union, whatever that might mean to him, as a stepping stone to the broader aim of the revival of a powerful Islam. Nasser would like to use Islamic solidarity primarily as a mean of extending the hegemony of Egypt and its Arabic-speaking hinterland. The current political contest between the two leaders thus has an intriguing element of confusion at its core.

The idea of Arab unity grew up as a progressive abstraction from the merely regional groupings initially aimed at during the remarkably sluggish inception of the national movement, when nothing was envisaged beyond local autonomy—"home rule"—for various portions of Syria or Iraq. This was complemented by the parallel but quite independent movement for Egyptian independence. For decades it never even occurred to anyone to generalize local demands like these into a program designed to encompass communities defined, essentially, as native speakers of Arabic who were not Jews (though theoretically, of course, in terms of this secular notion of nationalism, there is no reason why Jews should not be ardent Arab patriots, if there were an Arab *patrie;* Jews have in fact played roles in various local independence movements).

Perhaps it was the difficulty of attaining really serious regional alliances that led to a concentration on this abstraction of unity as such—precisely because it was so maximal a demand that its attainment could be put off indefinitely without causing any real disappointment.

It cannot be too strongly emphasized that the myth-making forces in the Arabic-speaking world are operating as it were abstractly, far more so than the superficially similar tendencies that molded the Western nations over the past few centuries. For more than a millennium the Arabic-speaking peoples have been in substantially the same cultural relationship to one another, yet the question of their constituting a nation did not arise until our own generation.

Contrariwise, the European nations whose consciousness was formed over a long-drawn-out period, against a background of a common religion, with the emergence of secular ideas congealing in the form of national languages, had time to become homogenized by the process; ethnic solidarity percolated more or less evenly throughout the nation in the process of becoming itself.

In our own day Arab nationalism has had to contend with the anti-national millennial consciousness of Islam—the faith of the great bulk of Arabic-speakers—plus sharply defined regional and to some extent national differences (as in Egypt).

The consequence has been that while in Europe national consciousness welled up from below and was merely shaped or expressed by the spokesmen for the elite, among the Arabic-speakers of the present day it is really a cerebral borrowing by the elite from the West; it has come to the Arabic-speaking world fully formed and has had to be imposed on the broad masses, still largely medieval-minded, from above.

This may account for the curiously abstract, hollow quality in the propaganda revolving around the unity of the Arabs. It may be because the material factors that might make it possible are simply not present, in spite of the rhetoric aimed at propagating the idea as such. Theoretically speaking, the basic elements of unity are, to be sure, there already—identity of language, religion, and past history—but there are so many other, more concrete dividing features, which are in fact simply more important, that the slogan of unity must be conceived of as a mere rallying cry. This may be the explanation of why the dozen states in the Arab League fail to unite despite all the talk. The only thing that stands in the way of union, in fact, is themselves.

Since the attainment of independence there have been a few regional alliances, to be sure, between Arab states, such as the dramatic formation in February 1958 of Egypt and Syria into the United Arab Republic, joined a little later by Yemen, making another short-lived state called the United Arab States, or the equally short-lived Arab Federation, formed around the same time, of Iraq and Jordan. Both organisms proved to be political mayflies, though Egypt still refers to itself as the United Arab Republic, in spite of the withdrawal of Syria from the union a short time after its formation.

These regional associations may of course foreshadow the method by which Arab unity may ultimately be realized through the conquest of power within the Arabic-speaking bloc by one major unit or another. This is, to be sure, a time-honored method of effecting political unification and has all the charms of simplicity. At present the ancient state of Yemen, still almost wholly medieval in constitution and custom, is being quite openly warred over by two of the members of the Arab League, Egypt and Sa'udi Arabia, the former with a relatively large population and the latter with a large revenue. There are similar contests and tugs-of-war between factional, communal, and state interests throughout the Arab world. It would be presumptuous to forecast the likelihood of any particular outcome in such a complex situation.

Yet Arab unity is quite independent, in its emotional appeal and general rationale, of such truncating regional associations. It is a sort of transcendental ideal, indeed, an ideology that claims to be the framework of a world view. It is also, of course, an absolutely fixed component of every public occasion. The phrase "Arab unity" is itself inviolate, since regardless of what may be the political reality in any given country, milieu, or social stratum, it has become a form of sacrosanct invocation that is bound to be accepted at least in public, regardless of the degree to which such acceptance is mere lip service.

I have referred above to the awakening of the Arabic-speaking world by the stimuli of European ideas that began inundating it four generations ago. As related to the Middle East, the European basic notion of nationalism revolving around a nation-state-language complex constituted a simple enough idea, from the point of view of the Christians of the Middle East and their Christian European mentors—escape from the Muslim ghetto they were in via the formation of a new synthesis based on the language they shared in common with their Muslim "compatriots."

That question was, very simply, to what extent could a fatherland, a *patrie,* be formed out of the disparate cultural traditions of Islam and the Christian communities within its Syro-Lebanese sector that were so easily inflamed by the European idea of patriotism based on language?

The Arabic language, which, as I have indicated so often before, was the axis of the Arabs' self-consciousness since they first emerged into history with Islam, is in our own day the matrix of the idea of Arab unity.

The respect due the language for reasons of piety is heightened and emotionalized by the love its speakers bear it for its own sake. Illiterates have the same feeling, apparently, and among literary people, of course, this respect is deepened by the vast storehouse of literature in the classical language, in all fields—the literature not of a nation but of a civilization. As mentioned above, this storehouse has been made available largely through European intervention, but the prestige of the past, which rests heavily on the language, has given it an almost unique position as the one common medium of communication throughout the far-flung and underpopulated stretches of the Arabic-speaking world.

It is true that the classical language is dead in the mouths of the common people, but the drive of the Arab revival, quite apart from contemporary considerations of its practical realizability, gives a tremendous impetus to the almost exclusive use of a modified classical Arabic as a written language. Except for fleeting and generally abortive experiments, it has never been possible as a practical matter to write in any of the vulgar dialects. Aside from their feebleness and undeveloped condition as mediums of modern communication, such an attempt in its nature cuts off the speakers of any given dialect from the speakers of all others. Also, since there is no "standard" spoken language in the European sense at all, the area of intelligibility of any given dialect can be contracted to an absurdity that makes it necessary to impose an artificial construction of greater utility on the dialect, since the absence of standards makes it possible to define a dialect with extreme narrowness. Furthermore, since the whole reason for having a national language in the first place is part of a larger movement of modernization in general, it would be *ipso facto* necessary to enrich even a relatively widespread dialect with modern terminology, turns of phrase, etc. Thus, in any case, a labor of construction, adaptation, and education is inevitable.

The classical language thus steps into a number of gaps, by virtue of its being both widespread and rich in potentialities, fulfilling its function both as the bond par excellence of the Arab world and as a modern medium of thought.

But the choice of the classical language, while perhaps inevitable (indeed, unquestioned by the great majority of educated speakers), brings difficulties of its own with it.

These difficulties have to do with the language itself and with the quality of the educated public in the Middle East and North Africa.

Though the language is singularly rich, its wealth is largely useless in the modern world. A great many terms relating to everyday, material life are irrelevant. A great many more having to do with emotions, intellectual reactions, and so on, are rather vague, a situation complicated by the extraordinary proliferation of synonyms. The dead, written language contains other words that might be usefully employed, but they are still awaiting an explorer. Old technical terms must either be defined or even be deciphered; others are obsolete. In addition, they must be discovered, since the works containing them are no longer read, quite apart from their being inadequate. Another difficulty is that Arabic does not lend itself easily to borrowing the Greco-Latin words that play so important a role in European languages.

There is still another, stylistic difficulty. The best periods of classical Arabic show innumerable examples of an extremely concise, laconic, personal style that would be quite in harmony with modern preferences, but unfortunately the literary renaissance that began at the outset of the last century took as its model the productions of an epoch of decadence in literature, characterized by a fantastic flatulence and flowery tortuousness of expression. Of course, there has been an enormous advance in the past two generations, facilitated by the daily press and even by certain "deformations" due to the colloquial speech, which have taken a great burden off the prose sentence. But there is still a very widespread prejudice in favor of a "classical" style, by which is generally meant a piling up of synonyms, a flood of sanctified clichés, a straining after an unusual or euphonious word, and the insertion of verses, proverbs, erudite allusions, etc.—in short, all the apparatus of a leisure-class ornament divorced to a large extent from the daily needs of the masses.

Scientific style is still in a period of groping. The ancient Muslim savants do not appear to have distinguished themselves by clarity, and since clarity in a modern scientific style is the chief goal it is difficult for a scientific writer to satisfy the demands of scientific expression and also the hordes of self-styled "purists" who lie in wait for a "solecism" in vocabulary of syntax.

Poetry is almost totally submerged in a traditionalism that places it beyond the reach of even well-educated people. Arabic poetry attains heights of incomprehensibility that can be scaled only by an expenditure of lexicographical energy entirely disproportionate to the objective. This has eliminated it as a source of day-to-day enjoyment and made it almost wholly a specialists' domain.

The three things that hamper a modern writer in Arabic are, to sum up, the difficulty of the language itself, its wide divergence from the spoken tongue, and, perhaps most important of all, the great attraction of foreign languages and the facility educated Easterners generally acquire in them. These combine to form a situation in which the classical language, while ikonized by enthusiastic amateurs, is in fact hated by the youth of all the more advanced countries. The methods of instruction are also stuffy and outmoded, so that in early life the youth acquire a virulent dislike of the written language that makes it almost inevitable for them to escape into the pleasant vistas of French or English for their intellectual expression. In addition, reading is unpopular in general, and certainly reading of "serious" Arabic literature in particular. For these reasons the horizons of even quite well-educated persons revolve around popular journals, reviews, cheaply sensational stories—in short, a "janitor's literature" that maintains the low literary level of the reading public.

Because of all these things it would appear that while the position of the classical language is, for the time being at any rate, quite assured and in no danger of being undermined by any outbreaks of a schismatic dialectal efflorescence, still it is very far indeed from being securely enthroned in the hearts of the people. It seems a remote and alien growth if we take into consideration the fact that the bulk of the Arabic-speaking world, through lack of education, would find it quite incomprehensible.

Modern Arabic literature naturally reflects the general reaction of the Arabic-speaking world to the Western flood of ideas. Yet with respect to the actual life of the people it has been rather insubstantial and ineffectual. The earlier literature of the nineteenth century wavered between a lifeless reproduction of medieval Arabic models and an imitation of Western models based on insufficient assimilation, with the inevitable consequence of sterility and feebleness. Neo-Arabic literature is, to the extent that it differs from the classical models, quite Europeanized. To the extent that it is traditional, it is no nearer the classical tradition than Europe is itself, since classic Arabic literature is not merely a parochial heritage of the Arabs but is part of the European past as well. This of course places Arabic writers at a certain disadvantage, since their own literary past is felt to be dead, and at the same time the bulk of their public is not really ready for or interested in entirely European styles.

In Egypt this duality of the old and the new persists with special force. Its seeds are sown in the schools, where Shaykhs from the largely medieval theological colleges and Western-trained university graduates teach side by side. This probably accounts for a certain well-marked cynicism in the educated classes. Because of this duality, which is largely a consequence of the conservatism of Islam, Christian writers have often been literary leaders.

Arabic literature is often intensely hated by the younger generation, which turned aside from the old-fashioned, pedantic, sterile, and exasperating ways of teaching literature no one was interested in reading and sought Western models. The Syrians tried to close this breach in tradition, but they failed since, as Christians, they could solve neither the stylistic problem of Arabic prose, nor the deeper psychological problem of Muslim reorientation in a changed world.

It must be recalled that Arabic literature, as a living force, had a relatively brief life—some seven centuries—before its revival in the twentieth century. The pulse of the literature began weakening perceptibly in Iraq by the beginning of the eleventh century, getting stronger along the perimeter of Muslim society in Syria, Egypt, Spain, and the Maghrib. It is generally agreed that the fourteenth century marked the end of the creative period of Arabic literature. Muslim Persian literature reasserted itself in Persia because of the persistence of the Persian people and its refusal to become assimilated into Muslim culture in the sense of accepting Arabic as a spoken language. Later the Turks, having passed into Islam through the vestibule, so to speak, of their Persian tutorship, developed a literature of their own, formed almost exclusively on Persian and to a far lesser extent on Arabic models.

There has been a curious reversal of advantageousness in the great Muslim cultural languages: Persian as well as Turkish, even when their literary forms were influenced by the transplantation of immense blocks of linguistic and stylistic material from Arabic, nevertheless remained living spoken languages. With the advent of the modern period the gaps between the written and the spoken languages have gradually been filled in by the efforts of many writers.

Arabic, by contrast, a classical language that became the medium for the whole civilization and was always slightly artificial even at the beginning, when it served as a "high language" uniting the otherwise different Bedouin tribes of the peninsula, has now become quite divorced from ordinary speech in those countries where it became a vernacular. In any given Arabic-speaking country, accordingly, there is a *de facto* state of bilingualism: A dialect or dialects are spoken by the people, including the educated people; then there is the high language, painstakingly and laboriously taught at school and used in journalism and literature with varying degrees of success. It is quite incomprehensible, never actually spoken, except as something of a *tour de force* that in any case remains inaccessible to people. This *de facto* bilingualism in Arabic has actually reversed the relation between literature and life as it was reflected in the three great languages of Islam: Arabic, Persian, and Turkish. Arabic, which began as a lively spoken language, finally over the past several centuries—since the thirteenth century at the very latest—has bogged down in an unbridgeable gulf between the traditional language and actual contemporary speech. Persian and Turkish literature, on the other hand, were the idioms of a courtly and aristocratic elite from the beginning and simply because the two nations managed to retain their linguistic and ethnic unity and identity have managed to make their way back to their original status as languages actually spoken by masses of people, quickly and successfully in Turkey and far more slowly in Persia.

The movement for the restoration of classical Arabic may, of course, be successful. The drawbacks mentioned above, while substantial, are mostly transitional and, if the Arabs become a relatively unified and modern people, will disappear automatically. The literary language has already undergone startling changes of a fundamental nature; there are already writers whose prose is light, clear, and comprehensible. If education is relieved of the dead weight of a clerical traditionalism that in any case is rapidly being corroded by the flow of modern ideas, it will become livelier and attractive to the youth. A more rational selection of classical texts, of undeniable power and charm, coupled with the appearance of more writers with a desire to please a wider public, will perhaps make classical Arabic not only a lingua franca between various Arab communities, but also a vernacular. Of course, it will not be "pure" classical; a good comparison might be that between American and Elizabethan English. In any case it seems probable that the radio, movies, and daily press, together with increased education, will give the modified classical language an unchallenged position in a revived Middle East.

It is possible, also, that Arabic will play a part in the future development of Africa as a whole—it is already the dominant language throughout two-fifths of the continent. It the Arabs become a nation in the modern sense, their long association and ties of blood with the native peoples, their prestige as the fathers of Islam, their nomads and tradespeople, who will probably have a great effect in spreading Islam and with it Arabic for some time to come, all seem to promise a considerable future to the Arabs, as they come to be defined more and more as the speakers of Arabic.

Islam stands with its feet in two camps. At one end it is part of the native landscape of Africa, primitive and untouched, at home in the backwardness and myriad superstitions of the native peoples. At the other end of its spectrum it is the belief of Europeanized Egyptians and Syrians. Its common denominator, for practical purposes, is Arabic. Wherever Islam pushes forward it is easy to teach Arabic. Islam has been advancing at an enormous rate since European penetration, and particularly since World War II. It is aided in this advance by the revulsion of the Africans against Europe, the need for refuge in a system of beliefs with prestige, the economic advantages derived from travel and trade in the vast Muslim world, the lack of racial feeling among Muslims, the spread of unofficial Muslim proselytizers along precisely the same lanes of law and order that were established by Christian Europe, and so on.

The curiosity is that the "opening-up" of Africa by European empire builders was to prove of long-range benefit mainly to Islam. The pacification of the great continent cleared an actual physical path for its organic diffusion. It also transformed the psychological status of African tribal society; by superimposing the overwhelming weight of the alien West on the Africans, whose multifaceted societies were not merely pulverized but whose morale was severely shaken up, European empire building created a favorable atmosphere for the mass conversion of native African society to Islam. Because of its long-standing roots in Africa, Islam is a quasi-native growth; at the same time it is sufficiently cohesive and self-assured to act as a counterweight to Europe.

Because of this it is not unlikely that a wave of Europeanization, or quasi-Europeanization, will spread from the capitals of the Arabic-speaking Middle East and North Africa and filter out through the whole of the very large area under the influence of Arabic.

There are, of course, other and more material obstacles in the way of fusing the disparate elements of the Arabic-speaking world into a viable state organism.

The socioeconomic backwardness is still very striking. Not only are great sections of the sedentary population still involved in a tissue of feudal relationships, but the problem of nomadism still plays a certain role. The split of the Desert and the Sown is very ancient; indeed, it may be the fundamental element in Middle Eastern history. Nomads contradict the possibility of a modern state; any attempt to create one must entail a radical settlement of the problems of nomadism.

It is true that nomads are now only of minor consequence numerically; they scarcely play a role in more densely settled countries like Syria and Egypt. But even here whole strata of the population are in transition from nomadism to peasant cultivation. Beyond its material weight the desert has always been a vital element in the Middle East and North Africa. Not merely has it performed a purely economic function (as a purveyor of the products of livestock, etc.), but it has been the principal source of manpower. The debilitating effects of eastern cities have been compensated for by a steady flow of life from the wilderness via the fields. In addition, the nomads have always been the "Arabs" par excellence, the repository of traditional Arab culture, even though from a statistical point of view speakers of Arabic have probably always been predominantly sedentary.

But there is nothing in the nature of nomads as such that makes it difficult to persuade them to settle on the land as farmers. On the contrary, the history of all nomadic groups appears to be a spasmodic struggle to attain the well-being, security, and comfort of a rural life and abandon the harshness and uncertainty of the incessant trek. Although Bedouin may sneer at peasants, when the pinch comes they are only to glad to be able to exchange the exhausting rhythm of their own lives for the security of a mud hut.

Nomadism prevails when the technical capacities of the nomads are only just sufficient to maintain them in a sort of precarious equilibrium with the exigencies of their environment. They are stretched taut from one season to another, barely eking out an existence by shuttling back and forth between grazing grounds with not enough of a breathing space possible to recuperate their powers and acquire enough technique for the taming of nature. They are always only just one step ahead of starvation.

Clearly, the only thing that could alter this finely drawn equilibrium would be either a sudden increase in the lushness of the environment, or else an exotically augmented power over nature, which would provide reserves for a community whose accounts at present just barely balance. It is precisely this increased power over nature that is supplied by modern technique and that puts the final seal on the doom of the nomads. Their settlement on the land in Arabia has been begun on a grandiose scale, inspired, in Sa'udi Arabia, by the religious fanaticism of the Wahhabi puritanical reform movement and elsewhere in the peninsula, as in Iraq, by more prosaic considerations.

But the social and economic backwardness of which nomadism was a single aspect is given a concrete and institutionalized expression in the political life of the whole area. The phenomenon of "leader-politics" is the direct outcome of this stagnation on a low level of economic intercommunication. Where production exists principally to satisfy restricted local needs, where there is no economic interchange of a scope broad enough to create a social class as its bearer, each village, townlet, valley, and tribe becomes a microcosm of social activity.

This accounts for the myriads of political spokesmen in the Arab world, for the independent diginity of each petty chief and village elder. This is why it has become a cliché to speak of the disunity of the Arabs and their incapacity to cooperate with one another.

Of course, social patterns are manifold, and the degree of disunity varies greatly. In some countries, as in Egypt, it has been almost entirely replaced by a bourgeois society with well-defined political groups in a quasi-Western style. In others, such as Syria, it is exacerbated by religious and ethnic schisms. In still others, such as the Sudan, life is almost primeval. The more primitive communities in the Middle East and Africa, in order to exist as political units, have generally crystallized around their own local bosses and wise men. In the more civilized areas the tendency to split up is pushed further by the existence of the great families, who themselves constitute political units. These family factions confront other, form similar, political units, and compose a balance or imbalance of power around themselves. The clan, family, and clique are the chief factors in the political arena; only recently have "movements" been superimposed on them.

The recent creation of petty national states has provided another locus of concentration for the economic and political forces at work. However, these national states, tardy arrivals in a world dominated by the supranational, cosmic interests of the great powers and subservient to their own backwardness as well as to these powers, are permitted very little scope for a tendency so familiar to us. It is the infantile character of these states that provides one of the strongest drives for unity, precisely as it is, simultaneously, one of the obstacles to that unity.

In some ways the belatedness of the Arab national states has smoothed the path to national unification. For the fact is that the basic cultural discord prevailing between various strata of Arab society applies with far less force to a unitary political organism than it does to the Arab world as it is now constituted. These cultural differences are found *within* every single Arab country; they were present during the efflorescence of Islam. However difficult the nomadic problem may be, it would be no more difficult for a unitary Arab state than it is for a handful of feeble, split-up dependent units. As a matter of fact, of course, the area of nomadism has been contracting rapidly during the past decades: The West has had its effect even on the Bedouin. The stronghold of Arabia itself has been passing under the spell of Europe. The Bedouin have been enmeshed in a relentless, organic process of settlement on the land, and even if the gap between the Desert and the Sown is never entirely eliminated it would be infinitely easier to deal with the complex relations of the Bedouin and the sedentary agriculturists within the framework of a unified governmental apparatus using similar methods than within five or six separate and often incompatible state policies.

The argument made from the enormous regional distinctions between various Arab communities and the absence of any genuine "national" consciousness in historic times merely exposes the capricious and artificial nature of most of the Arab states set up since World War I. For while no one might deny that a man from Baghdad and a man from Mosul are Arabs, it is true that each may be more aware of his difference from the other than of their common citizenship in the historically capricious Iraqi state. The argument from nomadism applies with even greater force here. What is artificial is not the concept of a unitary Arab state, which, regardless of the *material* obstacles to its realization, corresponds at any rate to a growing awareness of the Arabs of themselves as distinct from Europe, but the atomized states into which the Arabs are at present divided. The regional differences are much more potent between the sections of states already constituted than between the states themselves. Once again, that is, the argument against Arab union that is based on regional differences between Arabs is in reality more forceful when applied to small states than when applied to a larger union.

Minorities constitute a notorious problem in the Middle East. To the extent that minorities (particularly prevalent in Syria, Iraq, and perhaps Morocco) are rooted in religious schism and cultural particularism, they may eventually disappear. A Western system of government and education may bring the inevitable harvest of social homogeneity in its train, and in any case the minorities are not numerically important enough to form a serious obstacle to the unification of the Arabs as a whole.

As a matter of fact, the principal obstacles to Arab unification do not lie in the disharmonies outlined above, but in the pervasive rivalries among the political elite. In the more advanced countries bordering on the Mediterranean this may be a function of the character of the "Levantine" upper strata as a whole. There is a special quality in Easterners who have been educated in a Western manner that strikes most observers at once. As an intellectual class they give the impression of being flibbertigibbets.

The gap between the old and the new in the Arab societies that have felt European influence most thoroughly is so enormous and the economic backwardness of the overwhelming bulk of the population is so extreme that a difference in schooling acquires an absolute value as a specifically differentiating characteristic. The masses are steeped in such ignorance that education automatically involves elevation to an upper class, regardless of the precise economic status, which may or may not lag behind the social prestige created by education. This accounts for the persistent Eastern phenomenon of a growing class of these educated sprites, who belong socially to the upper strata, but exist in an economy too meager to have any interstices that they might squeeze into by virtue of the education that is their principal qualification.

Their only refuge is in politics, but even here the arena is restricted. The masses are backward intellectually (from the point of view of the elite) as well as economically; they are not receptive to the abstractions of Western political thought, which is one of the ornaments of the elite.

Accordingly, even in the political life that is the principal channel left open to this bottlenecked intelligentsia, they encounter precisely the same bottleneck: They are thrown back on themselves and on those members of the rising generation in the same position. The same gulf that separates the masses economically from the narrow apex of the elite also separates them intellectually. Providing no vent for the energies of the intelligentsia and so throwing it back on political activity, it also constrains this political activity into an abnormally shrunken, sterile, and self-stultifying arena.

This is largely responsible for the hectic quality, the mélange of an extreme intransigeance of form and poverty of content that is characteristic of intellectual groups in quasi-colonial areas. This instability, added to the personal and party ax-grinding inherent in this intellectual overpopulation, conceals genuine social and political needs in a mist of intrigue, factionalism, and wire-pulling, and impedes the emergence of any program organically related to actual conditions.

In Western Europe and the United States this phenomenon can be seen in perspective, since it is balanced by a certain stability in the educated classes as a whole. In the Middle East, however, it compromises the ensemble of all those elements in society that are affected by the "new life"; it is the hallmark of the modern intelligentsia per se and so acquires decisive importance as the intellectual matrix of contemporary Arab culture.

What we are contemplating, in short, is the grappling of the elite with the creation of a myth. We are witnessing, in a literal sense, the birth of a new identity.

For surely that is the point about Arab identity through the ages: It has *changed.* And the most potent factor in the creation of a new myth is the exploitation of the past. The fact that the basis of Arab identity today is quite different from what it was at the dawning of the Arab influence in history is quite irrelevant. There is no reason why a myth should not be confused, in some sense; factual accuracy is irrelevant to mythology. Since it is an ideal projection it can freely convert to its own purposes everything under the sun; it is all transcendentalized anyhow. To the mythological mill everything is grist.

The present-day Arab theory of the Arab past, like other such theories, is more important than the past itself, is more important than "mere" historical facts. Nevertheless, it is wise to recall that it is no more than one among many possible theories.

The point, after all, is that not only has the axis of Arab identity shifted in the past, it is still shifting before our eyes. I have already referred to Nasser's decision, made in mid-career, to project himself as an "Arab" instead of as an "Egyptian" leader. It was a mere decision, a simple act of will. Beforehand he had been very vociferous on behalf of his "Egyptianism." The motivation of the decision is obvious, especially when considered in the perspective of his political goal, the concentric circles of 50 million speakers of Arabic—*i.e.,* the Arabs, who are the hub—then the 250 million Africans in the next circle, since Egypt is, after all, African, too; and then half a billion Muslims making up the outer circle, the ultimate target for the propaganda of a Muslim government, since Nasser is, of course, a devout Muslim too.

If anything is odd about this, it is that it took such a long time for the idea to germinate. I should have thought that the myth of Egyptians as Arabs would have been launched many decades ago, with instantaneous success. But since a myth is plastic in its nature and subject to so many of the psychic and intellectual difficulties I have referred to before, the obstacles should be kept in mind in order to assess the chances of any particular myth.

It is incontestable that the Arab national movement has demonstrated a singular vacuum of ideas; the phrase "Arab nationalist ideology" implies little beyond itself. It seems that the whole of the Arab nationalist movement is a very narrow development of the intelligentsia alone, unlike the nationalisms of the various European countries it is ultimately modeled on. Perhaps the main point to remember is that the myth, before our very eyes, is putting on flesh and blood. It is, in short, *becoming.*

It cannot be denied that Arab nationalism, coming onto the world stage somewhat belatedly, after the movement of nineteenth century nationalism that engendered it had lost most of its momentum, has taken a rather rigid and hermetically self-enclosed form, in which the movement seems to exist almost for its own sake alone.

Contemporary Arab propaganda is obsessed by the twin problems of colonialism, or imperialism, now in fact simply outmoded, and of the existence of Israel, which surely occupies a disproportionate place in the minds of the political leadership if one simply takes into account the size of Israel in relationship to the vastness of the Arabic-speaking countries as a group. Yet both problems have played a key role in the general performance of Arab propagandists.

When nationalist movements in Europe, after achieving their objectives, often turned into currents of patriotism, more or less chauvinistic, the resulting political regimes were at least under the control or guidance of electorates that, despite the aberrations of Fascism, Communism, and so on, exercised some sort of control over political behavior. But the East in general, including the Arabic-speaking East, lacks the restraints due to liberal democracy or socialism, which acted as a balance for what might otherwise have been movements of unbridled chauvinism. Democracy is everywhere scarcely even a façade; the regimes throughout the area are more or less openly authoritarian and one-party. The word "liberty," indeed, is no more than a catchword used in a reaction against what is generally claimed to be the imminent depredations of the foreign imperialists so recently expelled.

The strife that continues nevertheless to make itself manifest beneath an appearance of orderliness is equally clearly the expression of continuing local rivalries, factional squabbles, and so on, rather than any large-scale politically programmed movement. The Socialism and Communism that in varying degrees have also played a role in the evolution of the modern Middle East have also been smothered by the hyperconcentration on nationalism in the contemporary formula.

In this complex process the Soviet Union has played different roles. Between the two world wars it generally tried to carry on its own autonomous agitation against the so-called bourgeois parties and classes of the various Arabic-speaking countries—with negligible effects, it must be admitted, which correspond, on the other hand, to a negligible effort—and also against Zionism, which in fact was made a penal offense in the Soviet Union itself. Since World War II, after a moment of uneasy confusion with respect to the nascent State of Israel, which the Soviet Union vigorously supported for rather short-lived tactical reasons, the Soviet Union has plumped for the support of Arab nationalism as a weapon against the West, primarily the United States. After reversing its position on the support of Israel, the Soviet Union seemed to accept "Arab nationalism" fully, soft-pedaling its support of its own Communist partisans and deliberately disregarding the question of social conflict or the class struggle. Thus the Soviet Union has lately found itself in the position of lending the weight of its revolutionary or pseudorevolutionary authority to regimes that are manifestly retrograde from any liberal and a fortiori Marxist point of view.

This double play has enabled the new Arab leaderships to straddle the fence very easily in their now well-known posture of "neutralism." Their relations with the Soviet bloc have been carried on essentially on a diplomatic plane, in which they have been able to profit by the material and spiritual support of the Soviet bloc without even considering the question of social reforms, which for that matter would be of no interest to the Kremlin anyhow. At the same time the strategic position of the Arabic-speaking states, located at vital points with respect to the Middle East, to the world of Islam as a whole, and to their African neighbors, has enabled them to go on enjoying torrents of advantages of all kinds from the West, especially the United States.

Hence foreign policy has more or less swamped domestic renovation. The socioeconomic problems of the Arabic-speaking states have not been solved to any appreciable extent, neither in the relatively advanced states like Egypt, Syria, Lebanon, and Iraq, nor in the downright "feudal" states like Sa'udi Arabia, Yemen, and Libya.

This "neutralism" of the Arab bloc is very relevant to the relatively recent incursion of the Soviet Union, and latterly of the Communist Chinese, into the immense arena of Islam and of Africa.

There is a curious confusion here concerning the relative provinces of theory and practice. Communist leaders very naturally claim that what they do is inspired by or at least in harmony with Communist—or Marxist—theory. Contrariwise, if national leaders establish institutions associated intellectually with a Communist view of the world, the institutions are often called Communist. For that matter the leaders are too.

Yet it would seem more sensible to understand the functional background, so to speak, of the problems that the leaders of the emergent nations are called upon to solve.

What, in fact, was the situation confronting the regimes that have come to the fore only during the past half-generation?

In concrete terms, the "backwardness" of backward countries becomes a source of explosiveness because of a sharp disproportion between the capital available for investment and the insistence on national renovation. Nowadays this renovation means industrialization; the intelligentsia has been swept into power, throughout the emergent area, by the mystiquc of the political ideas that have been churning up the whole world in the wake of Western technological diffusion. The new leaders of the Arab countries, too are now uniformly committed to the slogan made popular by the Bolshevik regime in its early days: Overtake and pass the West!

In underdeveloped countries, accordingly, the political leadership has embarked on a comprehensive overhauling of the national economy. This overhauling is of course no more than an attempt to achieve maximum self-sufficiency within the organizational framework of the new groups in power. Essentially these groups are drawn from the white-collar intelligentsia, which throughout the underdeveloped world has been multiplying in a lopsided ratio to the socioeconomic opportunities hitherto accessible. Their political medium is constituted by the volatile, feverish support of the other strata of the population that have been receptive to all fashionable political ideas since the end of World War II.

This phenomenon is worldwide and essentially unitary. It is the need for vast capital investment channelized through a parvenu leadership propped up on an undeveloped but insistent mass following. It enables us to perceive the problem confronting the leadership.

Where are the funds to come from? The entrepreneurial, potentially capitalistic middle-class elements were obviously far too exiguous for the new requirements, quite apart from the traditional hypercautious and essentially speculative nature of these fringe capitalists in backward countries. Not only did they lack the requisite funds, they could not even be absorbed into any large-scale program of centrally directed economic expansion.

On the other hand, the parvenu leadership felt the ground burning beneath its feet; it had to do something, and above all *seem* to be doing something.

It is doubtless this simple, glaring fact that explains the potentialities of a convergence between the somewhat bodiless ferment of the Arab nationalist movement and the structural dynamics of the Soviet bloc.

The various juntas of youngish men who have taken power in Egypt, Iraq, Syria, Algeria, Tunisia, and Morocco, whatever their personal opinion of Communism as theory, are in a situation in which they had to cope with this insistent demand for huge capital outlays, while in the eyes of their followers playing the role of charismatic executives.

The Soviet system, with its foreign-trade monopoly, its state economic planning and breakneck industrialization projects, all contained within the framework of a mass movement inspired by ideology, obviously fits this situation like a glove. It is in fact the only contemporary institutional complex that can enable newcomers to power in backward countries to make a show on the one hand of instituting elaborate programs of new construction, and on the other of clinging to power while paying lip service to the collective mystique that justifies their enterprise of renovation.

Thus Nasser and other leaders in the Middle East and North Africa make a constant point of "Arab unity" at the very moment they are clearly at loggerheads with one another on all practical issues, while on the other hand even the Aswan High Dam, which would seem to be a practical matter, is acclaimed as due to the renaissance of the "Arab spirit."

This institutional osmosis between the Soviet bloc and the Middle East has nothing to do with theory, however it may be adorned by it. It has still less to do with generalizations about the doctrinal irreconcilability of Islam and Communism. Even from a theoretical point of view, for that matter, it can be demonstrated that the historical structure of Islam has been built on institutions that are not at all alien to Communist ideas. The basis of Islam from its inception, after all, has been the triangle of the theocratic state (a centralized, God-sanctioned authority), the army (which engendered the actual organization of Islam in its primitive period and later), and the intelligentsia (the ancient scribal bureaucracy, plus the clergy, inherited from the defunct Persian and Byzantine empires). Thus, except for the mere belief in God, the actual organizational pattern of Islamic society is perfectly suitable for institutional adaptation to Soviet views once the right ideological key is found and the appropriate tactical accomodations made.

Because of this the Soviet Union can now maneuver in underdeveloped countries not only on the plane of normal power politics, but also by taking advantage of two factors peculiar to itself: both the mystique it enjoys as a backward agrarian country that in one generation moved up into the front ranks of great powers, and, more importantly, the above-mentioned institutional complex, which it offers not merely to the "impoverished masses yearning for a better life"—by now an empty and indeed meaningless cliché—but to the fermenting youthful intelligentsia that has come to the surface all over the former colonial or semicolonial world throughout Africa and Asia.

For it is the officers, students, and white-collar intellectuals, far more important in such countries than in the settled industrial West, that constituted the effective centers of political agitation in Africa and Asia. It is they who have been galvanized by the shifts in the balance of power between the West and the Soviet bloc, and latterly Communist China, which they see only through the prism of their own countries' limitless need for socioeconomic overhauling.

The attraction exercised by Communism over the Nasser regime, for instance, has nothing whatever to do with the charms of Marxist doctrine, an alien and irrelevant consideration. It is simply a model mechanism for practical politics. From the point of view of the Egyptian leaders, what the Soviet Union offered them was simply a cluster of techniques for the confiscation of property and the organization and control of the economy; it created a matrix for the new bureaucracy to operate in and demonstrated methods of building up a party-state apparatus, manipulating a mass following and the masses per se, and organizing propaganda both at home and abroad.

It is just because they have so little interest in doctrine as such that the new leaderships—not only of the Arabic-speaking states but all over Africa and Asia—can tack back and forth between the bigger power blocs. International tension naturally leads both the Soviet bloc and the West, led for the moment by the United States, to vie for the favor of the former colonial areas. Communist China, too, is busily maneuvering throughout these areas with growing skill and leverage.

The Arabic-speaking world, on the verge, perhaps, of ethnic crystallization, and in any case already functioning as a political complex, has appeared on the world stage at a singularly entangled conjuncture. It is a question whether its resources, mental and material, will enable it to keep pace with the improvisations of life.

BIBLIOGRAPHY

George Antonius, *The Arab Awakening,* New York, 1939.

Sir Thomas Arnold and Alfred Guillaume, (eds.), *The Legacy of Islam,* Oxford, 1931.

C. H. Becker, *Islamstudien,* Vols. I and II, Leipzig, 1924, 1932.

———, *Educational Problems in the Near East and the Far East,* London, 1933.

Richard Bell, *Introduction to the Quran,* Edinburgh, 1953.

Morroe Berger, *The Arab World Today,* New York, 1962.

J.-J. Berreby, *La Péninsule Arabique,* Paris, 1958.

Carl Brockelmann, *History of the Islamic Peoples,* New York, 1944.

R. Brunschvig and G. E. von Grunebaum, (eds.), *Classicisme et Déclin Culturel,* Paris, 1957.

Richard Burton, *A Pilgrimage to al-Medina and Mecca,* London, 1893.

Claude Cahen, *Leçons d'Histoire Musulmane,* Paris, 1961.

Joseph Chelhod, *Introduction à la Sociologie de l'Islam,* Paris, 1958.

Wendell Cleland, *The Population Problem in Egypt,* Lancaster, Pa., 1936.

Charles D. Cremeans, *The Arabs and the World,* New York, 1962.

Charles Doughty, *Wanderings in Arabia Deserta,* London, 1888.

Bishr Farès, "Difficultés pour un Ecrivain Arabe Moderne," *Revue des Etudes Islami Islamiques,* Vol. X, 1936.

Nabih Amin Faris, (ed.), *The Arab Heritage,* New York, 1963.

Francesco Gabrieli, *The Arab Revival,* New York, 1961.

———, *A Short History of the Arabs,* London, 1963.

Louis Gardet, *La Cité Musulmane,* Paris, 1961.

Sir Hamilton Gibb, *Studies on the Civilization of Islam,* London, 1962.

———, *Studies in Contemporary Arabic Literature,* Vols. 4, 5, and 7, *Bulletin of the School of Oriental Studies,* London.

———, (ed.), *Whither Islam?,* London, 1932.

Sir Hamilton Gibb and Harold Bowen, *Islamic Society and the West,* Vol. I, London, 1957.

Sir John Glubb, *The Empire of the Arabs,* London, 1963.

S. D. Goitein, *Jews and Arabs,* New York, 1955.

———, *Studies in Islamic History and Institutions,* Leiden, 1966.

Ignaz Goldziher, *Muhammedanische Studien,* Vols. I and II, Halle an der Saale, 1888, 1890.

———, *Vorlesungen über den Islam,* Heidelberg, 1925.
G. E. von Grunebaum, *Islam,* London, 1955.
Alfred Guillaume, *Islam,* London, 1954.
Sylvia G. Haim, (ed.), *Arab Nationalism,* Los Angeles, 1964.
R. Hartmann, "Die nationalen Bestrebungen der Araber," *Deutsche Revue,* July-September, 1921.
Arnold Hottinger, *The Arabs,* Los Angeles, 1963.
Snouck Hurgronje, *Verspreide Geschriften,* Leipzig, 1923.
———, *Mohammedanism,* New York, 1916.
Taha Husayn, *Fi al-Aql al-Arabi al-Hadith,* (in a special number of *al-Hilal: al-Arab wa-l-Islam*), Cairo, 1939.
Charles Issawi, *Egypt in Revolution,* London, 1963.
Reinhard Junge, *Die Europäisierung orientalischer Wirtschaft,* Vol. I, E. Weimar, 1915.
Hans Kohn, *Western Civilization in the Near East,* New York, 1936.
———, *Nationalism and Imperialism in the Hither East,* London, 1932.
———, *Die nationale Bewegung in Aegypten,* Zeitschrift für Politik, 1926.
———, *Der arabische Nationalismus,* Zeitschrift für Politik, 1927.
I. Krachkovsky, *Vozniknovenie i Razvitie novo-arabskoi literatury,* Vostok, Leningrad, 1922.
Reuben Levy, *The Social Structure of Islam, Cambridge,* 1957.
Bernard Lewis, *The Arabs in History,* London, 1950.
Louis Massignon, "Eléments arabes et Foyers d'Islamisation," *Revue du Monde Musulman,* Vol. 57, 1924.
Reynold A. Nicholson, *A Literary History of the Arabs,* Cambridge, 1930.
Richard H. Nolte, (ed.), *The Modern Middle East,* New York, 1963.
De Lacy O'Leary, *How Greek Science Passed to the Arabs,* London, 1949.
H. St. John Philby, *Arabia,* London, 1930.
———, *Harun al Rashid,* London, 1933.
Bertold Spuler, *The Muslim World,* Vols. I and II, Leiden, 1960.
Christopher Sykes, *Crossroads to Israel,* New York, 1965.
A. J. Toynbee, *A Study of History,* Vols. I, II, and III, London, 1934.
———, *The World After the Peace Conference,* London, 1925.
———, *Survey of International Affairs,* London, 1925.
Richard Walzer, *Greek into Arabic,* Oxford, 1962.
Hanna Zakarias, *De Moïse à Mohammed,* Vols. I and II, Cahors (Lot), France, 1955.
University of Chicago, *Near East: Problems and Prospects,* Chicago, 1942.

PERIODICALS

al-Hilal, Cairo
al-Muqtataf, Cairo
Foreign Affairs
Round Table
Der Islam
Oriente Moderno
Africa
Koloniale Rundschau
Hochland
Welt des Islams
Vostok
Revue des Etudes Islamiques
Revue du Monde Musulman

INDEX